D0147068

THE MANY FACES OF GAY

THE MANY FACES OF GAY

Activists Who Are Changing the Nation

ARTHUR D. KAHN

Westport, Connecticut
London

Library of Congress Cataloging-in-Publication Data

Kahn, Arthur David.
The many faces of gay : activists who are changing the nation / Arthur D. Kahn.
p. cm.
Includes bibliographical references and index.
ISBN 0–275–95366–1 (alk. paper)
1. Gay activists—New York Metropolitan Area. 2. Gay men—New York Metropolitan Area—Political activity. 3. Lesbians—New York Metropolitan Area—Political activity. 4. Coming out (Sexual orientation)—New York Metropolitan Area. I. Title.
HQ76.8.U52N54 1997
305.9′0664—dc20 96–26283

British Library Cataloguing in Publication Data is available.

Library of Congress Catalog Card Number: 96–26283
ISBN: 0–275–95366–1

First published in 1997

Praeger Publishers, 88 Post Road West, Westport, CT 06881
An imprint of Greenwood Publishing Group, Inc.

Printed in the United States of America

The paper used in this book complies with the Permanent Paper Standard issued by the National Information Standards Organization (Z39.48–1984).

10 9 8 7 6 5 4 3 2 1

Contents

Preface

In the spring of 1990, I heard Sam Ciccone, a retired police sergeant and executive director of the Gay Officers Action League (GOAL), describe how his organization (the first gay police organization in the nation) had evolved from a tiny underground cell of a few courageous officers into an officially recognized fraternal organization within the New York Police Department. Impressed with his account, I expressed my desire to write a history of GOAL as soon as I completed a work-in-progress entitled *AIDS, the Winter War: A Testing of America*. In December I informed Sam that I was at last free to begin work on the GOAL book. Sam agreed to arrange interviews with GOAL members. Within weeks, however, in this, my first experience in dealing with the police mentality, I found myself slapped down for "insubordination" by the ex-sergeant.

Rather than abandon altogether a contribution to the struggle against homophobia, I decided to turn my attention to the intensifying crisis in "gay bashing,"* a more urgent subject, it seemed to me, than a history of GOAL. Indeed, in my AIDS book I had touched upon the homophobic violence evoked by the HIV epidemic. In the context of the resistance within the New York Police Department to responding effectively to the antigay violence that was becoming more widespread and virulent by the month in New York

*In this book, I have adopted the definition of "gay" employed by the New York Lesbian and Gay Anti-Violence Project: "A man who is homosexual and identifies himself as a gay man; *it can also refer to homosexually oriented ideas and varieties of cultural expression.*" I employ it also, as is commonly done by both lesbian and gay interviewees, to cover both lesbians and gay men, speaking simply, for example, of the "gay" community.

City, as in the rest of the country, the interviews I succeeded in holding with four GOAL police officers would contribute significantly to the new theme.

As I was directed from one interviewee to another in my new project, the scope and ramifications of homophobic violence became ever more apparent; and after a year and a half of investigating, a broad and comprehensive theme emerged: *what it means to be gay in late twentieth-century America.* The coming-out experience provided the focus for that theme.

As activists, the interviewees for this book are not, of course, representative of the national gay and lesbian community, a community as varied as the general population. (People of color—African Americans, Latinos, Asians, and Pacific Islanders—comprise about one-third of the interviewees.) Almost all the interviewees are college educated; some are professionals. Several, including two state commissioners, two city commissioners, a city councilman, and a former director of the State Consumer Protection Agency, held important political positions.*

Although, with one exception, I limited my interviewing to people living in the New York Metropolitan area, the book is about *coming out in the United States.* New Yorkers share the experiences of gays everywhere in the nation. In addition, a substantial number of the interviewees grew up outside New York and underwent their initial and decisive coming-out experiences in other parts of the country and, in some cases, abroad. After completing my initial interviewing, I realized that my failure to include gay veterans restricted my treatment of the coming-out experience. I then added seven interviewees from this group.

In November 1993, two members of PFLAG (Parents and Friends of Lesbians and Gays), whom I met as fellow volunteers at the Gay Men's Health Crisis AIDS Dance-a-thon, assured me that parents of gays also undergo a coming-out experience that often proves a critical factor in their children's coming out. As a result, I interviewed several members of PFLAG.

Readers of this book, I think, will gain a sense of a gay community in motion as well as learn of the varied and complex coming-out experiences of a sizable variety of lesbians and gay men.

The coming-out experience involves every moment of existence and all aspects of life. Factors complicating the coming-out struggles, like race and religion, are treated in this book in separate chapters. Several interviewees expose the special problems of growing up poor and gay. Tracy Morgan expounds on the additional struggle of lesbians against male chauvinism in the gay community as well as in the general society. Ermanno Stingo, a se-

*I did not enjoy free choice of interviewees and was unable to find candidates for all aspects of the subject I was eager to investigate. In addition, of the six interviewees who either withdrew or were dropped by me, three were African Americans; their absence has limited my investigation of the particular struggles of black gays within both the majority and the African-American communities. The withdrawal of a Native American interviewee further circumscribed the scope of the book.

nior citizen, provides insights into the experiences of gays in past decades.

Winning acceptance in the immediate environment—among family, friends, schoolmates, and work associates (investigated in Part I of this book)—represents only the first stage of the coming-out struggle. Gays and lesbians must also struggle as a minority community within the general society, as the 1993 hullabaloo about gays in the military demonstrated. Indeed, several of the interviewees insisted that gays achieve a full sense of personal dignity and self-worth only through participation in struggles against the varied manifestations of homophobia in the general society. In fact, since the 1969 Stonewall "rebellion," the coming out of the community as a whole and of gays as individuals in New York (as in other urban centers throughout the country) has proceeded in tandem. Part II of this book is devoted to this culminating aspect of the coming-out process.

In exploring how their experiences at every stage of life contributed to their emergence as self-assured, "out" activists, interviewees collaborated with enthusiasm, submitting patiently to hours of prodding that often evoked painful and long-suppressed memories. "It is all part of the story," remarked Joyce Hunter, rejecting her initial hesitation to relate incidents of incest in her childhood. Convinced by an earlier interviewee that she must hold back nothing, Carla confessed to losing sleep for days before her interview, in turmoil at the prospect of relating harrowing events of a tension-ridden childhood. She insisted that her lover be present at the interview to provide emotional support.

A number of interviewees asserted that under the severe probing during the interview they achieved new insights into their own personal development. City Commissioner for Mental Health Billy Jones, for example, remarked at the start of the second session of his interview, "I thought about your saying that I have had a fortunate life. You don't think about such an idea. You know how you grew up and what happened to you; you don't make comparisons." Dennis de Leon, City Commissioner for Human Rights, declared upon reading the transcript of his interview that he had not realized how important a factor his relationship with his father had been in his life.

Delving into often-painful experiences evoked a rare sense of common humanity between the interviewees and me. Not only did I achieve increased sensitivity in regard to experiences that differed radically from my own, but in addition I arrived at new illuminations about my own life. It is my hope that readers will come away from this book with a new appreciation of the rich variety in our national mosaic and of the particular contributions to our society of lesbian and gay activists, with an increased sensitivity to homophobia, and with some new insights into their own personal odysseys.

In 1996, several years after the initial interviews were conducted, the publisher asked the author to obtain release forms from each interviewee. In signing the release forms, three interviewees asked to be identified solely by their first names; others are represented under first-name pseudonyms. The biographical sketches of some interviewees had to be omitted because their addresses could not be traced. Additional interviews were held to replace these eliminated accounts and those of interviewees who asked to be dropped from the book.

THE MANY FACES OF GAY

Part I

EXCLUSION IS VIOLENCE!

Estimates of the number of homosexuals in the United States range from 1 to 10 percent of the population, but whether the former (two-and-a-half million lesbians and gays) or the latter (twenty-five million) tally is accepted, gays and lesbians represent a community as large as, or larger than, the population of number of member nations of the United Nations. In any event, issues of civil rights and liberties critical to a democratic society are not decided in such a society according to the size of a community or the percentage of the population it represents.

Gays and lesbians are to be found in every aspect of American society, and as an integral part of that society they share its values and aspirations. The sixty individuals interviewed for this book related experiences of a society under extreme stress from pervasive violence, a breakdown of the family, and widespread drug and alcohol addiction, a society divided by attitudes of male chauvinism, racism, and anti-Semitism. Besides the general social problems, however, gays and lesbians suffer the additional burden of homophobic ostracism, an isolation that interviewee Ginny Apuzzo, an activist enjoying respect in the gay and lesbian community throughout the nation, equates to violence:

> Any and all attempts at isolating individuals for whatever reason represent a kind of violence. In ancient Athens, society ostracized individuals as an extreme penalty. Today gays and lesbians suffer isolation in families, in schools, on the job and in society at large. Violence includes sneers and epithets. *Exclusion is violence!*

"COMING OUT OF THE CLOSET"?

On the basis of Ginny Apuzzo's interpretation of gay exclusion, can one accept the standard metaphor, "coming out of the closet," as an appropriate metaphor for the complex process of coming to terms with the ramifications of the minority status of homosexuals? Does not the term "coming out" imply that a mere question of will is required to win full citizenship? If so, the appropriate injunction for gays would be: "Stop whining, open the door, slam it behind you, and step out into the sunlight."

"No," counters Ginny Apuzzo. "Coming out is the wrong phrase. We have always been 'out.' We have been trying to come *in,* in to a community, to security. When people come in for sanctuary and you throw them out, what are you doing to them? You are making political exiles of them. Like throwing people out of the manor during feudalism, leaving them to perish."

Indeed, upon the enactment of a Massachusetts law affirming the right of openly gay public school students to participate equally and safely in all school activities, the *New York Times* commented (December 13, 1993): "What made the lobby [in support of the bill] so compelling was the stories of the students' anguish. They told of being spat upon and called names, of being physically threatened and attacked, of feeling isolated and alone. Some had dropped out of school." Regarding the students' intensive letter-writing campaign, rallies, and candlelight vigils at the State House and meetings with the state senators or their aides, Bob Parlin, a high school history teacher and adviser to his school's gay-student alliance, declared: "These are some of the most courageous students I've ever seen."

Heterosexual men and women, no matter how astute and sensitive, have few clues to the painful isolation and undermining of self-esteem described by the interviewees in this book. Most interviewees as children were bewildered by a sense of difference from other children. The male interviewees generally resisted participation in boys' competitive sports and found the company of girls less challenging. Often they were ridiculed as "faggots" or "queers" or, if not taunted or physically attacked themselves, watched as gay classmates were humiliated or beaten. If, to compensate for poor athletic performance, they strove for academic achievement, they were often derided as "nerds."

The lesbian interviewees experienced such humiliations less often than the gay men, but on the other hand they had had to deal with aspects of the male chauvinism pervasive in society. (Many more lesbians than gays are discharged from the military services.) Resenting the limitations imposed upon their sex from their earliest years, they joined in boys' games and were ridiculed as tomboys.

As they approached adolescence, the gay and lesbian interviewees became aware that the indefinable difference they sensed in themselves as children turned out to be a difference in sexual orientation. While their straight peers freely expressed their attraction to members of the opposite sex, they kept silent about their crushes. Many made heroic efforts to behave like "normal" teenagers, dating and even engaging in sex with the opposite sex.

Some interviewees nursed a vain hope that their homosexual attractions represented merely a normal stage of adolescence. Pressured by parents or impelled by their own fears and shame, they attempted "cures" through psychotherapy. Others, in last-ditch struggles against their sexual drive, forced themselves into long-term heterosexual relationships that eventually proved destructive both to themselves and to their partners. (The experiences of interviewees—more women than men—who went through years of married life or other heterosexual or bisexual relationships before settling into an exclusively homosexual lifestyle confute the popular misconception that a "successful" heterosexual experience will "cure" homosexuality.)

Attempts at a "normal" lifestyle among both lesbians and gays, struggles sometimes lasting many years, prevented a normal evolution within their sexual orientation and delayed the establishment of a mature sexual adjustment. On the other hand, several of the women interviewees insisted that their heterosexual experience confirmed their lesbianism. Suffering most poignantly, with little prospect of an improvement in their condition, are transvestites and transsexuals, as the experience of interviewee Barbara de Lamere demonstrates.

Racial, ethnic, and religious factors complicated the coming-out experiences of most interviewees. African Americans and Latinos had to deal with the particular homophobia of their communities as well as that of the majority society. Roman Catholics especially confronted harsh rejection within their church. In addition, inculcated with the attitudes of the general society, both gays and lesbians experienced tensions within the gay community arising from racism, anti-Semitism, and male chauvinism. Some lesbians reject communication with all males, including gays.

The response of parents was decisive in the coming-out experience of all the interviewees. Sophisticated, humane parents facilitated the adjustment of their children. Parents who had assimilated the homophobia of society as expounded in literature, the media, and popular humor had to undergo a coming-out experience of their own before fully accepting the sexual orientation of their offspring.

Traumatic for both gays and lesbians during their years in the closet is the life of subterfuge they are compelled to lead. "Gays are socialized to hide," insisted one interviewee. "We instinctively know not to tell anybody. We lead this double life, and it's crazy. We're taught to manipulate throughout our entire lives." As social pariahs, gays and lesbians cannot establish relationships as freely as heterosexuals. Lesbians and gay men meet at bars, often for brief encounters in which the men especially confront the threat of HIV infection.

Gerri Wells emphasized that the impact of internalized homophobia in the undermining of self-worth among lesbians and gays often results in suicide. "Society everywhere is telling us that we're nothing," Gerri declares. "The gay bashers have been taught that we're evil and no good, and we have been taught that, too. You have to love yourself in order for other people to love you. Until we are able to deal with our own homophobia," she warns, "we will never be able to deal with the general homophobia and build the kind of community and community power that we need."

"Closet" isolation causes spiritual crippling, and the coming-out experience does not occur in a single liberating act accomplished from one day to the next. Rene Puliatti, a former naval lieutenant, compared the comprehensive transformation involved in the coming-out experience of gay men to the struggle that women wage within a male-dominated society. "Even more than women, gays," Rene asserts, "have to reevaluate all the premises on which society operates. Incorporating what society and religion say about them into their own psyches, to accept themselves, they have to reject society's values and standards and evaluate on their own, by their own standards, all aspects of the world. To achieve a sense of wholeness within a hostile society, I have had the choice to reject either myself or society."

The coming-out experiences recounted by interviewees in this book range from relatively painless emergence to emergence with minimal vicissitudes and up to emergence after lengthy and harrowing struggles. Several tried or thought of suicide. On the other hand, a few, like Matt Foreman, executive director of the Anti-Violence Project (AVP), and Marjorie Hill, director of the Mayor's Office for Lesbian and Gay Affairs, insisted that they experienced little or no distress in the process. Tom von Foerster, a founder of AVP, and Billy Jones, the New York City Commissioner for Mental Health, were spared the general travail because they had the good fortune of support at home. "My parents were always there for me," Billy remarked. Other interviewees, however, reported a gamut of reactions to their coming out in their families.

During his initial grappling with his homosexuality, M. was "in a tailspin." "I had to abandon the dream of a life as a married professor in a university community," he recalled. "My whole path in life was to be rejected because of my being gay. I had nothing with which to replace it." M. felt unable to discuss his problem with his parents; fearing he was disappointing them, he avoided seeing them.

"The unremitting struggle required in this society to become comfortable with being gay and to be effective as a member of society," recounted Alan Klein, a founder of Queer Nation, "has informed all aspects of my life. There are a lot of areas of one's life that need acceptance. You learn to take them one at a time, accepting your family for who they are, developing self-confidence and finally accepting yourself sexually and loving yourself for who you are. It's not easy to come out to your parents or on the job," Alan declares, but he wonders how he endured the secret life before he came out.

On the other hand, gay activists reported that in their coming-out struggles they achieved a firmer sense of who they were and increased confidence in their own dignity and self-worth. As Ginny Apuzzo put it, "Once you resolve the question about your own role in your freedom, once you ask yourself how much of my freedom is my responsibility, then you are a free person." Thus, in recalling her denunciation of the reverse homophobia among lesbian colleagues in the police department, Vanessa declared, "I knew what I believed in. I was a normal person. I was a good person. I had aspirations for a family. I had a wonderful woman at my side. I wanted everything that straight people had."

At a June 1992 "Lesbian and Gay Experience in the Criminal Justice System" meeting at the office of the Manhattan district attorney, Michael DeCicco, an official in the city department of correction offered a pragmatic rationale for his coming out. Confronting snide innuendoes from colleagues when he failed to appear at social affairs accompanied by a wife or girlfriend, he became aware that "out" gays were less likely to suffer insult and disparagement and did not have to remain constantly, minute by minute, on guard against exposure. He realized, too, that he was not alone in leading a secret life. Gradually he became more and more comfortable with himself and then even proud of his identity. In fact, when someone reported that a colleague had sneered at him in connection with a union election, Michael quipped, "That's the last time I'm going to sleep with him."

Bruce, a staffer at the Crime Victims Board, described the exhilaration he experienced in his belated coming out. "You've heard the term 'born again,' " said Bruce. "That describes what it meant to come out of the closet. I exploded out of the closet. But 'born' is better than born again. I ask myself how I managed to live before coming out. Human sexuality is a natural component no matter what your orientation, and if you suppress it you're going to have all kinds of problems."

The trauma experienced by gays before and during coming out sharpens their social sensitivity. According to City Councilman Tom Duane, "Many gays have a missionary syndrome and develop a high level of compassion out of their own social isolation." As a child, Tom recalls, he never participated in making fun of other children. "I knew exactly how they felt," he says. "To this day, I can't bear it when I see children making fun of each other." Gays, Tom insists, "have such a fundamental feeling that we are not good people that we go out of our way to show that we are good people. That's a lot of what drives a certain group in our community, certainly the people I tend to be with and to like."

"I think my being gay informs my fury," New York City Commissioner of Human Rights Dennis de Leon declares, concurring with Tom Duane's contention. "As a gay, you have a sense of outrage at what's been done to you. I think it's easier to understand someone else's outrage. I went through decades of confusion and struggle. Being part of the gay community helps me to understand all the different groups that we [at the commission] work with."

Chapter One

"I'm into Being Gerri Wells"

According to an estimate often cited by agencies maintaining statistics on violent crimes, one of four women and one of seven men experience sexual molestation before the age of eighteen. None of the gay interviewees related experiences of such assault, but two of the lesbian interviewees described childhood incidents of incest or rape. After divorce two of the lesbians were separated from their children. Generally becoming aware of their sexual orientation at a later age, often after years of marriage, lesbians not only suffer opprobrium as homosexuals but also undergo the humiliations of the sexism endemic to contemporary American society.

Reflecting on the experience of her lesbian daughter and on the experiences of the lesbian daughters of other members of PFLAG (Parents and Friends of Lesbians and Gays), one interviewee concluded that coming out is the result of a conscious decision more often among lesbians than among gay men. She had never heard a gay man say, "I've decided to be gay." On the other hand, she stated, lesbians, particularly those active in lesbian organizations, often declared that they had reached a decision to go with their lesbian tendencies. As women can more easily play a passive role in heterosexual experiences than can men, lesbians seem to enter into long-lasting heterosexual relations more often than gay men.

GERRI WELLS*

Among the lesbian interviewees, Gerri Wells enjoyed one of the least-difficult coming-out experiences. When she began to mature physically, her

*In 1993, a member of the Police Council and a Pink Panther (see Chapter 12). Note: Henceforth, for all interviewees whose experiences are divided between parts of the book, references to their appearance in chapters of Part II will be given as in this instance.

mother threw her dungarees in the garbage. "You are to stop dressing like the boys," she insisted. Gerri retrieved the dungarees, and the issue was never posed again. A lesbian friend frightened Gerri's mother by warning her that she had a dyke in her family and recounting her own suffering as a lesbian. Gerri believes that religion was also a factor in her mother's reaction. "I remember my mother looking out the window one day at me and my gay brother," Gerri relates, "and shaking her head and saying, 'Where did I go wrong?' He was playing with the girls, and I with the boys."

Gerri and her brother became aware of being gay at about the same time. "On Halloween," Gerri relates, "we went out as a couple. I dressed as a man. He wore spiked heels and a dress and put oranges in the top. He made me walk behind him up stairs to catch the oranges if they fell. We were fortunate," Gerri remarks. "Our parents gave us room to grow and to be. Most gay people I know haven't had that luck. My parents had artistic and beatnik friends, including gays. Their attitude was, 'As long as you don't hurt anybody or yourself, do what's natural to you.' My father would take us to Inwood Park to play softball. My brother would pick flowers for my mother. My father would never say to him, 'Get over here and play ball.' I enjoyed playing ball with my father.

"I'm into being Gerri Wells," Gerri declares. "That's who I am. That's how I grew up. That's how it should be." On the other hand, Gerri encountered homophobic attacks as a child and as an adolescent. At seventeen, at a Job Corps training school in Oklahoma, she was repeatedly harassed by homophobic fellow students. Stabbed on one occasion, she required several stitches in her head. After she warned the director of the school that if he did not respond to such attacks she would embarrass the school, the ringleader of the homophobes was expelled, and Gerri faced no more problems from fellow students. One day walking in town hand-in-hand with another lesbian, however, Gerri was badgered by a gang of adolescents. Suddenly she turned and punched one of her tormentors. He fell to the ground. The others backed off. "When kids in grammar school called me bull dyke," Gerri recounts, "I popped one of them. After that they'd say, 'Leave her alone.' You learn as a gay person," Gerri comments, "that if you don't respond to harassment with equal force, they'll keep it up."

Gerri's gay younger brother followed her example. For days a gang of boys taunted him as he jumped rope with girls on the block. "One day," Gerri recalls, "he stopped dead in his tracks and went crazy. He beat the hell out of the biggest bully. We had to pull him off the boy. After that he went back to his double Dutching as though nothing had happened. You bloody someone's nose," Gerri explains, "and they learn to leave you alone."

Gerri's brother, however, was not left alone. Once, outside a gay disco in Puerto Rico, a man pressed a knife to his throat, took his wallet, and called him a "fuckin' faggot."

TRACY MORGAN*

Of all the women interviewed, Tracy Morgan underwent the most complicated coming-out experience and arrived at the clearest insights regarding feminist issues involved in her lesbian identity. Born in 1962 in "a WASPish middle-class Jersey suburban town." Tracy is a child of schoolteacher parents. Growing up with a younger brother, Tracy declares, made her aware very early of women's position in society. Because her mother became upset when the house was in disorder, Tracy picked up her brother's socks and washed his cereal bowl. She could not fight back physically with him. "My power was in my mouth," she declares. "By attacking his ego, I could make him doubt himself. That is the strategy I have employed ever since with men of whom I have physical fear."

Tracy frequently slept over at the home of one her friends, Corey. She would position her hand on the bed so that if Corey, who was prematurely developed, rolled over, her breasts would fall into Tracy's hand. Before dinner during weekend visits with another school friend, Tracy and her friend would go into the guest room and roll around on the floor. "Let's pretend that we're married," they would say.

Tracy remembers hearing her mother express disdain for a seventh-grade teacher, an obvious lesbian, "who did everything," Tracy recounts, "but wear a tie."

At puberty Tracy began to have arguments with her mother. She could not understand why her brother was allowed to stay out later than she and why his comings and goings were never questioned. When he became sexually active, his behavior was accepted, while she was frequently "grounded" for coming home a half hour late or for moving on to a second party without giving warning. "When you're brought up with that message." Tracy declares, "you learn that you have to be more careful about yourself. The maturity that little girls have, in my opinion, is born of tragedy, not of privilege."

In high school, as corresponding secretary of the student council, Tracy developed a crush on the vice president. "She had beautiful hair," Tracy recalls, "and she was brilliant. I wanted to be just like her. I felt annoyed that she had a boyfriend. It was too scary for me to think about having sexual desire for her, so I dated her boyfriend after they broke up." As popularity rested on attracting the jocks, Tracy set out to win popularity and was even chosen homecoming queen. On the other hand, Tracy was aware that girls who slept around had their names scrawled on the walls in the boys' toilets and that she would be called a slut if she had sex with any of her dates. There were few epithets she could use against sexually active men in return.

*An ACT UP and lesbian activist (see Chapters 8 and 17).

"I was angered at the injustice, but I had to choose between opening my mouth," she recalls, "and opening my legs. I chose to talk back."

Tracy admired Margo, a bright, eccentric friend from the school choir. Boys called Margo "cow" because she was overweight. Called "cow" one time too many, Margo took to amphetamines. "Who did these men think they were?" Tracy asked herself. She announced that she would not go out with the jocks any more because of the way they treated her friend.

Delighted when she was the center of attention, Tracy's parents were dismayed when she suddenly isolated herself. She could not talk to them about what was troubling her. Her father also had a hard time communicating with her while she was a child and seemed even more at a loss when she became potentially sexually active.

During her senior year Tracy fell into a profound depression. "Let's do it," she said to Mark, a trusted friend since fifth grade with whom she had no fear of loss of respect or of idle talk. "I found it boring," she recalls.

Happy to be away from home, Tracy made an easy adjustment during her freshman year at American University in Washington, D.C. Bored after a few months with a conformist boyfriend, she became friends with a self-proclaimed bisexual, a "punk" who dyed his hair green. She began to think about bisexuality as a possibility for herself. Once in a conversation with a woman, Tracy blurted out, "If I wanted to have a relationship with a woman, I would." She wondered to herself, " 'Where did that thought come from? What am I telling myself?' It was kind of scary," she recalls.

During the summer Tracy dated Lewis, an effeminate young man, and with him had her first enjoyable sexual experience. The experience gave her confidence that she might eventually negotiate a lasting relationship with a man. She did have one problem: She could not look at his penis. Lewis's mother lent her a copy of *The Women's Room* by Marilyn French, a feminist book with a lesbian character. "Like a lot of other women my age, I was transformed by this novel," Tracy declares. "I realized that we accept the position of women in this society only at our peril. We get used to accepting it. We don't even complain."

Transferring to the State University of New York at Albany in her sophomore year, Tracy urged one of her roommates, a closet lesbian, to read *The Women's Room.* She was outraged by the issues it raised, but after kissing a woman, she looked in the mirror and was not sure she was the same person as before. Tracy assured her that she was not the same person. "As though I knew about such things," she comments in retrospect. After their conversation, Tracy thought to herself, "If she's a lesbian, what am I?"

At the final session of a psychology course, the instructor announced that all the books and articles the three hundred students had read had been based on studies of the behavior of men. "We know very little about the psychology of women," he declared. Tracy was infuriated. "I had sat there an entire semester generalizing about people—men," she thought. She hurried to the registrar and declared that she wanted to take a major in women's studies. She entered a program that was "a hotbed of lesbians with instructors so butch I thought they were men." Caught up in feminism, she broke up with her boyfriend. "I like you," she assured him, "but I don't want to have sex with you."

The Feminist Alliance on campus was split between "straights" and lesbians. Tracy resented the doctrinaire attitude among the lesbians that required that everyone wear a flannel shirt and boots. "How could I, a former homecoming queen, accept such attitudes?" she asks. "I wore skirts and still do. I wear makeup. How could I be a lesbian, if they were what lesbians were?"

Tracy ended up in the camp of the straight women, called "lesbophobic."

One of Tracy's lesbian classmates, Cris, a brilliant, attractive, and self-confident woman, particularly caught her attention. At home during intersession Tracy had nightmares about Cris. The next semester, in a women's studies seminar, Tracy found herself cramped in a tiny room with three other students, including "that woman"; but when Cris suggested that they do a project together, Tracy agreed. One evening she went to Cris's house, "a lesbian house." During their conversation, Cris asked whether she had ever kissed a woman. Tracy said she had not. The thought was scary to her. "It'll change my life," she declared. "As long as I'm not gay, I'm safe." Tracy suddenly realized that it was 4 A.M. Cris walked her to the door. "The thought came to me," Tracy recounts. "I'll kiss her! It was the first time I'd kissed a woman!" Cris was pleased. Tracy went home thinking, "O my god, now I am a homosexual."

Back at her room, Tracy found Hamilton, the closeted gay boyfriend of Tracy's roommate. She told him that she had just kissed Cris. "Hamilton was wonderful," she recalls. "Really?" he exclaimed. "Now what's going to happen?"

On Christmas Eve, at home a few months later, her father sat her down to talk things out. "What do you want to do with your life?" he asked. Tracy replied that she would like to get her doctorate and go on to teach. "Then what?" he insisted. Tracy asked what he meant. "Tracy, how far do you swing?" he demanded. He had never used such language with her. Tracy asked him to be more explicit. "Do you like women?" he asked.

"Yes," Tracy replied. He turned white as a ghost. She became anxious because he had a cardiac problem. "I won't tell your mother," he said. "It'll break her heart." But he did tell her mother. "I love you anyway," her mother insisted. Two weeks later, however, they called to inform Tracy that they were no longer going to pay for her college education. Learning of her parents' decision, Tracy's childhood friend Mark warned them that if they stopped paying for her tuition, he would provide the money. Confronted with this challenge, Tracy's parents reversed themselves. They assured her that she was merely going through a phase. "The dykes at school said the same thing," Tracy declares, "because I didn't look or act like them. I didn't feel that I fit in anywhere."

After a year and a half as lovers, Cris and Tracy broke up. Tracy then developed a relationship with a woman named Jill, a relationship that came to an end after a few months in great part because Jill, unlike Tracy, was not monogamous. "The breakup caused me to question my self-worth," Tracy recalls.

In 1985, moving to New York City after graduation, Tracy found herself bereft of the support of the women's studies program and of the protective world of the university. In Albany, Tracy declares, the lesbian community was small, and she could meet a woman at a bar and see her again at a rally. At the New York Lesbian and Gay Community Center and at lesbian bars, she found no sense of community. About lesbian activism in New York at the time she declares, "Talking is one thing, doing is another. I began to think that I didn't want to be a lesbian." She entered therapy. "My quest," she says, "was to get it all together, to see whether I could establish a relationship with a woman that was not threatening."

While supporting herself by freelance editorial work, Tracy served as a volunteer in drafting grant applications for the production of "Paris Is Burning," a film about cross-dressers in Harlem. She found herself in the company of gay men, few of whom had ever socialized with lesbians. "I wasn't meeting lesbians," she relates, "but I was certainly in a positive gay environment."

After relationships with women for two-and-a-half years, Tracy was astonished to discover the greater freedom she enjoyed in a relationship with a man she met at work. After a year with this man and another year alone, Tracy found another involvement, with a man who worked half the year in London. Tracy flew to England to visit him periodically and accompanied him on trips. "I'm a good campanion," Tracy asserts, "for men who don't want submissive women; but the minute I saw the gay community becoming visible, I felt this intense desire to return to the activity I had enjoyed in Albany. Suddenly in the gay community women were recognized. AIDS brought a connection between gays and lesbians."

Returning to lesbian life was not easy for Tracy. "I had control in relations with men," Tracy declares, "a lot of autonomy." With women she feared the problem of merging with another person, of being swallowed up, of not knowing where she stopped and her partner began.

In January 1990 Tracy helped to organize an ACT UP demonstration against the Centers for Disease Control in Atlanta. One evening at a lesbian bar, a woman came dancing up to her and said, "You're really cute." "No woman had said that to me for a long time," Tracy declares. The next night Heidi approached her again. "We danced together," she recounts. "I kissed her."

As Tracy became more involved in activist organizations, she and Heidi found themselves meeting at demonstrations. They became lovers.

ELIZABETH GARRO*

Liz Garro suffered a long and painful travail before achieving a clear and confident perception of herself. From early childhood, Liz proved to be the rebel among the seven children of a working-class Irish mother and Italian father, both "very Catholic and repressive." Liz's father insisted that every family had a "bad apple"; as the bad one, Liz was constantly punished for actions of her siblings. Once she was beaten for cheating in school. "I did not even know what the word meant," Liz recalls. "The boy sitting next to me and I both had perfect test papers, and I was accused of copying from his paper."

At the age of seven or eight, Liz already sensed that she was different from other girls. When her mother caught her playing with boys, she was confined to the house. At school, nuns sat her in the boys' section of the class to punish her for behaving like a tomboy. Though her grades were in the nineties, Liz suffered from comparison with her more studious, ladylike older sister. Once Liz overheard a nun ask her mother, "Does Elizabeth have the same father as her sister?" Dreading the prospect of four additional years of parochial school, Liz deliberately failed her high school placement examination. "I don't know what happened to her," exclaimed one of the nuns. Liz received one of the worst beatings of her life from her mother. (Years later Liz found out that her mother had been battered as a child by an alcoholic father.)

In public high school Liz learned that girls who wore a certain color were "lezzies," that is, girls who kissed each other. Liz thought that kissing other girls was something she would like, but she was warned to keep away from them; they might pull her into a closet! "Out" lesbians kept to themselves and assembled at their own candy-store hangout. Liz would have liked to get to know them, but she feared the reaction at home and at church. When Liz was sixteen, her mother took her out of school and sent her to Catholic Charities, complaining that she could not control her. When her father lost his job, Liz went to work for an optician. Her mother took her wages, granting her only enough for subway fare and lunch, but Liz was able to stay away from home the four evenings a week she attended night school. Friday evenings her mother allowed her to attend a religious hour and dance at church, but she did not allow Liz to go out on dates.

At eighteen Liz had a homosexual experience with a neighbor. The woman sat her down afterward and told her that what they had done was wrong. It was an experiment, she said, that Liz should forget and not repeat. Although protesting that she had enjoyed the experience, Liz was so overcome with guilt that when she left the apartment she felt that everyone knew that she had done something evil.

* Liaison to the gay community at the office of the Kings County (Brooklyn) district attorney (see Chapters 10 and 12).

At a new job in a bank, Liz began having lunch with Tony, a fellow employee, a newly returned Vietnam veteran. After grilling him, Liz's mother allowed Tony to take her to the movies or out for ice cream. He was, after all, Liz explains, Italian and a Catholic. When Liz announced, however, that she and Tony were becoming engaged, her mother flew into a rage. Tony gave assurance they were not having sex but insisted that they were resolved on marrying. Her mother, Liz insists, feared losing her income from her. "Besides," Liz declares, "I wasn't supposed to be happy." When Tony's parents dropped by one Saturday morning, Liz's mother announced: "She's dumb and bad. How can she get married?" After they left, she beat Liz, shouting, "How dare they come here? You're not getting married."

Liz and Tony made marriage arrangements on their own. The priest notified her parents, but they did not appear at the ceremony. Tony's father offered to walk Liz down the aisle, but Liz said, "You're not my father. I have to do this alone." Within months Liz found that she was pregnant. She confided in Tony her fear that she might be an abusive mother like her own mother. She also told him that she was attracted to women. He reassured her. He was macho, he insisted, and he would keep her straight.

After Lisa's birth, Liz befriended a neighbor who had a son Lisa's age. One day the woman put her hand down Liz's back and declared that she wanted to kiss her. Liz jumped out of her chair and ran home. "I was frightened by what she wanted to do," Liz declares. "I was having enjoyable sex with my husband. It was wrong."

When Lisa was old enough to begin school, Liz decided to continue her own education in college evening classes. To pay her tuition, she took a job at a child-abuse agency. Studying case histories of the clients, Liz relived and worked out some of her own childhood experience. Many children, she discovered, underwent far worse cruelty than she had suffered. Once, reading a report about a nine-year-old who required a reconstruction of her vagina, Liz broke down and cried.

Resentful of Liz's absence from home and of her attempt to surpass him in education, Tony quarreled with her. Their sex suffered. Liz resisted his demands for oral sex. Nevertheless, when a family counselor told her that she was going through a sexual-adjustment crisis, she denied having any problem. One day in an argument, Tony accused her of being a lesbian. Liz was insulted.

At work Liz confided her problems with Tony in a social worker named Yoly, an "out" lesbian who was in the process of breaking up with her lover. They kissed. "I had my first real kiss," Liz declares. "I was already thirty."

One day Liz admitted to Tony that she was undergoing an identity crisis. "I have to find out about myself," she declared, "and I cannot do it while we're married because I can't cheat on you." "All hell broke loose," she recalls. After ordering her out, he reconsidered and suggested that she experiment for a while, confident that after a fling she would return to him. When

Liz insisted that she could not lead a double life, he locked her out of the apartment and sued for divorce. For three years Liz battled in court for visitation rights with her child, "a degrading experience," she recalls, "with snickers from the judge and the court stenographer." Remarried, Tony persuaded Lisa to ask Liz to give up her rights as a mother so that his new wife might adopt her. Liz refused to do so, but for several years she did not see her daughter.

Only when Lisa reached nineteen did Liz reestablish a relationship with her daughter. Lisa even came to live with her mother, and Lisa and her boyfriend and Liz and her lover socialized. After a year, however, Lisa moved back with Tony. "Tony has a lot of money," Liz remarks, "and has spoiled Lisa. We speak on the phone once or twice a month. I haven't seen her in a year. The past is too difficult for Lisa to deal with. When she's ready, I'll be there."

FROM EDDIE TO BARBARA: THE COMING OUT OF A TRANSSEXUAL*

When the Gay Veterans Association changed its name to 'Gay, Lesbian, and Bisexual Veterans,' " recalled Barbara de Lamere, "I looked up at the wall and said, 'I've been every one of those.' " In fact, Barbara's account of her coming-out experience serves as a bridge between the coming-out experiences of lesbians and those of gay men, for she has been both and more.

Until her sex change at the age of forty-two, Barbara's name was Edmond, or "Eddie." (In the following account, the names alternate according to date and circumstance.)

Born in 1940, Eddie was one of three children and the only son of a French-Canadian factory worker and an Irish immigrant mother, who worked as a cleaning woman in a hotel. Eddie's parents had limited educations and were content with an existence of work, church, and beer drinking. When Eddie was still a child, his father brought his family to the Washington Heights section of New York City from his parents' chicken farm in Connecticut. They joined a community of members of their extended family, all with drinking problems.

It was a characteristic of the family to think that if they did not talk about a problem, its existence could be denied, and it might eventually disappear. Thus, when Eddie brought home a note from the school physician declaring that he required eyeglasses, his mother simply tore it up. Eddie was poor at games, unaware that his clumsiness arose from his restricted vision. Once while playing he crashed through a glass door and suffered the loss of flexibility in two of his fingers. "At the age of sixteen at a golf course where I

*A member of the board of the Gay, Lesbian, and Bisexual Veterans of Greater New York (see Chapter 15).

was working," Barbara recounts, "I said to another caddy, 'It's getting dark out.' It was noon. He took his glasses off and put them on me, and suddenly I saw. O my god! The sun came back."

Eddie began drinking at the age of thirteen. He was "plastered every weekend." After starting to work at the age of eighteen, he took turns with his parents and his older sister in furnishing a bottle for the weekend guzzling. "I thought of myself," Barbara explains, "as a 'garsoun,' a lout, and a garsoun thinks that in life you work, drink, and die. I didn't expect anything more out of life, and to me drinking was freedom." When years later, his mother became unmistakably an alcoholic, the family continued to deny she had a drinking problem at all. (Eventually she burned to death, after setting her room on fire while drunk.)

The major denial in the family concerned Eddie's cross-dressing, which he began at the age of three. They began to call him "Butch," apparently hoping that with such a manly nickname he would act like a "real" boy. When older cousins visited, they slapped him around, presumably to make him "tough." At Easter time, his parents gave his sisters "girl" presents; they gave him toy guns. After overhearing a relative remark on his effeminate walk and sneers that he threw a ball like a girl, Eddie became self-conscious about his every gesture. At some point, too, he became aware that "God did not like" his cross-dressing. Once in a novena he asked God either to cure his crippled hand or to end his cross-dressing. Deliberating a moment, however, he decided he would prefer a cure for his hand.

Eddie cross-dressed only when his parents were away. "I loved satins," Barbara recalls. Nellie, his older sister, entered into the spirit of his cross-dressing and joked about it with him. When Eddie was about sixteen or seventeen, his younger sister began to give him pointers about makeup. "My brother wears my clothes," Nellie announced upon introducing Eddie to her fiancé. Their parents made a joke of Nellie's remark, and Eddie, then eighteen, and his younger sister joined in the pretense. "Here Nellie was telling the truth," Barbara recalls, "and the rest of us were denying it."

In early photographs, Eddie never appears smiling. In fact, he often thought of committing suicide. As a teenager Eddie had a recurring dream of asking his mother as she lay dying, "Was it true?" She always answered, "Yes. You are a girl." If his parents ever found out that he was a transvestite, he decided, he would hang himself. "Of course, they knew," Barbara recalls, "but I was not supposed to know that they knew." (Not until Eddie was thirty-five, one evening when he and his mother were both drunk, did he admit to her that he was a transvestite.)

After puberty Eddie had no sexual fantasies involving either sex. On the other hand, he repeatedly dreamed of finding himself in the company of women in beauty salons, not kissing or fondling them, just being in their company. With the family, however, he boasted of crushes on girls, and it was a joke that he had twenty-six girlfriends. Any girl or woman he saw wearing something he admired he claimed as a girlfriend.

Eddie was aware that boys in the neighborhood were engaging in mutual masturbation. Once when Eddie went to study with two classmates, one of the boys said, "Let's give each other blow jobs." Eddie refused. One of the boys grabbed him, and the other pulled down Eddie's pants and tried vainly to arouse him. Giving up on him, they proceeded to do sixty-nine with each other. "I had no reaction to what they were doing," Barbara declares, "but I was annoyed that they tried to involve me against my will."

As a senior in high school, Eddie engaged in sex play with a girlfriend. Suddenly he ejaculated in his pants. He became frightened. At confession, the priest counseled, "Avoid all occasions for sin!" Eddie reported the priest's admonition to the girl and told her he could not see her any more.

By the time he graduated from high school, Eddie considered himself a transvestite, but not a homosexual. Anticipating being drafted, he volunteered for the U.S. Air Force. While in service he entered into a homosexual relationship; from 1963, the year he completed his military service, until 1967, Eddie and his air-force lover Larry lived together. (Eddie's military experience is described in Chapter 15, "Gays in the Military.")

Larry was aware of Eddie's transvestism while they were in the service. Afterward, he tolerated Eddie's cross-dressing indoors but would not escort him anywhere if he dressed as a woman. "You look like my mother," he sneered, "you look terrible." "In a sense it was a learning experience for me," Barbara recalls. "If I had gone out then, I would have been read [recognized as a transvestite] right away."

In 1967, Larry, who had long been expressing a desire to have children, announced that he was getting married. He promised that he would always be Eddie's friend, and Eddie was the best man at his wedding. At a bachelor party the night before, they had sex; and they continued to meet for sex occasionally until 1982. Larry had a serious disease, and Barbara fears that his silence thereafter signified that he had died. In 1994 Barbara still missed him. "Even today," she says, "I would love to live with him."

After Larry's marriage, Eddie went to New Orleans for the Mardi Gras and while there bought a complete wardrobe of women's clothing. Upon his return to New York, he was struck abruptly with a sense of his isolation. 'I looked out the window at night and saw cleaning women (like my mother) going to work together, in a community. I envied gays, too, because they had a community." On July 4th, Eddie put on heavy makeup and covered his head with a scarf, under which he had a wig fringe. After donning women's clothes, he took a couple of drinks to fortify himself. Glancing out the window, he looked up at the sky and declared to the world, "If I'm crazy, lock me up! Damn it, this is me, I have no choice." Venturing out to the street, he hurried to a telephone booth at the corner and pretended to be making a call. Returning inside, he shook for 15 minutes. He downed another drink and cried, "I did it, I did it!"

The experience became easier with practice. Occasionally Eddie was *read* as a transvestite, but he became increasingly more sophisticated about his attire, dressing more appropriately to his age. He went to the store in the morning as a woman, returned to the apartment to change, and set out for his college courses as a man. In the evening, once again he dressed as a woman. "I was changing my sex the way I was changing my clothes," Barbara recalls.

That same year, 1967, Eddie joined the Ridiculous Theatrical Company as a transvestite actor, using the name Onoe Bunny Eisenhower. That year, too, Eddie met Esther. A dedicated member of a small Communist sect actively opposing the Vietnam War, Esther had had lesbian affairs and was not dismayed at Eddie's transvestism. Aware that her political group would not accept her relationship with a transvestite, Esther left the group. Because of hostility to her in the theater company, Eddie gave up his acting. In 1970 they married in a Unitarian church. Esther's parents were in attendance. Eddie's father had died that year, but his mother came, drunk, "smashed to the gills."

Although Eddie and Esther occasionally quarreled and once even separated, their marriage continued for seven years. When Eddie let his hair grow and grew a beard, Esther thought that Eddie would cease cross-dressing outside the apartment. But Eddie did not stop. When he went out, he covered his beard with a scarf. "I couldn't help myself," Barbara insists.

In 1977 Eddie obtained a job as a proofreader in a law firm, a position Barbara continued to hold in 1996. The next year he and Esther obtained a divorce. She had fallen in love with another man. "I see my former wife occasionally," Barbara declares. "We're friends. I wouldn't want to have sex with her, and I like her fiancé."

Upon the breakup of his marriage, Eddie considered his options. He could, he decided, move to California and find work in Los Angeles as a female impersonator. "I could even become a woman," he exclaimed one day. The thought surprised him. It was the first time that that possibility had occurred to him. Through no choice of his own, he reasoned, he had the body of a man. He never expected to obtain any joy out of his body. He had a right to undergo a sex change. He had paid his patriotic duty by serving in the air force. His parents were both dead.

A therapist referred Eddie to an electrologist and an endocrinologist. He started hormonal treatments. At work, when his supervisor made caustic remark about transsexuals, Eddie defended them. "Why are you speaking up for them?" his supervisor asked. "Because I'm one of them," Eddie replied. The man walked out of the room. Within minutes he returned and demanded, "What the fuck are you talking about?" "I'm one of them," Eddie insisted. "You're joking." "I'm not joking," said Eddie.

The supervisor spread the word through the firm. As under the hormonal treatments Eddie increasingly developed female characteristics, colleagues began stopping by Eddie's office to look at "the company freak." As he let his hair grow longer and assumed ever more androgynous dress, Eddie found that while in the lobby of the building people thought he was a woman, in the office he was still addressed as a man. Unnerved by this switching of genders, he developed ulcers and thought of suicide.

Upon the advice of the office manager, Eddie made an appointment with a psychologist. A Catholic and the author of a book promoting the preservation of family values, the man had never had a transsexual as a patient, and his knowledge of transsexual surgery derived from a single article in a popular magazine. Opposed on religious grounds to sex changes, he offered Eddie no support. In two consecutive sessions he referred to Eddie as "a loser," and Eddie sat and cried. At his next and final session, he fought back. "You said I'm not happy," he declared. "I don't know anybody who is happy, who is accomplishing anything. Happiness! Everyone has to find happiness in his own way."

Paradoxically, the setback with the therapist strengthened Eddie's resolve to initiate the year during which he would have to live as a woman, a prerequisite to sex-change surgery. He had his alcohol-rotted teeth capped and stopped bringing beer and liquor to his apartment. To accumulate money for the operation, he began working long hours, depriving himself entirely of a social life. His fellow employees, already contemptuous because of his decision to undergo a sex change, resented his sudden industriousness. One man masturbated in front of him. Another announced he would like to hang Eddie up by his earrings.

"When the time comes for you to dress as a woman, let me know," announced his supervisor. "I'll find you another job." Eddie's self-confidence evaporated. "You want a man," he said to himself in despair, "I'll give you a man." He took to dressing in more manly clothes. He fantasized about beating up a gay man in the office with whom he had had sex.

During the office Christmas party, the general manager, aware of Eddie's emotional turmoil, called him into her office. Eddie broke down. "Everybody hates me," he cried. "The men think I'm after them. The women think I'm after them. They all tell me they can't bring their children here because I'll go after them. I don't go after children. I'm not a monster." The woman persuaded Eddie to make an appointment with a therapist of her acquaintance. The therapist proved to be compassionate and astute. For the first time in his life Eddie had someone to talk to.

One day, walking down the street, Eddie looked at women and said to himself, "They have what I'm going to have. It was the first time in my life," Barbara recalls, "I ever thought of a vagina as a part of my body. With the surgery, I would be able to go into a women's bathroom without being arrested."

The operation did not prove traumatic. "Much ado about nothing and anti-climactic," Barbara declares. "I had breast implants, had my trachea shaved, and underwent genital surgery. If it had been done when I was three, I would have been spared much suffering. Today I'm attracted to both sexes, but I am once again alone," says Barbara, "except for my cats. Heterosexuals are allowed to love. Why the hell can't lesbians or gays or transsexuals love? When I was a child I used to sing to myself: 'To be alone with just a memory, it is my destiny to be alone.' That's how my life has turned out, alone with just a memory."

Chapter Two
"What Beautiful Blue Eyes"

Because of the skewed conception of masculinity in American society, gays, "sissies," bear a greater brunt of homophobic scorn and violence than "tomboys." In elementary school, Tracy Morgan was aware that boys taunted as sissies or faggots were beaten up on the playground and generally terrorized. "That was a way," she thought, "of telling them that they weren't acting right. Women are not thought of as sexual beings before they're mature," Tracy explains, "and it is assumed that they're all going to grow up to be straight."

Homophobia, New York City Councilman Tom Duane is convinced, is instilled in little boys more than in little girls. As a child, Tom found roughhousing threatening, and like other gay children he lived constantly on the alert. "The dynamic of aggression on the playground," be says, "is not so different from that in prison. I think some of the drive is cultural and some of it innate in the species." Every attempt to play or work with others, he recalls, roused anxiety in him.

From her gay brother with whom she remained very close until his death of AIDS a few years ago, Gerri Wells came to understand that the catty behavior among many gay men that lesbians as well as heterosexuals find repellent is a reaction to the intense social hostility they encounter. "They internalize the hostility around and toward them," she says, "and express it in ripping each other apart."

The following coming-out experiences of some gay interviewees are presented in order of intensity of anxiety, beginning with Tom von Foerster's painless rite of passage and continuing with processes of ever-greater complexity and tension. None of the gay interviewees underwent the worst horrors suffered by many gay young people—physical abuse and expulsion from their families. (Such experiences are recounted in Chapter 13, on the Hetrick Martin Institute and the Harvey Milk School, institutions catering to troubled adolescent gays and lesbians.)

TOM VON FOERSTER*

"For a gay boy and young man," Tom declares, "I had an almost ideal situation. I do not think it could have been better." as a child, not athletic like his two brothers, Tom lived as a bookish recluse. Although concerned about his isolation, Tom's parents, sophisticated and tolerant intellectuals, exerted no pressures on him. Tom does not recall feeling unhappy as a child. He enjoyed school and did well in his studies. Although guilt and dissimulation were common among gay children and adolescents in the 1950s, he notes, he experienced almost no anxiety at his sense of being different. He simply did not think of himself as a sexual being.

By the time he entered college, though he had had no sexual experiences, Tom accepted that he was a homosexual. At the age of thirty, anticipating that his name might appear in the media as secretary of the Gay Academic Union, Tom came out to his parents in a letter. "A couple of days later," he recalls, "I got a call from my mother, who essentially said, 'Boy, are we relieved that you are now comfortable enough to be able to tell us.' She said they had known for a long time that he was homosexual. They thought that now that I had become comfortable with my sexuality I should not have any problems henceforth."

Even after coming out both at home and at Harvard, where he joined the faculty, Tom remained celibate. Asked at a Gay Academic Union conference whether he did not regret all the time he had wasted in an asexual existence, Tom replied that he had not thought of it as wasted. "I had a rich social life and did not miss sex," he declared. Whatever he experienced during those years, he noted, brought him to where he then was. Not until he was thirty-two did Tom experience his first sexual encounter and learn how to pick up men in bars. Thereafter, he declares, he made up for lost time. "I always wound up taking people home who were a pleasure to be with," he recalls. "Some still remain friends. The few disappointments were with people who picked me up. After the first experiences, I realized that if I didn't go home with someone, it was no great loss. For me sex had no neurotic component. I felt under no pressure.

"Every time I've taken a friend home to visit," Tom relates, "my parents have received him as part of the family." Tom's brother (his second brother had died young), on the other hand, adjusted slowly to Tom's sexual orienta-

*A founder of the Lesbian and Gay Anti-Violence Project (see Chapter 9).

tion, but Tom and his lover eventually were accepted by his brother and his wife and children.

ERMANNO STINGO*

Born in 1917, Ermanno, a dedicated volunteer at the New York Lesbian and Gay Anti-Violence Project until his death in May 1993, exemplified the experience of many gay senior citizens before the post-Stonewall emergence of a vigorous gay liberation movement. The eldest son among four surviving children of immigrants, Ermanno grew up in the Italian community in Greenwich Village. The Stingo family was warm, though conservative in values and attitudes.

When a doctor advised Ermanno's mother that his penis was too large for a child his age, "That bothered me," Ermanno recalled, "and I was always shy about that, even too shy to go into a men's room and urinate next to another man." When Ermanno was only five, a thirteen-year-old neighbor who lived in the same building showed him how to masturbate, and he continued to masturbate even though his father warned him that his brain would deteriorate. When he was nine, he and the neighbor engaged in their first sexual experience. Ermanno was the aggressive one in their encounters, which continued through his high school years, until his neighbor married. "I never felt guilty," he recalls. "I felt love. My relationship with my neighbor was in a separate world. I had no name for what we did. I didn't know the word homosexual, and the word 'gay' wasn't used until much later."

In school Ermanno became aware that he was different from other boys. He did not enter into competition for girlfriends. He developed crushes on boys but kept his feeling to himself. Slight of physique and called "Sissy Mary," he did not participate in sports. In high school physical training, he had difficulty chinning at the bar. On the other hand, he studied and read a great deal; while other boys won letters in sports, he was awarded a letter for his volunteer work in the school library. His closest friends were two girls who shared his interest in art. His mother objected to his constant association with them and refused to tell him when they telephoned.

His feeling of difference, Ermanno believes, hobbled his development as a self-confident and liberated human being. "If I had had a sense of who I was and what my needs were," he declared, "I might have progressed much further at work and in everything else. I would have been more decisive as a man. I let people push me around because I thought there was something wrong with me. I felt in some way inferior. I had done things that other people would not approve of. For six years my life was pretty barren."

*A volunteer at the Anti-Violence Project and board member at Parents and Friends of Lesbians and Gays (PFLAG) (see Chapters 9 and 16).

One day, embarrassed by the stares of a group of men gathered in silence in the men's room at the Christopher Street subway station, Ermanno was unable to urinate. Abruptly he realized that these were men interested in other men. He was not alone in his sexual attraction! Ermanno determined to move to his own apartment in order to have privacy for encounters. Braving his father's displeasure, he rented an apartment in the Astoria section of Queens in a building owned by a dancer he had met.

One day going down subway stairs, Ermanno, already in his thirties, glanced at a man coming up toward him. Their eyes met. "Sparks were flying," Ermanno recalls. "We talked. I took him home with me. That night was the most exquisite night I had ever had. I called the telephone number he gave me and got no answer. A letter came back marked 'Addressee unknown.' I was devastated. One day I met him in the subway again. He took me to his apartment. I had called at the wrong times, and the post office had made a mistake. I stayed that night and never left."

Boris had been out a long time. He taught Ermanno to appreciate himself as a man and helped him to accept his gayness. Until they were sure of their feelings, they were not monogamous. In the relationship, Ermanno declares that he became a stronger person. They remained together for forty years.

After Boris obtained work as a super at the Salmaggi Opera Company, Ermanno began to meet other gays. The couple started to read books about gay life. When they sent in a subscription to a Swiss gay magazine, the post office returned the envelope marked with a warning addressed to "Miss" Boris Maizel that the magazine was an illegal publication. At his bank Ermanno had to shout before the officers agreed to allow him to establish a joint account with Boris. Such, declares Ermanno, was the homophobic atmosphere of the day.

Like many other gays of the pre-Stonewall generation, Ermanno did not come out to his family or friends until he was in his late thirties. Neither his nor Boris's family accepted gays. "They talked," Ermanno recalls, "as though being gay was bad and as though gays lived in a separate world." Boris's mother came to call Ermanno her "other son," but she never spoke about their relationship. Ermanno's father had said, "If you don't marry an Italian girl, I'll disown you." Nevertheless, he did accept Boris, remarking, "What a nice young man, very bright." In Italian he added, "What beautiful blue eyes he has."

Ermanno's mother had died before Ermanno met Boris. His sisters accepted Boris, as did his brother and sister-in-law. When Ermanno turned sixty-five, however, a cousin remarked, "When am I going to have the confetti from your wedding?" Nevertheless, she sent Boris a birthday card. "He was just somebody nice that they liked," Ermanno declares.

ANDY HUMM*

Born in 1953, the fourth of five children of a Wall Street broker, Andy grew up in Baldwin, an affluent Long Island suburban community. Andy's family attended church regularly; and like his father and his brothers, Andy attended Catholic elementary and high schools, where, Andy recalls, the religious atmosphere was intense, and the nuns did not spare the paddle. One of Andy's sisters entered a convent briefly, and Andy as a child had an ambition to become a priest.

Andy recalls being severely chastised as a child for using an ethnic slur against a neighbor. Because of a sense of his own difference, he early developed a strong sense of compassion. It hurt him when classmates picked on an unattractive girl, and he made an effort to befriend her. Of the small minority of blacks in school, Andy says, "Something made me want to reach out and protect them."

Although he early developed crushes on boys, Andy had no insights regarding sex until he was in eighth grade. He remembers once accusing a friend of being gay. "He pulled me aside on the playground," Andy relates, "and said, 'You know what a homosexual is? It's a man who likes to put another man's cock into his mouth.' " Andy was shocked.

In the intensely competitive high school environment, Andy was often called a faggot because of his nonconformism. "I clowned in response," he recalls, "but I didn't enjoy being teased." He found being in the locker room with other boys both exciting and intimidating. He did not have a girlfriend and wondered what other boys felt about girls. James Kirby, a classmate, confided that one of the teaching brothers had propositioned him. Eventually Jimmy entered into a complicated relationship with another of the brothers. They went places together, but Jimmy refused to have sex with the brother and finally denounced him. The man was sent away to teach in Puerto Rico.

When Andy at last admitted to himself that he was gay, he thought of suicide. "This thing in my life," he recounts, "was out there and would catch up to me. I did not want anyone to know." He heard "fag" and "lezzie" jokes and saw the torment endured by effeminate classmates. The school nurse warned that "homosexuals were great ones for disease."

In 1971, after graduating from high school, Andy renewed his friendship with George, an elementary school classmate who was openly gay. One day at George's home, Andy watched as George and another young man kissed. "I had never seen men kiss," Andy recalls. "This was what I wanted." Though fearful of being caught in a police raid, Andy accompanied George to a Long Island gay bar. Men were dancing together. In the garden men

*Formerly a staffer at the Hetrick Martin Institute (see Chapter 13), he has been active on gay television programs and serves as moderator on a PBS discussion program.

were necking. Andy stared at them. He desperately wanted to have an experience with someone. No one propositioned him.

At the time he went off to the University of Virginia, Andy had had no sexual experiences. During his sophomore year he lived next door to the president of the gay student union. He could not understand why anyone would want to ruin his life by joining a gay organization. Nevertheless, Andy entered a "tumultuous, self-hating, closeted" relationship with another student, Keith. "One night," he relates, "we were up late. We fell asleep on the floor. We started to reach out and touch. I touched a man! Within weeks we had sex. I was totally in love in with him. It was wonderful to be able to kiss, hug, and love. I never thought that what I was doing was wrong." Although the two treated each other "horribly," the relationship lasted for three years. Andy did not want it to end. Where, after all, would he find another lover?

One day, entering a toilet at the university, Andy sensed a strange tension. Someone tapped his foot. It was a signal. Men were having sex in the toilets! Upon returning to New York, Andy began to meet men in gay bars and in bathhouses. He became aware of a community, and in 1974 he marched in the Gay Pride parade. "That was tremendous," he says, "seeing so many people and knowing that I wasn't alone."

In his senior year, Andy ventured into a meeting of the university gay organization during an election of officers and found himself elected president. No one else, he explains, was willing to sign letters and represent the group in public. "Suddenly I was an activist," Andy declares. Inspired by a talk from the renowned gay militant Frank Kameny, Andy responded to a homophobic article in the university newspaper. "I became," he says, "Mr. Gay Liberation on campus." After two gays were thrown out of a restaurant in the town's business district, Andy mounted a boycott. His name appeared in the newspapers. "I was never happier in my life," he recalls. "I had a sense of freedom. I didn't give a shit who knew."

On Easter Sunday Andy awakened to find that his car had been painted with slogans. He began receiving hate calls. When after graduation Andy applied for a teaching position at his former high school, he discovered that someone had sent newspaper clippings about his activities to the school, and the school officials suspected he was trying to trick them into a lawsuit. "It was ridiculous," Andy declares, "for me to think that my life was not going to be changed after I came out. Some people go back into the closet after graduating, but I couldn't."

In a résumé he submitted in applying for a position with the Associated Press, Andy acknowledged his freelance work for gay publications. "You're not going to flaunt this, Mr. Humm, are you?" demanded the personnel man. "Flaunt what?" Andy asked. "I'm gay. I intend to be as open about that as any heterosexual about his sexual orientation." To guarantee "objectivity," some of the media, Andy recalls, proscribed employee membership in political parties. Andy's membership in gay organizations was also unacceptable.

To come out to his parents, Andy chose a day on which Dignity, the Catholic gay activist organization, was holding a demonstration at St. Patrick's Cathedral. During the morning, anxious and testy, he caddied for his parents at their golf club. When his father dallied overlong, he barked, "Come on, hit the ball!" "If he had missed that putt," Andy recounts, "I don't think I would have been able to tell them for another week." His parents generally watched television before going to sleep. Andy came into their room and turned off the set. "Have you ever noticed anything different about me?" he asked. "You mean that you don't date?" his mother replied. "I do date," Andy rejoined. "I go out with men. I'm gay." "You seem to accept this," his father remarked, "and I suppose if we don't, we're not going to see much of you any more." Andy guessed that his father was right. "Well, there's your brother Johnny," his father noted. "We don't know what he is." They expressed their gratitude that he was sharing this intimate secret with them. His mother pressed him as to whether he was sure. Already twenty-two and with broad experience in the gay movement, Andy was able to respond convincingly. His mother began to cry. "I just think," she exclaimed, "that you're going to have a hard and lonely life."

The next morning Andy's mother said, "Your father said as he was leaving this morning that if I cried I would be crying for myself." Andy knew he would have to educate her slowly.

Andy encountered resistance from his younger brother. He resented Andy's receiving constant telephone calls regarding gay organization activities. A college athletic coach, he felt embarrassed when Andy appeared as a gay activist on television, but he did not reject Andy.

When Andy's mother admitted that Andy was gay, her sister replied that she had figured that out long ago. "I always tell gays," Andy says, " 'Don't think they don't know.' " He does not sympathize with people who say that their families know but that they prefer not to talk about it. "Why not?" Andy demands. "Why can't you talk about what you did last weekend with your lover?"

LANCE RINGEL, NEW YORK STATE DEPUTY COMMISSIONER OF HUMAN RIGHTS*

Born in 1952, the third of four children, one of whom died in infancy, Lance grew up in Decatur, Illinois, where his father worked as an engineer in a tractor company and his mother as a bookkeeper. By midwestern standards, Lance says, his parents held liberal views. His father had been excommunicated by the Lutheran Church for marrying a divorcée. When Lance's sister married a Jew, his parents' expressed annoyance when neighbors re-

*In 1996, Lance was serving as editor of a Long Island gay publication.

marked, "He'll take good care of her. Jews are such providers." Although the marriage ended in divorce, Lance's niece was raised as a Jew. The family adjusted also to Lance's brother's marriage to a hard-shell Baptist, a marriage as alien to the community as his sister's, though it did not provoke as much stir. Neighbors thought it strange that the family socialized and exchanged gifts with black houseworkers. During the Watts riots in 1973, white friends said they would seek safety at the Ringels' if the riots spread to Decatur.

As for himself, Lance declares, "I was one of the best little boys in the world, a straight-A student and high school valedictorian." Still he never felt that he was measuring up to his father's expectations. His mother assured him that his father praised him to other people, but he never said a word of praise to Lance. He was a strong personality who would not brook contradiction. Lance had a mind of his own, and they frequently argued. Lance recalls a heated clash they had over the Kent State incident, when several students were killed during an anti-Vietnam demonstration

Although Lance socialized with a clique of girls and boys (most of whom turned out to be gay), uncomfortable because of chronic acne and his short stature, he always felt as if he was an outsider. He was worse at sports, he says, than he needed to be.

When Lance was about eleven, his brother, three years his senior, called him a "queer." Lance's parents warned him never to use that word again. Lance did not understand why his parents became so upset. Soon thereafter on an election poster in support of his candidacy for class treasurer, someone scrawled the message: "Of the homo squad."

Upon reading an Ann Landers column on homosexuality, Lance asked his mother to explain the term. His mother was too embarrassed to do so. In response to his father's explanation, Lance exclaimed, "I like boys my age."

From junior high school on, Lance's sense of difference intensified. By the time he was thirteen, he felt like "a boy from Mars." At fifteen he developed a crush on a quarterback on the Oakland Raiders, and as a consequence of his new interest in football, he gained some jock friends. Although he had only one transient sexual experience in high school, Lance was beginning to realize that he was gay. He is convinced that his sexual orientation was no mystery to at least one member of his family—his grandfather, who a few days before his death wrote to Lance, "You don't have to be an athlete because you're a wonderfully caring boy." "It was almost," Lance recounts, "as though my grandfather was telling me to go ahead and do what I ended up doing."

During his first year at Georgetown University, Lance fell in love with his straight roommate and worked hard at building a relationship with him. On some nonphysical level, he says, his roommate, who claimed he had never had a close male friend, reciprocated his feelings. Transferring to Harvard at the end of the year, he expressed sorrow at parting from Lance. During Lance's remaining years at Georgetown, while admitting to friends that he thought he was gay, Lance kept his distance from openly gay men. Their lifestyle, he was convinced, was not for him. In fact, he became so involved in political extracurricular activities that he could spare little thought for his sexual problem or for his studies, and his parents were shocked at his B average. In his sophomore year, he worked in the Birch Bayh senatorial election campaign and thereafter served first as an intern on Capitol Hill and then as a low-level staff member. At the time, the Equal Rights Amendment was a major issue. Lance recalls someone's remarking to general laughter, "Next there will be ERA for homosexuals."

After graduation, at a summer film course in Southern France, Lance had his first homosexual experience with a Britisher a dozen years his senior. In 1975, he accepted a fellowship for graduate study in the theater department at the University of Pittsburgh. Here he met his future lover, Chuck. The following spring, upon receiving an invitation to serve as best man at the wedding of the Georgetown roommate with whom he had experienced a platonic relationship, Lance came out to his parents. Replying to his letter after some delay, his mother compared her shock to the shock she experienced at the death of his younger brother. One day she called to announce that she and his father were coming to visit him. Lance rejected their advice not to attend his friend's wedding.

In 1976, Lance served as a marshal at the last great mobilization against the Vietnam War and attended the Democratic national convention as a Carter supporter. That year, too, he moved to New York with Chuck. Shortly thereafter, they "crossed the line." They remained together thereafter. Lance's parents liked Chuck and accompanied him and Lance on a trip to Paris.

Withdrawing from political activity, Lance worked at a series of different jobs. As an assistant editor for a travel magazine, he traveled widely throughout the country and met gay people everywhere. He became aware of a community with an emerging culture of its own. "You have more in common with gay strangers," he says, "than with straight neighbors. That was the beginning of the concept of a Queer Nation." Nevertheless, he was not yet ready to engage in gay politics. "It would never have occurred to me," he says, "to participate in the Gay Pride parade. I rejected it as a continuation of sixties radicalism, with gays screaming and engaging in theatrical confrontational demonstrations." In 1980, however, intrigued by a notice that John Lindsay, a former Republican mayor of New York City, was speaking before the Lambda Independent Democrats, Lance attended the meeting. He was astonished at the political sophistication displayed by Lambda leaders like Peter Vogel and Ginny Apuzzo. "It was a revelation to me," he recalls. "I had no idea gays could sit still and be serious."

Invited to serve on the Lambda board, Lance assumed the editorship of its newsletter and in 1984 was elected its president. He recalls with pride a photograph of gay members of the New York delegation to the National Democratic Convention that year—Denise Alexander, Luke Guevara, Peter

Vogel, and Lance. "A Rainbow coalition," he declares, "including an African American, a Latino, a Jew, and a WASP; and if Ginny had been there when the picture was taken, there would also have been an Italian American."

When Ginny Apuzzo asked him to join the staff of the National Gay Task Force as administrator for its Fund for Human Dignity, Lance foresaw that his parents would learn through the media of his coming out publicly in his new post. Not since his exchange with them in 1977 had Lance discussed his sexual orientation with his parents, and he came out to them in a letter a second time. His mother replied that she regretted that members of the family, including Lance's brother, would now have to be told. The next day, however, Lance received a different kind of reply from his father. "My father had never written to me before," Lance recounts. "I opened the letter with trepidation."

Dear Lance,

We received your letter earlier this week, and I feel that I should personally respond because my reactions are not exactly the same as those of your mother. First of all, the announcement of your new job came as no surprise to me. Although I do not fully understand or condone, I have accepted the fact that you are gay. I also realize that any member of a minority group in order to survive among a hostile majority must either hide or unite and fight for rights, recognition, and acceptance. Since there is no doubt in my mind that I would take the latter course, there is no reason for me to believe that my son would do otherwise.

I know your mother has written to you, but I don't know exactly what she said, just as she will not know what I say here, but I am sure that you must sense that she has a problem, and it is very simply that she must face the fact that the acceptance of this job will most likely reveal to family and friends that you are gay. I am sure that she doesn't feel that the fact itself is terrible, but she is very much afraid of how this will change their feelings and regard for you. I hope you will understand that this is a natural mother instinct, which is further aggravated by her family's trait under which everyone strives to protect one another from what they perceive as an unpleasant situation. I think I can honestly say that I am not concerned what other people think and have argued that we should honestly and openly now inform anyone that we would ordinarily inform about your new job. Apparently your mother feels she can't handle this now, but I have prevailed in that we will tell your brother because I really believe he has a right to know. I also think we will tell the rest as time goes by and I hope this occurs before they are made aware by some outside source. In any event, I am not concerned about handling this situation whenever it occurs.

As far as I'm concerned, your acceptance of this new job does not change my love and regard for you, and I am sure your mother feels the same. We are, of course, concerned with the demands your new job will entail. I'm sure you realize that you will, at times, be faced with more scorn and hostility than you have thus far encountered, and it will hurt. I suppose all parents would like to protect their children from hurt, but mature parents know this is not possible.

With love,
Dad

In 1985, following Ginny's resignation, Lance took over as executive director of the Fund for Human Dignity. Early in 1986, however, under the pressures of the constant fund raising activities and the strain of being responsible for other people's salaries, Lance resigned from his post. Thereafter he helped to draft a report of the activities of the Governor's Task Force on Lesbian and Gay Issues, accepted a post on the task force, and joined the board and subsequently became president of the Institute for the Protection of Lesbian and Gay Youth (renamed the Hetrick Martin Institute upon the death of Emery Hetrick in February 1987).

In April 1987, at the dedication of a plaque to the memory of gay activist Peter Vogel at the New York City Lesbian and Gay Community Center, Governor Mario Cuomo announced that he was transferring responsibility for enforcement of his executive order forbidding discrimination on the basis of sexual orientation from the Office of Employee Relations to the Division of Human Rights. At Ginny Apuzzo's urging, Lance applied for a position at the division, and in September he was appointed director of a section charged with enforcement of the executive order.

When Ginny resigned as the governor's liaison with the gay community, with hesitation, Lance agreed to undertake the position for six months. When the National Gay Task Force urged the establishment of a State Office for Lesbian and Gay Concerns similar to the one established by Mayor Edward I. Koch in New York City, Lance found himself holding two positions, director of the new office as well as the governor's liaison person.

In April 1991. Lance resigned his posts. Two months later, however, he accepted appointment as the first openly gay assistant commissioner of the New York State Division of Human Rights. Although no white, openly gay man had ever held this post in the State Commission of Human Rights, his appointment was generally accepted as evidence of the recognition won by the gay community despite the failure in the legislature of a state antidiscrimination bill.

After years of working almost exclusively on gay issues, in his new post as assistant commissioner Lance became more aware of how the concerns of the gay community fit within the entire spectrum of human rights concerns. He was reminded that "a lot of people [were] going through the same kinds of experience. I see more clearly how problems of gays and lesbians are part of an overall social problem. It has also brought home to me how insular we gays can get sometimes."

TOM DUANE, NEW YORK CITY COUNCILMAN

In 1991 Tom Duane won election as a New York City councilman after a life long struggle against a crippling shyness that he now associates with the sense of unworthiness at being gay that clouds the lives of many homosexuals. A descendant of an ancestor who fought in the Revolutionary War and of one of the first mayors of New York City, Tom grew up in a conservative area of Flushing in the borough of Queens, where his father had long been active in the local parish. Tom's parents attended Mass every Sunday, and Tom and his brothers were enrolled in a parochial elementary school. Tom's parents pressured the boys to achieve excellence, and in school Tom was instilled by the nuns with a sense of discipline and of respect for authority. Tom constantly feared that he was not living up to his parents' expectations.

Tom's father coached Little League baseball for the Catholic Youth Organization. Every Saturday Tom, who disliked competitive sports, appeared for practice. "There are times," he recalls, "that I had to close my eyes and force myself to play. Duty offered no choice." ("Now," he remarks, "if the city council had a softball team, I would play on it, and I would be good. It wouldn't be compulsory. As a child, I was scared, but I couldn't let anyone know it. I was afraid of the ball. I was afraid to fail.")

At home the family watched little television. On rainy days Tom and his brothers were permitted to go to the movies. Otherwise time was to be employed more usefully. "Even today," Tom declares, "I am surprised how much fun it is going to the movies at night, just taking off without there being an obvious accomplishment, without saving the world for three hours."

From his earliest years, Tom sought to hide an indefinable difference he sensed in himself and strove to overcome extraordinary shyness, compelling himself to mingle with other boys and to speak about topics of interest to them. Burdened with religious guilt, he and his schoolmates, he says, suffered greater inhibition in regard to sexual experimentation than boys in public school. Sex was never mentioned at home; homosexuality, certainly not. (Only as an adult did Tom learn of homosexuals within his extended family.) In his freshman year in high school, Tom felt a strong attraction to a young man on the football team. In his presence Tom became tongue-tied. Once in the locker room he teased Tom, pulling off Tom's towel and flipping his own towel at Tom. Tom replied in kind, timidly. In retrospect, he recalls the event as a sexually charged moment. It was never repeated.

A classmate named Richard, more worldly than Tom, sensed that Tom was gay. "I knew that he knew," Tom recounts, "and he knew that I knew that he knew." Richard picked on Tom until finally Tom challenged him to a fist fight. Tom ended up with a black eye and Richard, with a bloody lip. "I don't know how I did it," Tom now exclaims. His father expressed satisfaction that the fight had ended in a draw. "This was an example," Tom remarks, "of how I coped with being shy. I said to myself, 'I'll just do it,' and I went out and did it."

Tom's political career had its origin in high school. Elected program chairman of the parish teen club, he helped to organize dances and ski trips. He also formed a team of members of the parish club and fellow high school students to participate in a Saturday remedial reading and recreation program at a Harlem school. From that experience he drew "enormous personal gratification. We were fulfilling a need with very young children who were dependent upon us. There was no sense of competition here."

The Vietnam War roused Tom's interest in politics. Reading about black liberation and women's liberation and later gay liberation further politicized him. He helped to organize Students for a Christian Society, the closest approximation to the Students for a Democratic Society they dared to attempt at the parochial high school. Members attended forums but never participated in demonstrations. All these organizational efforts, requiring working closely with others, proved a struggle for Tom in his shyness; and he developed skills, he says, in sizing up circumstances about him, skills that served him well through the years.

In his junior year, Tom and his closest friend confided to each other that they might be gay. (The friend turned out not to be gay.) The following year, Tom admitted to a Hunter College student some years older than he that he was gay. She arranged for him to meet a gay couple, also Hunter students, living in the Village. After an initial visit during which they smoked pot, Tom returned and had sex with them. He enjoyed it.

When Tom went off to Lehigh University, his father's alma mater, in Bethlehem, Pennsylvania, he had had only this one transient homosexual experience and a few unsatisfying experiences with women. "The sex drive at that age is strong," he explains, "and my attitude with women was, 'Let's try it.'" At Lehigh Tom fell in love with a neighbor in his dormitory. One day after a lengthy rehearsal of what he was going to say, Tom admitted his strong feelings and declared that he might even be falling in love. To Tom's delight, the young man declared similar feelings for Tom. After hefty drinking following the football game against the school's chief collegiate rival, Tom went to his friend's room, woke him from a nap, and had his first fully satisfying sexual experience with a man. After a few months, his friend became involved with someone else. The breakup proved traumatic for Tom.

During his sophomore year, Tom began to read gay publications. During vacations he attended meetings of the Gay Activist Alliance in New York, "to gain an education and to meet people." The summer between his sophomore and junior years, Tom came out to his older brother, John, who merely assured Tom that he loved him. Tom was hopeful of a similar reaction from his parents. They had not appeared dismayed when Tom's younger brother, Bill, expressed hesitation about entering the priesthood because of his suspicion that he might be gay.

"We were all sitting in the kitchen," Tom recalls. "I might have said in advance that I had something to tell them." He was gay, he declared, and was determined to be so publicly. "We always thought there was something wrong with you," his parents responded, "and now we know what it was." Tom resented this remark. In the past, he declared, he too had thought that there was something wrong, but now he was convinced that what he was

was not wrong. Reaching that conclusion, he assured them, was the result of a long process of reading and listening.

Tom's parents were unwilling to allow him to return to Lehigh to continue a gay lifestyle. At their request, Tom met with a psychiatrist. "He asked me all kinds of questions," Tom recalls, "and reached the conclusion that there was nothing wrong with me." Fearing that Tom, who had found work as a taxi driver and was preparing to move into his own apartment, would not finish his education, his parents relented and encouraged him to return to Lehigh.

Learning that the editors of the school paper had decided not to report in its Parents' Weekend issue on a panel on human sexuality in which he was participating, Tom demanded the publication of his letter of protest. Tom's letter provided the impetus for the formation of a gay organization on campus, with Tom and three other gay students who had been expelled from a fraternity providing the nucleus. Immediately they encountered hostility, even receiving obscene telephone calls. The university refused to grant them recognition as a bona fide school organization.

Completing his degree in American Studies/Urban Studies with courses at New York University, Tom wrote a paper on gay liberation before Stonewall, a theme, he says, that would have been unacceptable at Lehigh, where, in any event, he received his degree. From 1983 through 1988, Tom worked at various jobs at his father's Wall Street brokerage firm, in the publicity office of the city Department of Health, in public relations at the Westinghouse Broadcasting Company, and in advertising promotion for the gay publications *The Native* and *Christopher Street.*

Simultaneously, Tom was passing many hours in gay bars. "We're more directed toward bars to meet people," he remarks, "than heterosexuals, who have a broader choice of meeting places." Becoming dissatisfied with the time he was wasting, he joined the Chelsea Gay Association (active in the district immediately to the north of Greenwich Village), participated in the organization of the Chelsea AIDS Committee, and became involved in the Coalition for Lesbian and Gay Rights and in the gay Independent Democratic Club. That year he entered his candidacy for the office of city councilman. During the campaign he learned belatedly that an AIDS study in which he had participated six years earlier had shown that he was infected with the virus.

In 1991, two years after his first abortive attempt, Tom won election to the city council. "I did not think about my being HIV-positive during my first campaign. In my second campaign, I was completely open about my status. It provided an added incentive to my running, and I was confident that I could be an effective city councilman though HIV-positive."

In regard to his relations with his parents, Tom said, "It has taken them many years to adjust to my homosexuality. They have reached the point where they ask me whom I'm dating. They've met my present boyfriend and like him." They have also come to accept that Tom's younger brother is gay.

In reviewing his life, Tom asserts, he now understands that he engaged in a life of activism in an attempt to counter "the bad self-image that we all have as gays in this culture. We all use one device or another," he declares, "to overcome that self-image and to gain self-respect and dignity."

BRUCE*

"I wish," Bruce declares, "that I was going to school now when there are gay organizations like ACT UP. Even though I don't agree with a lot of what they do, they give young gay people a tremendous sense of belonging that I didn't have. I was in college at the time of Stonewall. I used to think, 'What are those crazy people doing?' It took me a long time to realize that those crazy people are me."

The oldest of three children of a loving Ukrainian mother and an aloof and unapproachable Jewish father, a distinguished professor of psychology at the graduate school of the City University who represented an inimitable model for his three children, Bruce experienced a repressed and unhappy life until he broke free by coming out at the age of thirty.

From his earliest years, Bruce was aware that something was wrong with him. Clumsy at sports, he suffered taunts from his classmates. In his schoolwork he made no effort to live up to the ideal that his father exemplified, and his parents made demands on him academically that they did not make on his sister. Bruce's brother made matters worse by maintaining a flawless school record.

In junior high school, aware of his attraction to other boys, Bruce was frightened when a gay boy caught having sex in the washroom was ostracized, while the other boy in the incident suffered not at all. At age thirteen Bruce was petrified when a man approached him in a movie theater. "I would never have taken the initiative," Bruce declares. "I was too broken in spirit." In high school Bruce was flattered when the "mayor of Midwood High School," a good-looking, popular boy he had known since second grade befriended him. "He bailed me out of fights when kids picked on me," Bruce recalls. Years later Bruce saw the boy's name among the credits to the movie *Cruising.* Subsequently, Bruce met him bartending at the gay club "The Spike." "I have often wondered," Bruce says, "what his torment must have been like, this all-American kid who was living with the secret of being gay."

In high school Bruce had three or four transient and furtive same-sex experiences. While at Long Island University, on the other hand, he went out on group dates and had occasional unsatisfying sexual relations with women. Once when he was studying in the bleachers of the gym, a jock came over to him and put his arm around him. "You're here to look us over," he said, "to check us out." "I felt dirty," Bruce recalls. "I got up and went home and

*Staffer at the New York State Crime Victims Board (see Chapter 10).

cried. 'What the hell is the matter with me?' I wondered. 'Did this guy catch on to something about me?' "

In defiance of his austere and domineering father, as an undergraduate Bruce became involved in right-wing politics. Among the Young Republicans, he felt a sense of belonging, though he met no one with whom he could talk about his private sexual yearnings. After graduating in 1970, Bruce joined the army reserves in an attempt to avoid service in Vietnam. "I was a hypocrite," he admits, "for I was in favor of the war."

In 1972 Bruce obtained a position with George L. Clark, Kings County Republican chairman; and at the 1976 presidential convention he served as an alternate Reagan delegate. Twice he ran for the state senate in a no-win district. In 1979, however, George Clark confronted a challenge to his leadership, and Bruce realized that if Clark were ousted seven years of his own life would go down the drain. "Here I am approaching thirty," he reasoned, "and what relationships do I have? What have I accomplished? I'm a lonely character with no future."

Nothing in the world, Bruce decided, could be worse than the suppressed sexual ferment with which he had been living. He steeled his will and went to Times Square to pick up a man. "I don't know," he recounts, "how I did it. It was not out of courage but out of desperation." On Eighth Avenue he saw "a tall, good-looking kid from Pennsylvania, an AWOL marine about twenty-one. I went up to him and said, 'Are you interested?' He was, and five minutes later we were in a hotel room. The first time he kissed me, Bam! If I was to have a first experience, this kid was the one to initiate me. He was the aggressive one, but I learned fast. It was the bursting of a dam!" Thereafter, Bruce declares, "I went wild, constantly picking up men. It was one glorious binge."

Three years later, after surreptitiously registering petitions with phony signatures for the nomination of an imaginary candidate in an election campaign, Bruce was terrified at the possibility of arrest and loss of the job he had in the meantime obtained through political influence at the Crime Victims Board. "I said to myself," he recounts, "is this the only thing I'm ever going to be known for—putting a dog and a cat on the ballot?" He decided to come out to his mother before he was arrested. "Ma, I've got something to tell you," Bruce declared. "I'm gay, and this trick I've played is the most significant thing I've ever done in my life." Bruce's mother replied simply, "You're my son. I love you."

Bruce's father was already dead. "I have wondered what would have happened if I had ever come out to him," Bruce declares. "I have wondered, too, how a psychologist with a reputation for brilliance in his field, a man trained in child development, failed to know about me. He certainly never said anything."

Looking back on his life, Bruce recalls all the years he lived a furtive and lonely existence hiding who he was, frustrated at work and suffering a constant feeling of guilt and unworthiness. "Emotionally speaking," he admits, "I was a cripple." Nevertheless, Bruce considers himself more fortunate than gay men who never awaken to who they are. In a bar during the 1988 presidential campaign Bruce met someone he had known years earlier in a Young Republican club. In a loud voice the man related how he watched police attack ACT UP members demonstrating against vice presidential candidate Dan Quayle. He encouraged them by shouting, "Kill those ACT UP faggots." "You fool!" Bruce snapped. "I don't agree with what they do a lot of times, but they're my people, they're your people." The man was unmoved. "One of these days," said Bruce, "I hope he'll wake up."

LUKE*

The second of five children of an alcoholic sheet metal worker given to outbursts of violent rage and a mother from a Pennsylvania Dutch coal miner's family in which alcoholism and its attendant violence were also problems, Luke had a background radically different from those of the other interviewees. He grew up in an industrial New Jersey town, in a cramped one-room apartment with no privacy for any member of the family. At the age of four, Luke ran away from home. He walked to a town more than twenty miles away where friends of his mother lived, before police found him. Alarmed at his disappearance, Luke's mother packed the family's possessions, and when his father arrived home, it was too late to stop the move into a larger apartment. The next night he came home drunk and fell into a fury, flailing at his wife and children. Upon the birth of another child, however, Luke's father on his own looked for a house to accommodate his growing family. A real estate agent persuaded him to join the Mormon Church, and the church became the center of family life. Luke's father stopped drinking. "The atmosphere in the house was transformed," Luke recalls. "He became a good father and good husband, and ours was suddenly a typical Andy Hardy household."

The idyll did not last. Within months, Luke's father resumed his drinking.

In junior high school, rebelling against his parents and the church, Luke "hung out" with a longhaired crowd, boys and girls who preferred smoking hash to studying or to participating in sports. At sixteen he joined a motorcycle gang. One day after cutting classes and failing his courses, he quit school. His mother asked why he had arrived home so early. His elder brother burst into the room, crashing open the door with such fury that the knob punctured the wall. Shouting, "You're a disgrace to the family," he hurled Luke to the floor. Then with their mother holding Luke down, his brother cut his long hair. Luke left home to stay with a friend. Lying about his age, he found a job. The next semester, however, he returned home and went back to school again.

Luke's younger brother became the most devout Mormon in the family. To

* Pink Panther (see Chapter 17).

gain acceptance into the Temple, a privilege reserved only to the most dedicated church members, he requested dispensation from the oath to honor his father. One evening after the family returned from a funeral of a great-aunt to whom Luke's younger brother felt a strong attachment, Luke's father began to drink. Luke's brother watched but said nothing. When his father fell into a funk, he got up and went to his room. During the night, he sneaked out and started the car in the garage. Luke broke down and cried at his brother's suicide. His father exclaimed, "Maybe he'll leave me alone now." Then he, too, broke down. "Now he's crying," Luke said to himself, recalling how his father ridiculed his brother for spending time sewing with his mother. For several weeks Luke's father stopped drinking. Once again, briefly, they were a close family. When he started drinking again, Luke quit school for a second time.

After returning from service in Vietnam, Luke's older brother turned to drink and became brutal to his wife, who divorced him. Luke advised his mother to seek a divorce as well. The church found her a lawyer. "Between me and her friends from the church," Luke declares, "we got her a divorce."

In early adolescence Luke was already attracted to boys. He was uncomfortable in the showers with the jocks, suspecting that they could read his mind. When he was fifteen he met the lover of one of his uncles and realized that this uncle was gay. Although Luke's father borrowed money from his brother and treated him warmly when he visited, he sneered at him behind his back and insisted that he would not stand for any of his children turning out to be a fag. By eighteen, after an unsatisfying heterosexual experience, Luke was certain that he was gay. He discovered a gay bar and became, he says, "a slut."

"During the day," Luke relates, "I was straight, and at night I was running around. It was a meaningless life. I was learning how hard it is to be gay." Once he was punched in the face by a man who thought Luke was making an advance. On another occasion, he was beaten by a gang of fag bashers. One day, on drugs and alcohol, he went berserk, tearing up his mother's house and terrifying her. Neighbors called the police. With plea bargaining, Luke received a three-year jail sentence. Enrolling in an experimental drug rehabilitation program in prison, he overcame his addiction, passed his high school equivalency examinations, and completed a course in auto mechanics. "Sometimes I wonder," Luke declared, "whether I would have been better off if I had not gone to prison. Jail for me was a growing up experience. Previously, I was going through all the confusion about being gay, living a day-to-day existence of anxiety and confusion. In prison I realized that I had been wasting my life and had to turn it around."

Luke moved from job to job, at night going to bars and meeting people for one-night stands. During the Labor Day weekend in 1988, he met Greg in a Village bar. Greg invited Luke to move in with him. Luke began to work and to go to school at night. "At last," Luke declares, "I had found someone to spend my life with. That was the end of my promiscuity, of my drugs, and of my alcoholism."

Chapter Three
Never Unaware of Being Black

Only artificially can one isolate aspects of the complex process of coming out. The process involves every aspect of life, far more than reaching an understanding with family members, schoolmates, neighbors, and associates at the workplace. With some interviewees, factors of race, ethnicity, and religion proved crucial in their struggles for personal and social integration.

None of the gay minority activists who volunteered to be interviewed grew up in inner-city ghetto environments, and experiences of people of color presented in this and the succeeding chapters are not necessarily representative of their communities. On the other hand, City Commissioner for Human Rights Dennis de Leon warned against dismissing middle-class blacks or Hispanics as somehow "not genuine." "That attitude," Dennis insists, "puts all blacks into a sharecropper category. I am atypical among Hispanics in terms of education, but if you say I am not 'a genuine Latino,' I think you have no understanding of what estrangement from a culture means for me. Maybe my whole life has been one big affirmative action."

African-American interviewees recounted varied and divergent experiences with racism. Even Billy Jones, City Commissioner for Mental Health, who enjoyed a sheltered childhood as well as an unbroken progression of professional and personal successes in his adult life, insisted that a black in this country is always conscious of who he is. "All I have to do is go out the door and attempt to hail a cab," he declared, "and I know I'm black." Black gays suffer not only from racism and the general homophobia in the society but also from the particular homophobia within the African-American community, where action against the spread of AIDS, for example, was long hampered by a widespread misapprehension that AIDS was a disease limited to white gays.

Lance Ringel and his lover Chuck experienced the virulent homophobia among black Muslims in a nearly violent incident in the subway. A member of the Nation of Islam was loudly denouncing gays as sinful. "Lies! lies!" Chuck cried. The Muslim approached and shook his finger in Chuck's face. "I put my hand up to separate them," Lance recounted. "We will get you," the Muslim shouted. "We will bury you."

BILLY JONES, NEW YORK CITY COMMISSIONER OF MENTAL HEALTH*

Billy Jones's earliest memories are of falling asleep in church in his mother's lap and of his father's reading the comics while Billy and his sister sat on his lap, presages of what was to prove a fortunate life. Born in 1939 in Dayton, Ohio, Billy along with an older sister and a younger brother grew up in a stable and closely knit extended family.

Billy's grandparents migrated from the Carolinas to Alabama. His father, one of nine children, had to leave school to help support the family as a coal miner. Billy's mother grew up in Kentucky and had some Indian connection in her family. She finished at least one year of high school. Billy's father worked in a factory and belonged to a union. He never spoke of racial problems he experienced on the job, but he never received promotions. Although the family lived in a segregated neighborhood, Billy went to an integrated school. His mother, a domestic worker, frequently visited the school to inquire about the progress of her children. Both parents had middle-class aspirations for their offspring. "Some of the kids I played with," Billy recounts, "later got into drugs and went to prison," but he recalls his childhood as a time of minimal stress. "My parents were always there," he says. Nor did the growing realization of his different sexual orientation prove especially troublesome to him, and he had no overt sexual experiences until he was in medical school.

Not a regular churchgoer during Billy's childhood, with the passing years Billy's father become more and more involved in the church and eventually became a deacon. As a young man, Billy played anthems on the organ and served as an usher. Billy declares that the religion of his childhood provided him with a philosophy to live by.

Billy's parents had white acquaintances but socialized generally with other blacks. Billy's sister, on the other hand, brought white school friends home, a rarity in those years. Billy had few white friends, but he recalls that when he talked about classmates, his mother would ask whether they were black or white, a question that did not strike Billy as important. He remembers in

*In 1996, Dr. Jones had returned to private practice as a psychiatrist.

first grade liking a white boy with whom he competed for the first seat as a reward for achievement, and in high school he developed a friendship with a white classmate. Billy did not take cognizance of the fact that all his teachers were white until he had a black teacher in high school.

Civil rights issues were rarely mentioned in his family, but Billy does recall discussion of the lynching of Emmett Till. During riots in the 1960s in Detroit, one of Billy's cousins was arrested. Billy's father traveled to the city to obtain his release. Although not as aware of race as other black youngsters, Billy was nevertheless early inculcated with a sense of responsibility to the stability and progress of African Americans. "I was raised to think that what I did," he declares, "would reflect on the family and on our people."

Having attended integrated elementary and high schools, Billy considered applying for admission to Ohio State. He decided not to do so not only because of his aversion to huge impersonal institutions but also because of a growing sense of his black identity. Billy's father dissuaded him from applying to Fiske University, declaring that he did not think Billy was ready to deal with the discrimination he was certain to encounter in the South. Sensing that in traveling away from home he would be free to investigate his sexual orientation, of which he was by now fully aware, Billy chose to accompany his best friend to Howard University, the alma mater of an aunt, a physician in Washington, D.C.

Subsequently, Billy continued his studies at another black institution, Meharry Medical College in Nashville. Here Billy had his first homosexual experiences. "I have never taken the initiative," he declares. "I never have known whether people were interested." Seeing everyone else marrying and having children, Billy wondered whether he wanted to spend his life as a gay man. Discovering a gay social world on visits to New York, he decided that he could live a rich existence as a gay man.

While engaged in postdoctoral work at Harvard Medical College, Billy faced a prospect of being drafted for service in Vietnam. He had never imagined himself as a soldier and was strongly opposed to the war. On the other hand, he felt that he could not ethically avoid a call to duty when so many thousands of young men with no options were being forced to serve. Thus instead of fleeing across the border to Canada, he reported for duty when called.

Billy's experience in Vietnam was scarcely typical of that of the mass of Americans. Arriving at the Saigon airport, he found a car waiting to drive him to his post, a military stockade at the naval base at Cam Ranh Bay. On the base, he became acquainted with Vietnamese workers. "I wondered why we were in their country," he declares. "These people," he thought, "should have the right to decide for themselves what kind of life they were to have."

Before going overseas Billy discussed with his analyst problems he might encounter because of his sexual orientation, and in Vietnam he exercised caution and remained celibate. He frequented the officers' club on the base and often traveled to Saigon on official business. Generally he found himself in the company of other doctors and therapists. The issue of his homosexuality never was posed.

Billy does not recall encountering racism in Vietnam. A white camp commandant, in fact, exhibited a more sympathetic attitude toward the prisoners in the stockade than the black officer whom he succeeded. Paradoxically, while on leave in Japan, at an international fair in Osaka, Billy confronted undisguised hostility from a man in charge of one of the African exhibits. Billy attributes the man's reaction to hostility toward the American uniform.

During Billy's tour of duty, black prisoners in the stockade rioted. They told Billy and the young black marine lieutenant assigned to negotiate with them that they wanted the world to know how they were being mistreated and broken in spirit. "What do you think will get back to the world?" Billy asked. "Who controls the information? These people are going to come in and beat your heads." Their indiscipline, Billy advised them, could threaten the commandant's military career, and he would be eager to arrive at a settlement. The presence of the lieutenant, closer in age to the men, and his concurrence in Billy's suggestions proved helpful in ending the riot without bloodshed.

To prevent further disturbances, Billy and others on the medical staff formed discussion groups involving both prisoners and guards. Since it was his responsibility as the highest ranking African-American officer in the unit to mediate tensions between African-American and white enlisted men, Billy also organized focus groups in the stockade and in other units to examine race relations and to probe for problems and causes of racial and other tensions. "In some respects," Billy recounts, "the class question took precedence over the question of race."

Clearly, Billy's sexual orientation not only did not prove to be a handicap in carrying out his duties, it actually proved to be an asset since it made him more sensitive to the needs of the personnel.

During his tour of duty, Billy recalls, it rained half the year, and there was a blazing sun the other half. "To live in such a climate," he recounts, "and to have to deal with your personal psychological needs in such a place for a year brought little cause for joy. Your one concern was to get through the experience alive and sane." The enlisted men, he recognized, had far less control over their lives. "That's what led to drug use," Billy declares. A black woman colonel, the head of the psychiatry unit during Billy's tour of duty, developed a mental health agenda directed particularly against substance abuse, "a problem," Billy says, "most people did not want to look at. If I had been an enlisted man, I don't know whether I would have got through it. Returning home was like being reborn. I figured I could handle any stress. I came back with the thought, 'My lord, I got through it!' "

Billy's good fortune resumed upon his return from Vietnam, for very quickly he met the partner with whom he was to share the rest of his life.

Asked how he accounted for the stability of their relationship in light of a widespread view in the "straight" community that gays are incapable of long-term marriages, Billy asserted that both he and Lewis worked hard at making their relationship succeed, considering it central to their lives. Relationships, he noted, frequently fall apart because the partners grow at different rates. He and Lewis, however, found fulfillment in the process of growth. In addition, he declares, they complement each other and share responsibilities. Billy easily displays affection, yet Lewis is the nourishing partner. Billy has made a career in public life; Lewis is a more private person. Billy feels incompetent around the apartment, and Lewis serves as the homemaker. A public accountant, Lewis balances the checkbook and manages the household budget. Billy plans their social activities. He is the one who buys the theater tickets.

Some years ago, encouraged by the example of gay friends who were successfully raising children, Billy and Lewis decided to adopt a child. They waited until circumstances were propitious financially and in other respects, planning, Billy declares, just as heterosexual couples do. In 1982, feeling secure after their sixteen-year relationship, they discussed whether they were prepared to commit the time required for bringing up a child. "We're not getting any younger," they reminded each other. "We don't want to have our son leading us while we're walking around with canes." For six months Billy made contact with child-care agencies. Learning that a black child was available in an agency that ordinarily handled overseas adoptions, on a Wednesday Billy telephoned. On Saturday he and his sister went to Washington, D.C., and brought the three-week-old infant back to New York. They named the child Alexander after Billy's deceased father. Billy took off work for three weeks. His mother arrived to help. "She's crazy about Alexander," Billy declares. "She has a grandchild she did not expect to have."

When Alexander was six months old, his parents enrolled him in a child-care center at the Bank Street School, a progressive elementary school in Greenwich Village. According to their schedules, Lewis and Billy alternated in bringing him to and from school. Eventually they placed him in a modified Montessori school, where he continued until first grade, when he entered the nondenominational Cathedral School at the Cathedral of St. John the Divine.

Alexander calls Lewis "father" and Billy "daddy." Although teachers have had difficulty in determining which of them Alexander is talking about, until the age of nine Alexander had no problems with other children in regard to his family. Billy and Lewis have told him that there are different kinds of families. Theirs is one kind. They have talked about their being gay and admitted that some people think that homosexuality is not right.

Billy and Lewis protect Alexander from potentially disturbing experiences. Thus after receiving an anonymous death threat, Billy did not bring the boy to the ceremony at which Billy was inducted as New York City Commissioner of Mental Health. When the *New York Daily News* planned a story on gay adoptions, Billy would not permit them to include Alexander.

"Our son is another aspect of my good fortune," declares Billy, "and a further factor in strengthening my relationship with Lewis. He has brought us much joy and transformed us from a couple into a family, adding another dimension to our lives. Now we think not only of ourselves and each other but of another person. We have entered the world of parenthood."

Billy does not see any difference between his family and a heterosexual family with a single child. He thinks Alexander has enjoyed a marvelous childhood without any unusual tensions.

Billy brought a rich background to his post as Commissioner of Mental Health. He had grown up in a closely knit, nurturing family with strong moral principles. His parents, eager that their children enjoy advantages they had not known, protected him from the hurt experienced by many black youngsters and encouraged him academically. His sister, to whom he remains close, provided him with a constructive role model. Strengthened by a positive and relatively trauma-free childhood, Billy was able to grapple with his homosexuality with a minimum of stress. He progressed through his education with confidence and competence, obtaining his degree in psychiatry at Harvard, one of the nation's most prestigious medical colleges. In Vietnam he experienced firsthand the race and class ramifications of fundamental national problems and became aware of the social aspects of mental health disorders among Americans. In his successful and dynamic relationship with Lewis, he grew emotionally. Adopting Alexander further rounded out Billy's experience, equipping him further for a municipal post of responsibility.

In his posts as city commissioner for mental health at the time of his interview and subsequently as director of the Health and Hospitals Corporation, Billy Jones had little direct involvement in the struggles of the gay community. In addition, in his personal life he had escaped homophobic assaults. Gay activist would be a misnomer for him, but he is an active gay, who demonstrates that homosexuality has no direct correlation to competence and to effectiveness as a governmental official.

MARJORIE J. HILL, DIRECTOR, THE MAYOR'S OFFICE FOR THE LESBIAN AND GAY COMMUNITY*

In retrospect, Marjorie Hill can claim that all her experiences during thirty-odd years prepared her for appointment in 1988 as director of the Mayor's Office on Lesbian and Gay Concerns. Although she escaped the most humiliating aspects of American racism, like Billy Jones she was always conscious of her blackness. Marjorie grew up in Bedford Stuyvesant, the large black community in Brooklyn, the only child of a factory worker and taxi driver father and a mother who worked as a beautician, a school para-

*Co-chair of the New York City Police Council (see Chapter 12). In 1996, she was serving as Commissioner of the New York State Workmen's Compensation Board.

professional, and a social services caseworker. Marjorie's mother served as a trustee in the church, and Marjorie sang in the choir and taught Sunday school.

With both her parents at work during the day, Marjorie grew up as a latchkey child. People in the apartment building checked on her, however, and Marjorie rang the bell of an elderly man who lived on the first floor to announce her arrival from school. Although drugs and crime, she points out, were not acute problems during her childhood, she was not allowed to go out when her parents were not home. After school, she did her homework or watched television.

During her childhood Marjorie's world was almost totally African American. The absence of blacks on television and in literature troubled her, but "there were lots of role models around, for I was aware of black doctors, lawyers, and other professionals in the community." In those days, Marjorie notes, even wealthy blacks could not choose freely where they wanted to live. "That's a problem," Marjorie remarks, "I have with integration. It promotes the separation of middle-class and professional blacks from the rest of the community." In addition, the church provided a strong buffer against a hostile outside world. The minister was politically astute, and politicians were accessible to members of the church. On the other hand, Marjorie recalls watching the riot in her neighborhood following the assassination of Martin Luther King, Jr. "It was scary," she declares, "though I didn't really comprehend the full racial implications."

Marjorie's mother taught her to read before she was ready for school and, considering kindergarten unnecessary, entered her directly into first grade, where she had her first encounter with a white person, her Jewish teacher. From second grade through junior high school, under the desegregation programs of the 1960s, Marjorie was bused to white schools. She recalls that during the first days of busing, many white parents kept their children home in protest, but the black children viewed the strike as a holiday. "My mother did not talk about it," Marjorie declares. "She didn't prepare me for a white environment."

In fifth grade, upset by the breakup of her parents' marriage, Marjorie became withdrawn. "My mother wouldn't explain to my teacher about the separation," Marjorie relates. "Her attitude was that if her child was doing well academically and wasn't throwing a tantrum, there was no reason for her to be called in for a conference. 'White people,' she complained, 'were always curious about what went on in black families and thought the worst.' " Marjorie did not share her mother's resentment against the white teacher. On the other hand, she thought there was something wrong in that from second through ninth grade only two other black children were placed in advanced sections, while all the others were assigned to slower and to special education (vocational training) classes. "I had more in common," Marjorie remarks, "with them than with my white classmates." Nevertheless, in general, Marjorie enjoyed success at school. "I didn't grow up feeling disenfranchised," she declares.

Marjorie does not recall any racial tensions in elementary school but does remember "a fair amount" in junior high school. Nevertheless, on the basketball team she found a friend in an Italian-American girl who had a black boyfriend. Marjorie especially liked the girl's mother. Marjorie does not remember, however, her friend's visiting at her home.

Marjorie traveled an hour and a half each way, making several changes, in order to attend the John Dewey experimental high school in Coney Island, at the far end of Brooklyn. Unlike most of her classmates, she recalls, she had already set her goal for the future; she was going to become a psychologist. In retrospect, she thinks her choice of vocation might have resulted from her own subconscious awareness of her different sexual orientation.

Loving to dance, Marjorie accepted dates with any black schoolmate who asked her out. She never went out with a white boy. "You didn't do that," she explains. "Besides, there weren't any white boys I liked." For three years she had a steady boyfriend, a young man some seven years older than she. She was not in love with him; she found their sexual relations "boring"; and the thought of living the rest of her life with him was scarcely appealing.

As a child and adolescent Marjorie had never heard the word "lezzie." Her parents did not talk about race; they certainly, she says, were not going to talk about "lezzies." Her mother did ask her why she had to do everything together with a junior high school girlfriend, but Marjorie gave the question no thought. When Marjorie started going out with the friend's brother, her girlfriend became furious. Abruptly, she announced that they could no longer be friends and refused to offer an explanation for her decision. Marjorie was devastated. After Marjorie broke off with the young man, the young woman said they could be friends again, but Marjorie refused the offer. Years later, when Marjorie ran into her at a lesbian dance, she explained that she had an intense crush on Marjorie and had feared that Marjorie would "freak out" if she confessed her attraction.

Marjorie's first encounter with "out" gays occurred at the age of fifteen or sixteen during a vacation in Durham, North Carolina, where the friends she was visiting socialized with transvestite students at a nearby cosmetology school. "They seemed like regular people," Marjorie recalls. "We went to a mixed club and had a good time."

One day when Marjorie was already in college her supervisor at a summer job warned her to be careful of the lesbians working in the office. "I closed the book I was reading," Marjorie recalls, "and asked, 'Which ones are lesbians?' " Her supervisor pointed to one woman who he said had been staring at her. Without delay Marjorie remarked to this woman, "You're always taking someone to lunch. I eat lunch." The woman looked at her with surprise. "I'll take you to lunch tomorrow," she declared. Within a year they were lovers. Six months later Marjorie came out to her mother. "I felt that I was going to be doing this for the rest of my life," she explains, "and there was no reason to keep her in the dark." Her mother's initial response was supportive. Reassured that Marjorie had no intention of quitting school, she posed no objections. "I love you," she said. "Now go to bed." Some days later, however, her mother announced, "Tell your friend not to come here any more."

When Marjorie was a junior in college, her adviser suggested that she not apply for graduate work in clinical psychology, warning that despite her high scholastic average she would encounter difficulty in being accepted. Marjorie never solicited the adviser's counsel again. In fact, as one of six African-American graduate students in clinical psychology at Adelphi University, Marjorie felt comfortable enough to be completely "out." She even took her lover to a class party. Nevertheless, although she chose black lesbian mothers as her dissertation topic, she did not otherwise make her lesbianism an issue in her daily life. "In my experience," she explains, "people don't talk about intimate experiences cross-racially."

By the time of her graduation Marjorie was already a lesbian activist. She served as program director of the Salsa Soul Sisters (subsequently, African-American Lesbian Women United for Change) and edited a newsletter directed to women in prison. Invited to talk about homophobia on Tony Brown's television program, she found herself suddenly in the public eye within the black community. In 1988 she served as a lesbian coordinator in the Jesse Jackson presidential primary campaign. Wherever she was active, she sought to persuade lesbian separatists, both minority and white, to collaborate with gay organizations. "I felt," she declares, "that gays and lesbians had more in common than differences and that we needed to support each other."

After completing her internship, Marjorie advanced from senior psychologist in a hospital to assistant director of a psychiatric clinic and then to director of an internship program and coordinator of psychiatric education. Simultaneously, she carried on a private practice and taught and supervised interns of color at both Fordham and Yeshiva universities. As president of the New York Association of Black Psychologists, she assisted in the formation of an AIDS task force. In 1988 she was appointed liaision between the Mayor's Office and the lesbian and gay community.

After Marjorie's parents separated, she had only sporadic contact with her father. He changed the subject when she attempted to come out to him. When she informed him that she was thinking of moving in with a woman friend, he exclaimed, "A woman? It's not good to live with women because they try to take away your boyfriends. But your mother is hard to live with so I can understand why you want to move out." Annoyed at his antifeminism and his hostile remark about her mother, Marjorie made no further attempt to come out to him, though she did introduce him to women she was seeing and at her college graduation introduced him to her lover.

In 1987, Marjorie's father invited her to drive with him to Washington,

D.C., where he was attending an evangelical meeting. On the way Marjorie informed him that she had accepted his invitation because she was participating in a gay March on Washington, which she had helped to organize.

Four years later, introducing her to his nursing home physician, her father noted that she had just returned from an international conference of gays and lesbians in Moscow. The doctor asked what he thought of his daughter's activities. "She has an important job," her father responded. "She works hard, and I know that the mayor is pleased with her work. Besides, what choice do I have? She's my daughter and I love her." That was the first time he had ever articulated such a sentiment. "That was nice to hear," Marjorie remarked.

KEITH CYLAR*

At a veterans hospital in Cleveland, where she worked as a dietitian, Keith's mother met his father, a blood technician and a minister. In 1958 Keith was born, "like a lot of blacks of my age," he says, "out of wedlock." Unable to raise him as a single parent, Keith's mother left him with her family in West Mundy, an entirely black village that has since been incorporated into the city of Norfolk, Virginia. She visited only during holidays, and Keith was raised by aunts and cousins, almost all female. The family lived in a house with an outhouse and a coal stove and with honeysuckle in the front yard. Keith was often lulled to sleep by rain falling on the tin roof.

The family were Southern Baptists. Some of Keith's relatives sang in the church choir. The husband of one of Keith's cousins was superintendent of the Sunday school. Keith's aunt was married to a Pullman porter, a member of the first black trade union and a man with a "sense of style and sophistication, who set the tone within the family." "It was important that you carried yourself with dignity," Keith recalls. "You weren't to have dirty fingernails. You were not to swear. You were to behave like a gentleman, and you were expected to do your homework. I was taught to be proud of being black," Keith declares, "and to be proud of my family. I also knew that I would always have to work hard and be twice as good as anybody white to get ahead." Everyone in his family worked, he recalls. No one was ever on public assistance. Keith's mother obtained an associate degree at a community college. One of his cousins went to college. Members of his family read poetry. Keith himself was taught to read before entering school. One of his cousins had comic books on Greek mythology, and Keith had daydreams about living in ancient Athens as an athlete and scholar.

Keith's great-grandmother was a slave, and from his aunt he heard stories about Jim Crow, about the violence she had suffered, and about how hard she had to struggle as a young woman. Members of Keith's family partici-

*Executive-Director, Housing Works (see Chapter 14).

pated in the 1963 March on Washington, when Martin Luther King, Jr., delivered his "I have a dream" speech.

When Keith was in third grade, the school principal rebuked him sharply for quarreling with a boy who constantly picked on him. Keith responded equally sharply. "I may have slapped her," he declares. He was suspended, and his family transferred him to a Catholic school. As the only boy in the village attending a parochial school, Keith became the butt of jokes. Because he was a good student, he was nicknamed "four eyes," and he was ridiculed because of the way he spoke. Like Marjorie Hill, Keith was struck by the fact that at his new school he and a black girl were the only students in upper-track classes; the second track was mixed, and the lowest track was all black. Upon his arrival, a boy called him a nigger. Keith hit him. "It was not so much what he said as how he said it," Keith recounts. "He was trying to put me down."

At the age of thirteen, about to enter ninth grade, Keith became rebellious and difficult to control. He yearned for a normal family life and wanted to live with his mother. He had been led to believe that his father was dead and suspected that his family was, in fact, preventing his father from seeing him. His mother found a larger apartment in Cleveland, and he moved in with her. As a newcomer at his new parochial high school, Keith at first felt isolated. He found no bond among the boys of color until he was seduced by two black classmates, Michael and Raymond ("a flaming faggot"). Though he spent weekends at Michael's house, he also had a girlfriend, and his mother had no suspicions about him. Michael and Keith remained lovers for years. Keith had no sense of guilt about their relationship.

At sixteen Keith began going to gay bars with his friends. It troubled him that Raymond hustled. His long Catholic experience, Keith insists, made him sensitive to moral questions. Paradoxically, however, from the time he moved to Cleveland, Keith began taking drugs. He and Michael stole Michael's mother's Valium and other sedatives, used marijuana and cocaine, and experimented with speed and LSD. At mass Keith drank the altar wine and drank otherwise during weekends. He took to drugs, he says, out of a sense of loneliness. On the other hand, Keith insists that he never lost control with drugs, alcohol, or sex. "I had the ideals of Ancient Greece," he asserts.

Although aware of racism from childhood, Keith always "fit in with white folks. I have never been hassled by the police," he notes. In high school Keith had white acquaintances, but he never exchanged visits with them. He also had a crush on a white girl but knew that he would never be able to go out with her. In fact, he emphasizes, all his close friends were black. "I was in my own world, a black world," he declares. Elected to the high school student council, Keith tried to help black boys who got into trouble. Once when he learned that a boy was being investigated for selling pot, he rescued a package of pot from the boy's locker before it was searched.

Keith admits that like other African Americans he has suffered day-by-day humiliations. “Every time you walk down the street,” Keith declares, “every time you get into an elevator with a white woman, and she clutches at her purse, it's there. It eats at you, it makes you angry. I have always been angry.”

Keith discovered that his father had been twice married and had several children. Learning that his father was in a hospital, Keith went to visit him. One day when his father's wife came to the hospital, his father refused to tell her who Keith was. Some years later, when Keith was about to leave for college, he says, his father suddenly assumed a paternal role, expressing opposition to Keith's leaving Cleveland. Keith reminded him that he had never acted like a father and had not contributed a dime toward his education or paid any child support. How did he dare, he asked, to tell him what he could or could not do? Keith never saw his father again, although he long harbored a fantasy of one day sending him an invitation to his doctoral graduation.

As a senior in high school, Keith began an eight-year affair with the thirty-three-year-old assistant minister, the leader of the church youth group. They continued to visit each other after Keith went off to Worcester State College in Massachusetts. When his lover found a position at Brown University, Keith transferred there, and he and his lover lived together. After a year, Keith, who was selling drugs and frequently getting high, began to find the relationship constricting. He transferred to Boston University. During two summers he held a job at a residential treatment facility in Cleveland, developing a program for disturbed young people. For his college internship, Keith worked with psychiatrically impaired delinquents in Boston.

Keith continued to visit his lover at Brown weekends and became, he says, dependent upon him in unhealthy ways. When his lover slept with Keith's best friend, they separated for good. Upset at the breakup, Keith entered therapy, and for a year he stopped drinking and taking drugs. He met many gay people and began to develop a gay identity. “As I established who I was,” he says, “I no longer wanted a relationship with a father figure, a mentor.”

Coming out as a gay man in the black community, Keith insists, was difficult. “How do you integrate being a jock,” he exclaimed, “running almost at an Olympic level on college teams, and being a gay African American? Automatically, you don't fit in, and I had no black role models.” In fact, Keith asserts, race became a pressing issue for him only when he began participating in gay life. He experienced “tremendous discrimination, subtle discrimination. When you talk to someone, all he wants to do is to sneak out of the bar and not let his friends see he's leaving with you.” He had a special problem dealing with “dinge queens” (white gays who seek black partners), he relates “men who were attracted to me merely to have sex. They bring a black-white issue into sex. I want people to want me as a person.”

On the other hand, Keith denies any connection between his drugs and alcohol addiction and tensions he experienced as an African American, insisting that he got into the habits solely because he was lonely. On the other hand, he attributes his addictions to the difficulty he experienced in being both black and gay.

REGINA SHAVERS*

Regina Shavers underwent a consistent, though scarcely painless, process in coming out as a lesbian woman, a process complicated by her increasing awareness of herself as an African American. Born in 1948, Regina grew up in a multiethnic neighborhood in Brooklyn. The white neighbors, Regina recalls, were primarily working class—Greeks, Italians, and Irish—while the blacks were generally middle class. Regina and her black friends, she says, "wanted to do things, to become artists. The whites were going to be priests, nuns, or laborers."

Regina's parents attempted to transmit their middle-class aspirations to her and her brother. "You always have to be better than white folks," they declared. "You have to control your emotions." On the other hand, Regina's parents were active in the civil rights movement. Her father, one of the first blacks to be accepted into the New York City Fire Department, admired Paul Robeson and Eleanor Roosevelt. On television Regina saw her mother being arrested in a demonstration at Downstate Medical Center. Both parents read poetry and encouraged Regina to recite.

Although Regina was not aware of racial tensions in her neighborhood and was close to some of her Irish neighbors, once when she was nine she had a fight with an Italian girl who called her a nigger. "I was hurt," Regina recalls. "I didn't trust white people. I had visited in South Carolina and had read a lot and knew what was going on. A black person is never unaware of being black. That's the biggest awareness you have with you all the time." The incident with the Italian girl, however, had an unexpected outcome. "The girls' grandmother called us both into the house," Regina recalls, "and gave her a lacing down."

Neighbors made remarks when Regina played with boys, but Regina's father, who had wanted to have a son, encouraged her. Her mother was confident that Regina would outgrow her tomboy behavior. In preparation for church on Sundays her mother dressed her in a pinafore and fixed her hair in Shirley Temple curls. One Sunday, Regina, then eleven, rebelled. "What can you do with her?" her mother exclaimed. Regina did not attend church again.

Although at the mainly black neighborhood elementary school she was in the top class, Regina remembers her experience there as unpleasant. "I felt I didn't fit in. I knew I was gay. I had lesbian fantasies as early as six. I had no words for it. I knew it was wrong. They always called me a tomboy. I

*Member of the New York City Police Council (see Chapter 12). In 1996 she had left the NYPD.

didn't want to be a boy, but I needed more freedom than other girls." When she and other students were transferred to a predominantly white elementary school, they were told that none of them could be placed in the all-white advanced class. The second-level classes were mainly black. The other, so-called special opportunity classes were almost entirely black. "I was in a war zone," Regina declares. "I never got into the advanced class."

Because Regina was a tomboy, teachers sent her to the boy's dean when she appeared out of control. He calmed her by giving her books of poetry to read. Regina's eighth-grade teacher, however, discouraged black students from applying to academic high schools and urged them to continue on instead to vocational schools. Regina's mother, however, had graduated from Erasmus High School, and she successfully insisted that Regina go there also. At Erasmus, Regina asserts, "I was in a bigger war." Most of the eight thousand students were Jewish. "They were not overtly hostile," Regina recalls, "just very insensitive." The fifty or so blacks, like the whites, came from more prosperous backgrounds than Regina's previous schoolmates. The black students stuck together, engaging in the same extracurricular activities. Regina did well in courses she enjoyed and played hockey and badminton. She was a good swimmer, but she did not try out for the swimming team. Swimming was scheduled for seven in the morning. "We used to straighten our hair," Regina recalls. "Natural black hair was considered ugly, and if I had swum, my hair would have been a mess all day. None of the other black girls would get their hair wet, and I needed their approval."

Regina discovered that to be popular it was necessary to go with certain boys. She felt no attraction to them and was frightened at having crushes on girls. At school she became aware of gays and lesbians. They were all white, and she did not mix with them. Having no one to talk to about her sexual "problem," she underwent such an emotional upheaval that the principal's office called her mother to find out what was wrong.

One day Regina went to the gay section of Riis Park, a beach on the south shore of Brooklyn, and had a long talk with herself. "I realized," she declares, "that getting married was an impossibility. Unlike my girlfriends, I didn't want a boyfriend. I didn't want to change my name. I didn't want anybody telling me what to do. I wanted to be my own boss. I decided I was going to live my life as a lesbian. Once I made that decision, everything else was anticlimax."

When Regina was in her senior year a notorious "out" lesbian classmate told Regina's best friend about a club in Greenwich Village, the Ace of Spades, and Regina and her friend started to go there. The lesbian friend and Regina talked regularly on the telephone. Regina reported each conversation to her girlfriend. One night Regina related that the other young woman had said that she was attracted to Regina's friend. "We giggled," Regina recalls. "My girlfriend was interested. I thought about that. I called her back and said that I liked her myself. That was how it started, our being lovers. We were both inexperienced and had to learn together."

When the girlfriend told Regina's mother that they were lovers, Regina's mother "had a fit." "She kept saying," Regina relates, " 'I knew it, I knew it.' " When her mother attempted to discuss the "problem," Regina refused to talk. Her parents decided to send her to a psychologist to be "cured." "I wanted their approval, but I was a teenager in rebellion," Regina explains, "living in a world that my mother didn't understand. I was living a life as a black lesbian in a society that negated me on both counts." Fortunately, an uncle proved sympathetic. "He came out on the stoop," Regina relates, "and talked to me. He advised me that in whatever I did, I should be the best. That helped a lot."

After graduating from high school, Regina enrolled at Brooklyn College. Discouraged by the impersonal atmosphere, she played cards all day and quit before the end of the term. At age eighteen in Regina's family, people were expected to be on their own, and Regina and her lover took an apartment in the East Village. They experienced homophobic assaults. "Any man felt free to say," Regina recalls, " 'If you're going to look like a man, I'm going to treat you like a man.' " One evening as they were walking down the street they saw a man in a car shouting a remark at a lesbian. She talked back. He jumped out with a tire iron and attacked Regina and her lover as well as the other lesbian. The three women fought for their lives. Passersby, including a high school friend of Regina's, ignored the fracas. The police arrived but took no action. On another occasion when a group of lesbians were leaving a party in Brooklyn, a gang of men began shouting at them, "Look at the bull daggers," and came running to attack them. The women grabbed garbage-can covers, and the men came to a halt. "We had no reason to expect protection from the police," Regina remarks.

While working as a laboratory technician at Maimonides Hospital in Brooklyn, Regina developed an alcohol problem and then a drug problem and was at the point of becoming unemployable. While under drugs she was trapped in a fire and hospitalized for several months. "I couldn't talk to my black girlfriends about being gay," Regina explains, "and I couldn't talk to my white friends about being black. At a very young age, I experienced the problems of being black, a woman, and a lesbian."

Regina lists as decisive events in her life hearing Malcolm X and Martin Luther King, Jr., in person; overcoming her alcohol and drug abuse; studying with the black lesbian poet Audre Lorde; becoming involved in the women's movement; and meeting her present lover.

Several of these experiences occurred after Regina enrolled at Hunter College as a mature student of forty-three in 1984. Audre Lorde, one of Regina's professors, proved a major influence on her thinking. She preached that "silence doesn't keep us safe" and encouraged Regina to write and to transform herself into an articulate "visible African-American lesbian." "I began to have words," Regina says, "to express myself. I had more confidence because I was more aware of what was going on around me." Overcoming her alcohol and drug problems, she began to work in a community addiction program. She also participated in publishing a magazine called "Returning Woman." From her association with black lesbian activists at Hunter College, Regina transformed herself into a confirmed and self-assured activist. At conferences of women's groups she discovered that she had something to contribute out of her own experience. At an international meeting in Cuba, she met writers, artists, and dancers from many nations. From this experience, she became convinced that in a society that did not allow for differences it was the people on the periphery of society who would have to insist upon change.

In October of 1991, after graduating from Hunter College, Regina, who that year had come out in every aspect of her life, was appointed to the Gay and Lesbian Rights Advisory Committee of AFSCME (the American Federation of State, County, and Municipal Employees), and two months later she received one of the annual awards from the New York City Commission on the Status of Women as an individual who had made "substantial contributions to the advancement of women in City government."

Regina met her present lover in 1989, an African-American lesbian ("Of course, she's black!" Regina exclaimed) who held a management position in NYPD. Younger than Regina, she nevertheless "calms me down and makes me a gentler woman. She draws me out, makes me communicate."

Chapter Four
The Silence of Machismo

More than gay men of other races or other ethnic backgrounds, Hispanic gay men confront particular opprobrium because of the tradition of machismo in their community. "It is more a disgrace in Hispanic families for a man to be gay than for a woman," declared Carla. "If a son is effeminate, they say, 'If you want to be gay, be conservative about it. Try not to show it.' " The theme of machismo recurs to a lesser or greater degree in all the interviews with Hispanics.

JUAN MENDEZ*

Born in 1965, Juan Mendez grew up in San Juan, Puerto Rico. His father, who came from a mountaineer peasant family, owned a successful automobile dealership. He and Juan's mother, a devout Catholic, exhibited middle-class prejudices. As a child, Juan heard his mother blame Puerto Ricans for deteriorating conditions in New York, where she had lived before Juan was born. She and Juan's father were scandalized when Juan's older sister married a black Puerto Rican. They were hardly reassured by his Afro haircut or his involvement in the movement for Puerto Rican independence or his battered Volkswagen Beetle. "My mother," Juan recalls, " cried and begged my sister to reconsider her choice for a husband. My father refused to attend the wedding." Juan's sister and her husband became models for Juan politically. A high school religion teacher reinforced their influence, teaching that people

*Staffer at the Hetrick Martin Institute (see Chapter 13).

should call each other "compañero" and criticizing missionaries for failing to address fundamental injustices in the world.

The family home was isolated, and Juan had no playmates. He disliked sports and was badgered at school because he was an "A" student and was called sissy or faggot. On the other hand, when during a wrestling tournament in sixth grade, the physical education teacher mocked him before his classmates, Juan won second place, defeating the class bully. "The win," Juan declares, "showed me I could do it." That same year Juan learned about sex for the first time. "The teacher drew a penis and a vagina on the blackboard," Juan recalls, "and explained how children were conceived. It was liberating but at the same time frightening because it was associated with sin." In eighth grade in the showers Juan gazed at an attractive, athletic older boy. The boy invited Juan to touch him. The incident was never repeated. Confident that he was merely passing through a stage, he was not troubled by his crushes on boys and on his teachers. Juan socialized easily with girls. "They knew I was no threat," Juan explains. For a week he even had a girlfriend. She broke off with him when he refused to hold hands with her.

Juan's bedroom faced toward a gay bar, and he could hear gay men talking in the parking lot. His father complained about the noise and scoffed at the men as degenerates. Juan's mother insisted that she had nothing against gays. "They were born that way," she said. Juan became aware of cruising at the beach, and one day in the showers he was excited by the sight of two young men engaging in mutual masturbation.

The last day of his senior year Juan ventured into a gay bar. He had no idea how to act or what to expect. The bartender engaged him in conversation and put him at ease. Moving on to another bar, Juan found a large crowd, with some people playing video games or billiards. "This is my world," Juan decided. He returned to the bar every day. One day he met someone. They kissed and went out and had sex in a car. The sense of danger, Juan recalls, added to the excitement. On another occasion, someone asked him how to play a video game. "When I turned around," Juan recalls, "I saw a beautiful man in his early thirties. He bought me a couple of drinks. I couldn't believe that this handsome flight attendant would pick me out. I thought I was overweight and badly proportioned. Besides, I wore glasses."

Rafael invited Juan home and was surprised to find that Juan recognized his Dali lithographs and was familiar with Mozart's music. They had "incredible" sex. Rafi took Juan to a party. "It felt great to dance with men," Juan declares. Certain that he was in love, Juan came out to himself. "It can't be bad," he assured himself, "because I am in love, and that is beautiful."

A year earlier, Juan's father had taken Juan to New York to investigate the possibility of his studying film work there. In the fall after graduating from high school, Juan spent the night with Rafael before departing for the city. They cried at the thought of separation. Rafi flew to New York with him and remained there two days with him. When he left, Juan's world fell apart. After two months, without warning his parents, who were making a considerable sacrifice to send him away to school, Juan returned to Puerto Rico. Rafi met him at the airport. Juan explained that he was not sure he wanted to study film. His mother was overjoyed. He enrolled in a small private Catholic college. His parents quarreled and separated, and during his last two years at school Juan moved in with Rafi.

The relationship did not evolve without difficulties. Rafi had an alcohol problem. When he drank, he became mean and domineering. On such occasions Juan returned home to his mother, now divorced and living with Juan's younger brother. In 1988, convinced that his lover would not overcome his alcoholism and that a continuation of the relationship was proving destructive to both of them, Juan left for New York. The four years, from age seventeen to age twenty-one, he spent with Rafi were not a loss, he insists. "I got an incredible amount of love and learned self-respect," he says. "In the good times we were able to build something very solid. I became independent and grew up." The experience taught him also to be cautious before entering relationships, to seek "a better balance between emotion and reality."

Early in the relationship, his mother found a letter from Rafi under Juan's mattress. She said nothing. She came to love Rafi, and five years after the two men broke up, she continued to call him. She could not bring herself, however, to discuss Juan's intimate life. "When I talk about love or seeing someone," Juan says, "she won't listen. We're still working on that." Juan's father also liked Rafi, but after his parents' divorce Juan lost touch with him.

Middle-class and college-educated, Juan admits that he has experienced little of the prejudice that other Puerto Ricans confront day by day. Indeed, Juan learned to appreciate his countrymen more in New York than he had appreciated them as a child and young man on the island. While working as a social worker at the Lower East Side Family Union, he became aware, he says, of "a proud community fighting to survive, fighting against institutional racism and classism and potential annihilation through AIDS. After more than fifty years of indoctrination," he declares, "they preserve their culture and patriotism. While in Puerto Rico people are trying to become more American, here they struggle to maintain their identity."

In his first Puerto Rican Day parade, Juan was struck by the pride and courage of the gay contingent marching in defiance of the parade organizers. They were greeted by jeers and missiles. The next year, however, a much larger contingent was greeted with applause; and people grabbed AIDS education flyers so quickly that Juan ran out of five thousand flyers within an hour. "People are experiencing AIDS closer to home," Juan explains. "Latinos tend to unite in time of crisis."

Juan rejects as exaggerated the common assertion of intense homophobia among Latinos. When during lectures on AIDS in high schools he announced that he was gay, he encountered, "a few gasps and some giggling" but no offensive remarks. In housing projects, Juan notes, gay individuals and couples face no problems, and he and other Latino activists move freely where other gays might fear to be seen. He recalled, for example, how he and more than a dozen other gay Latinos were warmly received in a crowded Lower East Side Mexican restaurant during a "happy" hour. The owner spoke to them about gays in her own family. "All the people in the restaurant," Juan relates, "started connecting with us. If we are open," he remarks, "people are willing to accept us."

GUILLERMO VASQUEZ*

"I never knew that I was a person of color until I came to the United States," declared Guillermo Vasquez, a member of the staff at the Gay Men's Health Crisis (GMHC). "In Colombia we are one community." Guillermo had, however, become inured to even more oppressive discrimination before emigrating to New York. During the years before he mustered sufficient courage to come out, he suffered under the pressures of Latino machismo. Under machismo, he explains, it is not wrong to have sex with someone of the same sex, but it is unforgivable to talk about it. "I could not disclose to my family or to my straight friends that I was gay," Guillermo declares. Indeed, his father complained at his going around with "faggots," but he refused to believe that Guillermo was homosexual. When, at eighteen, Guillermo announced that he was gay, his father responded with silence, "the silence," Guillermo insists, "of machismo."

Guillermo is the only son of a workaholic, shrewd, but not well-educated Colombian cattle rancher and of a religious and more cultivated mother. After obtaining a divorce while Guillermo was in secondary school, Guillermo's father remarried and had two daughters by his new wife.

By the time he was seven or eight Guillermo already sensed that he was different from other boys. At the age of ten, Guillermo had his first sexual experience, fondling a boy his own age. They had both heard a children's rhyme making fun of queers. "We knew," Guillermo declares, "this was something we weren't supposed to talk about." Subsequently, Guillermo did find two gay friends, Orlando and Oscar, with whom he could exchange confidences. "We had to deal with a lot of machismo, and when you have to live with machismo. . . !" Guillermo exclaims. "We were lucky to have each other."

At the age of twelve, to explore whether he was suited to a religious vocation, Guillermo left home to board at a seminary. His reputation as a queer preceded him, and Flavio, the handsome brother of one of Guillermo's elementary school friends, introduced him to sex life at the school. Because of the segregation of the sexes in parochial schools and the traditional Latin sheltering of young girls, boys engaged in sex with each other. How could his sexual activity be a sin, Guillermo asked himself, if what he was doing was so prevalent? Even priests made overtures to him. Guillermo organized a gay club that published a clandestine gossip sheet.

*Staffer at the Gay Men's Health Crisis (see Chapter 14).

Generally, straight boys at the seminary were not vicious to those who like Guillermo were recognized as gay. One boy, however, annoyed Guillermo by continually pawing him. Guillermo complained to the director, and the boy was given a warning. Guillermo himself threatened another boy who jeered at him as a faggot that he would let everyone know that they had slept together. "That was the end of that annoyance," Guillermo declares. Once Guillermo swung at a boy who called him a faggot and cut the boy's forehead with his ring. "I developed a reputation," he says. "I was a sissy, but one you had to be careful with."

At the age of fifteen abandoning all thought of the priesthood, Guillermo entered a secondary school. Orlando, who had attended another seminary, rejoined him. "If it weren't for you who sleeps around with everyone," Orlando complained, "they wouldn't know we were faggots." Guillermo retorted that the others would call them faggots in any case. "We might just as well be faggots," he insisted. "Orlando would have died," Guillermo declares, "to become straight."

Guillermo and his gay friends were not interested in going to brothels and out drinking like the "regular" boys. Too young to go to gay bars, they went to parties at the homes of older gays. "If I had not had those friends," Guillermo says, "I would have been home alone, frustrated.

"Machismo," Guillermo declares, "worked against me throughout my childhood and adolescence. We gays called ourselves queer so that when they called us queer it didn't hurt." At a school dance, indeed, he had a frightening experience. He drank too much and later could not remember what impelled a young man to pursue him out of the men's room. The friend whom Guillermo had fondled as an eight-year-old jumped up along with other young men at his table to Guillermo's defense.

Preoccupied with the disintegration of their marriage, Guillermo's parents had no suspicions about his sexual adventures. He had always felt closer to his mother. Soft-spoken, she taught him to behave like a gentleman. In adolescence, however, Guillermo came to resent her overprotectiveness. His father remained at his ranch about an hour's drive from town, coming home only on weekends. His father's partner had two sons close to Guillermo's age whom Guillermo's father took to horse races and to other activities he enjoyed. Offering excuses to avoid accompanying them, Guillermo sensed that he was not living up to his father's expectations.

After his parents' divorce, Guillermo's mother urged him to live with his father, arguing that she was emotionally exhausted and that his father could provide greater advantages because of his wealth. During vacations spent at the ranch, Guillermo was occasionally assigned tasks but generally left to himself. During the school year, living with his paternal grandparents, Guillermo maintained an active social life. His elderly grandparents went to bed early, always having a cup of hot chocolate before retiring. Sometimes Guillermo put Valium in the chocolate to guarantee their sleeping soundly. Then he and his friends would have a party. In the morning his grandmother would remark at how well she had slept.

After graduating from secondary school, Guillermo delayed his departure for a university in Europe until he could arrange to buy exemption from military service (an accepted practice in Colombia). Just before he was to leave, however, Guillermo and his father had "a silly quarrel," and he ran off to Bogota to share an apartment with a cousin. He discovered the gay life of the capital and began inviting boys home and eventually had a friend move in with him.

At nineteen, on a visit to relatives in New Jersey, Guillermo looked up a Colombian friend in Jackson Heights in New York City and discovered that it was possible to pick up people on the street. He moved to New York and in 1978, responding to pressure from his father, enrolled in prelaw and English-as-a-second-language courses at Columbia University. After graduating in 1982, he continued to take courses, supporting himself with money sent him by his father or earned at jobs in a department store and in a restaurant.

From 1984 to 1986, Guillermo simply "dropped out" into a life of drugs, alcohol, and sex. Rising at one or two in the afternoon, he dallied in getting himself together until it was time to go to the bars. He became a steady patron at the fashionable Studio 54, where, he says, pretty boys were willing to do anything for cocaine. He and his lover of the time traveled to Europe, South America, and the West Coast.

In the fall of 1986 Guillermo's best friend, a medical student, died of AIDS. "That," says Guillermo, "was the end of the party." It was then that Guillermo began to transform himself into a dedicated gay activist (a development described in Chapter 14).

DENNIS DE LEON, NEW YORK CITY COMMISSIONER FOR HUMAN RIGHTS*

In 1948, when Dennis was born, his father, who had emigrated from Mexico to Los Angeles eighteen years earlier, had just returned from service as an army captain in the Philippines. He found a teaching position at an all-black high school. Dennis's Spanish-born mother, "a radical activist who sees conspiracies everywhere," had worked in the pineapple fields in Hawaii and then as a welfare organizer in Los Angeles. When her mother remarried in Los Angeles and had a second set of children, she was forced to live in a toolshed. Speaking no English as a child, she underwent a heroic struggle to become, like Dennis's father, a school teacher. Dennis and his younger sister saw little of her, as she was constantly taking evening courses toward a master's degree.

*In 1996, executive director of the Latino AIDS Commission.

Although they spoke Spanish at home, both Dennis's parents were fluent in English. Language, Dennis says, never posed a problem. Color, hair, and facial features, however, were issues. His Mexican-born father was dark skinned and had Indian features. His mother was light skinned but had frizzy hair, as does Dennis.

Although sensitive about his olive-skinned complexion and called "a beaner" in elementary school, Dennis had no strong sense of being Mexican. "I associated everything Mexican with my father," Dennis declares. Tall and powerfully built, Dennis's father conducted a judo club for boys in the barrio. It annoyed him that Dennis, puny, asthmatic, and suffering from a speech defect, was not athletic. Dennis's sister, on the other hand, played baseball and socialized with the jocks in high school. One day, when Dennis was still in elementary school, as they were getting into the car, Dennis let his wrists go limp. His father "slapped the hell" out of him. "Don't ever do that," he shouted. "No son of mine is ever going to be a queer." Dennis did not know what the word meant, but the remark struck home.

Dennis's father had an alcohol problem. He harbored a constant rancor at whites and constantly complained of bad treatment of Mexicans. When he drank too much at family gatherings, he would scream imprecations about "the enemy." At any setback he got drunk and became abusive to his family, on one occasion, Dennis recalls, overturning the piano and smashing dishes. During these outbursts Dennis's mother ran off with Dennis and his sister. The children and their mother frequently lied to avoid setting their father off to drinking and yelling.

When Dennis was thirteen, his parents divorced. Eventually his mother remarried, to a WASP, "part of the ruling class," Dennis declares, "a nice man with no soul." Dennis's father also remarried, to a woman Dennis's age, and had a second set of children.

Climbing the rope in gym as a freshman in high school, Dennis had his first ejaculation. He remained hanging in midair, not knowing what had occurred. Unaware of how to masturbate, he spent hours in the backyard swinging on his father's gym bars, trying to renew the sensation he had had at school. Naive about sexual matters, he did not understand what classmates were talking about when they spoke of "a piece of ass" or a "blow job."

Academically oriented like his mother, Dennis helped to start a poetry magazine in high school. He joined the speech club and overcame a stuttering problem to the point of being able to participate on the debating team. He found friends among the bookish types. It was the only way, he says, he could isolate himself from the toughs. If he got in their way in the locker room, they shoved him away. If in the showers he glanced at their genitals, they exclaimed, "Do you want it?" In fact, he had fantasies "about the big guys doing things with the little guys. If certain boys came close to me," he recalls, "I would feel a rush of blood, an intense, almost uncomfortable feeling." Dennis did have a girlfriend. They engaged in petting, but girls roused no feelings in him, and he did not know what he was supposed to do with them. He became upset that no women appeared in his fantasies.

Dennis enrolled at Occidental College, supporting himself as a short-order cook and by tutoring. He felt alienated and nursed a constant rage at racial injustice and at a sense of being an outsider, feelings that in retrospect he thinks may have been motivated by his growing sexual fears. Since there was no Mexican organization on campus, Dennis joined a black group and let his hair grow. "I felt nonwhite," he recalls, "but I was unclear where I belonged. In the sixties everything was black and white. I felt viscerally uncomfortable with either, but more comfortable with the black community." Dennis ran for college office on "an angry platform of antiracism. I wanted so badly to be part of something." Membership in a Mexican group organized the next year brought him "a kind of radical chic." The group did tutoring in local high schools and mounted demonstrations on civil rights issues. "I began pulling together pieces of myself," Dennis declares, "clarifying how I viewed my father's family and culture. I began to feel more positive about being Mexican and to appreciate the role of the church in my life and as part of the Mexican tradition. I began to feel good about who I was."

During these years Dennis lived an asexual existence. "It seemed to me that you couldn't be both Mexican and gay. Besides, at that time it was okay to be black and against the war but not to be gay." When a lesbian came out to him and then publicly in the school paper, Dennis was astounded at her boldness. He foresaw a tragic end for her and was determined not to share such a fate. Nevertheless, he could not deny his crushes on men, especially strong men with powerful hands like his father's. ("As time has gone on," Dennis admits, "I have seen my relationship with my father and his treatment of me as having sexual overtones.")

Dennis emerged from college politicized and with an aspiration to change the world. Matriculating in a graduate psychology program at the University of California at Santa Barbara, Dennis encountered an academic rigor he had missed at Occidental, a school wracked by the anti-intellectualism of the 1960s. His enthusiasm for psychology, however, proved short lived. Rationalizing that at law school he would prepare himself to continue the kind of political activity he had engaged in at Occidental, with his mother's encouragement, he transferred into a Stanford program directed toward minority students. "In their eyes," Dennis recalls, "I was there as a Mexican, and I felt I had something to prove." In preparing a lawsuit in protest of the university's admissions policies, Dennis conducted a study that demonstrated that no correlation existed between academic performance and LSAT scores generally and only a marginal correlation existed between performance in law school and the LSAT. In his final year, however, winning a post on the law review, he began to think of himself less as a social activist. "I began feeling very confident. I had a skill, a trade. I acquired an identity as a lawyer, a technocrat."

Dennis experienced strong attractions to his straight associates, but while they went out with girls, he studied or worked out at the gym, lifting weights and running in an effort to lose weight and to improve his physique, "to become an Adonis." For the first time in his life he looked healthy. Nevertheless, on visits to the gay Castro district in San Francisco, he walked past gay bars, fearful of jeopardizing his career and of risking rejection. Once in a diner a counterman pointed at him and said, "I want that boy." He started a conversation and asked Dennis to come back at the end of his shift. Dennis passed the time at a pornographic movie. Confused and uncertain, he returned to the diner. Chris said, "Come home," and to his own astonishment, Dennis agreed. Chris was gentle. Dennis enjoyed the experience.

While at Santa Barbara, however, Dennis had met Rita, a graduate student, and was spending much time with her. Although he attempted to put his experience with Chris out of his mind, he frequently returned to San Francisco and remained overnight with Chris. "We were very close," he recalls. "I enjoyed sleeping with him more than with Rita."

Upon finishing at Stanford, Dennis performed his clerkship with Judge Robert Thompson, a member of a leading law firm and prestigious clubs, a man with broad political connections. With his assistance Dennis obtained an appointment at a wealthy Jewish Los Angeles law firm with about a hundred lawyers and such corporate clients as IBM and Baskin-Robbins. (Law firms in Los Angeles, Dennis explains, were classified as either Jewish or non-Jewish.) Troubled by a sense that he was selling out, Dennis promised himself that he would remain at the firm for only a short time. Still, the privileges were tempting—eating in expensive restaurants, staying in luxury hotels, being "a bird in a gilded cage." "The firm," Dennis declares, "became one's entire existence." Assimilation into a team player was encouraged by promotions and merit bonuses.

Although remaining prudently in the closet, with his firm's knowledge, Dennis helped to found the Bay Area Lawyers for Individual Freedom, "one of the first major politically gay things I did." A disagreement arose with his superiors, however, when Dennis refused to write a strikebreaking speech for a boss of a sausage factory. His superiors admonished him not to allow moral judgments to interfere with professional responsibilities but, self-conscious about the commitment to social issues that was a hallmark of the firm, they did not pressure him to a point of crisis.

After being introduced to a gay bar by Patrick, a gay colleague at the firm, Dennis returned on his own. It was "a big deal to Patrick," Dennis understood, "to be seen for what he was and to be able to share his private life," but gay life struck Dennis as a lonely existence. "I knew all the stereotypes about the lifestyle," he recalls. "I had the notion you couldn't form a good relationship if you were gay." In addition, reacting to his father's machismo, Dennis felt shame and even fear at his homosexuality. But while on a two-and-a-half-month assignment in New York, Dennis met someone in the Gay

Pride parade. One day, holding hands, they walked the ten or so miles from the George Washington Bridge to the Battery at the southern tip of Manhattan. "It was a joyous day," Dennis recalls. "He was a sweetheart, and he liked me." He was also a gay activist, and Dennis was impressed by his political sophistication. "That summer," he declares, "I began to sense the political aspect of being gay."

Dennis was anxious not only about his sexual orientation, he recalls, but also about his new class position among privileged whites. It upset him that he had to ask his colleague Patrick to go shopping with him to show him the kind of clothes to buy. At the law firm, Dennis's subjective struggle became ever more intense. "I did not want to be the kind of Mexican they thought I should be. They expected me to wear huaraches. I wondered what they said about me when I was not present."

Troubled by these conflicts, Dennis plunged himself into his work, spending long hours at the office night after night. "I was trying to prove myself," he explains, "and I had an anger I couldn't direct at anybody." One night in a petty but symbolic gesture of defiance, he stole a bottle of Tio Pepe from the firm's liquor cabinet. "As an act," Dennis declares, "it amounted to nothing, but for me it was that I was stealing something from them. I had got back at these people in some way. It was a Mexican drink, too!"

Invited to a firm pool party, Dennis discovered to his embarrassment that the caterers and waiters were Mexican. Then and there he resolved to renew his connection with the Latino community; with the firm's approval, he began doing pro bono work for farm workers and for undocumented aliens. Nevertheless, increasingly, he realized that he would never completely become a member of the team.

When in 1977 the dean of the Stanford Law School, newly appointed as president of the Legal Services Corporation, offered Dennis a job, Dennis accepted and moved to Washington. In a "groupie" house with a lesbian and three gay fellow tenants, Dennis found an instant family. Although the new position proved challenging, Dennis failed to adjust to his new circumstances. Anticipating dismissal for breaching the rule of going through channels, Dennis found a new position at the Civil Affairs Division of the Department of Justice.

Before starting at his new post, Dennis took a five-month vacation and read the eight volumes of Proust's *Remembrance of Things Past*, traveled in South America, and spent a couple of sexually charged weeks with a woman from the Los Angeles law firm, never able, however, to keep his eyes off men while he was with her. "I could have been one of the gay men who married, had children, and broke off at forty or so to live a gay life," Dennis declares.

Upon word that Patrick had committed suicide, Dennis flew out to Los Angeles, intending to continue on to San Francisco to propose to Rita, his friend from Santa Barbara. In Los Angeles Dennis met Bruce, a friend of Patrick's and a former Dominican seminarian. Bruce was the kind of lover

Dennis was seeking, and in San Francisco Dennis told Rita he did not want to marry her. Shaken by her outburst of anger, he sought refuge at Chris's apartment. Chris offered comfort, love, and acceptance. "I felt whole," Dennis says, explaining, "That was the main thing about having sex with men. It made me feel complete; there were no missing pieces."

Bruce followed Dennis to Washington, and on January 1, 1978, they moved in together. When Bruce obtained a position that took him overseas, however, Dennis returned to San Francisco to work with the California Rural Legal Assistance, supervising agencies rendering legal aid to farm workers. "During my two years there I learned about community organizing," Dennis declares, "and how to use public relations to get results." For the first time Dennis did not feel as though he was a member of a minority.

Weary of the constant struggle against cuts in agency appropriations by Governor Ronald Reagan, Dennis accepted an offer from the Koch administration to serve as a New York City corporation counsel and as executive director of the Mayor's Committee on Hispanic Affairs. In his new posts he became involved in issues of significance to the gay community, investing much of his energy in the enforcement of Koch's Executive Order 50, which prohibited discrimination in hiring on the basis of sexual preference by any organization doing business with the city. He succeeded in compelling the Roman Catholic diocese and the Salvation Army to submit to the order, only to lose the case on appeal. He negotiated for the establishment of an AIDS-issues division within the commission on human rights and hired the first attorney for the unit.

Interviewed for the post of deputy borough president of Manhattan under David Dinkins, Dennis asked whether his sexual orientation would prevent his obtaining the position. "Half my staff is gay," responded Dinkins. Upon Dinkins's election as mayor of New York, Dennis applied for and obtained the post of commissioner for human rights, a position where he could bring to bear all his previous experience. From the start he encountered homophobic opposition among the staff. "It has been interesting dealing with that hostility," he declares. "Much of it arises from the fact that most communities of color view gays and lesbians as white, not as blacks and Latinos. They look at them therefore as a kind of privileged class that have undeserved rights."

As commissioner, Dennis continued his efforts against discrimination suffered by people with AIDS and on behalf of gay domestic-partnership legislation. To demonstrate the critical need for a city gay rights bill, he ordered a tally of incidents of homophobic harassment in employment and housing and drafted a series of guidelines for a bias-free workplace. Under Dennis's direction, the commission conducted an "End the Hate" study of homophobic violence (extracts of which appear in Chapter 8 of this book.) "We distributed," Dennis reported, "thousands of survey forms to investigate the scope and the geographical diversity of anti-gay and lesbian violence and issued a report that I think will make a difference in getting bias-related crimes acknowledged."

Dennis and Bruce suffered sorrow at deaths from AIDS of people close to them, including Bruce's brother and a New York lawyer who had served as a mentor to Dennis. In 1984 and 1985, they parted when Bruce underwent a profound emotional upheaval. Bruce subsequently obtained a position at the Union Theological Seminary and experienced a revival of faith and found emotional peace. He took an apartment above Dennis's, and they resumed their relationship. Dennis is troubled about their political differences, "but we have a commitment," he declares, "and we continue to work hard on the relationship."

Regarding his struggle with his ethnicity, Dennis remarked, "I had always had my Latino identity in one box," Dennis remarked, "in one file cabinet, and my gay sensibility somewhere else. As I became more involved in gay life, feeling more comfortable in that world, I began feeling more comfortable about being Latino." Eventually, Dennis recounted, "I said, fuck it. I am who I am!"

After reviewing the transcript of his interview for this book, Dennis remarked: "What struck me was the interplay of my identity as a Mexican-Chicano and my gay identity. The transcript helped to crystallize for me that when I was young my Mexican identity always felt like a construct. A lot of that was due to my relationship with my father, for me the archetypical Mexican. My anger at him and my desire to distance myself from him put me at odds with my identity as a Mexican. In the process of coming to accept my own sexuality, I became more at peace with being Mexican because my own manhood, my identity as a man, developed as I became more confident of who I was as a gay man." Having achieved a clear sense of identity, Dennis was able to reach an understanding with his father. His father makes no negative remarks about Dennis's homosexuality. His mother, though not particularly expressive of her affection, always offers encouragement.

CARLA*

Born in 1959, Carla is the child of a daughter of a Philippine general and of a Puerto-Rican father who worked himself up from porter to maintenance supervisor in a city housing project. Carla's mother, who held a job in Wall Street, had traveled widely and was more worldly than Carla's father, who came from a humble family, closely knit but burdened with alcoholism, substance abuse, and dysfunctional marriages. He spoke Spanish with the children, insisting that they speak correctly.

When Carla was two years old, her mother abandoned the family. "She

*Co-director of the Outreach to Teens program of the Community Health Project (CHP), which provides health services to homeless gay and lesbian young people (see Chapter 13).

put on her hat and coat," Carla recalls. "Crying, she assured me she loved me but said she could not manage and had to move on." For years thereafter, when her father insisted that she and her two brothers respect their mother, Carla would respond, "Please, don't tell me what to do. You don't know what I feel." When her mother came to visit, Carla refused to talk to her. To her request that Carla call her "Mom," she would reply, "You're not my mother. I don't feel that in my heart." Her mother came down with tuberculosis, and Carla remembers seeing her under glass in an oxygen tent. As an adult, Carla came to understand that what she missed most all her life was her mother. "I was so angry with her," Carla declares, "that I never realized how much I loved her."

From the time her mother left, Carla had fantasies about families. She watched programs like "The Brady Brunch" and cried. In the Hispanic tradition, Carla's father did not consider homemaking an appropriate responsibility for a man. At the advice of the parish priest, he placed his children in a Catholic orphanage. Carla's two brothers were soon assigned to an older Hispanic couple, but after a brief stay in a foster home Carla was returned to the orphanage. The nuns, she recalls, were "nasty," impatient, and sticklers about rules. When parents came to visit during open school week, Carla felt all alone. "My father was always gallivanting," she recalls. In fact, from age seven to age fourteen, Carla saw her father only rarely, and it was necessary to make arrangements two weeks in advance to visit her brothers.

A gay uncle visited her at the orphanage and brought her bags of candy. Carla always knew that they had a special, unspoken relationship. (He died of AIDS in Puerto Rico two weeks before Carla was interviewed for this book.) Members of the family liked him because he had money and was generous with gifts, but behind his back they made fun of his effeminacy. When the family tried to persuade him to join a Pentecostal church as a born-again Christian in order to impel him to change his orientation, Carla assured him that he did not have to be ashamed of who he was.

Carla had two best friends, "blood sisters," and from childhood she knew she was different. "Looking as butch as I do," she asserts, "how can I deny what I am?" Her father thought it was cute that Carla and her girlfriend, the prettiest girl on the block, held hands. He dismissed her insistence that she liked girls, insisting that she was merely a tomboy. "I'm not a tomboy," Carla declared. When she played spin the bottle, girls picked her. When they played "run and tackle," girls hid with her. "Girls liked me, and I liked them. I never felt guilty about being gay."

Carla's father persuaded a married woman with whom he had entered a relationship to take Carla in along with her own six children. When the woman attempted to show affection to Carla, Carla pushed her away. The children, all older than she, tried to make her feel at home, but Carla preferred to play by herself. All her affection was directed toward her father. "He was my eyes," she declares. Her foster mother competed with Carla for his attention. If Carla kissed her father, she would cry, "Stop that, you're too big to be kissing and holding him."

Carla participated in youth activities at the local church and found a kind of family there. At fourteen, lying about her age, Carla obtained a job as counselor in a church children's program. "I like women," she confessed to the parish priest. "I know it's wrong," she said. "If you don't want me to work here, it's okay." "You're a child of God," he replied. "God loves everyone. As long as you love and don't hurt anyone, then it's all right to love whomever you love." Later when Carla met religious gays afraid to come out, she related what Father Angles had said to her.

Eager to get out of the neighborhood, Carla enrolled at Sheepshead Bay High School, a two-hour subway trip from home. "I wouldn't have made it if I had stayed in my neighborhood with all the gangs, muggers, guns, and drugs," she says. Carla enjoyed her years in high school, mingling with young people of varied backgrounds who were not as pressured as she in the daily struggle for existence.

In high school she was openly gay and had a Greek friend. She was never called names. "That was because of how I carried myself," she explains. "It was so natural. People respected me." At straight Latino or black clubs, which she attended, lying about her age, men bought her drinks.

Carla's relatives, however, resented her open lesbianism. "You're Manny's daughter," they exclaimed. "How can you do this to your father?" "Who are you to criticize me?" Carla snapped back. "You refused to take care of me when I needed you and let me go into an orphanage. Do you really think that I care now what you think?" Her father, on the other hand, sloughed off remarks from relatives, declaring, "She has her own lifestyle. I wish I could change it. I wish she'd give me grandchildren." Carla insisted that even though she was gay, she could give him grandchildren. (Indeed, Carla now thinks about having children, though she recognizes that she will encounter resistance in the Hispanic community if she does do so.)

Even before she graduated from high school, however, Carla's relations with her father began to deteriorate. Goaded by her stepmother's complaints about the company she was keeping and about her coming home at all hours, he began shouting at her. Once when Carla talked back, he took off his shirt and exclaimed, "You want to be a man, I'll show you what it is to be a man." Hearing the commotion, Carla's younger, gay brother came in, grabbed his father and ordered him to leave her alone. Carla had black-and-blue marks on her face and on her body. "When I die," her father snapped, "don't you come to my funeral. As far as I'm concerned you're dead. You're getting out because you're not going to lead that lifestyle in my house."

"I felt betrayed," Carla recalls. "He accepted his son's being gay but not his only daughter's, and he behaved like an animal."

After Carla left home, her father frequently looked for her at her high school. She refused to talk to him. Once, when he berated her for smoking,

Carla retorted that she did not live in his house any more and he had no control over her. During this period, Carla recalls, her social life consisted of "wild dances and parties, dating and carrying on." Wanting "to feel good," she took to smoking pot and drinking and took drugs, including cocaine, from age fourteen to age twenty-one. "I never went overboard," she insists, "but there was always something missing in my life."

After holding a series of jobs for short periods, Carla found a position at railroad yards north of the city. Here she encountered blatant sexism. She was given the worst tasks. "She wants to do a man's work," the men exclaimed. "Let her find out what it's all about." Subsequently, when working as the only woman mechanic at the youth shelter Covenant House, male employees complained that she attracted the women employees more than they did. One of the men taunted her before all the other engineers. "Carla," he said, "I'd like to see you in a dress up on a ladder." The foreman and the assistant foreman burst into laughter. Carla silenced them by responding, "You'd look better with a dress on the ladder than I would. I would cruise you." When Carla came out of the shower, they all said good night to her. From then on she was respected, she was one of the guys. "They don't teach you all they know," Carla explained, "but once you prove you can do a good job, they're the best friends you can have. But you have to bump heads."

Though she had no background of family stability, Carla succeeded in maintaining lasting relationships. For seven or eight years she lived with a woman with two small children. They had to keep their relationship secret because the woman's husband was seeking custody of the children. At the time of the interview for this book, Carla had established what she was confident would remain a stable relationship. She and her lover maintain separate apartments. "We have quality time together," she says, "but being fully dependent upon each other is too much. I am not looking any longer for a mommy. I want to be allowed to fall, to get hurt." Recently, Carla related, when she was nervous and unhappy about something that happened in her family, her lover looked at her and said simply, "I love you." Carla replied, "Thanks, but it's okay for me to hurt. Hurt is necessary for me to grow." Nevertheless, she admits, her lover's words were comforting and just what she needed at the moment.

Chapter Five
"I Feel Asian!"

FOUR CHINESE-AMERICANS

The Chinese-American interviewees described coming-out experiences different in various respects from those of most of the other interviewees. Among themselves, too, they expressed divergent attitudes regarding both their cultural heritage and the relationship between their community and the majority society. (A fifth Chinese interviewee was dropped from the book except for mention under a pseudonym in the final chapter.)

DAVID ENG*

David Eng, thirty-four, born and raised in New York's Chinatown, is the only child of a Hong Kong–born mother who came to the United States to study at New York University and of a high school–graduate Chinese-American father born in San Francisco who worked in restaurants and eventually became the owner of several restaurants. David's parents met "on the rebound" the very day their divorces from previous spouses were finalized. David was born before they married. (An uncommon circumstance, David declares, among Chinese.) The marriage, never secure, ended in divorce when David was in his late teens. Though inculcated with the Chinese traditional respect for parents, David never felt respect for his father. "I didn't know him well," David declares, "and still don't. We don't get along, and I

*Assistant director of communications at the Gay Men's Health Crisis (see Chapter 14).

don't like him as a human being. I hate Christmas because after I was about ten he never came home except during that holiday." Toward his mother, however, he continues to harbor "a tremendous sense of responsibility," especially because except for him she is all alone. David never wondered at her not remarrying. "We never discussed such subjects," he says. He and his mother lived isolated lives. They had no non-Chinese acquaintances and were not friendly with their neighbors.

David attended an all-Chinese public elementary school two blocks away from home. He was aware that all his teachers were Caucasian, and he wondered that on television he never saw his own people. At school, he recalls, he was often picked on because he was effeminate. He had to figure out the safest route home to avoid bullies. Still, he notes, he did not suffer from any violence, and the badgering did not prevent him from enjoying his schoolwork. Indeed, his mother instilled in him the Confucian tradition that good marks are necessary for personal advancement. He studied hard and won praise as a straight-A student. He suffered no ostracism for his academic success because many of his classmates were also outstanding students.

Because his mother, the proprietor of a garment factory, rarely returned home before seven or eight in the evening and worked Saturdays and sometimes Sundays, David often found himself alone in the apartment. "I early learned to be independent," he relates, "coming directly home and preparing food and doing the laundry." He spent time redecorating the apartment, practicing the piano, and reading. Most parents in Chinatown work, David notes, warning their children to avoid bad elements on the street; and David did not join the many Chinese children of all ages playing in the playground at the edge of Chinatown. He did, however, have one friend, a boy named Luther, who lived across the street. Luther's older sister served as guardian for the two of them.

One summer at his mother's suggestion David went off to camp. He felt uncomfortable in the unfamiliar surroundings. "I followed the schedule," he recalls, "and did everything expected of me. I always felt that that was how you became accepted, but I felt alone there."

David's mother brought him to her Presbyterian church on Sundays. When he was about twelve, she decided that he should become involved in church activities, and he began to attend Sunday school. In junior high school, he joined a youth fellowship group that engaged in Bible studies and went on excursions. "There followed," David relates, "the five most miserable years of my life. My brothers and sisters in Christ were constantly criticizing me. Every Sunday they pointed out something that was wrong about me. I did not dress properly, I did not walk properly. I was not masculine enough." They were shocked when he came to church in jeans with zippered pockets in the front. (Having a good allowance and earning extra money as a typist, David wore expensive clothes that he considered fashionable.) "I never could satisfy them. What's more, I thought they were right in their criticisms. I felt

I should conform better. Among Chinese, you're not supposed to be conspicuous."

David did not mention his discomfort at the fellowship. "I did not talk much about myself with my mother," he explains. "She worked late and hard. The time I was with her, I didn't want to bring up bad things. Chinese children don't burden their parents with their problems. You're supposed to take care of problems on your own." On the other hand, he is confident that his mother would have listened to him sympathetically, for she always let him do whatever he wanted and be what he wanted to be. Quite uncharacteristically for a Chinese, she easily exhibited affection. Indeed, he says, she was the only person to whom he was close, the only person who did not try to change him.

Having heard stories of gangs at the local Seward Park High School, David applied to Brooklyn Technical High School, where Asians also formed a sizable portion of the student body. During his second year he joined the English club and worked on the school magazine. He began having "weird sexual feelings" and developed bewildering crushes on men teachers. He was too timid to display his feelings. Troubled by emotions to which he had difficulty adjusting, his enthusiasm for his studies flagged. In his third year he joined the drama club and at lunch he listened with fascination as a flamboyant gay club member related his weekend adventures. In his senior year, developing a crush on Sam Weiner, a chemistry teacher, David found excuses to visit the chemistry office and volunteered to do clerical work there. At graduation Weiner wished David good luck and invited him to call if he ever needed advice.

When David was eighteen, his parents divorced. His father sat him down and asked him what his plans were. David reported that he had been accepted at the Parsons School of Design, one of the nation's leading schools of design. His father thought for a moment and then said, "I always knew you wouldn't turn out the way I wanted you to." David replied sarcastically, "I'm glad I haven't disappointed you." That, says David, was his last exchange with his father.

David looked forward to entering a new and more stimulating world at Parsons, expecting to meet new friends, especially gay friends. Instead, he found himself in an extremely competitive environment, where students were constantly fearful that classmates would steal their ideas. At the end of his first year, discouraged, David felt a need to discuss his disappointment with someone. He looked through his telephone book and came upon Sam Weiner's name. Weiner invited him to dinner. "We talked about everything except sex," David recalls. "I thought he was straight. We found we had a lot in common in our experiences in growing up." They met again the following week. This time Sam asked David whether he had ever been involved with anyone. David described his isolation. Sam showed David a picture of a former lover. "You knew I was gay, didn't you?" Sam declared. By the end of the year, Sam and David had become lovers, though they did not move in together.

David had never been able to express his feelings. His life could be falling apart, but no one would know it. It took about five years, David declares, before he could talk freely about his feelings and problems even with Sam. Initially, when Sam asked how things had gone during the day, he always replied that he had had a wonderful day. With time, however, Sam helped him to learn how to deal with his feelings. "He coaxed it out of me," David declares. "He would prod me by demanding 'What's wrong? Do you want to talk about it?' "

David decided that he would not come out to his mother until she posed the question, and for six years she did not learn that he and Sam were lovers. "I follow this pattern with everyone," he says. "When they're ready to hear, they'll ask." The subject came up almost casually while he and his mother were watching "An Early Frost," a television play about a gay man with AIDS, and brought no tension between them.

David declares he early lost all sense of identification with the Chinese community. Uncomfortable at sitting side by side with adult students at the after-school Chinese language and culture classes where his mother enrolled him when he was still a child, David rebelled, and his mother allowed him to drop out after only a year. When he went on trips with his mother, he did not feel uncomfortable outside a Chinese setting. In fact, he asserts, "the only place I did feel odd was in Chinatown." Now when he returns to visit his mother, he feels no connection with the neighborhood. His mother still speaks to him in Chinese, but he replies with ever-decreasing fluency.

"I cannot recall any happy times, particularly after elementary school," David declares. "I wouldn't want to go through that childhood again."

JUNE CHAN

Older than David, June Chan has had broader experience and has probed her experiences more profoundly. Family, church, and school, she says, were all factors in her development into an Asian lesbian activist. Coming out for her accompanied a growing feminist consciousness. From feminism, she moved to lesbian activism, increasingly in an Asian context.

June's mother and father were born in southern China, a region of dire poverty and the major source of Chinese immigration to the United States. Her paternal great-grandfather worked on the construction of the railroads in the American West. Chinese laborers were not permitted to bring wives to the United States, but he brought June's grandfather to this country, and he in turn brought over June's father. He grew up in Cambridge, Massachusetts, where June's grandfather washed and ironed the shirts of Harvard men. After graduating from high school and serving in the navy, June's father traveled to his native region in China to seek a bride. (June notes that it is still common for Chinese men to return to China for wives.) In 1955, he sent for June's mother and for June's older sister. June was born in New York's Chinatown a year later.

June's mother had little education. She and her brother, orphans, had been placed in different families as servants. During the Japanese massacre and mass rape in Nanking, she fled the city in a boat. She related tales of how in the panic women were separated from their children. She walked barefoot to find refuge in the mountains. On the plane ride to the United States, she asked for water for for her daughter and was astonished when the stewardess brought milk instead.

During her early childhood, June's family lived in a second-floor studio apartment in a building June's father owned on Mulberry Street in Little Italy, just outside Chinatown. He and June's mother worked in their print shop on the ground floor. June remembers playing with her older sister and other Chinese children on the sidewalk next to a ferris wheel during the annual Italian St. Gennaro festival. "We were taunted by the Italian kids," June recalls. "They would shout, 'Get out, you don't belong here.' " The family received occasional threats of arson. They did not, however, suffer any physical violence, and June does not remember feeling insecure. On the other hand, although her father talked little at home, he was a hail-fellow-well-met who socialized with Chinese and non-Chinese, including the Italian neighbors.

After the birth of two more sisters and with a third infant on the way, June's father moved his family into a four-bedroom flat in a building he bought in the Williamsburg section of Brooklyn. In Williamsburg, they found themselves among middle-class Hasidic Jewish and Puerto Rican neighbors. In the entire public elementary school, June and her older sister were the only Chinese children. June's mother impressed the kindergarten teacher by bringing June to school in Chinese finery. June remembers with affection her first-grade teacher, a Jewish woman named Mrs. Fishman.

After five daughters, June's parents at last succeeded in having two sons. With the business prospering, June's father began transporting the children in a Volkswagen bus to a school in Chinatown. "Don't you feel better now?" said June's mother. At the new school, June liked most of her teachers, all women and white, because, she says, they were generous, thoughtful, and caring. Afternoons, June and her brothers and sisters attended a Chinese school. June was struck by the intense patriarchy in Chinese culture. When a man entered a classroom, the students stood up. Someone would call out "bow," and the students bowed. The students learned by rote. June did so badly in this environment that her mother let her drop out.

In Chinese families, June says, men and boys were served first at meals and given the choice morsels. In June's family, however, though her father insisted upon his prerogatives, her brothers enjoyed no special privileges. June's older sister, a surrogate mother and role model for her siblings, took her sisters to school and to the park. Once when a boy and a girl, either black or Puerto Rican, began to push them, she shouted at them and routed them. "I was proud of her," June says, "I had complete trust in her. I would never have ventured out of the house without her."

June recalls watching with envy when her Chinese girlfriends were hugged and kissed by their mothers. "I was never hugged as a child," June declares, "except by distant relatives, who didn't know that such expressions of affection didn't happen in our family." On the other hand, June's mother kept after her children in their schoolwork, reminding them that she never had the opportunity to go to school. "She bragged about us to her friends," she recalled, "but never when we were present."

Except for teaching June and her older sister how to skate, June's father did not participate in the upbringing of the children. He never spoke to them except through their mother. On the other hand, on family trips to Macy's, he would say to June's mother, "Tell them to pick out what they want." Occasionally, he would take them to the movies in the neighborhood and, more rarely, on outings to Coney Island or to New Jersey to visit people whom his father had sponsored for immigration.

June's father never went to church, and June thought it odd that her mother had been baptized and had the children baptized. The Chinese Baptist church provided a social center for the children. They belonged to church fellowships composed of same-age groups and attended Wednesday prayer meetings and Saturday discussions of ethical and moral topics. Several members of the family, including June, sang in the choir. "We all gained an ethical sense that for me was later channeled into activist goals," June declares. "I'm no longer religious, but I live by the principles I learned at church."

June's father practiced corporal punishment only with her, for she was the only one in the family who dared to talk back to him. Worse, he frequently assaulted June's mother, throwing things at her, even hitting her and choking her. June recalls one night when her mother was knitting in the bedroom June shared with her elder sister, waiting for him to return home. When he came in, she said something to him. June woke up and saw him hitting her. "What are you doing?" June yelled. He stopped and left the room. June's mother was crying. She said that June had saved her life.

In 1980, when June was already twenty-four, the children encouraged their mother to seek a divorce. During the proceedings, June learned that her father had been cheating on her mother since the very night of their wedding. He treated women as sexual objects, June declares. "My sisters," June admits, "had a deeper understanding of what was happening in the family than I. My younger sister helped my mother through the divorce. I was a vegetable." After the divorce, he married a woman about the age of June's older sister, had a child, and then ran off. June and the rest of her family lost contact with him.

At the Chinatown junior high school, June encountered her first Chinese teacher, a man, a good English teacher with a sense of humor. June was taught to be afraid of whites and blacks. She was more afraid of blacks than whites. Her parents said there were black and white ghosts, not fully human. In school she was taunted by bigger black students. A black girl hall monitor, she says, "terrorized us, shoving and threatening to punish us." Nevertheless, she found junior high school exciting. She had girlfriends and played in the orchestra and engaged in sports.

When June went on to the prestigious Bronx High School of Science, for the first time, she says, she had to deal with a hostile outside world. On the long ride to school, she was badgered by men. Some even "flashed" in the subway. "And the way men looked at me!" she exclaims. "I was young and innocent. I didn't know what to do. I felt like a victim. They sense when you don't have street smarts. They can get away with it. I don't understand heterosexual men at all."

In high school June found herself among brilliant students and had to work hard to keep up. Five percent of the students were Asian; many of the rest were Jewish. There were few blacks and Latinos. June does not recall any racial tensions. "I got a good education," June relates. "I saw a bit of a different world, an elite. All of a sudden we home girls from Chinatown had a different set of friends coming from all over the city. That was a great thing about the school."

June's day otherwise consisted of the long commute to and from school and studying. She did not engage in extracurricular activities. "I was closed-in as an individual," June recalls, "very shy, very protected by my family. My social life was at the church."

Coming out for June was a lengthy and difficult process. She could not discuss intimate questions with her mother because her English was limited, and June herself did not have adequate vocabulary in either Chinese or English. Besides, she was utterly not self-aware. "The more I examine my past," June remarks, "the more I realize that I had a crush on my junior high school friends and then on my high school gym teacher. I never acted on these attractions." Once, June recalls, the National Gay Task Force sent a man and a woman to talk about homosexuality in a hygiene class. June was not particularly interested in the discussion. The lecturers, she thought, looked strange. What they talked about seemed totally unrelated to her experience. A boy in the class who was "a little fey" was teased because he exhibited especial interest.

Most graduates from the Bronx High School of Science went on to Harvard or Yale, but June enrolled at the City College of New York, where she found her courses unchallenging after the high standards she had encountered in high school. While at City College, June maintained "a harmless and asexual" relationship with a Chinese young man she had met in the church fellowship. They went to the movies and to dinner, and June enjoyed his company. After two years he left for graduate school in Utah. They kept in touch through the mail, and once June went out to visit him.

From 1977 to 1981 June pursued difficult graduate work in neurobiology at the State University of New York at Buffalo. She had no time for friends, and living away from home for the first time she was very lonely. Unhappy with her life, she thought her mood derived from her total immersion in her studies. In fact, she now realizes, she was preparing herself to come out.

A visit to one of her sisters at Smith College provided a decisive event in June's life. Her sister and her best friend, a lesbian, lived in a lesbian house. June was impressed by the self-confidence and lack of shame among the lesbians. They were comfortable with each other and with June's straight sister.

Back in Buffalo June found a feminist bookstore and started to read not just about feminism but also about lesbians. Feminism was a revolutionary concept for her, totally liberating, more liberating than religion had ever been. "Feminism was saying," she recalls, "that as a woman I was able to say, do, and be things, whoever I was." The model of her mother's marriage was ever in her thoughts. "I would be miserable in such a life," she assured herself. She broke off with her college boyfriend.

It was difficult for June to mesh feminism and lesbianism with religion. "I was at the point of leaving the church," she recalls, "and having my total support world crumble."

After completing her graduate work, June spent a month with her older sister, who had moved to London and married there. June did not discuss her inner turmoil, but she did a lot of soul searching. A poetry reading by Adrienne Rich, the American feminist poet, strengthened her feminist convictions. "Her books really spoke to me," June declares. "I was ready to move from theory to action." She realized that her best relationships had been with her sisters and with her girlfriends in high school. Through lesbianism she would be able to continue the way of life with which she had been most comfortable.

Coming out for her, June asserts, was totally an intellectual process. She had not met anyone, but she liked the idea that women could could make a life on their own or with other women. "For me," she says, "turning to lesbianism was a positive development."

June's progress into lesbian activism also followed a slow and complicated course. While her fellow high school and college students joined in anti-Vietnam war demonstrations, she remained aloof. In shunning involvement in politics, she was very Chinese, June asserts. "Chinese people don't feel empowered in a democracy. They don't trust authority." Upon returning from London, however, June joined a National Organization of Women (NOW) consciousness-raising group. She was able to talk with the sole lesbian she encountered in the group, a Jewish woman from an entirely different background from hers. "I got into what she was doing, progressive political work. I knew," she says, "I had to participate in that life." For six months they remained lovers.

June was not happy with the antilesbian atmosphere or with the hierarchical structure in NOW. "There was no way I could participate with a sense of empowerment," she says. In 1982, the night before the Gay Pride parade, with the family van, June transported soda and beer to a Lesbian Feminist Liberation dance. At the dance June saw two thousand women on the floor but only one Asian. She was too embarrassed to talk to her. "You're Asian," she explains, "and Asians are not supposed to be lesbians. It was as though I was seeing my sister." From simple volunteer work June advanced to organizing. They wanted to do things for lesbians, she explains, not just for women in general. "If we were going to talk about lesbianism," June declares, "we would have to do it by ourselves."

All the women June was dating at the time were Jewish, members of her social and activist circles. June felt a difference from these women, and in fact some of the women encouraged June to establish contact with other Asian women. In 1983 June met Catherine Hall, a woman of Chinese-Hawaiian and Irish extraction. Catherine was eager to organize Asian lesbians into a group of their own. She and June brought together at her mother's apartment about twenty Asian lesbians from a variety of ethnic groups, some born overseas and some born in the United States. "What do we have in common?" the women asked. The only thing June could think of was that they all ate rice. Catherine Hall, however, spoke of their common need to empower themselves and then, as an autonomous activist organization, to network with other groups of women. Their two worlds as Asians and as lesbians, she insisted, had to be brought together.

Asian Lesbians of the East Coast began to meet twice a month at members' homes. They published a newsletter and marched in the Gay Pride parade. Their attempts to educate the general Asian community about lesbians by speaking before various Asian women's groups did not meet with immediate success. When they presented skits exposing anti-Asian racism before Asian Women United, a group of straight, assimilated professional women, the women were confused, and some were uncomfortable. To display her tolerance, one woman boasted that she had seen *La Cage aux Folles* as though, June comments, that "bold" act made her a gay activist. At a meeting on stereotypes conducted by a coalition of ten Asian women's groups and subsequently at an Asian Pacific Heritage Festival, June heard people say, "Let's go look at the lesbians."

June's encounter with Asians from around the country during the 1987 Lesbian and Gay March on Washington brought a change in direction in her political thinking. In Washington a formal network was established. Two years later, about two hundred women attended a national conference and retreat in Santa Cruz, California. On this occasion, the national network was expanded into an international network. At a May 1992 international lesbian conference in Japan, June became aware that lesbians in Asia confront different issues from Asian lesbians in the United States. When a friend from Malaysia declared that a gay liberation movement was impossible in her country, June came to understand that in lands with total repression the gay struggle is interrelated with the general struggle for civil rights and democracy.

From 1985 on June devoted much of her free time to developing a slide show on Asian lesbians. She assembled a one-hour show of some eighty slides, images of Asian lesbian history culled from erotic art books, beginning with India, the most ancient source, as a tool for changing people's attitudes. Invited to make a presentation before the Berkshire Women's Conference on the History of Women, June accepted with hesitation, fearful of appearing before an audience of academics. "They were kind," she relates. "The slide show provides entertainment," she explains, "and is exotic and provocative. Lots of discussion followed."

One evening June's mother asked the meaning of the pink triangle June was wearing. June said it stood for homosexual liberation. "What's homosexuality?" her mother asked. June explained that it meant same-sex love. June's mother changed the subject. "That's how I came out to my mother," June declares. Though she never came out explicitly to her sisters and brothers, they realized who she was from her activities and from the mail she received.

At a poetry reading at a lesbian bookstore during a conference in Boston, June was introduced to Mariana, an Argentine poet. Thereafter she began to attend events where she thought she might meet Mariana again. They started to date. Since June had the better job, Mariana moved to New York. "I think it's a miracle that we met," June declares. "We have been together for eight years. We have not had to work at our relationship. We like each other. We have similar goals in life. When she lived at my mother's, we discovered how Chinese she was. My mother and sisters love her. Four years ago we moved into our own apartment."

June asserts that as an Asian woman she experiences racism as well as homophobia. "I don't look particularly like the stereotype of a lesbian," she declares, and "men approach me, white men." Once when June was in a Chinatown restaurant with her lover, a man started a conversation with her. Mariana ordered him to leave. He yelled back, and they hurried away. Every day, June relates, when she bikes to work she gets things thrown at her. "Men," she declares, "seem to want to knock you over when you're biking."

At her work as a laboratory technician at the Cornell University teaching hospital, on the other hand, June has no sense of any racism. She enjoys the respect of her colleagues and has been promoted as far as she can go without a doctorate. Science, she concludes, may provide an island of security for Asians.

June believes that Asian gays face different issues from Asian lesbians. White men have the ultimate power in American society, but the power relationship is different for Asian men than for Asian women. For lesbians Asians, according to June, choice of sexual partners has nothing to do with race, but gay Asians confront the epithet "bananas," "yellow outside and white inside," that is, Asian in appearance but white in mindset, while white gay men who seek out Asian sex partners are called "rice queens."

Through years of struggle June has achieved a sense of personal integration. "My identification as a lesbian made me a whole person," she remarks, "brought me to love myself as a complete person as a lesbian and a Chinese." Now after almost ten years of activism in the Asian Lesbians of the East Coast, June declares, "I don't feel just Chinese, I feel Asian. Racism doesn't care what your national origin is."

June and David agree in some respects in their attitude toward their Chinese heritage. "Scholarly achievement is a part of our culture," David declared with pride. Limited in job opportunities because of their problems with English, Chinese parents, David notes, want their children to advance beyond them and encourage them to study hard and earn good marks in school.

June is unabashed in her pride in her family and in her cultural heritage. She notes that her mother with scarcely any schooling and her father with a mere trade-school background produced a progeny of professionals. June's oldest sister is an architect, a younger sister has a Ph.D. in chemical engineering, another has recently passed the bar, and the youngest, a Smith College graduate, works in graphic arts. One brother has an engineering degree, and the other was completing a doctorate in divinity and was serving as pastor at the church the family attended. "I was brought up to be proud of being Chinese," June declares, "of having as a heritage an ancient civilization with numerous contributions to the world."

CHARLES C., A TRANSGENDERED CHINESE AMERICAN*

Charles C. was born in the mid-1950s in Manila, where he grew up and obtained his education. Early in the century, his father had emigrated as a child from Fukien province in China. His mother was born in Manila. They spoke Mandarin as well as a Fukien dialect. His mother, who had attended college, was also fluent in English. Although Charles's father had less formal education, he was well read in Chinese literature, played a Chinese musical instrument, and wrote with an eloquent style. He was recognized as a community leader, and Charles recalls that people often came to him for advice.

Charles was the youngest of seven children—four boys and three girls separated by intervals of one or two years. "It was a loving family," Charles recalls, "with few tensions among the children." Weekends the family often went on excursions, and Charles's mother often entertained. "Family meals," Charles notes, "were an important part of our social life. My mother came form a large family. I have eight aunts and many cousins."

Charles's father supported the family with an automotive parts shop. "We

*Member of the boards of the New York Lesbian and Gay Community Center, GLAAD, and Imperial court.

were middle class and never starved," Charles relates. "I'm sure my father had financial problems, but we never knew about them. He worked very hard and put us all through college." The family lived in an exclusively Chinese community, and all the children attended a Chinese school run by Episcopalian missionaries, a school their mother had earlier attended. They had English classes in the morning and Chinese classes in the afternoon.

As a child, Charles had many toys, hand-me-downs from his siblings. "I don't think my parents were concerned at my playing with dolls," he declares. "I didn't take a doll to bed with me. I played with my brothers' toys also." As early as six or seven, however, Charles had his "first taste of drag." Fascinated by Hawaiian dancing he saw on television, he made hula skirts for himself out of strips of newspaper and wigs out of coils of rope. His mother threw out the costumes and wigs, exclaiming, "What are you doing with all this garbage?"

As early as he can remember, Charles loved to draw, especially figures of women. Once, when he was in second grade, the teacher caught him doodling and held up his drawing of a woman and ridiculed him. The incident remained traumatic for Charles for a long time.

The brother a year older than Charles was much bigger and stronger than he. When they fought, Charles was always defeated. "I learned not to attempt to fight," he recalls. In school he thought of himself as a weakling because he was skinny and small. He played in the school yard during recess but never joined a team. "I was the cheerleader," he explains. Other boys called him "sissy," but the teasing was infrequent and without viciousness. "I was never beaten up," he recounts. "I was gregarious and an honor student. I had no sense of being isolated."

As early as age ten, Charles was aware of his gay tendencies. In grade school, he recalls, he helped to write a play and included a drag role for himself, in one scene emerging from a trapdoor as a princess. His classmates and teacher thought it was funny. "My sense of difference," Charles declares, "did not consume my life. My parents probably thought I was going through a phase. My life was highly structured and full—school, homework, and then to bed. We enjoyed little playtime after school. Besides, in the Philippines, he declares, being gay was an accepted way of life at least for fashion designers and hair stylists, who were envied for making a lot of money. On the other hand, gay teachers, doctors, or lawyers remained closeted. "I didn't know any existed," says Charles. Nor was he aware of any gays in his extended family or in the neighborhood where he lived.

On the other hand, Charles did know of a very famous actor who played gay roles, and one of the longest-running comedies on television had a gay character. "Being gay was not something necessarily evil," he recalls. "It was something to laugh about. Homosexuality was never mentioned in church, and I did not think of it as sinful. If there were any laws against gays I was not aware of them."

At the age of twelve or thirteen, Charles was already having erections, and one day in a movie house a man sat down next to him and started rubbing his leg. "I froze," Charles recalls. "I was shaking with fear and excitement simultaneously. The man moved his hand up to my private parts. I got up and walked away. But I was curious and kept returning to the theater in the expectation of another such encounter." Other experiences followed. One time a man persuaded him to leave the theater and brought him to a hotel. "It was awful," Charles recalls, "and painful. I was too scared to protest." He resolved never to accept such an invitation again. Eventually, however, he did yield, going with gentler men. On these occasions, he knew what to expect.

While a junior in high school, Charles fell in love with a man he met in a gay bar, a Filipino about ten years older than he. He was from a well-to-do and prominent family and did not live in Manila, and for the next seven years Charles saw him no more than a half-dozen times. In retrospect, Charles admits that "there was nothing special about this man. But he was my first love, and he was kind. For me he was the best-looking man in the world." One time when he and his "lover" went out together to a bar, a well-known television personality came over to them and suggested that Charles's friend leave Charles and go home with him. Charles's friend refused. "That flattered me," Charles recalls. "That was one of the best occasions with him."

At the Catholic University of Santo Thomas, where he studied advertising, Charles met other gays. He started to go to parties and to bars. While in his second year, however, he had a frightening experience that convinced him that he should eventually leave the Philippines. In a movie theater, a man began to touch him. When Charles reciprocated, the man pulled out an identification document, announced that he was a policeman, and ordered Charles to accompany him out of the theater. Several men were waiting on the street. They hustled him into a jeep, drove off, and parked in front of a police precinct, where they demanded money. Terrified, Charles said he had money at home, and after they drove him to his house, he gave them his savings, several hundred pesos. The men took his identification documents and set a place and time for him to give them more money. Charles's mother was angry at his returning home at 2 A.M. "What movie goes on until such an hour?" she demanded. Hardly able to control his tears, Charles said nothing, and his mother ordered him off to bed and declared that he was to remain home evenings henceforth.

Desperate, Charles appealed for help to a woman whom he helped to design clothing for her dress shop. She contacted a colonel in the army. He arranged for Charles to tell his story at a police precinct. The police advised Charles to report at the rendezvous where he was to hand over additional money, assuring him that they would be present to protect him. "I was trembling with fear," he relates, "fearful for my life. I expected shooting, killing." The blackmailers did not appear. He did not hear from them again.

After this traumatic experience, Charles stopped going to movie houses. But he could not remain indefinitely in isolation. Whenever he could sneak out of the house, he went to gay bars. "Some were sordid," he recounts, "where men engaged openly in sex acts; others were nice and classy. I went to both kinds." Because he never knew when he would be able to leave the house, he could not make plans with friends and had to travel alone.

After graduating from college, Charles found a position at an advertising agency, where he advanced rapidly to become a senior account manager, earning a very good salary. Despite his affluence, he continued living at home. "Unmarried Asian young people," he explains, "are expected to remain with their families." Charles's father had died when he was in high school. Living with his mother and one brother, Charles suffered loneliness, despairing of establishing a lasting relationship.

One day, while cleaning his room, Charles's mother discovered some gay publications. "We had a tearful confrontation," Charles recalls. "What did I do wrong?" she exclaimed. "Maybe you should see a psychiatrist." They never discussed the question again.

In 1979, Charles accompanied his mother to Canada to attend the wedding of one of his brothers. They were eager to continue on to the United States, a trip difficult to arrange inasmuch as consular officials refused visas to individuals like Charles, single and owning no property, assuming that they were planning to remain in the United States. "In the Philippines if you had a chance to leave," Charles explains, "you left. Life was depressing and becoming increasingly harsh. Under the corrupt Marcos regime, Chinese were compelled to pay bribes on every hand. Everyone who could leave did so. America was the dream country."

Charles succeeded in obtaining a visa, and he and his mother were able to visit the United States. When they arrived in New York, Charles decided that that was the city where he wanted to live. He was ready to give up his comfortable life in Manila, where he was served by three maids at home and did not have to contribute to the household expenses. He enjoyed his own chauffeur-driven car and had enough money for all kinds of luxuries. But in the United States, he saw an opportunity to study fashion design, his original ambition.

Admitted to the Barbizon School for Modeling in a one-year course in fashion merchandising, Charles was able to exchange his tourist visa for a student visa. "I turned out to be the best student the school had ever had," he relates. "My success gave me confidence." Nevertheless, although he lived rent free with in-laws of one of his sisters in Flushing, Queens, his savings were quickly exhausted, and the money he received from his family did not suffice to meet his expenses. A friend in school found him a job in a shoe store on the Upper East Side, where he was paid "off the books" because it was illegal to work on a student visa.

Charles did not want the family with whom he was living to think that he intended to impose upon them indefinitely. He rented a furnished apartment elsewhere in Queens, where he lived for two years while continuing his studies at the Fashion Institute of Technology and then at the Parsons School of Design.

During these years, Charles declares, he had no time for a sex life. "I was so busy," he recounts, "so fascinated with my new life, with discovering New York. I went to school, to work, and then home to bed. I had no friends, I had no money."

In 1982 Charles moved into a studio apartment near the shoe store where he worked. Having stopped going to school, he was no longer covered by a student visa and was liable to deportation as an illegal alien. Out of work after the closing of the shoe store, Charles responded to a help-wanted advertisement placed by STRUBCO, a gay mail-order company. Desperate, he begged for the job. "What is it," he asked, "that makes you hesitate to employ me?" The owner of the firm, Sean Strub, a gay activist and publisher of *POZ,* a magazine for HIV-positive people, hired him, "impressed," Charles declares, "by my being out and by this time engaged in gay community fundraising activities as a drag queen."

During this time, Charles's social life remained restricted. He went to bars by himself and occasionally developed brief relationships. "There were few places where Asians felt welcome," he relates. It was not that he experienced overt discrimination. "I did not hear hostile remarks," he declares, "and I could go everywhere, but from the beginning I had the impression that most people were not interested in meeting Asians." Charles frequented the Sapphire, a rice-queen bar, where he thought it more likely that he would meet someone looking for Asian men. "I wasn't eighteen years old any more," he remarks.

Charles did establish a relationship with an older married man who made occasional trips to New York from Toronto to visit two gay friends and to spend evenings at the G & H bar, where older gay men congregated. Charles often went to another bar around the corner, but before returning home he would stop in at the G & H, always certain of having a good time as one of the youngest men in the bar.

After living in New York eight years on a student visa and then illegally, Charles took advantage of the law passed in the mid-1980s granting amnesty to aliens who had arrived in the United States before 1982. "That was the beginning of my real life," Charles declares, "the end of living in fear and of earning little money." In the meantime, at the G & H bar Charles met his current lover, another Charles, whom he calls "my Charles." "We met in 1982," he recounts, "and have been together now for fourteen years."

Before her death in 1991, Charles's mother visited him twice a year. She had already shown him that her love was unconditional, Charles recounts, and she and "my Charles" became "the best of friends." It was not necessary, Charles declares, for him to come out to his brothers and sisters, who are now scattered about the world. "At some point they realized I was gay," he says. "We don't talk about it. There has always been unconditional love in the family. I've been there when they needed me. I know they will be there for me if I need them."

Summing up his coming-out experience, Charles declares, "Except for a few traumatic incidents, I have had a life without major struggle. I worked hard and excelled in school and at work. In coming out I was not burdened by financial problems. I have never felt guilt at being gay, never wished I was straight. I charge the ease of my coming out to the kind of family in which I grew up."

Transgendered Activist

In 1984, secure in his relationship with his lover and at his job in a gay mail-order firm, Charles was ready to embark on a life of gay activism. Learning about the prospective opening of the Lesbian and Gay Community Center on Thirteenth Street, he volunteered his services. "My first involvement in an organized gay activity," he recalls, "was stuffing envelopes for what was to become an annual garden party."

Charles was invited to join the Center dance committee, which organized the biweekly Saturday-night dances at the Center and subsequently took over the running of the annual garden party and of the Pier Dance Party after the annual Gay Pride parade. Charles remained on the committee for eight years, serving as its chairman for two years. By 1992, other commitments made it impossible for him to continue.

"That was the beginning of my gay family," he declares. "I began to assemble a circle of real friends. The Center became my life except for my life with my Charles."

One activity led to another. In the late 1980s, Charles joined Asians and Friends, an organization dedicated to bringing Asians together socially with non-Asians. Later, he began serving as host for shows at the "rice-queen" bar, Club 58. In 1989 Charles was invited to join the board of the Community Center. Three years later he became a member of the board of directors planning the Gay Games and worked on the preparations until the games were held during the 1994 celebration of the twenty-fifth anniversary of the Stonewall Uprising. In 1993 he was one of the gay individuals pictured on a GLAAD (Gay and Lesbian Alliance against Defamation) subway poster, appearing in drag and identified by his drag name, Coco Lachine. The next year he became a member of the board of GLAAD, at a time when the Los Angeles and New York chapters were being merged into a national organization.

Charles's first experience with drag dated back to his Hawaiian hula skirts and rope wigs in his childhood. After graduating from college, he had attended a few drag affairs in Manila, initially in men's clothes and then in drag. In 1986, appearing "dressed" for the first time in New York at a Prom Night dance at the Community Center, he was chosen the Center's first homecoming queen.

Charles's first drag appearance away from the Center came at the 1988 Imperial Court "Night of a Thousand Gowns," a drag ball at the Waldorf Astoria Hotel. The Imperial Court is a national organization with over sixty-five chapters throughout the nation, all run by small committees that plan annual drag balls along with other fund-raising activities in support of gay organizations and AIDS/HIV causes. In 1990, when the Imperial Court of New York was at the point of dissolving, Charles and three colleagues undertook to revitalize it. They transformed the Imperial Court into a not-for-profit membership organization and applied for tax-exempt status. With money borrowed from the Community Center along with their own individual contributions, they mounted a "Night of a Thousand Gowns," donating the profits to the Community Center. Each successive year they achieved greater success, raising during five years more than one hundred thousand dollars from the ball and other drag events for donations primarily to AIDS organizations. Chosen in 1993 as Empress of New York, Charles began traveling across the country fund-raising with drag performances for local chapters of Imperial Court.

"Over the years," Charles declares, "I have become one of the most visible drag queens in New York City. If any organization needs an Asian and a drag queen, I'm it. I am asked to judge contests. Dressed in drag, I have been invited to all kinds of official events. I have been introduced to three mayors, Governor Cuomo, and President Clinton. I was present at City Hall for the first press conference for Gay Games IV."

The day after he was interviewed for this book Charles was attending a benefit for Deborah Glick, the openly lesbian state assembly member, and a special screening for the new gay movie *The Birdcage.*

Charles asserts that he never encountered hostility when appearing in public in drag. "I have been to some of the fanciest restaurants in the city," he declares, "the Top of the World, Four Seasons, the Rainbow Room, going to dinner after an event where I was in drag. I look fabulous in drag. I pass very well. I'm comfortable in drag. I'm a completely different person. You would not recognize me."

"There is an entire spectrum of 'transpeople,'" Charles notes, "including transgendered, transvestites, and transsexuals. Most of those you see in gay bars don't consider themselves to be transgendered. They identify themselves for the most part as gay men who occasionally dress in drag to do shows and perform." Between this group and the transsexuals (those who undergo a sex change), Charles declares, is the range of transgendered, who do not necessarily identify themselves as either gay men or women. "They consider themselves simply as transgendered persons." He points out that there is also a range among transsexuals. "You don't have to go to the point of undergoing a sex change," he says. "If you have started hormone injections, you are a transsexual."

A transgendered individual himself, Charles points out that he has no intention of becoming a transsexual. He considers himself to be "a transgendered, enlightened drag queen, first and foremost a gay man, and a drag queen and Asian second. I am one step beyond being a drag queen," he explains, "because I identify with the problems of the transgendered. It is not just a question of my standing on the stage and blowing kisses during a performance. When dressed in drag, I assume another identity, one with which I am comfortable."

Straight people and many gays, Charles recognizes, cannot distinguish among drag performers, the illusionists, the transsexuals, and all those in between. "It's a community," he insists, "composed of varied segments, a minority of whom do the shocking things in the Gay Pride parade." The media have always singled out the "outrageous" segment, Charles asserts, and have established a stereotype shocking to conservatives. "The media," he remarks, "don't make an effort to know the transpeople." Two nights before he was interviewed for this book, at the annual GLAAD media-awards function, Charles, "dressed," had his picture taken with Barbara Walters. "I have met a lot of important people," he declares. "I am one of the lucky ones. Most drag queens don't have such opportunities. If I have a chance to be with people, I can command their respect."

In 1996 Charles decided it was time for him to advance to a new level of activism in helping to develop at APICHA (Asian and Pacific Islander Coalition on HIV/AIDS) an outreach program for the gay Asian drag/transgendered community. "We want to know what their lives are like," Charles declares, "what problems they encounter with discrimination, violence, family relationships, and sexual practices."

Charles has long been aware that the transgendered and transsexuals confront special problems in their day-to-day existence. There are few places where they can go to meet partners. As they have difficulties in holding down jobs or in maintaining lasting relationships, many drag queens, especially the younger ones, turn to prostitution and substance abuse. Faced with poor prospects for survival, they will have sex with a john without using a condom. Transvestites and transsexuals frequent either the few sleazy bars catering to their clientele or, more often, cruise the streets, where they can more easily meet the bisexuals or straight men especially attracted to them. They are targets of violence and disease.

At the first APICHA discussion, eight "girls" were in attendance. Charles, who served as host, was gratified. "We chatted for two hours," he reports. "We learned a lot about their lives and their fears and about the kinds of situations they encounter when 'dressed.' "

The topic for a second session was makeup and grooming, a subject certain to draw a larger audience. Injecting the issues discreetly, Charles spoke about safe sex and about programs offered at APICHA. He asked how many of those present were carrying condoms in their pocketbooks. The majority, he discovered, did carry condoms. One had a whole roll of condoms. "She was really prepared," remarks Charles. ("I always use the word 'she' with drag queens," Charles remarks. "When I'm dressed, I appreciate people who respect me for the person I am, addressing me according to my identity. By using 'she' in speaking about me, they are displaying their acceptance of me.")

"What we have just been talking about," noted Charles in concluding the interview, "is where I am now directing my interest and energies. What I was doing previously was related to diversity education and the promotion of visibility. What I am doing now is more tangible, more personal, more human. I can touch people more directly in this activity than by being on boards of organizations. It is more fulfilling. What I hope the APICHA sessions will achieve is that one day when they are in trouble, they will know whom to call, not necessarily me, but APICHA, the Anti-Violence Project, or a sympathetic lawyer or doctor. I hope they will develop self-respect and learn to be comfortable with who they are, that they will love themselves and realize that they are no longer alone."

SCOTT HIROSE, A JAPANESE AMERICAN

Scott Hirose, a twenty-nine-year-old second-generation Japanese American, is one of four children (he has two older sisters and a younger brother) of a surgeon father and schoolteacher mother. As exemplified in their choice of his given name, Scott's parents wanted their children to belong to American society as fully as possible. They did not teach any of their children to speak Japanese. Scott learned almost nothing about his grandparents. His parents, he says, were equally ignorant about their parents' early lives. "My parents' prime goal was to make us Americans," he relates. "They believe that if you display an aura of being accepted and belonging, people will accept you. Work hard, do your job well and don't make waves, they say, and you'll have no problems."

Living on the West Coast, Scott's mother, unlike his father whose family lived in Denver, was relocated during World War II to a camp in Poston, Arizona, where she remained for three years. She rarely speaks about this experience, Scott says, always emphasizing positive aspects. On the other hand, she has recalled that in the camp only a single piano was available, and many young people had to wait on line for a chance to practice. "Members of my generation express more anger about the internment," Scott declares, "than do my parents and grandparents." Nevertheless, he is aware that his mother harbors deep feelings about the internment, which she declares broke her parents' spirits. His father, too, does not talk about life during those harsh anti-Japanese years.

Generally, Scott relates, he grew up in a warm and nurturing family. Both his parents wanted their children to experience the world. "They worked very hard," he declares. "They didn't want their kids to experience what they had experienced." Although their parents did not exert overt pressure on them, their mother attended all the parent-teacher conferences, and the children knew they were expected to do well in school.

Although he recalls his childhood as a happy time in his life, Scott remembers often being alone, shy, and introverted. He found few Asian children in his neighborhood or at school, and in school he was sometimes the butt of jokes. He recalls a rhyme about "Japanese with dirty knees." "It did make me feel that I was different," he relates, "that I was being singled out, but I didn't go home crying about it. We didn't talk to our parents about what troubled us as children."

In retrospect, Scott recalls an event that presaged another aspect of difference besides the racial. "We had a daily fifteen-minute silent reading period in second grade," he relates. "I always read the same story—about Damon and Pythias, about the love between two brothers, one willing to take the place of the other in prison. I read that story every day for a whole school year." He recalls a swimming instructor for whom he developed a strong admiration. "He was very good looking, blond, an Adonis, and was the only one of the instructors "who got in the water with us." He encouraged Scott to join the school swimming team, and Scott competed through high school.

In seventh grade Scott remembers feeling an attraction to one of the boys in his gym class and to another who sat next to him in mathematics class. When he took a shower with other boys, he was ashamed at his desire to stare at their bodies, but he could not help himself. He was too insecure ever to speak about his feelings. In high school, when dating became more intense, Scott did not date. He did attend a prom, but only because a girl invited him to go. His parents did not take note of his failure to go out with girls. "We didn't talk about sex at all in the family," Scott notes. "My family was very repressed, as though sexual feelings weren't normal." Besides, Scott had an excuse for not dating. He was engaged in many activities—the swimming team, student government, the yearbook, the newspaper, the honor society, and a special club in which they studied Russian. He assured himself that things would change in college. Some day he would meet a girl.

Scott did receive warnings from his parents about homosexuality. He recalls his father's relating how before his marriage, while staying at a YMCA on a visit to New York, he had punched a man who made a pass at him. Scott was aware that no one talked about the gay uncle of one of their neighbors. "I recognized that I had no interest in girls," he declares, "but I didn't allow myself to accept that I was interested in men."

On the other hand, Scott did not shower "with the better-looking guys on the swimming team, only with the nerds," afraid he would become aroused and be found out. He heard degrading jokes about women, and one of the boys was accused of having sex with his pet rabbit and was teased about it. "Sex other than with women," he says, "clearly was not okay." Scott saw, too, how people taunted effeminate boys in school, knocking their books on the floor as they passed in the hall, slamming the doors to their lockers, and mimicking them cruelly.

The coach of the school debating team was gay, flamboyant with his Hawaiian shirts and swishing. In this teacher's company Scott developed a tremor in his hands, so bad that he could not take notes in class or insert his contact lenses. His parents feared he had a brain tumor, but a CAT scan revealed no physical cause. "In retrospect," Scott declares, "I think I was getting in touch with people's reactions to gay people. Whether or not I called myself gay, I was getting in touch with such feelings."

Scott went off to Carleton College, a small liberal arts school in Minnesota at which social activities were not permitted to interfere with serious study and where Scott was not confronted with tensions about dating. During his first year he was engaged in adjusting to his new independence in a new environment, and the sex issue remained latent. On the other hand, he became more aware of being Japanese. Scott's advisor, an Asian, urged Scott to seek out the office of Third World Affairs, where students of color gathered. "I was curious," Scott relates, "to find out about my Asian identity. I had had no association with Asian groups. I had always felt that I should hang out with whites," he declares, "in order to be more accepted."

In the Third World group, Scott relates, he found understanding and a common language. "The group," Scott points out, "broke down my isolation and helped me to identify repressed feelings that weren't confirmed by my family. Suddenly I discovered a community and an identity." He developed friendships with blacks and Latinos. He saw, he says, how color was a factor in the lives of all people of color. "I got in touch with a lot of anger of which I had never been aware," he declares. "In my family the attitude was that such feelings merely got in the way of accomplishing things."

A significant issue discussed among the students of color was that of being color-blind, of people saying, "You're our friend. It's okay that you're Asian. We're all alike." "They want to look at the similarities," remarks Scott, "rather than at the differences, whereas you want to be treated as though you're different but also able to belong."

Carleton prided itself on the diversity of its student body. In fact, Scott insists, the diversity was not real. A lot of white students, he recalls, felt threatened when the people of color ate together in a separate room. "Why should we not be able to have dinner together?" he asks. A number of black students dropped out because they did not feel at ease.

In partial fulfillment of a college core requirement, Scott enrolled in a course in Chinese religious thought. He found himself resonating with the ideas he encountered as he had never done with other ideas. "I read texts," he recounts, "and said to myself, 'This is so me.' In studying Confucianism, I readily accepted the thoughts about how you learn from other people and by example and how you are to use your life. That's how I was raised," he declares, "even though my parents did not consciously preach such thoughts. It's as though it was in my blood."

In a Bible course Scott came upon a book entitled *Jesus Christ and Mythology* by Rudolf Bultmann, which proposed a way of looking at the Bible that Scott found compelling. In studying the parables in the New Testament and the Pauline epistles, he encountered many issues relevant to his life that he had never thought about. As a result of his experience in religious courses, he switched from science and mathematics to a religion major. Scott insists that he was not interested in a church religion. "I have never attended a Christmas service," he declares.

If Scott achieved new clarity about his racial identity and cultural heritage, he still faced the problem of his sexuality. Although he was aware of a gay group on campus and every year during orientation week looked with curiosity to see who sat at the gay information table, he was too frightened to display interest in the group. He also recalls having crushes during his freshman year. He made a point to be in the dormitory when an attractive man came to vacuum the hall. "It was exhilarating," he recalls, "to feel an attraction for someone. The word 'gay' was occurring to me because I realized that I had never had a significant romantic attraction to a woman. The thought emerged all the more because I was away from my family. The Third World experience, too, encouraged my sense of independence and my sense of who I was."

During training as a peer counselor for orientation week at the beginning of his sophomore year, Scott heard reports by gay students about their experiences. "Tell your students that they can talk to us if they have questions about sexuality issues," they announced. "What they've been saying is totally me," Scott exclaimed to himself. The realization proved upsetting, but also energizing. "I was happy to find that there were gay people out there whom I could respect," he relates, "people who had dealt successfully with their sexual identity."

In a conversation with one of his best friends, a straight Chinese woman student who was also in the training program, Scott mentioned how the gay reports at the training session started him thinking. "I think I'm gay," he declared. She urged him to give the issue more thought and to talk to the gay counselors. Scott also had a discussion with his two roommates. One, a Caucasian young man, reacted sympathetically. He thought that all men, including himself, had bisexual tendencies. But the other roommate, a Chinese, responded angrily. He urged Scott to see a psychiatrist. "That wasn't what I needed to hear at all," Scott declares.

Scott met with a gay counselor over lunch and declared that he thought he might be gay. His major concern, he said, was in regard to the morality of homosexuality. The gay peer counselor, a senior, was also a religion major. "Whether or not you're gay," he said, "is nothing that can be helped." He offered some comments about homophobic passages in the Bible, mentioning interpretations of the Sodom and Gomorrah incident, for example. What one considered "normal," he pointed out, depended upon who was making the definition. Summers working on a farm, he had realized that homosexuality was pervasive among animals as well as human beings. His arguments convinced Scott, "I wanted to be persuaded," he admits. Besides, he found the gay counselor very attractive. "I never mustered the courage to do anything about it," he declares.

Scott engaged in further conversations with religion majors about morality issues, and morality became for him a nonissue.

At Christmas break, Scott tested his elder sister. She had advised him that college was the time for personal exploration. She mentioned that she thought that two of her friends at college were lesbians. In fact, she had once wondered whether she was a lesbian, but at school she dated men and discovered that she was attracted to them. When Scott declared that he was undergoing the same kind of questioning, his sister "freaked out," he recalls, and changed the subject. Subsequently, without Scott's knowledge, she repeated what he had said to their mother. In telephone calls after Scott returned to school, his mother started ending their conversations by assuring him, "We all love you, we still love you," words she had never used before. Scott confronted her, asking, "Has Lorie told you something intimate about me?" She started to cry. "I've never kept anything from your father before," she declared. "It's been three weeks. I don't know whether I should tell him." Scott urged her to do so. "What did we do wrong?" she exclaimed.

One night a week later, Scott's father telephoned. "He said horrible things," Scott recounts. "This is a dangerous game," he declared. "What's the matter with you? Don't you have balls any more?" Although the telephone was in a public hall, Scott, angry at his father's statements, shouted back, indifferent to whether anyone heard him. "I can't have a conversation with you," he announced at last, "if you're not going to listen to what I have to say." He hung up the phone. "I had never spoken to my father this way," Scott recounts, "or raised my voice to him.

"I'm so angry," Scott declared, reporting the conversation to his roommates. "Well, write to them what you're thinking," responded his sympathetic roommate. "Forget your homework tonight, the letter's definitely more important." Scott took this advice and wrote to his parents that he could not have a conversation with them because they were not able to hear him on his own grounds. He described the feelings that he had for the gay counselor. His father called to say that he was coming to visit. Scott forbade him to come.

Scott had planned to study Russian that summer at Middlebury College, but his parents ordered him to return home instead. "You're never to speak to that man again," his father insisted. "I felt as though he was cutting me off from this avenue of exploring who I was sexually," Scott declares. "He didn't keep me from talking to the gay counselor again."

That summer at home Scott engaged in frequent discussions with his parents. They suggested that he have a talk with his pediatrician. Scott refused. They did not ask him to see a psychiatrist, but they posed what he considered to be ridiculous questions. His father asked whether Scott was afraid of being castrated. "We simply were not able to communicate," Scott recounts. "I was gay, it had nothing to do with what anybody thought."

During most of those tense weeks, Scott's father continued to make insensitive remarks. "He also cried a lot," Scott recalls, "and asked for my forgiveness for treating me so badly." Both parents blamed themselves. "From what I've read," Scott remarks, "a quite standard reaction. AIDS was mentioned, too." At a certain point, however, Scott relates, discussion ceased. His parents offered no advice when he returned to college. Nor was the subject broached during the next two years. "I was very angry every time I went home," Scott recalls. "Why can't you change?" he wondered. "What's so hard about it? I constantly repeated that I was the same person I had always been." He could not understand why Jennifer [a high school friend] could be so supportive of him and his family could not.

The summer between his junior and senior years, Scott spent at Middlebury College studying Russian. Although he hesitated at first, he did come out to close friends in this new environment. He would broach the subject by saying that he had had a lot going on with him recently and add, "I've realized that I am gay." He encountered no hostile reactions.

His last two years at Carleton, Scott was appointed a resident assistant. People on his floor knew he was gay, but again he encountered no hostile reactions. "I was respected for who I was," he asserts. During his senior year, Scott found a gay friend with whom he went to gay bars in Minneapolis. "I found it exciting," he recounts. "I felt more alive than I ever had before. To know that there were so many other gay people was an eye-opening experience. I liked dancing with my friend, but I couldn't imagine what it would be like to be in a relationship with someone, and I never went home with anyone. I came out backwards," he insists. "Most people have sex before they come out to their parents. In my case, their disapproval really kept me from having sex."

In 1988, after graduation, Scott went to Leningrad on a four-month study program. When he was about to leave, his mother said to him, "They mention taking condoms. Do you want to do that?" Scott replied that he was not sexually active. "Mom," he said, "you know me, I wouldn't do that." It was clear, Scott comments, that his mother was more comfortable in discussing sex than he was.

There were two openly gay men in Scott's study group. At a dance, noticing that Scott held a young woman at arm's length, one of them said to him, "The way you were dancing with that woman makes me think that you're gay." Scott admitted that he was. One night shortly thereafter the man invited Scott to his room. They had a long conversation. The man asked Scott whether he felt any attraction for him. Scott admitted that he did but said that he was too paralyzed to do anything. "If you can't," said the friend, "I will." They slept together that night and several nights thereafter. "It was a relief that someone took the initiative," declares Scott. "It was the first time I had sexual relations with anyone, and it felt good. I was twenty-two."

Scott's friend wanted to continue the relationship, but Scott was unready to enter a lasting connection. Besides, the man lived in Washington, D.C., and Scott decided to live in New York, where his Chinese woman friend from Carleton was living as well as another friend from high school, a straight woman who invited him to stay with her. He remained with her in a studio apartment for five months. They slept together in a double bed without any discomfort.

For two years, Scott recounts, he led a lonely life. He did not go to gay bars because he did not feel comfortable cruising. "Partly because I was Asian," he explains. "I knew that there were specific tastes in the gay community. Being Asian or black was not an advantage in the bars." One evening in 1990, however, Scott went to the Lesbian and Gay Community with a black gay friend from Carleton. They discovered that a racism workshop was taking place under Don Kao, a longtime Chinese American activist. When the workshop broke up into separate racial groups, Scott joined the Asians and Pacific Islanders. Don Kao proposed a continuing gay Asian organization. "That's when my life completely took off," Scott declares. He became one of the first members of GAPIMINY (Gay Asian and Pacific Islander Men of New York); as it expanded in membership he served as its contact person, that is, received its messages on his telephone.

The group met weekly in Chinatown over dinner to share their experiences of isolation both as gays and Asians. "We wanted to be proactive rather than reactive politically," Scott recounts, "to make our existence known, to bring our particular agenda to the gay community and the general Asian community." Discussions over the dinner table often centered around racism. In bars, for example, they questioned whether it was out of racism that they were ignored; racist when people were attracted to them because they were Asian; racist when people attempted to flatter them by denigrating other racial groups. "I had thought," Scott recounts, "that there was something wrong with me for not feeling comfortable in mostly white settings. Now I found my reactions validated."

In May eleven members attended a retreat at Don Kao's farm in upstate New York. In workshops they sought to define their purpose and goals. "No one had sex during the weekend," Scott relates. "We weren't there for sex. We got to know each other well. We were there to define ourselves."

Scott remained active in GAPIMINY for about three years. Once he participated in a public broadcasting program on gay issues along with black and Latino gay men and a lesbian. From his experience in GAPIMINY, Scott says that he learned a lot about organizing and about how to reconcile conflicting points of view. "We tried to run our group so that it would include everybody, to bridge language and cultural differences between American-born and foreign-born and between young and old members. I became even more aware of being Asian, and I was completely out."

GAPIMINY provided the impetus, Scott recounts, for the formation of other Asian and Pacific Islander organizations with more specific agendas like the Silk Dragons, an Asian drag group; the Korean Lesbian and Gay Organization; and the South Asian Lesbian and Gay Association for Indians, Pakistanis, and Bangladeshis; and, as the HIV crisis grew more intense in their communities, APICHA (Asian and Pacific Islander Coalition HIV/AIDS).

After three years of membership, Scott ceased his activity in GAPIMINY. The organization, he says, had grown large and lost its sense of intimacy. Besides, with the addition of new members, discussions became repetitive and of declining value to Scott. Nor was he content with a primarily social agenda, for he had assembled a circle of friends of his own.

While active in GAPIMINY, taking advantage of a tuition reimbursement program at the Ford Foundation, where he worked as a secretary, Scott enrolled first at the Columbia School of Social Work and then at the Union Theological Seminary, where he found courses offering closer analysis of factors like ethnicity and gender. Although he obtained a Master of Divinity degree, he had no intention of entering the ministry. "I didn't share the culture of the church," he explains. "The church has done a lot of damage to some of my gay friends."

While at the seminary, Scott entered his first lasting love relationship with a fellow student, a Scandinavian, a relationship that lasted for three years. The first time Scott and Eric visited in Colorado, his parents put them in separate bedrooms. One evening during a game in the living room, when Scott's siblings were displaying affection to their partners, Erik put his legs about Scott, who was sitting on the floor. The others became obviously uncomfortable. During a second visit, things were more relaxed. Scott and his partner were assigned a bedroom together.

Scott never had any sense of racism in his relationship with Erik, but they faced problems in dealing with other people. Asian friends tested Erik to be sure he was not racist, and they had questions about Scott's associating himself with a Caucasian.

While in this relationship with Erik, Scott became associated with GAMCOG (Gay Asian Men Coming Out Group). "That group was part of my community," he declares. The group dissolved, however, after about eight months. Continuing as contact person for GAPIMINY, Scott continued to receive calls from people who were just coming out of the closet. In August 1994, to assist these people, Scott suggested to APICHA that GAMCOG should be reestablished. Funded by the Paul Rappaport Foundation, GAMCOG was still meeting twice a month in 1996. At each meeting held over dinner, the group decides on a topic for discussion, generally a topic related to problems involved in coming out to the family and with religious beliefs. Overcoming loneliness is a frequent topic. To introduce the participants to the gay community, the group organizes field trips to gay centers in the city.

GAMCOG did not attract a large group, and the participants were constantly changing. But Scott was proud of its accomplishments. He points to one man who lost a facial tic that had previously appeared whenever he spoke about his life. "There are many intangible results," he adds, "like developing a sense of community, overcoming a sense of isolation, and dealing with feelings. The participants become more articulate, more helpful to each other."

In July 1995, Scott broke off with Erik. "I felt," he explains, "that my life was moving in another direction, professionally and emotionally." Single again, Scott found dating difficult. "Once you become used to living as one of a couple," he declares, "it's hard to start looking again."

While studying at the seminary, Scott worked at a battered women's shelter and in a child abuse prevention program, where he continued along with a job at the Greenwich House Children's Safety Project. He matriculated at the Bank Street College of Education, taking courses to become a children's psychotherapist.

Scott is convinced that his entire past experience prepared him for work with children. "I grew up in a repressed environment," he explains. "My parents didn't know how to make sense of emotions. I needed to heal a major part of myself and to overcome the hurt of their rejection." On the other hand, he insists that he owes a lot to his parents for providing him with so many opportunities. They also helped him, he declares, in learning how to deal with children. "To this day," he says, "I use therapeutic interventions that my father and mother used with me. They taught me that you don't choose the life that you end up with. What you do get to choose is how you deal with that life. I want to help children to meet such challenges and to make it easier for them to resolve their problems."

A FILIPINA: JOMAL ALCOBER, A STAFF MEMBER OF THE NEW YORK CITY HUMAN RIGHTS COMMISSION

In discussions of racism, Americans think primarily of relations between the white majority and the African-American minority and secondarily of relations with Latinos. Rarely do they mention as an element in the mix that makes up American society the one million Filipino Americans, an ethnic minority with one of the lowest school dropout rates and highest college graduation rates in the nation.

"I've always felt different," insists Jomal Alcober, a human rights specialist and investigator at the New York City Human Rights Commission. "I knew that my skin color and hair were different. Teachers liked to touch and play with my hair and talked about it to the other students. I could never pretend to be white."

Joyce Maria (she uses her nickname Jomal) Alcober was born in 1958 in

Washington, D.C., the youngest of the four children and only daughter of Filipino parents. A daughter is prized in Philippine culture, she reports, because of the matriarchal traditions in the society. "I knew from an early age," she declares, "that I was special." Jomal's parents came from modest backgrounds in the Central Provinces. During World War II, Jomal's father served in the Philippine scouts, a guerrilla force that tracked Japanese movements on the island of Leyte. Advised by American officers to flee the country, he joined the crew of a merchant vessel and made his way to Washington, D.C., where he had an uncle. Subsequently drafted into the army, he served in the Korean War.

In Manila, Jomal's mother, then in her late teens, met a black American soldier eager to return home with a Filipina wife. Back in Texas he changed his attitude and began treating her like an indentured servant, even beating her. With the aid of a Filipina friend, she ran off to Washington, where she met Jomal's father. She had not gone beyond grade school and worked as a beautician. Jomal's father, a high school graduate, had a job as a waiter. Jomal remembers her parents returning home evenings angry at incidents of humiliation they had suffered at work. Her mother often felt compelled to change jobs.

Jomal was early made aware of the history of the Philippines and of the Filipino community in this country (a history, she notes, that dates to the seventeenth century, when on a stopover at New Orleans a boatload of Filipino laborers escaped from a Spanish slave ship and dispersed throughout the Louisiana territory). Jomal learned as a child that men brought from the islands to work on the railroads during the last century were, like their Chinese fellow laborers, forbidden to bring their wives with them. They married black or Native American women and often, later, Jewish women. She recalls her father's relating how once when he was playing ball with other Filipinos, someone yelled, "Immigracion!" Having obtained his citizenship as a result of his military service, he was safe, but all the others jumped into the nearby Tidal Basin.

Jomal's parents and their friends were deeply involved in Philippine politics and numbered among their friends leaders of the pro-Aquino Movement for a Free Philippines. Instead of hiring a babysitter when they went to political meetings, they took Jomal with them; from her earliest years she listened to political discussions. "It is part of the culture," Jomal notes, "that adults express interest in their children's opinions." As a child, she was shocked by a photograph in a Philippine newspaper of a man decapitated for stealing a can of sardines. She recalls the anxiety in her family when her mother visited the islands in 1972, when the country was under the Marcos declaration of martial law. "In the Philippines if you were related to an anti-Marcos person," Jomal declares, "you could lose your job, and some of my relatives did lose their jobs."

Until Jomal started school, she spoke Warai, her parents' native tongue.

Schoolmates, however, exclaimed, "You're an American now, speak English!" Encouraged by her parents to lose any trace of accent in English, Jomal forgot her Philippine language. Jomal's parents laid great store on their children's education. Her father conducted spelling bees or games with multiplication tables. Aware of her brothers' unpleasant experiences with the nuns in parochial school, Jomal insisted upon going to public school.

Occasionally at home Jomal heard racist remarks about whites and blacks, but she herself did not confront racism until junior high school. Then, abruptly, she faced the color issue. When teachers were asked to take a census of their students, classing them as either white or black, a science teacher listed Jomal as white. Jomal protested. When a history teacher subsequently listed her as black, Jomal denied that she was black. The teacher put the question to a vote, and Jomal's classmates voted that she was black. In vain Jomal appealed to the vice principal, insisting that he list her in another category.

In junior and senior high school Jomal became aware of inner-city violence. Eight of her high school classmates, she recalls, died either from gunshot wounds or from drug overdose. One girl was murdered by her father when he discovered that she was pregnant. One day a boy in her homeroom was shot in a park near the high school in a drug-related incident. A locker search uncovered some one hundred guns. She also saw Washington burn in an explosion of black rage. "Discrimination," she says, "was happening all around to everyone except white people. When your friends are being hurt, you can't just sit by and do nothing."

Caught up in the excitement of the civil rights movement, Jomal participated in a demonstration to demand the right to wear slacks to school. When classmates were picked on, Jomal, who was big for her age and stockier than some of the boys, intervened. Once she herself was cornered by a gang of black girls. She remembers clenching her fists to defend herself. Angry and overwrought, she ran to the gym teacher, only to be frustrated when the teacher dismissed the incident, noting that Jomal had not been hurt physically.

Jomal's first sexual experience occurred as a child in first grade when a white teenager brought her into the woods and molested her. Jomal reported the incident to a neighbor, an older girl. She, in turn, told Jomal's brothers. Word spread throughout the neighborhood. Jomal was confined to the house. Her "rapist" was beaten up by the boys of the neighborhood, and his family was forced to move. Jomal remembers that she felt guilty for causing the trouble. "I didn't know it was wrong," she explains. "He was gentle and did not use force."

Years later, when a colleague in a Lesbian Sensitivity and HIV Training program at the AIDS Training Institute of the New York City Department of Health asked her to define when she became aware of her lesbianism, Jomal, by then thirty-three years old, recalled that in fourth grade she had a repeated dream in which she embraced her teacher, a married woman with two children. In fifth grade while visiting a friend who had formerly lived in her neighborhood, she had her first same-sex experience. "I didn't feel guilty," she relates. "I was merely worried we would make too much noise and get caught." Both girls were confident that eventually they would marry and lead "normal" lives.

In high school Jomal had an affair with a man teacher. She dated briefly a young white man who dealt in drugs and went out with blacks, Hispanics, and Asians. When the brother of her best girlfriend said he wanted to have sex with her, Jomal agreed. "He forced me to go down on him," she recalls. "I found that disgusting."

In her senior year Jomal worked for an art teacher who she had been told had had relations with her previous assistant. One day the teacher invited her to her home. Sensing Jomal's nervousness, she did not attempt to seduce her. Jomal asked to be released from her program. Years later, however, Jomal ran into her and had sex with her.

After graduation, Filipino friends took Jomal to a gay club without warning her in advance what to expect. She was shocked at seeing cross-dressing. Nevertheless, her curiosity aroused, Jomal returned to the bar on her own. When high school friends she met at the club asked her whether she was gay, she replied that, as far as she knew, she was not.

In 1979, after completing a two-year program at a community college, Jomal, then twenty-two, found work at a hospital in Hawaii. She stayed with relatives and was surprised to discover that a gay cousin of hers enjoyed easy acceptance in his family.

Upon Jomal's return to Washington, a neighbor brought her to Morgan's, "the hottest lesbian club in D.C. at the time." For the first time Jomal saw a woman she was eager to meet, "a southern belle." The woman was even less experienced than Jomal and not at all comfortable with her sexuality. They soon parted. Then Jomal met Linda, whom she calls her "transitional woman," and spent a weekend with her. "The sky opened up," she recounts. Arriving home "with a huge smile" on her face, she found her brother giving a description of her to the police. Jomal merely said that she had met someone, but her mother apparently had a "sixth sense." "Are you sleeping with a woman?" she demanded. Jomal said that she was not. Six months later, when she acknowledged the relationship, her brother insisted that she was merely passing through a phase. "No, she's not," her mother retorted, blaming herself for the "disgrace." On the other hand, Jomal overheard her father exclaim, "Mommy, people are different. It's okay. She's our daughter." His acceptance of her lesbianism, Jomal declares, enabled her to feel more at ease in her relations with people generally. "I had a base," she says.

Despite her mother's initial reaction, Jomal remains convinced that in Philippine culture "people are accepted for who they are." Her maternal grandfather, indeed, had left her grandmother to live in Manila with his male lover. Jomal's Philippines-born parents, she notes, exhibited more understanding than her three brothers. If they had grown up in the Philippines, she believes, they might have been more tolerant.

While Linda, an army reservist, was away at military exercises, two gay friends told Jomal that Linda was seeing other women and was on drugs. "Here I was in a marriage," recounts Jomal, "and the last one to learn that my lover was engaged in an affair." The two men urged Jomal to have an extramarital affair and pressed her to accompany them to a lesbian bar. She protested that after so many years of monogamy she did not know how to pick up another woman. The men gave her pointers, and she succeeded in meeting someone. "It was like the Star Spangled Banner all over again," Jomal recalls.

Confronted by Jomal, Linda admitted that she was back on drugs and was "fooling around" with other women.

Depressed at the breakup with Linda, Jomal continued seeing the woman she met at the bar. This woman was in the process of ending a relationship. Fearing that she might once again be a victim of unfaithfulness, Jomal broke with her. Even today, she says, she retains love for that woman and compares other women to her. "My father's pick!" she adds.

At a lesbian bar Jomal developed a friendship with Anthony, a gay bartender. She married him to enable him to remain in this country. They discussed having a child. When a former sex partner of his died of AIDS, Jomal asked Anthony to be tested. He proved to be HIV-positive. "That brought the AIDS crisis home to me," Jomal declares. Volunteering to serve as a buddy, she was assigned to a woman of color infected by her IV-drug-user lover. Moved by her client's plight, Jomal became active on the D.C. Women's Committee on AIDS and served as coordinator for the first Women and AIDS East Coast Conference. At the 1987 Gay March on Washington Jomal fell in love and subsequently followed the woman back to New York, where two years later she helped found the Asian and Pacific Islander Coalition on HIV/AIDS. Thereafter she moved from leadership offices in one organization after another. Learning of an opening at the New York City Commission on Human Rights, Jomal applied for the position and, in December 1990, began working at its AIDS Division.

Jomal found life in New York quite different from life in Washington. She missed the warm relationships with gay men she had had in the nation's capital. In New York, Jomal declares, gay men close themselves off from lesbians. "I have to have male as well as female company so as to create a balance in my life," she declares. "In this respect, I am far from being a separatist."

Jomal asserts that she became an activist not "because of racism and homophobia in the United States but because of civil rights violations in the Philippines. Although I know I was born in this country," she declares, "I have always felt Filipina first. That's my heritage. We are strong people, we have retained our culture after centuries of Spanish and then United States rule. For a people living on seven thousand islands to unite as a nation is a great achievement." The Filipino culture, she believes, is more humane than any in the West.

Chapter Six
The Warning of the Holocaust

The very term "the Jewish people" demonstrates that Jews are not simply a religious group like Catholics or Protestants. "A Jew is one who defines himself as a Jew," declared the British philosopher and historian Sir Isaiah Berlin, "one who is accepted by the community as a Jew and one who joins freely in the fate of the Jews." Because Jewish Americans during the last century have proved to be the most upwardly mobile community in the United States and are, except for a tiny minority, Caucasian, anti-Semitic verbal and physical attacks as well as vandalism against synagogues and cemeteries are often dismissed as isolated incidents perpetrated by a lunatic fringe. A December 1992 report on bias-related crimes in New York City during the first eleven months of the year, however, revealed 186 anti-Semitic assaults compared to 99 against African Americans, with a substantial increase of the former and decrease of the latter over the previous year.

A number of the non-Jewish interviewees expressed warm sentiments about the Jewish community and sensitivity to anti-Semitism. Juan Mendez reported that his mother expressed a high regard for Jewish people she had known while living in New York City. Juan himself spoke with respect and affection about a middle-aged Jewish divorcee, a "Rosalind Russell type," who was his superior while he was working at Orion films. She was, he recalls, politically sophisticated and liberal in her opinions. She and Juan exchanged and discussed clippings from newspapers. She took him to movies, including a Yiddish film, *The Dybbuk*. From her he became aware of the Holocaust.

As a child, June Chan had heard about the Chosen People in Bible class.

At the Bronx High School of Science, she learned about the Holocaust. "It horrified me," she recalled, "the pictures and images." Speaking of the activists she encountered in the women's movement, she declared, "It is an amazing thing that Jewish women had such an influence on my life. They had a tremendous sense of social responsibility. They felt a burden, a duty to change the world. They taught me everything."

David Eng described the richness he was experiencing in his relationship with his Jewish lover Sam Weiner. "He and I wanted to know more about each other," he declared. "He's always been interested in Asia and is frustrated that I don't associate myself with Chinese culture." With Sam he attended his first Seder. "I loved it," he said. "I have noticed parallels between our cultures," he declares, "in the sense of family, intellectual aspects, what parents expect from their children—success in education and professions."

Dennis de Leon, city commissioner for human rights, recalled how his father would exclaim upon turning on the television set, "All Jews, all Jews!" He considered that Dennis was selling out in taking a position in a law firm headed by Jewish attorneys, but Dennis was impressed by the social consciousness of the members of the firm. Rereading the transcript of his interview, Dennis remarked, "Regarding my statement about there being a lot of Jews in the law firm, I don't like the insensitive use of the term 'Jews.' In the *Amsterdam News* they'll say 'a carful of Jews.' I'm sensitive to that kind of insensitivity."

Both Tracy Morgan and Chris Hennelly noted that Jewish gay activists were uncomfortable about ACT UP demonstrations within St. Patrick's Cathedral. Indeed, regarding the Stop the Church action, Sharon Levine declared, "I was in favor of demonstrating against Cardinal O'Connor at his residence, but I thought it was not right to upset the congregation. We expect him to treat our [gay] community with respect, and we have no right to walk into a church and deprive people of their right to pray." Aware of a possible association of such an action with attacks on synagogues over the centuries, Chris Henneley, an enthusiastic participant in the St. Patrick's action, declared, "I could not demonstrate inside a synagogue."

Without exception the Jewish interviewees, including Jay Blotcher, Jewish by adoption, and three others who were children of Jewish mothers and non-Jewish fathers, were conscious of their Jewish identity and proud of their heritage. All but one were raised in homes where at least the High Holidays were celebrated, and all attended either secular or religious Jewish schools. All the men had been bar mitzvahed. Joyce Hudson, the daughter of a Jewish mother and a black father, spent her childhood in an Orthodox orphanage, and Steve Ashkinazy transformed himself from a secular to an Orthodox Jew in adulthood. As teenagers, Fred Adler and Howie Katz were active in Jewish youth organizations. Naomi Lichtenstein and Steve Quester sojourned for long periods in Israel.

THE HOLOCAUST

Although all the Jewish interviewees associated discrimination against gays with the millennial discrimination against Jews and viewed the Holocaust as an event with special meaning to them in their struggle against homophobia, only two interviewees had immediate connections to the Holocaust: Giselle, a PFLAG (Parents and Friends of Lesbians and Gays) member and mother of two gay children, who had suffered directly in the cataclysm; and Ruth (the pseudonym for an interviewee whose interview is not included in this book), whose father's family had fled from Germany in the 1930s. While growing up Ruth was constantly reminded that she was Jewish and warned that if another Hitler arose she would be killed. Ruth felt the discomfort of growing up in a neighborhood where her family were the only Jews, but that, she understood, was part of being Jewish. "It was instilled into me," Ruth declared, "that we had to think about poor people, all people who were deprived. From earliest childhood," she recalls, "I knew you were expected to do things of social significance that made you uncomfortable."

Only as an adult did Ruth learn that her grandmother, missing her friends and unhappy in New York, had returned to Nazi Germany and subsequently died in a camp. To reclaim her family's history, Ruth visited her father's native town. A woman who had known Ruth's grandparents took her through the family's former home. "In Germany," Ruth declares, "I felt Jewish in the sense that I didn't feel that I belonged there."

"Now do you understand," Ruth's father asked when she returned from her trip, "how lucky you are to be alive? You never know what's going to happen, when you may have to pack up and move again."

During the gay rights bill hearings in the 1970s, when an Orthodox Jewish rabbi proclaimed that gays should be isolated on an island, quarantined, or killed, Fred Goldhaber jumped up and screamed, "You haven't learned from our Holocaust and you're as bad as the Nazis." Fred was, he declares, "devastated that a prominent Jewish spokesman could fail to understand that we're all human beings. Gays are just another oppressed minority. The Holocaust makes you understand better the situation of gay people."

HOWIE KATZ*

As far back as he can remember, Howie had questions about his sexual orientation. As a boy he was attracted to the son of a famous football player, a boy in Howie's brother's Cub Scout den. In high school he felt more at

*Fund-raiser for the Lesbian and Gay Anti-Violence Project and lobbyist for the New York State Civil Rights Act (see Chapter 9). In 1996, he was working on the staff of a state assemblyman.

ease with younger boys and never confident in the company of his peers or with older males. At George Washington University in Washington, D.C., while attending a meeting of a visiting gay activist group, he was fearful of exhibiting too great an interest in their program. "There were a couple of people at the meeting I wanted to notice me," he recounts, "without the others noticing my interest." He was aware of a gay group with an office on campus, but he never went near it. "I had a macho self-image," he explains.

Troubled by his "unnatural" attractions, Howie confessed to a classmate that he might be gay. "We didn't talk about it in any detail," Howie recalls. "I was suicidal. He calmed me down." Subsequently, he wrote to his parents about his suspicions. At his mother's suggestion, Howie sought help from a Washington psychiatrist. Howie yearned to talk about his sexual orientation, but the psychiatrist merely wanted to explore why Howie did not like women. "It wasn't that I didn't like women," Howie insisted. "I was attracted to guys. It was uncomfortable enough for me to try to talk about the subject. I just gave up."

As a camp counselor the following summer, Howie, then twenty-one, developed a Platonic relationship with a thirteen-year-old camper and admitted to him that he was gay. "I knew that he loved me so much that if I told him," Howie explains, "he wouldn't reject me. If anything, my telling him strengthened our friendship." They continued to correspond until the boy's mother brought the relationship to an end. "That was the worst thing that could have happened," Howie declares. "I became suicidal."

One night during his last semester at college, rebuffed by a girl whom he asked to go to bed with him, Howie decided, "This was my last chance!" He drove around until he picked up a man. "At his apartment, I decided to go with the flow," he recounted. "We smoked a little pot. We went to bed. Whatever he did, I did." When he saw that his partner wanted merely to use him, Howie felt cheated. "I wanted mutual feelings of tenderness and love and enjoyable sex," he recalled, "making my partner enjoy it as much as I enjoyed it."

After graduation, Howie decided to enter his father's paper-box manufacturing plant. His father was pleased that alone among his children Howie, with his long Afro haircut and scraggly Fu Manchu beard, showed interest in taking over the business. Neither he nor Howie's mother ever spoke about Howie's "problem." In despair at his life of subterfuge and at having no one to talk to, Howie sought out the college friend to whom he had first come out. "We sat on a rock in Central Park," Howie related, "and I told him again that I was gay. He remarked that the least I could do was to waste a few evenings to find out for sure."

Emboldened by his friend's sympathetic response, Howie came out to another college friend. This one replied that he had suspected Howie might be gay because of Howie's problems in dealing with women and because of Howie's choice of male friends. Subsequently, he sent a letter expressing gratitude for Howie's sharing with him this most intimate confidence. The next time they played basketball, he declared, Howie could still feel free to give him "a pat on the ass." A third friend, Howie's college roommate, used to talk about punching fags. Upon Howie's admission of being gay, he changed his vocabulary. "He liked me," Howie explains. "None of my friends rejected me."

Howie moved into his own apartment and began answering personal ads in the *Village Voice.* The first response came from a man about his age, who was, Howie declares, "a bit more effeminate than I like, but he was pleasant and gentle. Within a couple of days I came down with the clap. We went out to dinner again, but no sex." Howie next established a relationship with a man he met in a bar, Michael, a hairdresser, "a pretty boy, not especially effeminate. The first six months," Howie declares, "were great. I was learning that I could feel love and be comfortable in a sexual relationship with another man."

Encountering no difficulty in coming out to his brothers, Howie resolved to speak to his parents. "I announced that I had something to tell them," he relates. "I admitted that I didn't believe gay people were happy. I was not happy being gay." Howie's parents cried. They assured him that they loved him and would not reject him. "My dad said he did not know how much he could talk about it," Howie recalls. "They had assumed that I had worked out this problem with the shrink."

After coming out to his parents, Howie was able to bring Michael to visit, but his father asked Howie not to come out to the extended family. It became increasingly obvious, however, that Howie and his lover had no common interests. When Howie insisted he needed time to himself, his lover became angry. "He came from an Italian family," Howie recounts, "where people yelled and said the nastiest things they could think of to each other and then declared they were sorry, and everything was forgotten." Howie began striking back with equal nastiness. During an argument, he kicked in a stereo speaker. His lover challenged Howie to hit him. They broke up.

Howie entered analysis once again, this time with a psychiatrist he had seen while in high school, when he was fearful of bringing up the subject of his sexual attractions. "Now," Howie recounted, "I wanted to find out why I was gay so as to end up not being gay. In the back of my mind, I was still thinking that maybe this was a phase I was going through, that if I went to another psychiatrist I might figure out why I was gay, why I stopped developing at that stage—and then go on to live a heterosexual life like the rest of my family." Over a period of two-and-a-half years, Howie recalls, with the psychiatrist he examined all the stereotypical explanations for why people are gay. None of them seemed appropriate, but Howie was becoming more comfortable with himself.

Ever an enthusiastic athlete, Howie joined a gay softball team and in short order was appointed team manager and then commissioner for the twelve to sixteen teams in the New York gay league. He presented a monthly report on gay sports on WBAI, New York's publicly supported Pacifica radio station. The year his team won the gay world series, he says, was the happiest of his life. In 1979 at a softball tournament in Toronto, Howie met Peter, a ballplayer from Boston and spent the night with him. Within a year Peter moved to New York. Peter was college educated. He had a responsible position with the New York City Parks Department and was a bright and pleasant person. Howie's parents liked him and accepted him as a member of the family.

After yielding for a couple of years to his father's prohibition against coming out to other members of the family, Howie came out to a few relatives individually. Depressed at a big family function, Howie got up from the table and walked outside. His mother followed him. Howie started to cry and said, "I can't do this, it's too painful." She said, "Then don't do it." "But dad. . . ?" Howie protested. "It's his problem, not yours," replied his mother. "He'll have to deal with it."

Invited by his cousin Janice to another family gathering, Howie called and asked her husband whether he could bring someone. "Oh, you're living with someone," he replied, "bring her." Howie said, "It's not so easy. There's something I've got to explain." "Oh, you're going with a black girl. That's ok." "No, in fact, he's white." "Oh, bring him." "I'm really pleased that you say that," Howie declared, "but I want you to make sure that Janice has no objection." They called back the next day. "Bring him." "That's how I came out to the extended family," Howie relates. He faced no problems. One of his cousins who had been forced to break off with a gentile boyfriend expressed her admiration for Howie's courage. When people were saying goodbye, however, an uncle remarked, "We used to be worried about Kenny, but he got married." His wife poked him. If Howie's father was in turmoil, he didn't show it.

In 1981 Howie's father announced that he was taking the entire family to Israel to celebrate the marriage of Howie's brother. He asked whether Howie would share a room with a cousin or preferred to have a room by himself. "I've been living with someone for a couple of years," Howie retorted and walked out of the room. "I was pissed off, too," Howie related, "that my brother had not responded to a letter in which I asked whether Peter was invited. I didn't know how he would react, especially since he was living on a kibbutz. I sent him another letter. My brother wrote back, 'Of course, Peter's invited.' "

Howie bought a ticket on his own for Peter and informed his dad that Peter was going with him. That, Howie thinks, was the moment when his father realized that there was no turning back. "This is my family," Howie was announcing, "my choice, my lover, my partner. My father was not to treat Peter differently from any of the other in-laws. He did not pay for the ticket, but he paid for everything else for us in Israel."

In 1986, after a relationship of six years, Howie found out that Peter was involved with someone else. Howie's parents, who had come to consider Peter one of the family, sought unsuccessfully to persuade them to reach a reconciliation. "At one point," Howie related, "my lawyer was battling with his lawyer over the ownership of the apartment and the house in the country." When the former manager of their softball team died of AIDS, Howie called Peter to tell him about the funeral. Peter was not able to attend, but the next day he called, and they came to an agreement as to how to divide up their property.

After they split up, Peter tested HIV-positive. Howie was negative. "I was one of the lucky ones," he says.

"Being gay has enriched my life in lots of ways," Howie declares. "It's made me a full and whole person able to love unconditionally. To have someone love you unconditionally is probably the essence of what human beings strive for more than anything else."

Howie Katz's older brother is a reformed rabbi. His other brother married an Israeli and lives on a kibbutz. Howie's sister, previously not religious, now attends a temple with her children. His father became religious with age. Though the Holocaust, Howie says, was a reality to his parents and his brothers and sister, his parents did not succeed in making him understand as a Jewish child that he was never to be complacent, never to believe that what happened in Germany couldn't happen again. As an adult, Howie recognizes that his Jewish background has had a lot to do with forming him as he is. "The culture, the community," Howie remarks, "teaches one about being oppressed, makes you realize that other people can hate you. I like the fact that Judaism teaches that everyone has a place in the world to come whether you believe in Judaism or not, that if there is such a thing as an afterlife everyone will be measured by deeds in this life. In the Jewish tradition you have to give charity. When I had money, I gave it away. Now I give my time, my work." In lobbying for the passage of a state hate-crimes bill, his prime responsibility as an AVP (Lesbian and Gay Anti-Violence Project) staffer, Howie notes that his closest collaborator has been Michael Riff, the associate director of the Anti-Defamation League of the B'nai B'rith. "I'm sure our common Jewish culture has something to do with that," Howie declares.

SHARON LEVINE*

Sharon Levine's mother wanted her children to undergo religious instruction in order to be able to make an intelligent decision about religion as adults. Sharon felt free to discuss intimate personal problems with the family's rabbi. "The rabbi is our teacher," Sharon declared, contrasting her experience with that of her Catholic lover, "whereas a priest tells you what to do.

*A member of Queer Nation and the Pink Panthers (see Chapter 12).

The priest warns you will go to hell if you don't play by the rules. The rabbi never used the word *sin*. What people want is the right to live their own lives. You don't discriminate against people because they have a different way of life."

The neighborhood where Sharon grew up was primarily Jewish, and there were no tensions among the neighbors. "One Halloween," however, Sharon recounted, "we had a swastika painted on our door in shaving cream, which sank into the wood so that it couldn't be removed. We felt that we had been violated. Because of the anger so many people feel toward Jews, I was always terrified. I didn't want a mezuzah [a small metal strip containing the Ten Commandments] at my door because I didn't want people to know that mine was a Jewish home." In Sunday school Sharon was horrified by pictures of the Holocaust. On the other hand, as a Jew she also felt a certain security. "Anti-Semitism brought my family closer," she notes, "made it more supportive. I know many other people don't have that."

When Sharon was about sixteen, she became aware that there was something different about her. She enjoyed being in the women's locker room. When she visited her father (her parents divorced when she was still a child), she studied the naked women in his copies of *Penthouse* and *Playboy*. In any case, Sharon was fortunate in having understanding parents. In fact, she declares, "I just assumed that all parents wanted to know what was going on in their children's lives. I was surprised that my friends were jealous of my open relationship with my mother." She remembers sitting at the kitchen table and listening as her mother warned her brother David that if he ever got a girl pregnant it would be his fault for being irresponsible. Once when Sharon remarked how unsatisfying she found her dates, her mother suggested that she try going out with different kinds of young men. Sharon followed her mother's advice, to no avail. "If I was having sex," she recalls, "my heart broke because he was trying so hard and I was simply bored."

One evening, while a junior at a boarding school, Sharon returned to a friend's room after they had been out drinking at a bar. They went to bed. The next morning Sharon declared to herself, "This is what I am and what I'm going to be. All this time," she says, "I slept with men to prove what I wasn't. It was a relief to know for sure what I was."

One morning during a summer vacation, Sharon's mother asked her whether she was a lesbian. "You either are or aren't," her mother insisted. "You have to know, and I want to know." Sharon declared that she was, indeed, a lesbian. "I don't think she wanted me to change," Sharon says, "but she wanted me to be sure that I knew what I was getting into. She warned me that lesbians face a difficult life. She feared I would be devastated once someone said something awful to me." When Sharon came out to her father, he asked whether there was anything he could do to help her change. Sharon was dumbfounded. "We're not talking about what I'm going to order for lunch," she declared. "We're talking about my life!"

Her mother's first meeting with her lover, Sharon declares, was "horrible." When she expressed concern at having no word from Sharon for a long time, Sharon's brother quipped sarcastically, "She's probably dead." Sharon's mother drove with David to New York. She waited in the car, while he went up to the apartment. "When I saw David," Sharon recalls, "I said to myself, 'My god, what's he doing here?' There were five of us sharing a one-bedroom apartment—Sharon, her lover Denise, a friend Joey, Joey's lover, and a roomer. All worked nights and were just getting up. Dishes were piled high in the kitchen sink. Sharon called Denise out to meet her brother. "David," Sharon recounts, "behaved like a saint. He hadn't known until that moment that I was a lesbian. He didn't bat an eye. He shook her hand and said, 'Nice to meet you.' "

Sharon's mother insisted upon coming upstairs. "No matter how disgusting it may appear," she declared, "it will ease my mind." Sharon telephoned to report that she would not be at work and went out to dinner with her mother and brother. David was angry. "Don't you think," he declared, "that one of you could have told me over the years? I'm mad because you should have known I would love you anyway."

After this experience, Sharon and Denise began having dinner with David and his girlfriend and with Sharon's mother and her friend. Sometimes they all went out together.

Sharon associates her gay activism with her sense of her vulnerability as a Jew. During the Holocaust, she declares, "people who were terrorized still raised their hands and said, 'Yes, I'm Jewish.' In my family the Holocaust meant that you always had to stand up for what you believed in. I am a Jew, and nobody's going to take that away from me. I am a lesbian, and nobody's going to take that away from me."

ALAN KLEIN*

Alan Klein was born in the New York City borough of Queens in 1964, the son of a short-tempered father who worked long hours as a certified public accountant and of a prototypical "Jewish mother." ("Some people," he remarks, "call that nurturing, some people call it 'nudging.' ") With his sister, three years his junior, Alan constantly quarreled. Indeed, Alan recalls, there were always tensions within the family, "inevitable," says Alan, "when there is a Jewish mother." Only as young adults did Alan and his sister learn that both parents found their marriage stifling. They divorced while Alan was in college.

"Nevertheless," Alan admits, "Reform Judaism is supportive, and I was brought up to be caring and thoughtful and responsive to issues. Our history, including the Holocaust, is meaningful to me and it makes me critical of anti-gay Jewish rhetoric."

*A founder of Queer Nation (see Chapter 14).

Alan's father insisted that Alan join the basketball and baseball Little Leagues and served as coach and commissioner in one of the leagues. He was an ideal coach for a Little League team, Alan declares. He shielded players from their fathers when their participation was disappointing. He neither exhibited favoritism toward Alan nor exercised special pressure on him.

At a summer camp Alan attended when he was in the sixth grade, some of the boys engaged in mutual masturbation. Once a counselor took down Alan's pants and began to fondle him. Alan resisted. "I felt as though I was being pushed into something I wasn't ready for," he recalls. The next summer, Alan agreed when another camper suggested mutual masturbation. He was embarrassed, however, when the camper told another boy what they were doing. The other boy exclaimed, "Alan, do you do that?" Alan grudgingly admitted that he did. The boy suggested they go outside. He pulled down Alan's pants, got down on his knees, and approached Alan's penis with his mouth. Shocked, Alan asked what he was doing. "A blow job," he replied. "You're not really going to do that, are you?" Alan exclaimed. "Oh no," he replied, "I just wanted to see what you'd say."

When Alan was in eighth and ninth grades, he "fooled around" with a classmate who came to Alan's house to use the swimming pool. After a while, Alan relates, they started using hand lotion on each other, and finally reached blow jobs. They never kissed and never came. Alan enjoyed the activity immensely. In high school Alan had girlfriends and tried to have sex with one of them, but she became anxious. That was as close as he ever came to having intercourse with a woman.

The summer before he entered college, Alan served as a counselor on a European tour. On bus trips Mike, one of the students in his charge, would sit next to him and rest his head on Alan's lap. Alan did not know how to deal with him. When the group arrived in Rome, Mike invited Alan to a party in his hotel room. Alan knocked on the door. Receiving no answer, he entered. The room was dark. Mike motioned Alan to come into bed. He pulled off Alan's T-shirt. They caressed each other. "All of a sudden," Alan recounts, "I saw his face approaching mine. I drew back at first but then moved forward, and we kissed." It was Alan's first kiss. "This is it!" he exclaimed to himself. Mike and Alan spent the remainder of the six weeks together.

Alan still thought of himself as a straight guy who liked having sex with me. "I didn't know what gay was," Alan declares. At Ithaca College, however, it became obvious to him that the world would not accept a straight guy who liked to have sex with men, "especially a rabble-rouser like me, who was not accustomed to being treated badly by anyone, except my mother. I came to realize that I had to give a little and that society had to give a little." Nevertheless, when he entered a brief relationship with a young man named Steve, his mother challenged him, "Are you gay?" Alan was taken aback. He replied that he was having a relationship with Steve. Yes, he was gay. His mother wanted to know how long he had known he was gay and whether he was sure.

In his junior year Alan met Karl. Nineteen, two years younger than Alan, Karl had had no sexual experience. They remained together for seven "fabulous" years.

Alan believes that he had a less anxious experience in accepting his sexual orientation than most people his age. On the other hand, whereas in the 1990s many sixteen- or seventeen-year-old gays do not give being gay a second thought, he did not come out to himself until his sophomore year in college. It was not until a year later that he became aware of what it meant to be gay. "Coming out," Alan declares, "meant first of all coming out to myself, getting to the point where I could say I was gay without feeling a tremor of uneasiness." Only after meeting Karl did Alan develop confidence about his homosexuality.

With Karl, Alan's mother started off on the wrong foot. "Mothers always love me!" Karl exclaimed in astonishment at her hostility. Alan's mother and Karl never got along. Indeed, according to Alan, it took her years to come to terms with his being gay. "I don't know that she has done so fully even now. That is not my concern."

During his last year in college Alan came out to his father during a lunch at a Chinese restaurant. "Our relationship was not good at the time," he declares. "I was unhappy with the way he handled things with my mother during their divorce. I didn't know what his reaction to my coming out would be, but I couldn't hold it in any more." At one point in the meal Alan said that he had something serious to talk to his father about. His father asked whether he was well. Alan replied that his health was fine. "Karl is my lover," he said. "I'm gay." After a moment's silence his father asked how long Alan had known. Alan replied that he had fantasized about men since the first grade. "But you are healthy?" his father asked, concerned at the possibility of HIV infection. Alan said he was. "I want you to know that I love you," his father continued, "and I'm really glad that you've shared this with me. I'm glad that you've let me into your life. Nothing will stand in the way of how I feel about you."

"We hadn't had such a talk in years," Alan declared. "It was the catalyst to making our relationship what it is now. After the divorce he had changed a lot, but I had not appreciated the change. In addition, I had an impression that he was more 'macho' than he actually was. Now I realized that he was a giving and loving human being."

Alan's father and his second wife Barbara accepted Karl as a member of the family. The extra bedroom in their summer home was reserved alternately for Alan's stepsister and her husband and for Alan and Karl. "My father is supportive," Alan declares. "He feels it is important for people to be who they are." His father and Barbara attend meetings at the Lesbian and

Gay Community Center and seem at home there. His father considers himself a political conservative, but, according to Alan, he has come a long way. "He understands what ACT UP is about," Alan says. "He's proud that I was a cofounder of Queer Nation."

Alan's sister found out about him while he was still in college when she read a letter he had left on his desk. "She was a little uneasy at first," Alan declares. Now she marches in the Gay Pride parade with her brother and even accepts invitations to lesbian parties without finding it necessary to explain that she's straight. "I call her an honorary queer," he says.

JAY BLOTCHER*

In 1961 when Jay Blotcher, the grandchild of Nicaraguan immigrants, was one year old, he was adopted by a Jewish couple in Randolph, Massachusetts, a Boston suburb. They later adopted a little girl, three years younger than Jay. His adoptive father, whom Jay describes as "old school," worked as an automobile parts traveling salesman; his mother, a native of New York and better educated than her husband, remained at home as a housewife. Like other Jewish children, Jay remarked, he expected more from his parents than other children. On the other hand, like "typical Jewish parents," he notes, they rarely gave him a pat on the back. If he came home with a B grade, his father would say, "Why didn't you get an A?"

By the age of eight Jay was already aware that he was different. He recalls flirting with a counselor at a swimming pool and feeling an attraction for other boys. By age eleven he began having sexually charged dreams. In junior high school he was embarrassed when he showered with other boys. He was not teased for not liking sports or for being chubby and "maybe slightly effeminate." He did suffer humiliation, however, because of his darker skin. "I was called nigger," he recalls. "I harbored a sense of outrage and got into fights."

When his family drew up a list of guests for his Bar Mitzvah, Jay could offer few names. His mother prodded him, saying, "Come on, isn't there anyone else?" His father said, "He's a loner, leave him alone." Jay thought, "I am a loner? I wasn't quite sure what they meant." In elementary school, Jay did have a friend, another "nerd." During one summer vacation, they started fondling each other, engaging in "kid stuff," which, they assured each other, they would end after their Bar Mitzvahs. In the eighth grade, however, Jay began having sexual experiences with other boys. Although they felt no shame, they knew they had to keep their mouths shut. On the other hand, Jay was popular with the girls because he was not as shy as other boys. "You become friends with girls," he decided; "with boys you have sex."

After his Bar Mitzvah, Jay, who looked older than his age and had "chutz-

*Like Alan Klein, a founder of Queer Nation (see Chapter 14).

pah," began going to the "combat zone" in Boston and having anonymous sex in porno movie theaters. He received a dollar or two for masturbating men. He recalls arriving late for Passover dinner after an experience in a car behind the Boston Public Library. When he was in eleventh grade, a boy started calling him and breathing into the phone. Jay found out that he was doing the same thing to others in the drama club. Once, when the boy came to Jay's house, Jay was annoyed that he wanted nothing more than sex and would not consent to a fuller relationship. Jay was not satisfied with "quickie" experiences, but they were all he could find with other gays in the drama club.

In his freshman year at Syracuse University, Jay had a woman friend stay overnight with him, the first man on the dormitory floor to do so. Though, in fact, they had merely slept together, the others on the floor celebrated and called him "Jay the Stud." On the other hand, on an another occasion someone came into Jay's room and cried, "You'll never believe this. My roommate's gay. I read his diary." Jay warned the roommate. They became friends. When Jay's roommate discovered gay magazines among Jay's things, he announced on the floor that Jay also was gay. Since the others had already come to accept him, they did not reject him outright, but suddenly he became "Jay the homosexual." People came to him and asked what gay sex was like. Some even wanted to experiment with him.

In his sophomore year, Jay had intercourse for the first time with a woman. "She knew I liked guys," he relates, "and introduced me to a friend who was troubled about his sexual orientation. He came over and stayed for two weeks." It was Jay's first relationship that was not just a one-night stand. Jay found himself sleeping with both a man and a woman, sometimes in threesomes. "I was so liberated," he recalls, "I could do anything. Sex became the center of my life. I also became involved in drugs—hallucinogens. My grades dropped."

Jay insists that he has never really suffered from being gay. When he came out to other people, Jay found that they either said that they had long since known or simply remarked, "What does it matter?" Because of his evasiveness, they had thought that he was ashamed of being gay. When Jay began going to bars (his parents had moved to New York), he gave noncommittal answers to his mother's questions about where he had been. Dissatisfied with his replies, she asked directly where he stood. Somewhere in the middle, he replied. "She became skittish," he recalls, "and dropped the subject."

One day Jay showed his mother an article he had written for the gay publication *Christopher Street.* "What are you trying to tell me?" she exclaimed. "Do you expect me to jump for joy?" "I want you to know," he replied, "that I'm going to be working for gay magazines when I move back to New York after graduation."

Obtaining a job on a gay television program, Jay sought unsuccessfully to conceal from his parents the kind of show in which he was involved. "At least get them to pay you," his mother advised. Jay was annoyed by her comment, and for a month they did not talk. In the spring of 1988 Jay was arrested in an ACT UP demonstration, and his picture appeared in *USA Today*. Aware how concerned his parents were that people might find out about him, Jay assured them that association with an AIDS group did not represent evidence of being gay. His mother exclaimed, "Oy, my son the activist!" (Nice Jewish boys don't get arrested, Jay explained.) Nevertheless, his parents felt a grudging pride in his activity. His mother posted the clipping on the refrigerator.

Only after his mother died did Jay come out explicitly to his father. "I guess I knew that," his father remarked, "but you're my son and I love you." "People in New York love me not despite the fact that I'm gay," Jay grumbled, "but because I am an activist and have been involved for so long. It's not a stigma, it's a plus." A year later after undergoing open-heart surgery, Jay's father sent him two clippings, one announcing Reform Judaism's acceptance of gay rabbis and the other describing a gay pride parade in Fort Lauderdale. "It means a lot to me," Jay responded, "that you support me in what I do." "It isn't that you're breaking the law," his father replied, "and you're my son." He gave Jay his mother's wedding ring as a token of full acceptance.

NAOMI LICHTENSTEIN*

As a child, Naomi was as good as her brother in sports. She played games with his friends even though they made fun of her, hitting her and making jokes about her. Large for her age and overweight, she was sure that no one would want her. She was attracted to girls and suspected that she was "queer." At summer camp she heard two disabled girls jeered as "lezzies." The discomfort they endured frightened her. At camp, too, she felt pressured at being with boys at social events. "Once I literally jumped out the window of the recreation room and ran off," she recalls.

In the tenth grade, Naomi underwent a crisis because of her parents' sudden divorce. She had never been close to her mother. As for her father, with whom she went to live, "In his way," she says, "he was fond of me, but I had to do things in order to get his attention. He was not able to say, 'Whatever this child is, I'm going to care for her.' "

During summer vacations in high school and college, Naomi served as a camp counselor. One summer she had particular success in working with blind children. "I gained tremendous self-esteem," she declares, "because I did something well. People liked me and praised me. From the moment I returned home in September I marked off the days until I would go back to camp."

*A staff member at the Lesbian and Gay Anti-Violence Project (see Chapter 9). In 1996, she was working as a clinician in a private institution.

Naomi's brother and sister attended prestigious schools on scholarships. Naomi, however, chose to go to a small college far from home, Rockford College in Illinois. "I was scared about the academics," she relates. "I never thought I was on par with my sister and brother, and I didn't get much support from my parents. My sister was the firstborn and my brother was the boy. I was an afterthought." As "a Sunday school dropout" by the age of nine, it was not until Naomi was a student at Rockford in the heart of the Bible Belt that she discovered her Jewish identity. An African-American fellow student was harassed, and she herself experienced a sense of isolation. "I was nervous walking around," she declares. "I felt that I didn't belong." In addition, in group therapy Naomi became convinced that she might, indeed, be a lesbian. Nevertheless, she was strongly attracted to a young man. Even twenty-four years later, she says, she continues to think about him. At the same time she was troubled by her attraction to Toby, a woman in the town several years older than she. In February 1968, at eighteen, beginning to suffer from what she calls "sexuality headaches," Naomi transferred to State University of New York at Stony Brook, where there were many Jewish students. At least in this regard she felt more at ease. She also discovered that many of the students were experimenting with both drugs and sex. "I was hurting inside," she relates. "I started on marijuana and hashish."

A traveling lesbian-feminist dramatic group presented skits affirming their sexual identity. "Gay and lesbian sex was not talked about until the early 1970s. They opened my eyes," Naomi asserts. "I saw that I was not alone."

After graduating in 1971, Naomi remained at Stony Brook, continuing in group therapy. When a woman on whom Naomi had a crush refused to have sex with her and went off with another woman, Naomi became suicidal, taking the rejection as proof that she was unlovable. A close friend had killed herself after being jilted. Now Naomi was jilted. "At the time that all these things were happening," Naomi relates, "coming out, being jilted, suffering from depression," she went off to Sikkim, where her brother was living with his wife. When a Tibetan tailor asked Naomi to become his second wife, her brother rejected the request. "I actually considered the offer," Naomi recounts. "I thought I was no good for anything else. I was flattered that he asked."

From 1972 to 1975, still unsure about her sexual orientation, Naomi lived a hippie existence in Brooklyn, drinking and drugging, having affairs with women and dating men. She was convinced that until she experienced heterosexual sex she would not know whether she was really a lesbian. When she became pregnant, she realized that sex had to be taken seriously. She underwent an abortion. (Lesbians, Naomi notes, do not like to admit that they have had abortions because it shows that they have had sex with men, but many lesbians, she insists, have sex with men.) After this traumatic experience, Naomi remained exclusively with women in short-term relationships. In the Gay Pride parade in 1978, however, Naomi met Ellen, a friend from

Stony Brook on whom she had once had a crush. They became lovers the following January and remained together thereafter.

Naomi relates her experiences with anti-Semitism to her experiences with homophobia. "In earlier years before I was out as a lesbian I was taunted for being Jewish," she declared. "I was always on guard." She also likens the mounting spate of homophobic violence throughout the United States to what happened to Jews in Germany and to blacks in the South. "It is open season. We live in an extremely violent culture, and no one is doing anything about it."

STEVE QUESTER*

Born in 1963, the elder of two sons of a Protestant chemical engineer and a Jewish schoolteacher, Steve was raised as a Jew in Upper Saddle River, a suburban New Jersey community across the Hudson River from New York. Considering it important to expose her children to a Jewish education, Steve's mother joined a Reformed temple. His father came to the temple as a parent of children in the congregation, but the family also visited Steve's paternal grandparents at Christmastime. It was not until Steve was a young adult that he learned that his parents' marriage had caused a family scandal. His maternal grandmother had been "beside herself," but she came to love her son-in-law. "My brother and I," Steve insists, "always felt completely accepted by both sides of the family." Steve's father died when he was nine, and his mother did not remarry.

As a child Steve rarely encountered anti-Semitism, but he learned about the Holocaust in Hebrew school. "I was educated to see myself as an object of bigotry," he declares. "I was taught that it was my responsibility to oppose bigotry in all forms because of our two-thousand-year history."

In school Steve was a straight-A student with eyeglasses and a dislike of sports, a nerd, he says, even in his name—Herbert Steven Quester. He suffered the opprobrium of being called a sissie. In seventh grade he suddenly realized that it was because he had a crush on the vice president of the class, a popular, handsome football player, that he joined a classmate in tormenting the boy. Steve was not so much troubled at being attracted to boys as at not being attracted to girls. It was all right to be bisexual, he thought, but not to be gay. From the media and from his mother he had gained the impression that gay men were somehow repellent. Once in a barbershop his mother mimicked and made snide comments about a boy with long hair. In fact, she often made such comments.

During heavy petting with a girl in the front seat of a car, Steve realized "in a flash" that he did not want to do what he was doing. Sensing that he was upset, the girl called the next morning. He told her he was gay. She was

*An ACT UP activist (see Chapter 14).

supportive. "I didn't know what to do about being gay," Steve relates. "I was dying to meet someone gay. I even left an anonymous note in a friend's locker."

Steve met his first gay friend during a summer study program in Israel. Upon their return to New York, the friend introduced him to a lesbian student at New York University. She in turn brought him to a gay party. It was there that he came out to himself. After graduating from high school and establishing a relationship with a lover, Steve came out to his mother on a drive back from Cornell, where he was applying for admission. "I simply said to her," Steve recounts, "I'm homosexual." She responded just as simply, "No matter who you are or what you choose, I love you." She admitted that she had had her suspicions since he was in sixth grade. Nevertheless, upon reflection, she wondered aloud what she had done to cause his deviation from the norm. Steve assured her that such self-blame had no basis in reality.

Gradually, Steve relates, his mother adjusted to his situation. When a clerk at the Oscar Wilde gay bookstore in Greenwich Village suggested that she read a book on loving a gay, she replied that she did not need such a book, she already loved a gay man. After attending a convention of Parents of Gays and Lesbians, she sent copies of the organization's literature to relatives.

Steve asked his mother not to say anything to his brother until his brother finished high school, but his brother subsequently insisted that he had known about Steve for several years. When, during a visit to a cousin in Kentucky, Steve was subjected to antigay remarks from the cousin's husband, his mother and brother decided not to have anything more to do with the homophobe. Subsequently, at a family Passover gathering at the home of another cousin, when Steve mentioned that his graduate school advisor and his lover had just adopted a child, the cousin remarked, "That's going too far." "Here he is in his thirties," Steve thought, "with an income in six digits, a house, a wife, and a child. How does he dare to deny *them* what he has!" The cousin insisted that he was not speaking about Steve. "I was different." He said people had to consider the social stigma that the child would suffer. His wife, Steve's mother, and an aunt argued with him. Steve's brother tried to change the subject.

Steve expresses pride at his mother's coming to parties and mingling with his friends. "She is completely free about my being gay," he says.

FRED GOLDHABER, A JEWISH PRESBYTERIAN

Fred's mother had learned to value education from her immigrant parents. She inculcated a similar respect for learning in him. Forced to help to support her family, she did not finish high school. When her parents set as a condition for her marriage to Fred's father, then a struggling law student, that he work in their liquor store, Fred's mother helped him through school by cleaning floors and by working at whatever jobs she could find.

Younger than his only brother by six years, Fred experienced warmth and affection from his parents until he was about seven, when, abruptly, all physical expression of affection ceased. He was confused by the sudden end to hugging and kissing and frequently had outbursts of rage. One day when a friend pelted him with pebbles, Fred picked up a stone and hit him in the forehead. He ran home and hid under the bed, terrified. He promised himself he would never commit any such violent act again.

Although Fred's parents did not keep a kosher house, they did not eat pork or unkosher seafood. One Yom Kippur Fred asked why they did not drive to the synagogue near his grandmother's house. His parents explained that they did not want the neighbors to see them riding on a High Holiday. Fred had the impression that religion was something "you took out of the mothballs and put on once or twice a year for the sake of the neighbors." Fred hated the synagogue services, conducted in Hebrew and unintelligible to him. Nevertheless, Fred was bar mitzvahed and continued to attend synagogue with his parents for a few years thereafter.

In elementary school Fred put together a scrap book on the Holocaust, assembling his material primarily from *Life* magazine articles. "I'll never forget," he declares, "the picture of the little boy with his hands up in front of SS men and the heaps of bones. I know that I am a Jew and that that could be my fate, and I worry when I see anti-Semitism in high places." As he grew older, he became aware that other peoples suffered also.

Overweight, unathletic, and a bookworm, "a nerd," Fred suffered badgering from classmates. He was bewildered when classmates made fun of him and his first girlfriend. One boy even wrote a short story mocking them. On the way to school boys would seize his sneakers or his baseball hat and throw them up on telephone wires. When Fred was twelve or thirteen, his parents sent him to a camp where his brother worked as a counselor. Fred was treated cruelly by the other campers. Packages he received from his parents were rifled. His comic books were stolen or torn. Fred's parents had taught him not to play with himself, not even to look at his genitals, and he was embarrassed when boys played with each other in the showers and when one of his bunk mates insisted upon displaying his erections.

Although he had intimations of his homosexuality as early as eight years of age, Fred dated girls in high school, Jewish girls, and expected to follow his brother's example by marrying a school sweetheart. In his junior year he dated a laboratory assistant. She wore thick glasses and never looked into Fred's eyes. They went out on double dates with an Egyptian friend and his girlfriend. "I thought of the Jews in Egypt," Fred recalls. "This was cool!" His friend's girlfriend liked poetry. She and Fred read to each other and fell in love, or rather, Fred suggests, "in love with love." They never went further than holding hands and staring at each other. Next Fred became friendly with Carol, the accompanist for the chorus, who taught him open-mouthed kissing, but when after rehearsals he dropped her off and continued driving boys to their homes he was happier to be with them.

Fred developed a crush on a handsome boy in the choir. Once, when the boy visited Fred at home, they wrestled. After his friend left, Fred tried to recreate the pleasant erotic experience of the physical contact and had his first orgasm. He was shocked. He thought the semen was pus. He suffered with this secret for months.

Fred saw a television program entitled "The Homosexual" in which a hard hat confided to a fellow worker that he was unable to achieve an erection with his wife. The man told the other workers, who made fun of him, calling him "a queer." In response, the man raped his wife. Fred was struck by the necessity of defending oneself against the charge of homosexuality. Wondering whether the term applied to him, he looked for an answer in books and was not reassured.

Fred's first homosexual experiences proved unsatisfactory. "I wanted affection," Fred declares. "They merely wanted to come." Sometimes, mistaking signals, he made approaches and was roughly rebuffed. An openly gay man in the chorus with a drinking problem embarrassed Fred by coming on to him in front of other people. Fred helped him through a painful withdrawal and then introduced him to two other friends. One night, when Fred's parents were away, the three engaged in a threesome upstairs, while Fred sat downstairs reading the Bible aloud. "I made myself more and more ridiculous to myself and to my friends," Fred admits.

On rare occasions at Brooklyn College, Fred ventured to the gay corridor for quick, furtive encounters. Once frightened by a blunt come-on, Fred ran out of the men's room, leaving his high school and college rings at the sink. "That was typical," says Fred, "wanting but fearing." After graduating from Brooklyn College, Fred developed a friendship with a colleague at the high school where he was teaching. They went on trips together. "If you ever want to hug or hold my hand," Fred declared one day, "I'd like that." To Fred's dismay, the man became enraged. "Are you queer?" he demanded. Thereafter he would not remain alone in the office with Fred. A boy with whom Fred was working on the school yearbook expressed surprise at the teacher's abrupt change in attitude. Distraught, Fred admitted that he was homosexual. "I had to tell somebody," he says. The student said he liked Fred though he felt no attraction to him. "That really struck me," Fred recalls. "Here this kid appreciated me better than the adult, better than I appreciated myself."

Steve Ashkinazy, a college friend and subsequently a teaching colleague, introduced Fred to the gay world. Fred found the bars trashy and repellent. When Steve took him to the Fire House, the gay community center at the time, Fred joined a group sitting in a semicircle at a showing of a horror film. During scary scenes, the men shrieked and grabbed each other in mock terror. "They were having a wonderful time," Fred recalled. "Suddenly the guy next to me grabbed me. I grabbed back." After the showing, a seminary student invited Fred back to his room. "The sex wasn't great," Fred declares, "but it was honest." In the morning he walked Fred to Grand Central Station and gave him a passionate kiss on the train platform, ignoring the stares of passersby. "I had crossed the line," Fred says. "I would never turn back. I was not alone, everything was fine. I had no guilt. Nothing anyone could say to me would hurt me any more."

In 1971 Fred joined Gay Activist Alliance (GAA) committees and developed a circle of gay friends whom he drove home after meetings. One night he found himself alone with Paul, a blue-eyed, red-haired Irishman. They talked until 4 A.M., parked near Paul's house (not in front of it; Paul would not permit that). They admitted their loneliness to each other. The next week at a GAA dance, Paul showed Fred some poems he had written, violent but beautiful, exhibiting, Fred declares, an extraordinary command of language. They agreed to become lovers and drafted a contract in which they promised to be faithful. After being certified as medically dead on a battlefield in Vietnam, Paul had been revived. He saw life as a constant struggle in which happiness was unattainable. "I wanted someone to love me and take care of me," Fred declares. "I couldn't find such a person, so I tried to love and take care of him." He and Paul had sex, anonymous and unsatisfying, three or four times and then never thereafter. For eight years Fred remained sexually abstinent.

One night, driving to the airport to pick up Fred's parents, Fred pressed a reluctant Paul to remove his gay-power and Lambda buttons, fearing to create an incident with his parents. During the ride back Fred's parents described a movie they had seen on the plane, ridiculing a gay character in it. They also related that they were planning to watch the "fegeles" [fairies] in the Halloween parade in Greenwich Village. Paul listened in sullen silence.

The next weekend Fred sat his parents down, declaring that they needed to have a talk. Fred began by mentioning that for many years his father [a lawyer] had sought to introduce him to daughters of clients. He would never again agree, Fred announced, to date a client's daughter, and they would have to abandon their expectation of grandchildren from him. The person they had met the night before, he declared, was his roommate and the person he intended to live with for the rest of his life. "I spoke as gently but as forcefully as I could," Fred recalls, "because they needed to know that what I was saying was not open to discussion. This was simply how things were."

When Fred recounted how hurtful had been their talk about the movie and the parade, his parents listened in silence. As soon as Fred finished speaking, they reacted as he had anticipated, weeping. "Where had they gone wrong?" they exclaimed. To their request that he see a psychiatrist, Fred replied that no psychiatrist could persuade him to love a woman. A psychiatrist might, he admitted, persuade him not to love anyone. What was important was that he was able to love at all, and Paul was the person he had chosen to love. Fred suggested that, rather than looking to blame him or each other, they accept that he had been undergoing a process for a long time and now at last knew who he was. He assured them that he loved them and had not spoken as he had to hurt them. He could not bear lying to them any longer.

As Fred was leaving, his mother declared that she expected him for dinner on Monday night as usual. His father said that Paul would be welcome at the house but not to share a meal. Fred replied that he was glad that Paul would at least be welcome. "We will see where we go from there," he added. At his parent's request, Fred saw the movie *Fiddler on the Roof*. As he watched, he realized that they were trying to show him what harm he was doing to their lives and his own, and he wept throughout the film. As the months went by, Fred and his mother moved closer. Eventually, he was able to speak freely to her. When he confessed that he and Paul were not having sex, she assured him that a celibate life was not healthy and urged him to look for someone else, aware that that someone would be another man.

With Fred's father, reconciliation required more time.

Increasingly, Fred appeared on television in connection with gay political actions. His father would not talk about his activities. "For thirteen years," Fred declares, "I did not know that he even liked me."

In 1983, a student at the Brooklyn high school where Fred was teaching picked him out in a television report of a Christmas concert by the Gay Men's Chorus. Subsequently he accused Fred of making a pass at him. Fred was exonerated, but that evening, in despair, he went to a gay bar. Larry, a black gay man, a computer programmer at Queensboro Junior College, comforted him; and eventually he and Fred became lovers.

When Fred's mother suffered an attack of emphysema followed by a heart attack and lingered in a hospital for five months, Fred spent many hours with his father. For the first time in many years he went to his father's office. On the wall Fred saw plaques and newspaper articles about himself. "I was astonished," Fred declares. "I had no idea that he was paying attention to what I was doing. There were things about me all around the office."

During those months Fred and Larry took a trip to Toronto. Upon their return, Fred showed his mother a scrapbook with pictures of the trip. She looked at the photographs and smiled but advised him not to show the pictures to his father. Nevertheless, Fred left the scrapbook in the room, certain that his father would glance through it. The next week Fred introduced Larry to his parents. His mother responded with a bright smile. "Dad," Fred recalls, "was standoffish. I had warned Larry in advance. We were both scared because we didn't know what fireworks to expect. As we were leaving the hospital, Larry held the door for my father. Thereafter once or twice Dad went to a restaurant with us. He invited the two of us to go to Barney's, his favorite clothing store, to help him pick out some clothes. I was not sure which of two jackets I preferred, but Larry was definite as to his choice. Dad then bought whatever Larry suggested, and suddenly the two of them were good friends. My father, I believe," Fred declares, "loved Larry, and Larry was always looking for a substitute father, his having died when he was eight. We spent a lot of time with my dad while my mother was still alive, and after she died we had dinner with him every Saturday."

In June 1987, abruptly, Fred experienced extreme weakness. He was unable to lift a carton of books at school. He fell down in the street and had to be helped to his feet. Belatedly he learned that in a National Institutes of Health study in which he had participated several years earlier he had tested HIV-positive.

Two years later, after a former lover of Larry's came down with AIDS, Larry, too, was diagnosed as HIV-positive. The infection progressed to a point where Larry, who had reacted with denial to Fred's diagnosis, was at last forced to accept medication. By the fall of 1990 he was immobile and completely dependent upon Fred. Though seriously ill, Larry, formerly a Jehovah's Witness, expressed a desire to be baptized and to go out as a missionary. Fred began to attend Jehovah's Witness services with him. "I thought," he relates, "he's a great guy and if this is his religion, maybe the religion isn't so bad." After members of the church recognized Fred's picture in newspaper and in television reports on the Harvey Milk School, they summoned Fred to appear before a council of elders. At Larry's request, Fred obeyed. "When you lie down with pigs," the elders proclaimed, "you come up smelling like a pig." In response Fred reminded them of the biblical injunction, "Judge not, lest ye be judged."

One day Fred found Larry in tears. "You must tell Fred to leave the apartment," the elders had announced, "and you must give up this kind of life." Fred offered to move to another apartment in the building and to continue to take care of Larry. After some deliberation, Larry asked Fred not to move. Larry grew weaker and required more and more attention, but except for one man who had formerly been gay, none of the Witnesses offered to care for Larry or even came to visit. Members of a nearby Presbyterian congregation, however, took turns in caring for Larry.

One day in October 1990, Larry was unable to raise himself onto the bedpan, and Fred was not strong enough to help him. Rushed to the hospital, Larry sank into a coma. Later that day, at school, Fred received a call that Larry had died. At the hospital, finding attendants wrapping Larry's body, Fred took Larry's Bible and read one of the Psalms.

No Jehovah's Witness attended Larry's funeral.

Fred says that his father had a hard time dealing with Larry's death. He attended the funeral and went to the cemetery. "In many ways," Fred says, "my father's become a hero to me. He has overcome so much prejudice. Lack of contact with other kinds of people led to ignorance. He has turned into a really wonderful person."

Fred continues to attend services at the Presbyterian church and calls himself a Jewish Presbyterian.

STEVE ASHKINAZY, AN ORTHODOX JEW

While his two brothers enjoyed a "normal" childhood and subsequently married, Steve experienced a stormy and stressful childhood and adolescence. From his earliest years, Steve says, he was aware of being different, and he knew that being different was somehow wrong. At four years of age, when a little girl declared she was going to marry her father when she grew up, Steve insisted he was going to marry his father also and felt frustrated at being told that he could not do so. In kindergarten when the teacher went around the room asking each child's favorite color, Steve hesitated to say red, thinking that red was a girl's color. He was careful not to carry books "like a girl" and was constantly on guard with his gestures. He spent so much time alone in his room that his parents and two brothers nicknamed him the hermit. He often cried when he was by himself.

Aware that Steve had problems, his parents dragged him to psychiatrists, but Steve never exposed to therapists his anxiety at being different and his fear of death.

Prematurely sexually aware, in fourth grade Steve was fascinated by illustrations of naked gods in a book on Greek mythology and was already staring at other boys and even fondling them. At twelve he orchestrated situations to wrestle with boys in their underwear. By then, too, he was masturbating obsessively. He felt great relief upon learning in biology class that semen was constantly being renewed. At fourteen he developed crushes on his best friend, on other boys, and on his teachers. He was pained when he saw other gay boys mocked and mistreated. In gym the teacher forced a heavy effeminate boy to run and then joked about how his breasts bobbed up and down. In a health-and-hygiene class, the teacher ridiculed an effeminate boy who dyed his hair, calling him to the front of the class and sneering at him. The boy dropped out of school. "I think about him often," Steve declares, "because now I work with kids who undergo similar humiliations."

In a newspaper Steve read about a campaign to rid Times Square of drug addicts, prostitutes, and homosexuals. He resolved to go there before all the homosexuals were chased away. Never having traveled to Manhattan by himself, he was very nervous. At Thirty-fourth Street, the subway station before Times Square, he began to wonder how he would identify a homosexual and what he would do if he met one. Before he got off the train, a man approached him. Steve accepted his invitation, though he did not find the man attractive. "I had waited so long," Steve recalls, "that I wasn't going to say no to the first person who came over to me." On the way home, however, Steve was sure that everyone on the train was staring at him, aware of what he had done. Three days later Steve went back to Times Square, and thereafter for several years he returned at least twice a week. All this time, by offering credible excuses, Steve kept his mother from being suspicious. By the time he was an upperclassman in high school, his family had become accustomed to his being "busy at school."

The years on Times Square Steve remembers as being "an incredible combination of sleaze and glamor in the hunt for momentary affection." His success in seducing older men added to his self-esteem. "One time," he recounts, "I might go to an SRO [a single-room-occupancy hotel room], and another time to a penthouse." Men took him to the opera and to fancy restaurants. Some insisted upon giving him money, suspicious of his motives if he refused. For all his promiscuity, Steve never came down with a venereal disease. He wonders that he has remained HIV-negative.

Steve made advances to teachers and slept with three of them in high school. At Brooklyn College he slept with several more. He spent a summer with a professor who directed an opera festival. At college he joined an underground gay clique that met in a corridor outside a men's room, a favorite cruising spot. With this group, Steve says, he had his first sense of an openly gay society.

At college Steve was completely apolitical. While his friends were participating in anti-Vietnam War actions and in a general student strike protesting the Kent State incident, which resulted in the cancellation of classes during the last three weeks of the term, Steve remained aloof. "I saw political issues as having nothing to do with me. I was the perpetual outsider." On the other hand, Steve became involved in dramatics and began to support himself with jobs at theaters. After graduation he continued earning a good income as a set and costume designer, competing with people much older and much more experienced than he.

Steve's parents sent him to Europe as a graduation present. On the trip Steve discovered that he belonged to an international gay fraternity. "I have always found," Steve declares, "that sex is one of the easiest things to find in the world. It's on everybody's mind. When people say they can't find sex, I assume they're either afraid or really don't want it."

After returning from Europe, Steve, who had previously kept aloof from the gay community, began to frequent the Community Fire House. He fell "head over heels" for one of the leaders at the center, a man in his fifties. Since the man set total openness as a condition for a relationship, Steve was compelled to come out to his parents. Apart from his father's occasional disparaging remarks about "queers," Steve's only recollection of talk about gays at home was of conversations after his parents' annual attendance at a transvestite show. Once his mother complained at finding herself in the ladies room with "fairies." "I didn't quite understand why they laughed about the entertainers," Steve recalls, "but I knew that somehow I had a vested interest in the event." Now convinced that his macho father would find it impossible to adjust to his "shameful" confession, Steve came out to his mother first. He asked her to set a time when they could have a serious talk. Sitting down in her bedroom, Steve had difficulty in getting the words out, "I want you to know that I am homosexual," he said at last. She began to cry and to blame herself for failing as a parent. She insisted that he had no reason to make this confession except to hurt her, and she demanded that he say nothing to his father or to his brothers. For weeks thereafter she came repeatedly into his room and cried. She still loved him, she declared, even as she would have loved him if he had committed a murder. She had some savings concealed even from his father that she wanted him to use to pay for a cure through psychiatry.

One evening, realizing that Steve was not going to repent or to undergo a "cure," Steve's mother summoned him into her bedroom. While Steve stood by in silence, she appealed to his father to set him to rights. "My father," Steve says, "is a nice and generous but not a thoughtful man." He listened. "I don't know what you want me to say," he declared at last, "or how you want me to react. I don't want to say anything foolish. Let me think about it, and let's talk about it another time soon." At the subsequent conversation, Steve's father, his mind poisoned in the meantime by Steve's mother, announced, "This is craziness, you don't know what you're getting into. Don't you want to marry and have children? We have given you an example of a good family life. Let's send you to a psychiatrist."

Steve's parents informed his brothers about Steve's "shame," and during a tense year Steve braved the family's hostility by persisting in coming home on weekends. Somehow the family learned that he had been arrested at a demonstration. At the arraignment, he discovered his parents and brothers assembled in the courtroom. "It was my first arrest," Steve relates, "and I felt exhilarated, but my family were horrified to learn that I was not only 'sick' but also a criminal." Driving home after the hearing, they exclaimed, "This is what it has come to!" "They were not prepared," Steve realized, "to accept that I was proud of being arrested. They expected that it would be the shock that they thought I needed."

Although, from then on, Steve, his parents and his brothers could not be in the same room without screaming at each other, Steve still went home on visits. It hurt him when his older brother announced that Steve could no longer play with his nephews and nieces. His younger brother said that the very thought of Steve's sex life made him want to throw up. One time, screaming insults, he drove a friend of Steve's out of the house.

The experience of living and talking through a crisis was unprecedented in Steve's family. "But gradually," Steve says, "they began to see that I was still the same person I had always been. They loved me, and their love made a resolution possible. They needed time to get over years of misinformation and misconceptions and prejudice." There were times, Steve relates, "when I regretted my continuing to go home to face the family's hostility, but in retrospect I am glad I did. I relate my experience to young people who are about to come out, to let them know that the pain can be temporary, that you need to be patient."

After a year, Steve declares, the atmosphere in the family changed absolutely. Steve was once again permitted to play with his nieces and nephews, and his friends were once again welcome at his parents' home. The family came to the gay restaurant in which Steve held part ownership. His mother even began cutting out articles on gay rights and sending them to him. She called whenever she saw something that she thought of interest to him and was upset when a story about the Harvey Milk School in the *New York Times Magazine* failed to mention that he was the school's director. Steve began to take her to gay affairs. She even attended a dinner of Parents of Gays and Lesbians.

Eventually, family members began to employ Steve as a go-between in periods of tension. "My mother will call me," Steve says, "and ask me to talk to my brother because he's doing something crazy. I have gone from being the outcast," Steve declares, "to being the kingpin of the family. I hold the family together."

While struggling in high school and college with problems associated with his gay identity, Steve lost all sense of his Jewish identity. Steve's family attended synagogue on the High Holidays and had their sons bar mitzvahed. His mother related how she experienced anti-Semitism while visiting his father at an army base down South during World War II. She became friendly with other wives, but when they found out that she was Jewish they would have nothing more to do with her. On the other hand, Steve does not recall any discussion of the Holocaust or of Israel, although his family made a contribution toward the planting of commemorative trees in Israel.

After he became a gay activist, Steve was struck by the fact that no one with whom he associated was Jewish. All his Jewish acquaintances he knew from years earlier. In fact, if anyone referred to him as Jewish, he became defensive. When he invited old friends to meet his WASP lover, he asked them not to be "too Jewish." He outraged his family by refusing to come home for the Passover celebration.

Steve frequently spoke before gay organizations, especially religious groups, but he never seemed able to fit the gay synagogue into his schedule. In 1977, on a whim, he decided to stop by for Friday night services. "I looked out on the sea of Jews wearing yarmulkes and praying in Hebrew," he relates, "singing melodies at least slightly familiar to me. I was so overwhelmed by a feeling of belonging and of coming home that I cried." He wondered at the paradox of his working in programs to help people struggling to come out as gays while suppressing his own Jewish identity. He became an active member of the congregation and participated in demonstrations and fundraising drives in support of Israel. His family were delighted that he was becoming a Jew again.

In 1979 Steve attended an international lesbian and gay conference in Israel. "I had no desire to visit Israel," he declares. "There were so many important places in the world that I had not yet seen." In order not to waste time on the trip, he arranged a three-day stopover in Athens. In touring Israel with a gay guide, however, Steve was impressed with how much everyone else in the group knew about the country. "Although I had learned to be proud of my Jewish identity," he says, "I had no knowledge of what it was to be a Jew." Returning home, he set himself a regimen for a year to learn something about Jewish history, law, and identity. At a gay demonstration against the movie *Cruising,* he wore a yarmulke (skullcap). "It wasn't a religious statement," he insists. "It was an identity statement." In a fracas with the police, an Irish cop pulled off his yarmulke and beat him with his club. During his two weeks in a hospital, Steve began his Jewish studies. He came to believe that to be a Jew, one had to be an Orthodox Jew. "I will never do justice in trying to explain why I believe this to be so," he admitted. "Jewish law is a binding obligation. Jews are supposed to keep kosher and observe the sabbath. I have done that for twelve years. It isn't just that the rituals enrich my life. It's what they're part of, an entire orientation, seeing my life in a context of an eternal picture."

In one sense, Steve declares, his orthodox religion did not change his life. "I have always been ethical," he insists. "Now I have more understanding of why and how I do things." On the other hand, he admits that obedience to the rituals inhibits his social life. He is not free Friday nights or Saturdays. He will not eat in nonkosher restaurants. He does not drink alcohol in bars.

Steve had spent years wondering what life was all about, whether he was seizing all that there was to be had in life. In Orthodox Judaism, he declares, he found answers to these profound questions. On the other hand, with his dedication to Orthodox ritual, Steve once again became an outsider and resumed some of the isolation he experienced as a child.

JOYCE HUNTER, BLACK AND JEWISH

"I see myself as biracial," declares Joyce Hunter, one of the founders of the Hetrick Martin Institute, and, indeed, during her life she has experienced the pain of both racism and anti-Semitism.

Joyce's maternal Orthodox Jewish grandparents, immigrants from Lithuania or Byelorus, sat shiva (the ceremony of mourning for the dead) when Joyce's sixteen-year-old mother declared her intention to marry a seventeen-year-old black high school classmate. Joyce was born in 1939 in a home for unwed mothers. Her grandfather never acknowledged her as his grandchild. Two years later, after her parents married, Joyce's brother was born. He was followed by six other children. At the insistence of Joyce's grandmother, all the children were brought up as Jews.

Joyce does not recall what happened in her life before age five. With her mother ill with hepatitis and her father away in the navy, she and her three-year-old brother were placed in the Orthodox orphanage in a Brooklyn shore community. (They were subsequently joined by a younger sister, Arlene.) The other children at the orphanage noted her difference as a black Jew, and some of them taunted her as not being really Jewish. The staff intervened to protect her. "We don't call people names here," staff members insisted. "We're all in this together." Learning that, according to rabbinical law, membership in the Jewish people depends upon the mother's origin, Joyce silenced her tormenters by retorting, "My mother is a Jew and that makes me Jewish."

At the public elementary school to which the orphans were bused, Joyce fought with gentile children when they called her names. Her hair was different. She had a dark complexion. She was called "a mulatto" or jeered at as a "high-yellow Jew." Joyce felt an identification with a black girl in one of her classes. The girl was not badly treated, Joyce recalls, but certainly suffered isolation. She herself, she thought, was "neither here nor there. I wasn't white enough, I wasn't black enough."

Joyce attended Hebrew school every day and synagogue services on Friday night and Saturday morning. "Religion was an integral part of my being," she says. "It was very important to me. It gave me a foundation, a structure. I was brought up as an Orthodox Jew, and I remain proud of being Jewish. It is my religion and my heritage. It has a lot to do with who I am now. We were never taught as Jews to dislike other people because of their color or religion. They should have taught me a little more about my black identity and culture, but they weren't capable of doing so."

From 1945 until 1954 the orphanage welcomed children from displaced-persons camps in Europe, survivors of the Holocaust. "They brought," Joyce recalls, "a tremendous impact as to what it meant to be a Jew and the suffering that Jews undergo." She was profoundly moved by *The Diary of Anne Frank.* "Being a Jew," she realized, "meant that you had to fight for survival. I understand that also from being black in this country."

For the first five years at the orphanage Joyce sat at the gate on Sundays, waiting in vain for visitors. Then her mother began to come occasionally along with Joyce's grandmother and an aunt. On rare occasions when her mother took her to visit her grandparents, her grandfather would not speak to her. (Contrary to her parents' often repeated contention, Joyce is convinced that her grandfather was upset because her father was not Jewish, not because he was black.) Neither Joyce's mother, grandmother, or aunt ever mentioned her father. Until she was about twelve, Joyce never asked about him. Then, suddenly, seven years after she had last seen him, her father began accompanying her mother on visits. Weekends, Joyce and her younger brother and sister were allowed to visit their parents; and when Joyce was fifteen, the three of them left the orphanage. "It was a traumatic day when our parents came for us," she recounts. She was scared because she was going home with comparative strangers. Besides, on the weekend visits, she had seen that her father had a drinking problem. The more he drank, the more abusive he became.

At the public-housing project apartment, Joyce found an additional four siblings awaiting her. With her mother away at work, she undertook their upbringing. Eventually, three, those with darker complexions (so Joyce's mother later explained), were placed in foster care. At the apartment her father continued to abuse her. "He beat me one time," she relates, "when I tried to get away from him. My mother took me to a hospital. She knew that he picked on me. She never understood why we were always fighting."

"I don't know why even now I hesitate to talk about my father's abuse," she declared, hesitating in her account. "Maybe it's because I felt so betrayed by somebody I really wanted to be part of my life."

The trauma from the incest was coupled with Joyce's conflicts about her lesbianism. ("I believe there is no correlation between sexual abuse and sexual orientation," Joyce cautions.) As early as ten years of age, Joyce was aware that she was more attracted to girls than to boys. She had no one to turn to for reassurance about her "problem." The staff at the Orthodox orphanage was puritanical. They taped the mouths of children who used profanity and ordered them to stand in a closet. Although the children engaged in sexual experimentation and some of the staff members sexually abused their charges, sex was never talked about. In seventh grade Joyce began to suffer criticism as a tomboy. Staff people at the orphanage tried to put her in dresses. "Now you're getting ready for high school," they insisted. "You have to change the way you dress." Joyce's association with religion, her source of stability, became problematic, she says, as she became aware of her lesbianism. "It was not an easy childhood," she remarks.

In the housing project, Joyce had boyfriends, some black and some white. The 1950s, Joyce notes, were less sexually permissive than the succeeding decades, and she was able to avoid having sexual relations with the boys she knew. On the other hand, she was called "high-yellow Jew" by the blacks and "nigger Jew" by the whites. "It was good to be neither in those days," Joyce recounts.

Joyce heard faggot remarks in the neighborhood, and in high school for the first time she encountered the word "lezzie." She did not dare tell her best friend that she was in love with her. "I was afraid to act on my lesbianism," she recalls, "but I wasn't sure what I was afraid of."

A few months after Joyce moved in with her parents, a social worker asked her if she wanted to return to the orphanage. Joyce, overwhelmed by her father's abuse and her fears about her lesbianism, said that she did want to go back. "She should have pursued my request," Joyce notes in hindsight. "By that time, I was already broken. I didn't see a way out, I didn't think anybody believed me when I spoke about my unhappiness." At a friend's house, Joyce thought about jumping out the window. Her friend came in the room in time to distract her. A few weeks later Joyce again began thinking about hurting herself and locked the door to her room. Her mother forced her way in. Seeing that Joyce was distressed, she took her to the hospital. "I really didn't want to kill myself," Joyce admits. "I wanted to get out of my situation. I told the doctor what was happening," Joyce recounts, "thinking they would take my father away and let me go home. I looked at my behavior as rational in a no-win situation. They let him stay in the house. They hospitalized me."

The first night at the orientation area of the hospital, a converted prison, Joyce, the youngest patient in the institution, shut her door in fear and cried. "It was like something out of a James Cagney movie," Joyce recalls. "The refectory was a tremendous hall, where people slopped food on your tin plate. The food was foul. I refused to eat it and dumped it out of my plate.

Immediately a crowd of staffers pounced on me. They gave me a tranquilizer." The next day on the food line, a young man handed her a package of food and introduced himself. Of Scotch-Irish extraction, Sean was also a teenager at risk for suicide. "Don't ever dump your food again," he warned. He began slipping her food regularly from the staff dining room, where he worked. If she was well behaved for the next thirty days, he assured her, she would be allowed to go to the library, where they would be able to talk. He taught her how to survive, how to smuggle out mail, and what not to do. She felt safe in visiting her family accompanied by Sean, whom she had arranged to meet after they both left the hospital. Sean berated her father for abusing her. He listened in silence.

Upon her release from the hospital, after a brief time at home, Joyce moved in with two women friends in the housing project. When Joyce admitted to one of her roommates that she was becoming attached to her, the woman expressed shock, and Joyce was forced to move. About to enlist in the army, Sean asked Joyce to marry him. She did not love him, but she saw a chance to get away; he was, she says, her first real friend. She followed him to his post in San Francisco. "We should never have married," Joyce declares, "but the good thing was that we have two wonderful children, Debbie and Mark, both now in their thirties, and five grandchildren."

Joyce returned to New York for the birth of her first child and stayed with her mother, by then separated from Joyce's father. Completing his tour of duty, Sean came back east. Joyce's mother fell ill, and Joyce took over the care of her youngest siblings. When Joyce was pregnant with her second child, she fell in love with a neighbor, a married woman with children. ("Most lesbians I knew were married," Joyce remarks. "I knew a lot of married lesbians with relationships with other women, particularly in my age group. People have more options today because more people are out and there is a supportive community.") Since she worked nights and Sean days, Joyce was able to spend time with her neighbor. Weekends they went to lesbian bars. During the two years of this relationship, Sean had no suspicions about her other relationship.

After breaking off with her neighbor, for seven years Joyce continued to lead a double life, constantly forced to invent alibis for absences from home. Introduced to the gay community center at the Fire House, Joyce for the first time saw lesbians in an environment other than a bar. "For me," she declares, "it was like a homecoming; I felt that this was where I belonged." She met people who had lived as lovers for years. She had not known such a life was possible. "Now I wanted to come out of the closet," Joyce recalls. "I couldn't live with the secret any more," she declares. "I felt that I had to come out of the closet in order to live a full life."

When Joyce came out to Sean, he declared he had long been aware that she was a lesbian. He had thought he could change her. (They had never discussed the problem during twelve years of marriage!) Since he had become interested in another woman, he readily agreed to a separation. In 1971, when Joyce was already thirty, she and Sean decided upon what Joyce calls "by anyone's standards, a civilized divorce."

When neighbors began making remarks about her lesbian visitors, Joyce decided she had to have a talk with her children. One day she sat them down. She spoke about sexual differences and told them that she was gay. Some day, she said, she probably would have a woman in her life. After some questions, they said they wanted to go out to play. When Joyce came out to her mother, her mother reacted with exclamations of guilt.

After coming out, Joyce says, she got her life together. "It was nice to be open and frank," she declares. "I felt alive and honest." Obtaining a high school equivalency diploma, she enrolled in college. "I blossomed," she declares. "It was a total liberation. I became a better parent. I was more honest with my kids." There were problems, however. "Kids," Joyce points out, "want their parents to be like everybody else." When they began "acting up" in school, Joyce entered therapy with them. "They got to know who I was," Joyce recounts. "On the other hand, the therapy allowed me to be at ease with them. They saw that mommie could make mistakes and accepted that mommie was different." Nevertheless, they were unhappy that their friends were no longer permitted to visit them, and Joyce was forced to move. At their new home the children found themselves without any friends. They were troubled, too, that their father no longer came to visit them.

Three years after the divorce, Joyce lost custody of her daughter to a family member; while it was a difficult period, Joyce and her daughter remained close.

As a gay activist in college, Joyce received threats on her life. Her son, about to graduate from high school, declared he wanted to go to the same college to protect her. "Please go to the school for other reasons than protecting your mother," Joyce replied. Subsequently, while working at the Hetrick Martin Institute, Joyce received threats not only on her own life but on the lives of her children. "That was scary," Joyce declares.

"I see my children all the time," Joyce says. "I spend weekends with them, do all kinds of family things with them. They are close to Jan, my lover, and I'm close to Jan's three children. I have five grandchildren, she has six; we have eleven grandchildren between us. Our grandchildren like each other.

"Some members of my family had problems with my being a lesbian," Joyce relates. Although some of her siblings still retain rage against their father, "None of us," Joyce declares, "denies our father despite everything. He did love us in his own unhealthy way. He did try to provide for us." Joyce realizes that her parents suffered great hardships at a time when mixed marriages were taboo.

"When I work with kids today," Joyce declares, recalling her own childhood, "I think of what my childhood was like. That is why working with youth today is very important to me."

Chapter Seven

Catholic Gays: "Sinful and Evil"?

Roman Catholic interviewees experienced more intense trauma than other interviewees in coming to grips with their sexuality. As Alan Klein noted, "I never felt any stigma about sex. That was one good thing about growing up in a Jewish family, where there is not as much tension about sex as in Catholic families." Similarly, Sharon Levine noted that her lover, who came from a religious Catholic family, had a guilt problem that she herself had never known. "Her brother," Sharon recounts, "repeatedly reminds her, 'You're born Roman Catholic and you are Roman Catholic. Don't let anybody tell you you're not.' She would love to go to mass, but she doesn't go."

Most of the Catholic interviewees fell away from the Church and experienced only minimal guilt in doing so. "I was upset by Catholic condemnation of other religions," Pete Guardino of the New York Police Department (NYPD), a lapsed Catholic, reported. "As a Protestant, my mother was considered evil, and I couldn't go to her church." Transit police officer Jerry Cox numbered among his relatives a Jesuit priest, a Christian brother, and a nun who dropped out before taking her vows. Like many Irish Catholic youngsters, Jerry had an ambition to become a priest. Discovering girls, he realized that priesthood was not for him. By the time he came out to himself he had drifted away from the Church and carried no burden of sin.

"Catholicism teaches that we're sinful and evil," declares Gerri Wells. "At thirteen or fourteen, I stopped going to church because I felt that I wasn't welcome. That was very painful. The church that talks about spirituality, holiness, and compassion has caused a lot of hatred toward me." "Catholicism was something to overcome, the guilt, the sin," concurred Tom Duane.

"Catholic schools seek to put everyone in a mold. Even before I was aware of being gay, I thought of myself as a bad person. I stopped going to confession at sixteen or seventeen. I was not going to believe in something that said that what I was was wrong. At the point that I decided to have sex with other men, I still had remnants of guilt about sinning." On the other hand, Tom insists that he never lost the social activism he gained from Catholicism as a child.

Guillermo Vasquez attended a Catholic seminary as an adolescent. He repeatedly received absolution for his thoughts and deeds by reciting Hail Marys. Eventually, a priest suggested that since he knew that he was going to repeat his sin he should do ten Hail Marys on his own every Sunday. "It'll save your time and mine," the priest declared. As a gay activist, Guillermo objects to the Church's opposition to the use of condoms. "We at GMHC [Gay Men's Health Crisis, where Guillermo was on the staff] go against the teaching of the Church," he declared. "I see myself as doing good work," he insists, "and not hurting anybody, really doing what Christ asked—to love and help one another."

Ermanno Stingo saw his mother tip a priest to obtain permission for him to receive confirmation before communion so that she would not have to buy him a second set of clothes. In the confession preliminary to communion, when Ermanno admitted that he masturbated (he did not confess to same-sex experiences with his cousin), the priest refused to grant him absolution. Reminded by Ermanno that he had permission to receive confirmation before communion, the priest retreated and assigned him "I don't know how many Our Fathers and Hail Marys." Ermanno wondered that a man should have the right to tell him what was sinful and to absolve him by assigning a few prayers.

TRACY MORGAN

As a fifth grader Tracy Morgan experienced a need for a religious experience and began attending a Catholic church with Maria, her devout best friend. One Easter they spent almost an entire day at the stations of the cross. Not knowing the ritual in taking communion, Tracy mouthed the words with Maria and imitated her as she stuck out her tongue for the wafer. "At that moment," Tracy declares, "I realized that I was doing this without its having any meaning."

Tracy accepted an invitation from Janet, her closest friend in high school, to join her at a religious retreat. During that weekend, Tracy underwent intense indoctrination. "You get no sleep," she relates. "You keep repeating, 'I know Jesus, I love Jesus,' They give you a cross as a sign that you've been through the retreat. In high school people who wore the cross were somehow special." Tracy's religious fervor faded, however, after a few days of catch-up sleep. "I wasn't that interested in the religion," she admits.

For Tracy the ACT UP Stop the Church action at St. Patrick's Cathedral in December 1989 was a positive experience. "To help in planning an action and to go out at 9 A.M. in cold weather with five thousand people screaming in front of the church!" she exclaims. "I hadn't known I had it in me." She was not shocked at the desecration of the Host by one of the demonstrators. "I thought it was wonderful to see a Catholic," she declared, "Take a bold stand and say, 'Sorry. If you refuse to recognize me and my community, why should I recognize you?' " The action, Tracy was convinced, solidified the gay community and brought a lot of people into action. "We have to stop waiting to be recognized," she is convinced, "stop waiting for someone else to tell us we're okay. We'll decide what's screwed up and what's not, what's our way and what's not. The Catholic Church has made me feel guilty about sex."

DENNIS DE LEON

When he was in sixth grade, Dennis relates, "My father informed us all of a sudden that we were Catholics. I hadn't known." Dennis started to go to church and was confirmed. "I took religion very seriously," he recounts. "I prayed a lot. I left a space in my bed for my guardian angel. I hit myself when I had bad thoughts." For a year Dennis attended a parochial school. He recalls seeing a priest pull a boy out of confession, grab him by the collar, and announce, "I don't want to hear any more of this masturbation stuff." Dennis cherished a card with a beautiful image of the Archangel Michael and prayed to the archangel. He even thought of the Church as a vocation. "I have some high school diaries full of religious martyrdom," he relates, "I wanted to be on the cross. I was looking for a cause for which to sacrifice myself."

After high school, developing more self-assurance, Dennis declares, the Church vanished from his life. "I didn't need to hang on the cross any more."

ANDY HUMM

Andy Humm's German Catholic family, he insists, had a less restrictive conception of the Church than many Irish, Italian, or Polish Catholics. In sixth grade at parochial school, however, after his class was told that it was a mortal sin even to have impure thoughts, Andy began going to confession if he so much as lingered over an underwear advertisement in a magazine. The priest would tell him, "If you keep this up, you are going to become a slave to sex." Andy thought, "Oh, my God, what are you putting on me?" He looked at boys and girls who were becoming interested in sex as "horrible people."

When he began to sense that he was different from other boys, Andy decided that he would escape from his problem by entering the priesthood. After a priest refused to give him absolution unless he confessed that same-sex relations were a sin, however, Andy declared to himself, "It's not wrong." As soon as he uttered these words, he recalls, "I knew it wasn't wrong." While at college Andy served on the parish council of a local church and taught at the Sunday school. Upon his coming out publicly, parishioners complained about him to the priest. "What am I to do?" the priest responded. "Get rid of him? Shall I get rid of all the people who commit sins? I don't want you people coming in and whispering about little sins like masturbation," the priest announced. "Hating people, treating people badly—that's what sin is." Andy remained on the parish council.

After graduation, back in New York, Andy was disappointed to discover that not every gay was "into gay liberation." In Dignity, the Catholic gay organization, "Everybody was is the closet." In an election, a group of activists with whom Andy associated himself lost. "We all left Dignity," Andy recounts. "I had had it with the Church. There were bright Jesuits in the group. I learned a lot from them, liberation theology, relating the Gospels to social justice, the obligations of religion to make this a better world. Even when I lost my belief in God, I kept the values of service."

VIRGINIA APUZZO

One of Ginny's first memories is of her grandmother taking her by the hand early in the morning and pulling her off to church, Ginny's feet scarcely touching the ground. Ginny watched as old women in black dresses raced with the priest in reciting the prayers and sang terribly out of tune at the top of their lungs. Born in 1951 in the Bronx, the daughter of working-class Italian-American parents, Ginny and her younger sister were latchkey children who fended for themselves after school. Her mother had always wanted a little girl with curly blond hair and blue eyes, "a little lady," but, Ginny says, "as soon as I was able to walk and talk, it was clear that that was not the direction I was going in. I couldn't stay in frills for thirty seconds without ripping them. She put me in a bra when I was about ten. I was a big girl," Ginny explains. "I'd go out and play stickball with the boys and as soon as I hit the ball, the straps of the bra would rip."

Like many Italian men, Ginny's father wanted a son. He took pleasure in Ginny's boyishness. She frequently fought with the boys in the neighborhood. When her mother called down from the window, she would often find Ginny lying under a pile of boys in a brawl. Parents in the neighborhood forbade their daughters to play with Ginny because they considered her "a bad influence."

Ginny recalls that at gatherings of her extended family, everyone shouted to gain attention. "I learned early," she declares, "how to make myself heard."

Ginny also remembers a lot of violence during her childhood. One time her father found her wrapping cards with pictures of saints in cellophane. He kicked at the cards, scoffing. In retaliation, Ginny ran up to her parents' bedroom and ripped up money he kept in the top drawer of the bureau there. Her father beat and kicked her. In fact, he constantly applied corporal punishment, often in anger. "Somehow I thought it was fair if my mother did it," Ginny recalled, "but not fair if my father did it. It was probably all unfair."

From the age of ten to twelve Ginny was sexually abused by her youngest uncle, who served as her baby-sitter. (Ginny declared that she had never mentioned the experience to anyone before being interviewed for this book.) "At the time," she recounts, "I was embarrassed and ashamed, guilty. I had all the symptoms associated with such an experience, and I have never been able to eradicate the experience from my life, but one goes on living. It was an incident that had to do with that particular person," she declares. "It had no effect on me at school. I don't for a minute think that that experience is the reason why I am a lesbian." In the course of her life, she remarks, she had "enormous feelings of intimacy and warmth toward men" though she never had sexual relations with them. Her uncle subsequently died in a fire. His death caused Ginny's father a lot of pain. That he died such a terrible death, she believes, seems a just punishment. "God does not accept such evil!" she declares.

At ten Ginny said to her best girlfriend, "When we grow up, I want to marry you." To Ginny's surprise the girl expressed shock and broke off their friendship. Subsequently, realizing that attraction to other girls was sinful, Ginny feared that she would never enjoy salvation. Indeed, from the incident with her girlfriend, Ginny declares, she began to grapple with the theological implications of her homosexuality. "My grandmother." Ginny recounted, "went to church out of faith, not intellectually, but when you become aware of who you are as a gay person at the age of ten, you have to develop cunning. You recognize that your survival depends upon your ability to anticipate, to mobilize. I needed to have a mind to survive in the world."

Ginny never mentioned her fears in confession, but one time she asked a nun, "If I had been born with three arms and had learned to use them all well, would God be pleased at my using my extra power?" She was disappointed that the nun was bewildered by the question.

Because many of the girls in the neighborhood were becoming pregnant and being forced to marry, Ginny's parents sent her to the all-girls Cathedral High School. Ginny participated in sports and was a good student, but the nuns were dissatisfied with her because she was not sufficiently ladylike. Ginny felt attracted to fellow students but had no overt sexual experiences. She made trips to Greenwich Village on her own. She liked the atmosphere, but she had no idea where to look for lesbian meeting places. When a classmate came to stay at Ginny's home, however, the two became lovers. One day, after Ginny had already gone off to the State University of New York at New Paltz, her mother discovered a letter the young woman had written to Ginny. She called the girl's family, ordered the girl out of the apartment, and summoned Ginny home. Ginny denied the relationship. In retrospect, she feels guilty at lying to her mother.

After graduating from New Paltz, Ginny obtained a teaching position in Upstate New York, eventually becoming supervisor of social studies in grades K to 12. At the age of twenty-six, however, she left her position and entered a convent. "I had to decide," Ginny relates, "what I would do with the rest of my life as a lesbian, what I would do with the fact of my life." She saw an opportunity to make a deal with an institution. "You take care of me," she recounts, "you relieve me of Con Edison, the A & P, car payments and everything else, and I will do what I can for you, teach and teach well. I will learn and learn well and I will pose for myself the most significant spiritual question in my life—the extent to which redemption is possible for me as a lesbian."

In the convent, Ginny declares, "I thought, I prayed, I worked. I studied theology with distinguished theologians at Manhattan College. It was the time of aggiornamento. Not just John XXIII but the whole Dutch church," Ginny recalls, "was awakening and talking about things that were significant, dealing with the reality of people's lives and the capacity of the Holy Spirit to touch your life. We were part of a movement that was looking at poverty and recognizing that we couldn't live in protective shells."

Ginny obtained her doctorate in the politics of urban education at Fordham University. Simultaneously, wearing a habit, she taught at Cathedral High School, where she developed a course on problems of minorities. After three years, having resolved the problem that had plagued her since she was ten, Ginny was ready to reenter the world. "When I walked out of the convent at twenty-nine," she declares, "all I had was on my back, but I walked out the freest person in the world because I had answered my question."

Ginny considered that her next task was to determine what to do with her new awareness. "I believe that you must always act on your knowledge," Ginny asserts. "I saw that the gay community was shortchanged in every social, economic and political institution. I felt that that injustice had to be addressed."

In 1981 Irene Impellizzeri, the dean of education at Brooklyn College, appointed Ginny to a teaching position, which Ginny held for five years. Although in 1992 she achieved notoriety as one of the most uncompromising opponents of the rainbow curriculum among the members of the Board of Education, Dean Impellizzeri offered full support after Ginny came out on national television along with her black lesbian lover Betty Powell. "Betty and I conducted a course as a team and were cited as master teachers," Ginny notes. Their gay students, Ginny says, were enthusiastic. Other students were puzzled at having a pair of lesbians as teachers. Ginny could never determine whether the hostility she encountered among colleagues was based on homophobia or on resistance to the curricular changes she and Betty were promoting. "I don't walk through the world looking to be aggrieved," Ginny explains. "I do what I have to do to get a job done."

At Brooklyn College Ginny joined the Lesbian Feminist Liberation and the Gay Academic Union, her first gay organizations. "The meetings of the Gay Academic Union were wonderful," she recalls, "hearing about the lesbians in the WAC [Women's Army Corps] during the war and about other aspects of our gay culture that had been hidden from us. I always wanted to become a 'we.' It's very lonely being an 'I.' Sometimes it means becoming a couple, then you long to be part of a tribe. The Academic Union people were the first people of my tribe."

While they were at Brooklyn College, Betty became cochair of the National Gay Task Force, and Ginny became cochair of the Gay Rights National Lobby. Thus they found themselves at the center of the national post-Stonewall coming-out struggles. Neither of them, however, had had experience with gay social life. A housepainter named Sean took them to Marie's Crisis, a gay piano bar in Greenwich Village. "There were all these guys singing, dancing, laughing, having a great time," Ginny recounts. She asked Sean whether there were any similar bars for women. He took them across the street to the Duchess. They had difficulty persuading a big fat bouncer at the door to let Sean come in with them. The bar was dark. Nobody was singing. Nobody talked to them. Everyone glared angrily at Sean. Only after returning several times did Ginny find the kind of support she was looking for. "There were so few places for lesbians to socialize," Ginny declares. "Women had to struggle so hard to find a safe space that they were reluctant to open up to strangers."

Following upon her varied leadership roles in gay organizations, Ginny was appointed to one state official post after another. In the mid-1980s as deputy executive director of the New York State Consumer Protection Board, Ginny promoted investigations of AIDS therapies, pressured pharmaceutical companies to reduce the cost of AZT and pentamidine, and organized community and administration meetings on conditions of insurability, on confidentiality legislation, and on bias-related violence against people infected with the virus. Appointed by Governor Mario M. Cuomo as vice chair of the state AIDS Advisory Council, Ginny assisted in formulating a comprehensive AIDS program for New York State.

In every post, Ginny was an "out" lesbian. People coming into her office (in 1993 Ginny was serving as executive deputy commissioner of the New York State Division of Housing and Community Renewal) saw on the walls pictures of Ginny being arrested at the White House, a letter from the mayor of San Francisco with the message, "We did it," and proclamations from the mayors of Boston and Houston. "I may meet legislators who voted against a bill fifteen years ago," Ginny noted, "and now need something from me. I say, 'You don't remember me, but I testified before the city council on the Gay Rights Bill.' I see the shadow come over their faces. 'Will she hold a grudge?' they wonder. 'I was one of the Independent Democrats,' I may announce at a meeting. 'They just gave me an award.' Then everyone in the room realizes that I am lesbian. It's my way of reaffirming who I am and where I come from. I'm a member of a tribe that has special needs," Ginny declares. "People like to forget the less-comforting things about you. We have to remind them."

At conferences of Dignity, the Catholic gay organization, Ginny has frequently recounted her religious odyssey. "I am a politician," she declares. "I know that institutions by nature are prone to be less than perfect. My relationship to the Church is like my relationship to the Democratic Party. I believe that the Church is a corrupt institution that has brought pain to gay men and gay women. It harms people who demand the right to choose. It closes its eyes to racial minorities. One could and must argue whose church it is. Is it a church of old white men? I separate the Church from the message inherent in my faith. The message summons me to service. We can bring something to the gay community because we are summoned to serve. My religious investigation was directed toward clarifying how to serve, in what context."

Decisive to her understanding of the status of the gay community in the United States, Ginny declares, were her speaking tours throughout the country while cochair of the Gay Rights National Lobby. "Unlike many who held national positions in the gay movement," she recounts, "I did not restrict my travels to the East and West Coasts. I went to Columbus, Cincinnati, Oklahoma City, Tulsa, Selma, and cities in Texas. At every stop I learned how hard it is to be gay in America. It is one thing to sit in the Duchess in Sheridan Square and to talk about our pain living in New York. But go to Birmingham, Denton, Texas, to Binghamton, or to a truck stop in Columbus and you learn about gay America. Sitting in a Metropolitan Community [gay] church in Oklahoma City and watching people standing up to sing hymns in a church that was in danger of being bombed—MCC churches were set on fire in Oklahoma and Texas and even in Denver—I could be very proud of that tribe."

In contrast to Ginny, who matured into a strong, proud, and integrated personality, her sister, ladylike even as a child, accepted the male-supremacist concept that a woman could get married without seeking to obtain a full education. When her husband left her after many years of marriage, she had no skills for making a living. She did not remarry and lived on the edge financially. "She was critical of my behavior when we were children," Ginny declares. "Now, although we love each other, there is a distance between us."

A PROTESTANT CLERGYMAN

DONALD LEMKE, LUTHERAN PASTOR

Don Lemke was born in 1952, the oldest of three children, two brothers and a sister, of a mother of mixed Northern European extraction and a father whose immigrant parents where German settlers in Russia, known in the Dakotas as German Russians. Both Don's parents' families had lived on the land, and they themselves worked a twelve-hundred-acre stock-and-grain farm just north of the North Dakota–South Dakota line. The nearest neighbor was three miles away.

Don's father, a traditional German, expected to be obeyed without argument, but both Don's parents were patient and soft-spoken. Although they did not understand why he thought and acted differently from other boys, they were supportive of almost any decision he made.

"When I arrive home," Don recounts, "my dad cries, and he cries when I leave.

"I was best little boy in the world," Don declares. In the one-room school to which he was driven every day, Don showed himself to be the smartest among the ten or twelve students. At a rural school, he declares, "You learned to get along with people. You might not like the other students, but you had to compromise to get along. Older kids helped younger kids. We helped each other all the time." On the other hand, Don was uncomfortable at being exceptionally heavy, tall for his age, and very awkward. He did not enjoy engaging in rough-and-tumble play and disliked swearing and "dirty" talk, and he was always the last chosen in games. "Almost as far back as I can remember," he recounts, "I preferred the company of girls. I was not at all competitive." Boys called him "sissy," but he decided that names could not hurt him. Only when at the age of twelve or thirteen, when he learned what the epithet meant, was he troubled by the jeering.

"I always felt alone as a child," Don recalls. "I was happier by myself than with people who didn't understand me."

At six or seven, Don was already leafing through the Sears and Montgomery Ward catalogues looking for the advertisements of men's underwear. For an eighth-grade writing project he submitted a paper advocating rights for homosexuals. He does not recall how he came to choose the topic. "Probably from something I read," he declares. "I was aware that that was the direction in which I was moving." He looked in books and articles for information on homosexuality. "What the books said didn't sound right to me," he recounts. "I thought if that's what somebody feels, why is it wrong?"

As early as four or five and until he was fourteen, Don played at celebrating mass at home as though he was priest. "I have always had a sense of the presence of God or the divine in my life," he declares. At the local high school, Don joined the Luther League, a church youth group, and sang in the church choir. He wrote a play recounting the Nativity, which was produced in one church after another in the region. He also served pulpit supply. Religious questions about homosexuality never occurred to him. The subject, he says, was never mentioned in sermons.

From seventh grade through his early years at high school Don had "a sort of girlfriend." He remembers saying to himself when he was with her, "I like holding your hand and taking walks with you, talking to you, going to movies with you, but I never have a sense of anything wonderful." He did not confront any sexual demands. Early sex was not generally practiced, although Don was aware that some students were having sex as early as their freshman year. Some girls disappeared from school for nine months.

Once after a physical education class, a handsome boy came up behind Don and pressed his erection against Don's buttocks. Don experienced a sense of exhilaration. ("Even today when I think of him, I drool," Don declares.) "It was just horseplay," Don explains. "Raging hormones can do amazing things." Neither the boy nor Don ever mentioned the incident.

Don investigated nude male and physical-strength magazines and bought a few, particularly copies of *Physique,* a porn magazine that featured pictures of nearly naked male bodies. Once his parents opened a magazine wrapper and exclaimed, "What is this stuff?" They said nothing more, however. One day while driving with Frank, a high school friend who worked with Don at the local hospital, Frank leafed through the copies of the magazine. Suddenly he opened his fly, took out his penis and ejaculated. He begged Don not to tell anyone about the incident. "What's the big deal?" Don replied. "We're just two guys helping each other to learn about sex. I knew I was lying," Don admits.

Frank began staying overnight at the farm. He and Don slept on a feather tick on the floor. Sometimes they engaged in mutual masturbation. Occasionally, Don performed oral sex on Frank. Once Frank attempted anal sex, but Don resisted. It was frustrating to Don that Frank did not like to kiss.

In his senior year, impelled in part by his relationship with Frank, Don chose as the topic for his senior paper a defense of marriage rights for homosexuals. It was, he recalls, only months after the Stonewall "rebellion," which he had read about in *Time* or *Newsweek*. "My teachers," he declares, "did not agree with my position, but I got an A." Neither the teachers nor his classmates made any connection between the topic of his paper and his own personal life.

Abruptly, Frank and Don had a falling out over some incident at work. At school Frank began to gossip maliciously about Don. "For the rest of my senior year," Don recalls, "my nickname was 'Midnight Cowpie," after the movie, *Midnight Cowboy.* I was miserable." Don told his parents about the jeering he was suffering. For them, he was the good little boy. He was different, they assured him, and the town was too small; there were no people around with whom Don could be comfortable.

"I felt totally alone," Don recalls. He declares that he still experiences twinges in recalling the trauma at Frank's rejection.

Before graduation, Don had a sordid experience with a local Catholic priest with whom he discussed the possibility of his converting to Catholicism. After the rupture with Frank, he became convinced that he could not be a pastor and be gay. "If I were a Roman Catholic priest," Don explained to the priest, "I wouldn't have to worry about women." The priest invited Don to his room and asked what Don liked to do for enjoyment. "Stand on my head and take showers," replied Don flippantly. "Well," remarked the priest, "we can stand on our heads in the shower here, if you like." Don was not attracted to the priest, who was heavyset. "It felt wrong," he declares. The priest subsequently invited Don out to dinner in a further vain effort at seduction. Don had in the meantime found out that the priest had made a pass at a minor, a boy whom Don knew.

During the summer of 1970, on a trip to New York as a delegate from his parish to a Luther League convention, Don developed a crush on a handsome straight companion named Rod, with whom he roomed at the Biltmore Hotel. When they walked to Madison Square Garden for the convention sessions, Don noticed men in tight jeans and realized that they were wearing no underwear. He and Rod were frequently cruised, a new experience for Don. During an excursion to the Palisades amusement park, a man actually grabbed Rod's crotch. "That guy's weird!" Rod exclaimed. "He's probably gay," Don replied. "Why didn't he make a pass at you?" Rod asked. "You're good-looking," Don remarked. "But I'm not that way," Rod insisted.

In the fall of 1970 Don entered Augustana College, a Lutheran institution in Sioux Falls. He was still suffering so sharply from Frank's rejection that he was in no condition to seek another lover. Walking in town, he frequently passed through areas that he later found out were cruising areas, but he was "blissfully unaware that men were so readily available." Serving as a trainer on the gymnastics team, he had the opportunity, he relates, "to perfect my massage skills on the team." In a college psychology course, the question of whether gays were acceptable as pastors was posed, and the response was negative. In a health course he heard homosexuality described as a deviant behavior subject to treatment. "A part of me believed what I heard," Don declares. "I wanted to believe it because I wanted to be like everyone else, to have friends like everyone else."

The next year Don transferred to the University of North Dakota at Grand Forks and entered the fine arts program. He recognized that some of the art, music, and drama majors were gay. When Don's roommate attempted the "I'm drunk, can we have sex?" routine, Don did not understand what his roommate wanted. "I came to this university determined to make an effort to become straight," he explains. Indeed, he sought help at the university counseling center. The counselor assured Don that he was going through a phase. When he urged Don to date, Don made attempts at going out with women.

When he was with a woman, he kept asking himself, "What am I supposed to do? This doesn't feel right." Having worked in a nursing home and then in a hospital, he often saw women naked. He said to himself, "There's nothing here that attracts me."

At length Don found a woman on campus whom he liked, and they maintained a relationship for the next four years. When she hinted that she would like to have sex with him, he countered that premarital sex was not something good Christian boys engaged in. (When Don finally came out to her, she told him that whenever he hugged her she felt that she was being hugged by a friend or a brother instead of a potential lover.)

Don served as a deacon at the Lutheran church on campus and as a production manager for musical activities at a very conservative local Lutheran church. He also joined three campus religious organizations: the ultraconservative Navigators, Inter-Varsity, and Campus Crusade for Christ. At a meeting of a small action group of the Crusade he announced that he was praying daily to receive Jesus and to be healed of his attraction to men. "They promised confidentiality," he declares. "I've always been a naive fool!"

During the summer between his sophomore and junior years, Don attended a religious conference in Dallas, traveling with men from Inter-Varsity and Campus Crusade, on one of whom he had developed a strong crush. In his effort to be a "regular guy," he brought along a copy of *Playboy,* which he offered to lend to the others. "We don't read such magazines," they informed him.

Don took swimming classes so that he could be naked with other men. Occasionally he invited one of them to go out with him or to join him at the dining hall for dinner. One man rebuffed him by announcing that he was straight. Others did not understand what he wanted of them.

Shortly before Don's graduation, at an action meeting of the Campus Crusade, when members were delivering personal testimonies, Don was not permitted to offer his testimony. He was offered no explanation for his exclusion beyond a vague allegation that he was not sufficiently "mature in the Lord." "If I'm not good enough to give my testimony," he assured himself, "then something's wrong here."

Upon graduating from the University of North Dakota in 1964, Don entered the Wartburg Theological Seminary in Dubuque, Iowa. Here he met a number of obviously gay seminarians. One of them lent Don copies of the *Advocate* and other gay publications. "I read them from cover to cover," Don recalls, "and became aware of organized gay activities for the first time." He began to assemble a gay library and displayed his gay literature openly on his bookshelves. "I say to myself," Don remarks, "that I've been out longer than I know I've been out. Before I reached the point where I started telling people outright, I just lived who I was. At that point in my seminary years there was no longer a struggle."

Don's adviser at the seminary, the campus psychiatrist, advised Don to add overtones to his speaking voice and to curb talking with his hands. "People may suspect that you are homosexual," he declared. "You're not, are you?" Don replied prudently that he was not.

During his second year at the seminary, Don noticed a loner named Doug and decided that he was at least "somewhat gay." During Christmas vacation Don and Doug both remained on campus. One evening sitting with a group of men in the TV lounge, Doug expressed a wish for some ice cream. Don went out and bought a half gallon for him. The next day Doug knocked at Don's door and suggested that they go out to dinner together and then to a movie. When they returned to the dormitory, Doug asked, "Are you gay?" "I think so," Don replied. Doug declared that he was bisexual. He liked Don and asked whether Don wanted to spend the night with him. They slept together for several nights until Don left on an assigned excursion to monasteries in Michigan and South Dakota.

Don used the trip to investigate the possibility of his becoming a monk, a possibility he had first thought about back in high school. At the monastery in South Dakota, Brother Michael, upon welcoming him, commented how wonderful Don's lips were and how deep his eyes. Don replied that he felt no attraction for Brother Michael, and the monk apologized for his remarks, explaining that he had drunk too much.

Upon returning from his trip, Don renewed his relationship with Doug. Sex with Doug did not prove entirely satisfactory. Doug displayed little passion, and Don did not feel a strong and positive connection with him. "Doug liked boys more than men," Don recounts, "and women more than boys."

During the summer following his junior year at the seminary, Don attended a clinical pastoral education program in Tacoma, Washington, at which he met Bruce. Bruce admitted that he was gay. In fact, he had a partner. "Well, I'm gay, too," Don declared. "It was the first time I had said it in so many words," Don recounts. "It was a big moment in terms of being able to say it openly and with confidence."

From Tacoma Don traveled to Bethel Park, Pennsylvania, to serve his vicarage in a parish under a very conservative pastor. The pastor was single. His best friend was a organist pastor. (Church organists have a reputation for being gay.) But the pastor claimed not to understand what being gay was all about. Occasionally he would make provocative remarks like, "What do these homosexuals want?" "To be treated like people," Don would respond.

Don had his own apartment and enjoyed considerable freedom. He went to gay bars in Pittsburgh and East Liberty. Receiving a response to a a personal advertisement in the *Advocate,* he drove up to Butler to meet Bill, a social worker and a married man who was just beginning to come out. In Bill, for the first time Don encountered a body type that he found attractive. The two men developed a satisfying emotional and sexual connection. They spent a week together at a seminar on drug and alcohol addiction. "I had a crush on him," Don relates, "and it could have turned into love."

Bill came out to his wife, confessing his relationship with Don. "He made me responsible for the unpleasantness that followed," Don declares. "I wasn't ready to be responsible for someone's coming out."

After Don had an accident in which his car was destroyed, Bill came to the hospital to drive him back to Bethel Park. Some days later, Bill came on a visit. "I wasn't feeling well," Don recalls, "not feeling at all sexual." The experience proved unsatisfying. Bill telephoned subsequently and complained that he felt used and abused. "I didn't want to hurt his feelings any more by saying that I felt the same way," Don declares. "We ended on a bad note." The relationship had lasted about three months.

After finishing at the seminary in June, Don returned home to North Dakota, where he was ordained and assigned his first parish. He also had an experience with gay organizing in establishing a chapter of Lutherans Concerned, which he sought to integrate with Integrity and Dignity, the organizations of Episcopal and Roman Catholic lesbians and gays. Using a pseudonym he agreed to be interviewed by the Minot paper about gay and lesbian issues.

Don did not come out to his parish, but he did come out to one of his pastor friends, who as a result delivered a sermon gratifying to Don on racial, ethnic, and gay and lesbian stereotypes. "People declare," he said, "that all homosexuals are molesters, promiscuous and going to hell, but when my best friend came out to me, I knew that the things we all know aren't necessarily so."

But the big event of the year for Don came with his meeting another Doug, a student at Minot State College, "whom," he says, "to this day I love. I was so happy with him," he recounts, "that I went to Minot every Sunday night and came back on Tuesday, carrying out my parish duties during the rest of the week."

On November 10, 1978, Don recalls the precise date, while driving with his father and mother to visit his grandmother, Don and his mother talked about a seventeen-year-old young woman in Don's parish who had decided that Don was good husband material. Don insisted that a relationship with her was inappropriate. "How so? She's attracted to you," his mother replied, "and you like her." "It doesn't matter if I like her," Don insisted, "it's not appropriate with a girl her age. Besides I'm gay. I don't want a relationship with a woman."

Don's parents reacted with dead silence. Don went on to relate how happy he was in his relationship with Doug.

Later that evening Don's mother came into his room and asked him whether he was sure. He was. "Did we do wrong?" she asked. Don assured her that they had done nothing wrong. He reminded her that he had told her that he was in counseling while in college. "I wanted to find out," he explained, "whether there was something wrong. Now I know that it doesn't matter whether it's wrong or right. I am who I am."

"Are you happy?" asked his mother. "Yes," Don replied.

Nevertheless, for a long time Don's mother continued to ask what she had done wrong and to hope that at some time he would change. When she suggested that he visit a psychiatrist, he replied, "I've already been there."

Don's father said nothing.

Don gave his parents books to read.

Some months later, "out of the blue," Doug broke off the relationship with Don. He could not deal, he declared, with a relationship with a member of the clergy. In fact, a short time earlier, Doug had visited Don in a hospital where Doug's father had died in that month some years earlier. Doug had emotional difficulties, and the association of Don with his father, Don insists, was more than Doug could handle.

"For me," Don recounts, "the rejection represented a repetition of the experience with Frank, but it hit me harder. Doug was more of a person. He had never hurt me before. With Frank, there was always the excuse, 'This is what we do because we're learning about sex.' With Doug, it was, 'This is what we do because we love each other.' " Don declares that he gained a valuable lesson. "I learned," he declares, "what it is to really love someone."

Don informed his parents of his hurt. They came to visit him. His mother asked. "Have you met any nice girls yet?" Don's father looked at her and said, "The question is whether he's met any nice boys yet, or should I say men?" "I understood," Don declares, "that he was telling me that it was all right and that he understood."

Don realized that the parish in which he served was not for him. In the fall of 1979, Don attended the Institute for Advanced Studies of Human Sexuality at San Francisco for training in counseling gays, lesbians, and bisexuals. While at the institute, he had two intense, short-term relationships and became convinced once and for all that sexual attraction without emotional interest was not his way. "I don't go in for one-night stands," he insists. "I say, 'If there's no connection, Herman doesn't stand.' "

Don went on to spend a week in Hawaii to investigate at the university what was one of the best sexuality programs in the United States. Some straight Hawaiian women brought Don to gay bars frequented by Native Hawaiians, where he met warm and wonderful people. Going on to another bar just off the Waikiki beach he walked in on a private party. The people insisted that he remain, and he enjoyed himself. "Those were the first and only times," he declares, "that I have ever felt welcome in a gay bar. People were accepting me not for possible sex but out of friendship."

Returning to his parish in North Dakota, he remained until February of 1980, when he resigned, having served there for a year and a half. He felt empty. He had been rejected by people he loved. He considered that he had failed in his parish.

In August, after serving as an interim pastor at a parish north of Minot, Don accepted a position as a chaplain intern at Memorial Sloan-Kettering

Medical Center in New York. Before leaving North Dakota, he had a short-term relationship with a man who was prepared to move with him. At the last moment, he changed his mind. Don was rejected once again and arrived in the city with low morale.

At Sloan-Kettering, Don did counseling and pulpit supply, preaching and celebrating the liturgy. He joined Lutherans Concerned. A month or two after his arrival, he came out to the clinical group to which he was assigned. His announcement complicated his chaplaincy. His supervisor in the clinical pastoral experience was trying to deal with his alcoholism and to come out of the closet at the same time. "He couldn't deal with my being out," Don relates. At the end of May 1981, instead of remaining to complete his internship, Don resigned.

On November 1, 1981, at a church where he was preaching in a celebration for Lutherans Concerned, Don met an architect who would become his lover. With David, he went to a performance of *Torch Song Trilogy.* He fell sick before they arrived at the theater. "I was scared," he recounts. "Something did not feel right. I was thinking how good it felt to be attracted to someone again, yet I was fearful at the possibility of another traumatic rejection."

During the twelve years they remained together, David subjected Don to psychological abuse. Don continued in the relationship because, he says, "I am a good clergyperson. I kept trying to make the relationship work. I bent over until I was a pretzel. Finally, I started to break."

Don left David in 1993.

From this long relationship, Don gained an important insight. "There are good things and bad things in a relationship," he came to realize, "but you don't have to try to correct all the bad things. You must either live with them, change them if they are in yourself, or get the hell out. With David I was doing all the changing."

Thinking back on his life, Don declares, "In my childhood, I was almost always alone. I had to learn how to develop and maintain intimate relationships. It took some time before I could answer the question, 'What am I really looking for?' "

Don serves as the convener for Lutherans Concerned of Metropolitan New York. In the Lutheran congregation of which he is a part, he has succeeded in pressing for an affirming welcome to lesbians and gays. He volunteers for the hot line at the New York Lesbian and Gay Anti-Violence Project and attends meetings of Parents and Friends of Lesbians and Gays (PFLAG) and appears as a speaker before the group.

"Would it be easier to be straight?" Don asks rhetorically. "Not any more for me. I've found my center. As long as I am true to my center, it's not hard. It's hard being something other than you are."

Don does admit that if he were straight he might find it easier to meet women than it is to meet men as a gay man because there are more women than gay men looking for a good man. It might also be easier for him to work within the church, but, he insists, "I wouldn't be as good at what I do if I were straight." Citing *The Wounded Healer,* a book by Henri Nouwen, a Benedictine monk, Don contends that "only those who have been wounded can reach out and heal the wounds of others."

"During my life," Don declares, "I've touched many people's lives. It's not often that you can have someone tell you that your life has healed their life. But it has happened to me often. As long as I have been able to do that, I am confident that I have lived a life of value."

Part II

COMING OUT TO THE WORLD

"Do you know how many gay men and women I have met across this country," declared Ginny Apuzzo, "who have told me, 'I have been out there on rent issues, in the civil rights struggle, on the picket lines'? We have been engaged in all these struggles. Now it's our turn [to fight for ourselves and our community]."

"You come out a million times," Ginny Apuzzo contends, "in a million different ways and during your entire life." The first stage of this continuous process occurs within one's immediate circle—family, friends, schoolmates, fellow church members, and colleagues at work. Gays do not achieve first-class citizenship for this first stage, for they still confront general social threats to their community such as homophobic legislation or hate campaigns mounted by groups like the Christian Right. The 1969 Stonewall riot in New York's Greenwich Village issued a clarion fight-back call to gays throughout the world. Prior to that outburst of frustration and pent-up rage, gays in New York as well as in the rest of the United States lived a furtive, underground existence, ostracized by the general society. They feared to report homophobic assaults and were often victimized by intimidation and blackmail. "Stonewall," declared Ginny Apuzzo, expressing a general sentiment among gay activists, "galvanized in one convulsion the feeling I had all my life: 'Enough is enough.'" The outburst of militancy unleashed by Stonewall provided the impetus to the mass coming out of lesbians and gays who had previously feared to expose themselves to the world.

Success in the coming out of the community, asserts Ginny Apuzzo, "is measured every day by the number of us who begin to live our lives as who we are. Our success is that you can find me. When I was growing up, I didn't know where to find you. I didn't know where to look." In a broader sense, she says, success is measured according to the level of empowerment of the gay community. "When I can call NYNEX [the New York Telephone Company] in here," declared Ginny (at the time of her first interview, director of the State Consumer Protection Board), "and say, 'What do you mean you won't list GLAAD [Gay and Lesbian Alliance against Defamation] in your telephone book?'; and the guy answers, 'You don't need it in the book.' 'Okay,' I say, 'pick up this phone. Make believe that your daughter is a lesbian and she needs help of a legal nature and you want to call a gay lawyer. You call information. Tell me who you ask for. Do you know there's a Lambda Legal Defense? If you haven't heard of it, how can you find out that it exists?' I handed him the phone to call information. He said, 'Okay, you win.' "

In the 1980s an increasing number of lesbians and gay men became known by running for public office or by being appointed as "out" gays to posts at all levels of municipal and state governments. Often braving overt homophobia, they aggressively voiced the demands of the gay community. Among the interviewees following this path of activism inside the system were the two commissioners Dennis DeLeon and Billy Jones, as well as Bruce of the Crime Victims Board and Liz Garro, a liaison person at a district attorney's office. Others, including Commissioners Ginny Apuzzo and Lance Ringel, Director of Lesbian and Gay Affairs Marjorie Hill and City Councilman Tom Duane, pursued their coming out first through activity in gay organizations and then in public office.

Stonewall also provided impetus to the establishment of well-funded, completely led gay organizations. Indeed, the New York gay community developed the complex network of agencies and organizations—social, cultural, political, legal, medical, and so on—required by a community that represents a sizable city within a city. A number of interviewees worked on the staffs of or as volunteers at gay agencies like the Lesbian and Gay Anti-Violence Project or the Gay Men's Health Crisis. The majority of the interviewees, however, progressed in their coming-out process to active participation in gay mass organizations. The chapters of Part II explore how the early experiences of interviewees determined their particular kind of activism and trace how each achieved maturity through activism. Indeed, the coming-out process, as the experience of almost all the interviewees demonstrates, culminates when gays embrace the struggle against threats to their community as a whole. "In my experience," insisted Alan Klein, a founder of the activist Queer Nation, "a lot of people find that the self-empowerment that comes with political activity is helpful in defining themselves as individuals. As they gain a better sense of self, they're able to fight more effectively. They become inspired with a more realistic sense of values and then will accept nothing that is less than right. Without my awakening in ACT UP and Queer Nation," he went on, "I can't imagine myself being as fulfilled, as aware as I am. I know that being an active member of the gay and lesbian community is right."

Concurring with this view, Steve Machon, a dedicated member of ACT UP, divided the gay community into three categories: "homosexuals," who ignore or deny their association with the general community; "gays," who have come out but do not participate in community activism; and "queers," who dedicate their lives to the struggle for dignity and full civil rights.

The most aggressive mode of exclusion against which the gay community struggles is homophobic violence, and the next chapters explore the history and extent of homophobic violence and the ways the community has mobilized it.

Chapter Eight

Gay Bashing: The Extreme "Exclusion"

"The first day I entered upon my post as deputy director of the State Consumer Protection Board," reported Ginny Apuzzo, "I received a letter in that wonderful European script. 'I was a concentration camp inmate,' my correspondent wrote. '*You* should be in a concentration camp.' If you have lived through a concentration camp," Ginny wondered, "how can you wish another person to undergo the same experience? That is the kind of vicious rancor against gays that explodes into vicious homophobic violence."

Before the Stonewall riot in 1969 evoked a mass upsurge of activism, only a few courageous gays dared to reveal to the people in their immediate environment and certainly not to the world who and what they were. Twenty-five years after Stonewall, homophobic violence persists as a growing threat to the community even in New York City, where gays have achieved a high level of militant organization. Indeed, disregarding State Attorney General Robert Abrams's warning that "Hate crimes directed against lesbians and gay men appear to be the fastest-growing form of bias-related crime in the nation," the New York state legislature, in contrast to legislatures in three neighboring states and in a total of nine other states, repeatedly failed to enact a law imposing stiff penalties on people found guilty of hate crimes, including those based on sexual orientation.

Homophobic violence, including judicial execution of gays, is hardly a twentieth-century phenomenon. As early as the thirteenth century, under church initiative, sodomy was declared illegal in most of Europe, punishable by castration, torture, and death. One theory has it that the term *faggot,* in fact, evolved out of the burning of gay men at the feet of witches or heretics.

In New England, executions of gay men took place as early as 1646, and in New Haven death was decreed nine years later for lesbians as well.

In Europe and the United States, where the nineteenth-century medical conception of homosexuality as a mental illness persisted into the 1970s, "cures" included castration, hysterectomy, lobotomy, drug therapies, and shock treatments. During the 1930s and 1940s, under Nazi persecution gay men (lesbians were overlooked) suffered the most intense homophobic violence in European history. Some fifty thousand were imprisoned in concentration camps, many were subjected to brutal medical experiments, and up to fifteen thousand perished.

During the witch-hunts of the McCarthy era in the United States, gays, singled out as presumptive security risks, were dismissed, often in disgrace, from government agencies. Twenty years later, Anita Bryant, a spokeswoman for the Moral Majority, expanded her national crusade against women's rights activists to include a call for quarantining gays and lesbians. A 1980 change in policy toward homosexuals in the military services resulted in a witch-hunt against gays and lesbians, hundreds of whom received dishonorable discharges. Violence against servicemen and women intensified.

According to a 1987 National Opinion Research Center general social survey, the homophobic views of the Moral Majority reflected those of most Americans. The poll revealed that 82 percent of the population considered homosexuality "always wrong" or "almost always wrong." Hostile respondents fell into three categories: (1) a small number of activists who went out of their way to find homosexuals to assault; (2) opportunists who were not sufficiently motivated to seek out homosexuals to victimize but would assault them as the occasion arose; and (3) the remainder of the 82 percent, who disapproved of homosexuality but not strongly enough to engage in gay bashing.

The messages about homosexuality "that this culture sends out through the media [and] religious and education institutions," explained Gregory Herek, a University of California psychologist who has studied and written extensively on homophobia, "are often intolerant and negative—that this is not an acceptable lifestyle, that it's immoral, criminal, sick." For many homophobes, Herek declared, antigay prejudice is a means to an end—a way to affirm other values. "Hating gays helps people define who they are. A strong negative stand against homosexuals, for example, can make someone feel he's a good fundamentalist Christian."

In a 1988 report a governor's task force on bias-related violence announced that in the spate of bias violence on New York college campuses, "The most severe hostilities are directed at lesbians and gay men." Among teenagers, the report noted, gays and lesbians are "perceived as legitimate targets that can be openly attacked." In New York City, according to "End the Hate," a 1991 report drafted under the supervision of interviewees Dennis de Leon of the New York City Commission on Human Rights and Marjorie Hill of the Mayor's Office for Lesbian and Gay Affairs, acts of homophobic violence registered with the police had nearly tripled during the previous three years, with approximately 75 percent of homophobic assaults going unreported. In addition to suffering epithets and threats, graffiti on doors and windows, arson, mugging and robbery, being spat upon or chased on the street or forced off the road by hostile drivers; respondents to the End the Hate questionnaire reported stabbings, stomping and assault with guns, rocks, bats, broomsticks, bottles, lead pipes, fists, mace, acid, and tire irons. Some had been harassed out of their apartments by superintendents, neighbors, and local teenage gangs or forced out of their jobs by supervisors or co-workers. A sizable number, both men and women, reported being raped, even gang raped; one man had been raped in a subway car in front of other passengers. On-lookers to such attacks, respondents noted, rarely intervened, and police often refused to take action against perpetrators and even jeered at the victims or, worse, engaged in homophobic violence themselves.

"Attacks against gay men," says Melissa Mertz, Director of Victim Services at Bellevue Hospital in New York City, a hospital treating many victims of homophobic assault, "[are] the most heinous and brutal I [have] encountered. They frequently involve torture, cutting, mutilation, and beating, and show the absolute intent to rub out the human being because of his [sexual] preference."*

Kevin Berrill of the National Lesbian and Gay Task Force (NLGTF) set the intensifying wave of homophobic assaults during the 1980s within a national environment. "It should come as no surprise," he declared, "that anti-gay attacks are widespread when [Bush] White House counsel C. Boyden Gray unapologetically uses the word 'fag' in a [November 1990] speech, or when characters in an NBC television comedy ["The Fanelli Boys"] make 'queer' jokes or when rap songs [Audio Two] include lyrics such as 'I hate faggots. They're livin' in the Village like meat on some maggots.' "

The *Anti-Lesbian/Gay Violence in 1995,* a report issued in the spring of 1996 by the National Coalition of Anti-Violence Programs and the New York City Gay and Lesbian Anti-Violence Project, declared: "Using the past as a guide, the nation appears poised on the verge of another surge of violence against gay men, lesbians, bisexuals and transgendered persons." The report continued:

*Quoted by Kevin T. Berrill at a June 1988 National Institute of Mental Health workshop on "Mental Health Aspects of Violence Toward Lesbians and Gay Men: Research Issues and Directions." According to the New York Anti-Violence Project (AVP), gay men undergo a greater level of harassment, physical violence, and intimidation than lesbians. On the other hand, lesbians suffer more verbal harassment by their families and harbor more fear of violence. In addition, violence against lesbians is often difficult to distinguish from general violence against women. AVP records of homophobic assaults for 1989 and 1990 listed 71 percent of the victims as Caucasian, 13 percent as Hispanic, and 12 percent as African American. The latter groups, the AVP report noted, face a higher risk of general violence in their communities. Sixteen percent of AVP clients are heterosexuals attacked because of a misperception of their sexual orientation.

During 1995, the lesbian and gay community was under attack from many sides. The attacks had many faces: statewide and local anti-gay ballot initiatives, federal and state legislative struggles, electoral campaigns, and hate-filled media programs. Together they provided justification and encouragement to those who harassed, intimidated, assaulted and sometimes murdered lesbians and gay men.

Throughout the year the religious political extremists racheted up their anti-gay rhetoric and organizing. Measures to deny civil rights protections for lesbians and gay men were presented to voters in Maine and West Palm Beach. Anti-gay bills were introduced in nearly two dozen statehouses. Montana's State Senate passed a measure to require anyone convicted of violating the state's "deviant sexual conduct" law (which includes homosexual activity) to register with the police. Its sponsor said gay sex was "even worse than a violent sexual act." On the floor of the U.S. House of Representatives, gay men and lesbians were referred to as "homos." In the Senate, Sen. Jesse Helms said that "deliberate, disgusting, revolting conduct" was responsible for AIDS. In all, People for the American Way documented organized anti-gay activity in 43 states, the District of Columbia and Puerto Rico, concluding that "the climate for homosexuals in America is growing *more* hostile, not less."

SHELLEY NEIDERBACH AND THE CRIME VICTIMS COUNSELING SERVICE

Unreported in official statistics are the side effects of homophobic violence, often lasting for years—anxiety and paranoia, reduced self-esteem, self-hatred, inability to display affection to friends, eating disorders, insomnia, nightmares, and dependency, as well as loss of concentration at work or at school. All these traumas Dr. Shelley Neiderbach, an "out" lesbian, a counselor at the Jersey City State College, and former chairperson of the Mental Health Task Force of the National Organization of Victim Assistance, experienced herself as a crime victim. One night in 1975, stopping for a red light near her home in Brooklyn Heights, Shelley found herself looking down the barrel of a gun. While one man ordered her to move to the passenger seat, his partner, entering the rear of the car, forced her to slump down in her seat. Gripping her about the throat, he began beating her about the head with the butt of a gun. During an instant when he removed his arm, Shelley opened the door and rolled out onto the street. To her good fortune, the men drove on.

Within twenty-four hours, both perpetrators, men in their late teens, were captured and subsequently brought to trial. Although the assistant district attorney (ADA) deposed nine felonies, the grand jury brought a charge of mere second-degree assault. It was very hard, the ADA explained, to prove intent to murder. "We know you were assaulted," he declared. "You are in bandages. We have the hospital reports. But we have to follow the New York fifty-stitch rule. You have only forty-three stitches."

Shelley quipped that the ADA would have had a better case if the men had murdered her. "No," replied the ADA, "then we wouldn't have had a witness." With plea bargaining the charge was further reduced to assault one.

Although thirty-five million crimes are reported annually in the United States, and the National Institute of Justice estimates that a twelve-year-old American has an 80 percent chance of being the victim of a serious crime at some point in life, Shelley found that in New York City no agency was equipped to deal with her problems as a crime victim. Psychiatrists working with Vietnam War vets had defined post-traumatic stress disorder (PTSD) as a disease, but mental-health practitioners were not being trained to treat the syndrome among the general population.

In 1979, to fill a need that had not been met for herself, with a group of professional colleagues Shelley founded the Crime Victims Counseling Service. Networking with social service organizations and agencies as well as with the police and district attorneys, she and her colleagues obtained referrals for the crime-victim group therapy they evolved. In 1982, invited by the director of the newly founded New York Lesbian and Gay Anti-Violence Project (AVP) to conduct group therapy sessions with gay crime victims and to train staff members for such work, Shelley investigated both the rationalizations promoting homophobic assault and the characteristics of trauma specific to gay and lesbian crime victims.

Homophobes often denounce gay men for their promiscuity, which Shelley prefers to label "compulsive sexuality." Generally suffering victimization during childhood, Shelley points out, such gay men find it hard to bond with people. Living repressed, anesthetized existences, they feel alive only during the sexual act. "For them it is like drug addiction," says Shelley. "They need a few moments of orgasm to feel ok, and then they have to go out for more."

The effeminate voices of some gay men and the truck drivers' bellow of some lesbians represent, according to Shelley, identification with the oppressor (mom for men, dad for women). The lisp and limp wrist and sashaying and other gross mimicry of females demonstrate the desire of some gay men to get out of their bodies and to be treated as women. For these men, Shelley declares, a violent assault reinforces their effeminacy, which is already in conflict with their bodies.

In general, according to Shelley, victims' internalized histories are pushed to the surface, especially when individuals are victims of bias crime. At crime-victim group therapy sessions, Shelley says:

> We're just dealing with the latest event in our clients' lives. If you are lesbian or gay, you are probably in a mental health crisis even if you have never suffered direct violence. It is very difficult to thrive in our culture without internalizing some of the homophobic surround. . . . When lesbians and gay men are attacked, to the immediate trauma the therapist must add societal/medical/legal/psychiatric/cultural victimization (frequently originating with parental rejection). . . . "Closeted" gays and lesbians experience the attendant subjective anxiety of being found out; for those who are "out," there's "only" the world to contend with. . . . In the event of sustained parental violence, assault by a lover or attack by a stranger and/or selected victimization via

hate crime—the diagnosis with gays is likely to be "PTSD Plus." . . . The observable effects include a high rate of attempted and completed suicide among lesbian and gay youth; higher than average self-medication leading to alcoholism and drug abuse; hyper- or hyposexuality; dysfunctional domestic relationships; lack of trust; despair.

In a bias attack the implication, Shelley declares, is that the victim is deranged, sick, or evil, someone to get off the face of the earth. "Crime is bad enough," declares Shelley, "but when on top of it you're picked out in a bias crime, it's 'Shit, here we go again.' " Crime victims feel ashamed to begin with. "Why did I let this happen to me?" they exclaim. "I must have done something wrong." Such self-denigration and self-rebuke, according to Shelley, are exacerbated among gays and lesbians.

The excessive fear of men among some lesbians, Shelley believes, originates in early childhood abuse. Shelley's father, for example, repeatedly expressed his disappointment at not having a son. To please him, Shelley became a classic tomboy. Upon the birth of her brother, Shelley had to transform herself overnight. "I wasn't physically abused," she admits, "but I did suffer psychological abuse."

A major component of lesbian sexuality, Shelley declares, is a desire for affection rather than for genital sexuality; and for a lesbian who has chosen not to have sex with men at all, rape, a man's forcible entry into her body, vaginally, anally, or orally, is a horror that evokes incalculable rage and humiliation.

For many sociopaths, lesbians are, in effect, saying, "You can't control us because we don't need you. We're happy by ourselves." Assaults on lesbians represent, therefore, according to Shelley, not just a means of punishment but also an expression of control and contempt. The men are essentially announcing: "All you need is a hot beef injection and you'll go straight."

THREE TYPICAL CASES OF GAY-BASHING

Julio Rivera (gay-bashing by homophobic hoodlums)

In the early morning of July 2, 1990, Alan Sack saw Julio Rivera staggering out of the yard of Jackson Heights Public School 69. Rivera was screaming for help. Alan raced toward him. "Julio's blood," he subsequently reported, "was everywhere—his head was full of holes. I bent over and asked if he knew who'd done this to him. He shook his head." Alan called 911. An ambulance rushed Rivera to Elmhurst Hospital, where he died a few hours later.

A handsome, deeply troubled Puerto Rican in his late twenties, Julio worked as a bartender, prostitute, and gigolo. He was just blocks from home when he passed the dark schoolyard known as Valley Alley, a popular gay cruising area also frequented by small-time drug dealers. Attacked, he was stabbed repeatedly and beaten on the head with the claw end of a hammer.

Because cocaine showed up in the autopsy, police labeled the killing as a drug murder and refused to classify it as bias related. Although they pursued the case with a minimal sense of urgency, evidence regarding the perpetrators mounted. A witness reported seeing three white men running from the scene. A month after the murder, a man told the police that a skin head in the schoolyard boasted that he and his friends had killed Rivera. As this witness was known to be a male prostitute, the police ignored his evidence.

The Rivera case roused the gay community to anger as an earlier Bensonhurst racist killing had done among the Afro-American community. Matt Foreman, director of the New York Lesbian and Gay Anti-Violence Project (AVP) noted, however, the contrast between the public outcry at the racially motivated murder of a black man and the silence at the vicious slaying of a gay man. The Queens gay community, previously, according to Alan Sack, "appalled and terrified about coming out," on August 18 rallied to a Julio Rivera Gay and Lesbian Anti-Violence Coalition and conducted a candlelight vigil and the first-ever gay-rights march in the borough. (Jackson Heights, after Greenwich Village, is the second-largest gay community in New York City.) A reward fund of $3,500 was raised. "Now," proclaimed Alan Sack, "we are all realizing there is a certain social and political consciousness to being gay."

"One thing [the Rivera murder] did was put a brown face to gayness in the city," commented Rafael Ruiz-Ayala of the Latino Gay Men of New York City. "There are a lot of people who think that Latino gays are twice the scum of the city. This [crime] has created a new awareness. It acknowledges [we] exist."

To publicize the case and to awaken New Yorkers to the intensifying street war against homosexuals, gay organizations held press conferences. Matt Foreman and other activists met with police and city officials, unsuccessfully lobbying to have the murder classified as bias-related so that additional resources might be assigned to find the perpetrators. In October activists besieged Gracie Mansion, the mayor's residence, to prod Mayor David Dinkins to speak out. At a gay political action meeting at the Waldorf-Astoria, members of the newly organized Queer Nation heckled Dinkins. One of them shouted, "Julio Rivera can't be here tonight because he's dead."

Three days later, three months after the crime, the mayor announced a $10,000 reward for information leading to the conviction of the killers.

On November 13 the police reported the arrest of two twenty-year-old Jackson Heights residents, Daniel Doyle and Eric Brown. Charged with second-degree murder and with possession of deadly weapons, they were held without bail. From Doyle, the son of a former NYPD detective, arrested at Union College in Schenectady, where he was a student, the police obtained both videotaped and written confessions. Brown, the son of a Con Edison engineer and a student at the Art Students League, turned himself in. The arrest of a third perpetrator followed shortly thereafter. Younger but tougher than the other two, Esat (Ed) Bici, eighteen, a high school dropout who lived with his grandmother and worked at odd jobs and wore a shaved scalp and a tattoo with the letters DMS, the initials of the Doc Marten Skinheads, a gang of Queens punks who took their name from a brand of combat boots they favored.

Upon the announcement of the arrests, Matt Foreman declared, "We refused to let [the Rivera case] case die. We kept up the pressure, and if we hadn't, I'm convinced there never would have been an arrest in this case. That's typical of how the police have responded—or failed to respond—to the crime wave against gays and lesbians."

Following a showing of Doyle's videotaped confession at the trial in March 1991, *New York Magazine* commented in its April 8 issue: "Rivera's murder was perhaps the grisliest in a wave of hundreds of assaults against homosexual men and lesbians. . . . With all the marks of a classic gay-bashing—young whites traveling to a homosexual area and using savage weapons to prey upon someone they'd never met—the Rivera murder became a galvanic issue in New York's gay community: not just because of its ugliness but because it remained unsolved for more than four months while police refused to classify it as a bias-motivated attack."

According to Doyle's testimony, the evening of July 1 began with a social gathering at the apartment where Doyle lived with his sister and his parents. At 1:30 A.M., after four hours of beer drinking, Doyle, Eric Brown, and Esat Bici, the last of the revelers, decided to go for a walk. As they left the house, Bici slipped a claw hammer into the waistband of his shorts. Brown took a plumber's wrench and a silver-handled knife from Doyle's kitchen. Brown and Bici proceeded to the gay cruising area called Valley Alley, while Doyle took off for a grocery to buy more beer.

"As I came around the corner," Doyle testified, "I saw Ed, Eric and a third man . . . involved in a scuffle. The man . . . was in a defensive posture. . . . I saw Ed take hold of what appeared to be a carpenter's hammer. I saw Ed swinging the hammer . . . as hard and as fast as he could."

On the videotape Doyle brought his arm down sharply to demonstrate how Bici smashed the hammer into Rivera's skull. (A total of ten blows with the claw end, according to the medical examiner.) Rivera screamed but did not fall. "I went and punched the guy," Doyle continued. "I hit him once or twice with my fist, and then I probably kicked him in the gut." Rivera still did not go down. "I noticed there was blood on the hands of Eric and Ed. . . . Eric had a knife in his hand. . . . I took the knife and I swung it down, and it entered the guy's back. . . . It didn't go all the way down—it just went halfway and stopped. I pulled it back out and looked at it, and I was horrified with myself."

On screen Doyle exhibited no horror at his brutality. He continued impassively: "At the point the gentleman was crouched over. . . . Ed started bludgeoning him with the hammer again. . . . [Eric] pulled from his pant leg a plumber's wrench and swung it up and—the man was bent over—hit him in the facial area. Then Eric dropped the wrench. That's when I started saying, 'Maybe we should leave.' "

In an hour and twenty minutes of videotaped confession and in two written statements, Doyle offered no motive for the crime.

Detective Jorge Sanchez testified that a woman in the neighborhood informed him that the three "disliked homosexuals and that Doyle, in particular, hated faggots." The woman also said that all three belonged to the DMS gang. A DMS member said Doyle had admitted that they had "really beaten up that fag down at the schoolyard," and an eyewitness picked Doyle out of the lineup.

The grand jury returned indictments for second-degree murder.

Ignoring the obstinate resistance of the NYPD, the Queens district attorney denominated the murder a hate crime. Four days after the DA's announcement, the NYPD belatedly adopted the official FBI definition of a hate crime. (For almost a year AVP had been pressing the NYPD to accept the FBI definition of a bias incident as one in which the "offender's actions were motivated, in whole or in part, by bias.")

Matt Foreman wrote in the AVP newsletter:

> As the Julio Rivera murder trial ground on during the last three weeks, I became depressed. We had pressed for the prosecution to be aggressive and forthright about Julio's life—his gayness, his supportive family, his close circle of friends, his cocaine use. Instead, the prosecution stepped past these issues, knowing if they didn't bring them up, technically neither could the defense. But that didn't stop Brown's and Bici's attorneys from asking disgusting and sleazy questions. . . . the innuendo that Julio "got what he deserved" hung in the air like a poisonous gas. . . .
>
> On the last day of testimony, things changed for me. While the medical examiner testified in amazingly understandable and crisp language, pictures of Julio on a slab in the city morgue were shown to the jury. . . . Hammer blows visible on his forehead. Bruises from the pipe wrench running across his cheek. The end of his nose split open. . . .
>
> Even the defendants looked away. . . .
>
> After 16 months of talk and protest and formulating strategy, I'd lost sight of Julio. He'd become a tragic symbol, a rallying cry, an issue. With those pictures, however, he leapt back to life. Just as suddenly, legal technicalities clouding the acts of the defendants fell away. . . . those pictures . . . showed a human being whose life was ended by violent, hate-filled blows. They reminded me that we do this anti-violence work not for a cause or for political reasons but because virulent, senseless bigotry continues to plague each one of us every day.

When Brown was released on bail, three hundred people met at the schoolyard and marched to his apartment house, a few blocks away. They carried placards and chanted, "Shame! Shame!" On Saturday, March 5,

1991, AVP in conjunction with Marjorie Hill, Dennis de Leon, and local lesbian and gay organizations led marches in all five boroughs of the city to protest antilesbian and antigay violence. In Staten Island the marchers commemorated the gay-bashing murder of a mentally disabled local gay man, Jimmy Zappalorti. Speakers proclaimed that Jimmy would still be alive if the state legislature had passed the hate crimes bill.

Transported by buses from Staten Island back to Manhattan, the demonstrators assembled at Third Avenue and St. Mark's Place, site of a brutal antigay slashing, where the violence had been compounded by sluggish police response. At 1 P.M., between four and five hundred demonstrators marched past the Purity Diner in the Park Slope district of Brooklyn and then rallied in front of the Seventy-eighth Precinct to protest police inaction in regard to a violent attack on lesbians at the diner. Dennis de Leon proclaimed, "My lover and I have run from people shouting 'faggot!' I'm not going to run any more."

Of the government officials who addressed the Brooklyn demonstration, only District Attorney Charles Hynes, universally respected as a confirmed defender of civil rights, was not booed. At the reading of a proclamation from Borough President Howard Golden, the demonstrators shouted, "Words, words, words! We want action." After Dennis de Leon read a statement from the mayor, the crowd chanted, "Where is Dave? Where is Dave?"

Doyle, who had testified against his accomplices in return for a promise of a shorter sentence, was convicted of second-degree manslaughter, the other two of first-degree manslaughter (mandating fifteen to twenty-five years' imprisonment).

Tracy Morgan (McCarthyite hounding of lesbian activities)

While other gay demonstrators assembled in December 1990 outside St. Patrick's Cathedral in the second demonstration organized by ACT UP against John Cardinal O'Connor, Tracy Morgan and her lover Heidi Dorow joined the worshipers inside the church. After the service, as they left the cathedral, Tracy had the impression that a hundred cameras were focused on her and her lover, singling them out because they were holding hands. Reporters crowding about them asked what they were doing in the cathedral; Tracy answered, "We were just being ourselves."

The next day Tracy and Heidi's picture appeared on the front pages of the *New York Post, Newsday,* the *Daily News,* and the *New York Times.*

Three days later Tracy and Heidi participated in a Women and HIV conference in Washington, D.C.; they also participated a few days later in demonstration against the Centers for Disease Control in Atlanta.

Two days thereafter they began to receive obscene telephone calls, generally at 3 A.M., increasingly vicious and disquieting.

On January 5, 1991, at an ACT UP strategy brunch, Tracy, a featured speaker, proposed an end to meetings with government agencies. Her remarks evoked sharp opposition. Within days the telephone harassment changed character. "We're forming a new lesbian and gay group," announced one male caller. "Do you want to join? At the end of our meetings, we get kinda wild."

Throughout January, calls, especially hang-up calls, persisted, though with declining frequency.

On February 26, two days after a conference call during which leaders of ACT UP women's caucuses throughout the country voted to impose a six-month moratorium on meetings with government officials in protest of the handling of women's AIDS issues, a man with a West Indian accent called one of the three Brooklyn women's health clinics at which Tracy worked as a counselor and caseworker. He asked whether Tracy and the woman answering his call were lesbians.

What amazed Tracy was how he knew that she was present at that particular clinic on a day she was not scheduled to be there.

The next Sunday, while Tracy and Heidi were sitting on a stoop on Houston Street having a snack, a black man wearing a Pink Panther (a gay defense organization) button, malnourished, very likely homeless, approached and explained that he was from ACT UP San Francisco and in New York for the rally on women and AIDS that afternoon in Tompkins Square park. He asked whether they were going. (They were wearing no ACT UP insignia.)

Tracy knew that no rally had been called that day at Tompkins Square. "I looked at Heidi," she recalls, "and at him and thought, 'Is this really happening?' " This was the kind of guy, she realized, to whom the cops slip ten bucks.

Tracy prepared a memorandum about the hostile calls and the strange event on Houston Street, and Heidi handed out copies at the next ACT UP meeting. After the meeting Tracy spent the night at Heidi's. About 1 A.M., the phone rang. On Heidi's machine they heard the message Tracy had recorded on her own answerphone. Within minutes Jane Auerbach, another activist in the women's caucus, called. Her phone had been ringing since she returned home from the meeting. She was especially upset because her invalid mother had been disturbed.

Three-way phone calls continued almost daily to Heidi, Jane, and Tracy.

All three women reacted with alarm, Heidi especially. One evening the previous summer, when Heidi and a woman friend embraced on a street in Greenwich Village, a young man, one of a group of a dozen young people, approached and shouted, "Lezzie, kiss me, don't kiss her!" When Heidi and her friend attempted to push past him, he punched Heidi in the head. When her friend grabbed him, he punched her, too. The rest of the gang leaped into the melee, and within seconds the women were kicked and punched to the ground. Heidi's friend suffered a concussion. Both women were bruised and in shock. They entered a complaint at the police station to no avail.

In early March, women's ACT UP caucuses throughout the country decided to "zap" a Washington meeting of the National Institute of Health's AIDS Clinical Trials Group. Heidi engaged in a noisy argument with Rebecca Pringle-Smith, a member of the ACT UP Treatment and Data committee and an opponent of militant tactics. "The government has you in the palm of their hand, you're selling us down the river!" Heidi exclaimed. That night Rebecca found on her answering machine the message, "You're selling us down the river." At the next ACT UP meeting she accused Heidi of responsibility for the verbal assault. The heated exchange that followed aggravated the tension between the Treatment and Data people and the women's action group.

One day Rebecca found excrement outside her door. Shots were fired through her window.

Someone painted a swastika on the door of Jane Auerbach's apartment; and one evening when Jane was out walking with her mother, a man screamed, "You fuckin' dyke." As she entered her apartment, she heard the phone ringing. "I'm going to kick your fuckin' dyke ass," snapped a male voice.

At 1 A.M. on a Saturday morning during the women's caucus demonstration in Washington, someone in Boston called the employer of a mother of an activist to say that the woman's daughter, Kerry, one of the few women with AIDS in ACT UP, had died. That afternoon, at an office social event, people expressed shock at seeing Kerry's mother. "How can you be dancing?" they asked. Alarmed, she called Washington. "Mom, I'm fine!" exclaimed the perplexed daughter. That evening Kerry's mother found an anonymous condolence message on her answerphone. Thereafter Kerry herself began receiving calls from a person who screamed when Kerry asked her name.

Viewing her own harassment within the broader context of violence she encountered in her social service work, Tracy quit her job and moved out of her apartment. She informed no one of her new residence. Jane did the same. Calls followed both of them. Tracy obtained an unlisted number. Two days later the calls resumed. Once again Tracy changed her residence. The calls followed her. Jane had the same experience. Heidi, too, continued to suffer telephone harassment.

Jane, a former IV-drug user, found needles in front of her door in packages addressed to her mother. Someone purporting to be from the Lesbian-Gay Community Health Project, no doubt aware that Jane's mother had threatened to order Jane out of the apartment if she resumed her addiction, called to request Jane's social security number, asserting that Jane had been coming in for needles and offering to place her in a drug treatment program.

Reporting their continuing experiences at an ACT UP meeting, Tracy and Jane were listened to in silence. Two weeks later a sheet of paper was found at a meeting, reading, "Attention Jane Auerbach: Why are you following Tracy Morgan and her robot-like girl friend, Heidi Dorow? Life Force [an organization of HIV-positive women and their supporters to which Jane belonged] doesn't want you to do what you're doing. All this stuff about their being harassed is a joke. Watch where the first stone is thrown."

The police declared that they could do nothing to stop the harassment.

Private investigators demanded a $5,000 retainer. A lawyer at the Center for Constitutional Rights characterized the harassment as typical FBI tactics but advised that nothing could be done beyond making an inquiry under the Freedom of Information Act.

"I knew from reading about the Black Panthers," said Tracy, "that nothing stops these people. We might finger one or two infiltrators in ACT UP, but they would send in more.

"We are still under surveillance," Tracy reported almost a year after the harassment commenced. "My phone is tapped. When I talk to people I warn them not to reveal anything over the phone that they would not want the government to hear.

"My mother," says Tracy, "is terrified for me." Tracy insisted that her father be told what was happening despite the fear of aggravating his heart condition. "If somebody calls and says I'm dead, as they did with Kerry in Boston," Tracy argued, "he'll have a heart attack and die, when in fact nothing will have happened to me."

Tracy and Heidi had their fear of violence reinforced one day in April 1991. Going down the steps to a subway station, they were waylaid by four young men. A struggle ensued. The men were arrested. At the trial, the defense lawyers, pointing to the gay friends of the two women in the courtroom, concocted a tale of lesbian lovers engaged in a violent quarrel which the young men had attempted to break up. One of the young men was sentenced to ten days of public service. The others were acquitted.

"The only people in this country," Tracy declares, speculating on the motive for the harassment she was experiencing, "who are visibly active are the lesbians and gays, the only moving targets around. Our activity is considered a threat." Upon the report of controversy between members of the women's caucuses and the ACT UP leadership, some government agency, Tracy believes, saw an opportunity to split the movement. Indeed, such a split did occur in the San Francisco ACT UP.

"Such persecution," Tracy declares, "changes your whole life. I live with a sense of powerlessness that I have never known. What's going to happen? When will this stop? People who are unpolitical and don't participate in any actions think I'm paranoid, but black people, straight or gay, understand immediately." Tracy pointed out that "the gay community is under a lot more of this kind of attack than many people realize."*

* Few ACT UP members had been born at the time of the McCarthyite persecution of nonconformists. Except for surviving victims of that witch-hunt, few Americans find credible the warnings of a possible revival of repression of opponents of official policies or Moral Majority values. In fact, the author of this book was deprived of his passport during the 1950s and was grilled by the House Committee on Un-American Activities. Subsequently, he lost a teaching position at a New York college because of his radical past.

The harassment of gay activists, in the late 1980s and early 1990s almost the only significant force challenging the dominant national ideology, provides a warning that, as has repeatedly been demonstrated in the history of this country, "the price of liberty is eternal vigilance."

Chris Hennelly (police violence against gays)

The incident of blatant homophobic brutality against Chris Hennelly substantiates the admonition from Liz Garro, gay and lesbian liaison person to the district attorney of Kings County (Brooklyn): "We were illegal in New York until a decade ago, and the police still perceive us as outlaws."

The incident had its origin not with any action by Chris Hennelly himself but in one committed by Scott Sensenig.

On February 3, 1991, accompanied by Dolly, a lesbian college friend, and Dolly's lover Chris, Scott went to Dobbs Ferry, a town a short distance north of the New York City, to protest an antiabortion demonstration there. Outraged when Cardinal O'Connor invited the demonstrators to New York for a special blessing and announced plans to organize a national network of Pro-Lifers, Scott urged his friends to join him in spray painting a protest slogan outside the cardinal's residence. "I hoped," Scott explains, "to make a statement anonymously about the cardinal's position on safe sex education and condoms and on homosexuality and reproductive rights."

On February 5, 1991, at two in the morning, just as Scott and Dolly were completing the painting of "O'Connor Spreads Death" outside the door to the cardinal's residence, Chris, their look-out, cried, "A cop!" Scott and Dolly tarried long enough to finish their slogan before taking to their heels. Suddenly they found themselves hemmed in by police and unmarked cars. Demanding to know where they had hidden their paint can, the police stood Dolly and Chris against the wall and threw Scott against a car. They hit him in the face with their fists and poked him and whacked him on the head with their nightsticks. Knocking him to the ground, they kicked him, spat at him and jeered "faggot." When they stood him up again, "I looked them in the eye," Scott recalls, "and said, 'Do you feel better now?' " At this challenge, the cops hurled him to the ground again and resumed their kicking. "Ordinarily they know just how much force to apply," says Scott, "and later they were surprised at the bruises on my face and body. When they beat up blacks, the bruises don't show."

At the station house, officers mocked Dolly and Chris. "We're going to videotape you dykes," they cried, "and jerk off as you have sex." At central booking, in front of other prisoners, the police asked Scott whether he was a "homo." At meal time a guard shouted: "Go to the end of the line, you mother-fucking faggot. There may not be anything left for you." He was called out of the cell three times to be fingerprinted and beaten some more.

Scott's misadventure set off a far more destructive event.

Five days later, at the February 11 meeting of ACT UP, members voted to march that very evening on the Midtown North Police Precinct, the precinct responsible for the manhandling of Scott and his two accomplices.

One of the four marshals appointed at the meeting from among the most dedicated activists and provided with distinctive red armbands was Chris

Hennelly, a twenty-nine-year-old former Franciscan friar. After suffering violence and poverty during childhood, adolescence and early adulthood, Hennelly had at last entered upon a new life. He had established a lasting love relationship and found rewarding employment with a computer consulting firm. Three weeks earlier, as a singer and entertainer in a program he had developed with his lover, Chris had a sold-out show at the El Moro night club. They were scheduled to repeat their show at other clubs. Chris was enjoying satisfaction, too, as an activist. Two months earlier, he had won publicity in the media with an impassioned speech at the Board of Education in which he antagonized the church people present with an account of his disillusionment as a Franciscan friar and with his outspoken support of the distribution of condoms in the public schools.

At the February 11 demonstration Chris's life underwent an abrupt and tragic transformation.

No incident occurred during the march from the assembly point at Times Plaza to the precinct on West Forty-second Street, but arriving at the police station at ten o'clock that evening, the three hundred or so ACT UP marchers discovered police drawn up in ranks outside their headquarters. (ACT UP members assert that plainclothes informants and provocateurs sit in on their meetings. The decision for this demonstration had been made only two hours earlier!) Forming lines in the street, the demonstrators faced the cops. While two photographers from the gay cable television program "Out in the Nineties" and another freelance photographer filmed the event, speakers berated the police for their brutality against Scott and Scott's friends. (Ordinarily, declares veteran ACT UP member Steve Quester, the police remain docile in front of TV cameras. They were not to do so on this occasion.) A demonstrator hurled pink paint onto the street. Some of it spattered the shoes of Deputy Inspector Carl Jonasch, commanding officer of the precinct.

As the demonstration began to disband, the four marshals linked arms to block off the ACT UP marchers from contact with the police. Immediately, as videotapes subsequently revealed, Deputy Inspector Jonasch gave a signal. Fifteen policemen raised their clubs and, smirking, advanced on the demonstrators. They attacked individuals fingered by Jonasch, ACT UP marchers who had been the most vocal during the demonstration. They seized cameras of two of the photographers, arresting one. (Subsequently the police insisted that one of the cameras contained no film.) The third photographer they hurled to the ground and clubbed.

In the assault Deputy Inspector Jonasch grabbed Chris and pushed him to the ground. As Chris fell, a cop struck him on the temple with a two-handed swing of his nightstick. Chris screamed and momentarily blacked out. Later he recalled receiving eight or nine blows to the head and kicks to his back and kidneys. Ignoring his insistent cry that he was a marshal charged with preserving order, the police, Chris subsequently testified in court, "beat me, and I kept begging for mercy! It was like they were playing croquet."

When he attempted to crawl away, they pulled him back by the feet and beat him about the head and the body. Dragging him up the steps into the precinct building, they resumed their bashing. (Three other demonstrators arrested suffered minimal violence and were released without charges.)

Some time after midnight, after booking Chris on charges of disorderly conduct, assault, and resisting arrest, the police called the Emergency Medical Service; and Chris was transported to the emergency room at St. Luke's/ Roosevelt hospital.

Matt Foreman of AVP, a participant in the demonstration, called Katie Doran, gay community liaison at the office of Manhattan District Attorney Robert M. Morgenthau, to ask when Chris would be freed and to arrange that he be provided with asthma medication, which was being denied him. Katie Doran promised to investigate Matt's charge of police brutality.

The next day, accompanied by Matt Foreman and several members of ACT UP, including Suzanne Philipps, a "straight" physician and long-time AIDS activist, and his lover, Chris was transferred to St. Vincent's Hospital, where initial diagnosis showed a cerebral concussion, postconcussive syndrome, multiple blunt head traumas, and injuries to the neck, back, and extremities. The precinct arrest photograph displayed a bruise on Chris's right temple. Pictures taken at St. Vincent's Hospital indicated further injuries to his head and knee and in the kidney area. At a news conference two days later, Dr. Phillips reported that Chris had lost his senses of smell and taste and was experiencing impaired hearing, probably as a result of a severe concussion caused by at least eight billy-club blows to the head. Disoriented, Chris was unable to walk and was suffering classic post-traumatic stress symptoms, which Dr. Phillips declared might prove irreversible.

As weeks passed, Chris began to suffer from blurred vision, dizziness, impaired motor control and coordination, and severe pain in the head, neck, and back. Worse, he experienced fits resembling epileptic seizures and partial paralysis of his right side. He was not able to move from his bed without assistance.

In a letter to Mayor David Dinkins, Matt Foreman demanded an investigation of the actions of Deputy Inspector Jonasch and Jonasch's immediate suspension from duty as well as a review of general police procedures at demonstrations. "It is clear to me," he declared, "that the police charge was ordered to pick off and arrest a few demonstrators in order to intimidate the group and to punish the demonstrators for exercising their rights. The charge came without warning and without provocation on the part of the demonstrators and even though the demonstrators were separated from the police by a line of marshals." Joining Foreman's call for an investigation of the event and of police procedures at demonstrations were State Assemblywoman Deborah Glick, Manhattan Borough President Ruth Messinger, City Council President Andrew Stein, and Councilmember Ronnie Eldridge.

The request was denied.

Katie Doran subsequently insisted that her office "tried to begin an investigation of the charge that [Chris Hennelly] was beaten by the police." She invited Chris to come to the office with his lawyer, promising that nothing he said would be held against him during his forthcoming trial. "He chose not to talk to us," Doran reported. Matt Foreman, she said, agreed to assemble witnesses to meet with the deputy chief of the DA's corruption unit, but the DA demurred at Matt's insistence that he interview the witnesses in advance.

Katie Doran did meet with an ACT UP delegation inquiring about actions the DA's office was planning. Spokesmen for the DA refused to make any statement until evidence and testimony were assembled for evaluation. Doran complained that no one for ACT UP or other gay organizations was providing essential information. "If people want to talk to us," Doran said, "they're welcome to come in."

"We see no reason for dealing with law enforcement officials," responded Matt Foreman, "especially when they are the ones who should be on trial." In fact, while rationalizing their failure to investigate the charge of police brutality, Katie Doran and her colleagues at the Manhattan DA's office vigorously pursued the indictment of Chris Hennelly.

In preparing for his initial trial, Chris recounts, his lawyer warned him that law enforcement officials did not want him exonerated. "You have been involved in the church," his lawyer insisted. "You have been outspoken on many issues." Hennelly was fortunate, however, in having the Honorable Edgar G. Walker as presiding judge at the hearings on the police charges against him. The defense enjoyed an additional advantage in the appointment of the prosecutor, a young assistant district attorney, Stephen LoSquadro, obtuse in argumentation and insolent not only to the defendant but to the court as well. In a judgment dated September 30, 1991, Judge Walker condemned the ADA's behavior during the hearing. "The ADA's responses to the court's inquiries," he declared, "were . . . often evasive and occasionally misleading." The ADA, for example, had charged that the defendant had "deliberately withheld" from the court copies of the emergency room records from St. Luke's–Roosevelt Hospital, records never in the defendant's possession that were actually withheld by the ADA. The judge noted also that the two videotapes of the February 11 demonstration confirmed the defendant's description of events and his allegations of police brutality. "The videotapes make it perfectly clear," declared the judge, "that the defendant did absolutely nothing after he was clubbed to the ground. It is hard to conceive of what resistance the defendant could have put up while being surrounded and beaten by the police. The act of attempting to crawl away from such an onslaught can hardly be considered resisting arrest." The judge also exposed inconsistencies in the testimony of the plaintiff's witnesses. A policeman who alleged that Chris had bit him in a struggle on the street, for example, had not even been near Chris at the demonstration. The judge also rejected the prosecution's charge of guilt by association based on Chris's membership in ACT UP, calling it "a concept which is anathema to our concept of law and justice." Finally, the judge noted that "the defendant [has] already been summarily sentenced by the police to a lifetime of pain punctuated by epileptic seizures. No purpose," he insisted, "would be served by the court imposing any additional sentence. The defendant's motion," the judge concluded in his ruling, "to dismiss the information in the interest of justice is granted."

During subsequent tense weeks, Chris and his lawyers awaited an appeal of Walker's decision to a higher court. District Attorney Morgenthau, however, apparently decided not to risk another rebuff and further unfavorable publicity.

In November, after Governor Cuomo denied a request for the appointment of a special prosecutor to investigate the case, Chris's lawyers filed a civil action against the City of New York and against five police officers as well as Deputy Inspector Carl Jonasch. They charged "police misconduct including false arrest, malicious prosecution, utilization of excessive force, and a cover up." They sought "relief for the violation of [the plaintiff's] constitutional and civil rights and his rights as otherwise protected under the laws of the United States and the State of New York."

As complainant in this new suit, Chris charged that the rank and file of the NYPD and its command personnel sanctioned "policies, practices and customs . . . grounded in anti-gay bias and police misconduct practiced by the rank and file against individuals who are gay and who are otherwise engaged in protected conduct . . . because of the anti-gay bias that permeates the rank and file and which is allowed to fester by command personnel . . . including the false arrest of gay rights activists and the malicious persecution of said individuals and the utilization of excessive force against them."

Interviewed for this book while preparing for his civil rights case against the police, Chris mused over his future as a gay activist. "My responsibility now as a survivor of police brutality?" he said. "I must do what I can. Part of my lawsuit deals with the homophobia prevalent in the police force. The intolerance preached explicitly or implicitly by the commissioner and by the department helped create such hostile tension that night and on previous occasions. I am not primarily seeking damages; I'm going for the broader issue."

As for his personal future, Chris declared, "I'm trying to see how the epilepsy will play itself out. The doctors say it will be lifelong. I'm on a lot of medications that are making me gain weight. I have no reflexes on the right side of my body. I still have double vision." As for the future generally, Chris declared, "When I graduated from eighth grade, I was given a copy of the Constitution. I read it frequently. It's too bad that they're trying to shred it. We still haven't recovered from the lying and cheating of the Nixon Era. I'm twenty-eight. I have to have hope that as I see some of my young friends die at twenty and twenty-five years of age that people of this country will eventually turn out those who have caused so much pain and hurt. It will take a monumental effort. It took a monumental effort to fight this case, just one little case."

POSTSCRIPT

In a news story headlined "Man Beaten by Officers Settles Suit," the *New York Times* of February 17, 1994, reported that Chris Hennelly had won a $350,000 settlement in his lawsuit against New York City. Hennelly, the *Times* declared, "remained bitterly dissatisfied with the official handling of his case, particularly the fact that the Police Department did not discipline the officers who beat him with billy clubs and a radio on February 11, 1991. 'This will happen again and again because the city ratifies their conduct,' he said." The *Times* went on to quote Chris as declaring, "I used to be a controller for a Wall Street firm, and now I can't even add a restaurant check. I have double vision, significant cognitive disfunction and a seizure disorder."

In a letter dated February 23, 1995, the Civilian Complaint Review Board (which deals with complaints against the New York Police Department) advised Chris of the disposition of the complaint he had filed with the board on February 14, 1991. "A full investigation has been conducted," the letter declared, "by investigators of the Civilian Complaint Review Board. After careful review of the evidence presented, including your testimony, the Board found the complaint to be substantiated. The complaint will now be forwarded to the New York City Police Department for appropriate action."

The board found that because of a loophole in the city's contract with the Police Benevolent Association, which requires that disciplinary proceedings be brought within eighteen months of an incident, the officers responsible in the beating of Chris Hennelly would not be punished.

Chapter Nine
The New York Lesbian and Gay Anti-Violence Project

The Stonewall uprising was triggered by a police raid on a gay bar, and a first goal of the gay community in its post-Stonewall coming-out experience was to ensure the community's security, a task that became increasingly critical during the backlash against the community following upon the AIDS epidemic. In 1992 homophobic propaganda in support of right-wing initiatives in Colorado and Oregon provoked an immediate tripling in the rate of antigay violence in Colorado and a tally of 968 incidents of antigay violence in Portland, Oregon, a number surpassing that in any other city in the nation.

Both the backlash and the mobilization of the gay community against intensifying homophobic attacks were exemplified in an August 9, 1991, *New York Times* report from Houston, Texas:

HOUSTON POLICE SET TRAP TO QUELL TIDE OF VIOLENCE AGAINST HOMOSEXUALS

Two officers posing as a gay couple were sprayed with Chemical Mace on Friday night hours after [a decoy] program began, and another undercover officer was beaten with a baseball bat early Monday. The decoy program, which homosexuals here helped the police develop, arose in response to the July 4 beating and stabbing death of 27-year-old banker, Paul Broussard. As Mr. Broussard and two companions left a gay bar, they were chased down by 10 young men wielding [nailed clubs] and knives. One companion escaped, and the other was wounded. . . .

The Houston Police Department fell under heavy criticism from gay and other human rights groups after the incident, especially because homicide detectives initially said there was no evidence the attack was a hate crime. . . .

> In response to the Broussard slaying, more than 1,000 neighborhood residents, organized by the group Queer Nation, rallied in Montrose [the area in which the murder occurred] on July 13, blocking traffic for several hours and chanting at the police. . . .

The ten perpetrators, typical of teenagers (mostly white) in cities across the nation who drive through gay areas on weekends "shouting epithets and sometimes throwing rocks and bottles or attacking with baseball bats, knives, clubs, bottles or hammers and then speed away," were apprehended and brought to justice.

The Houston undercover action provided an education for the participating officers. "These incidents tell us there is definitely a problem," Captain John Adamson of the Houston police admitted, "and it is a persistent one that we are going to have to deal with until it's done with." "You see," reported one of the police decoys to the *Houston Post,* "what [gays] go through on the streets out there, just for being who they are." (Commented *New York Times* columnist A. M. Rosenthal wryly: "For all Americans to learn [what this Houston policeman learned], we may have to wait until some famous and admired American is shown on TV, beaten to a pulp but with enough strength to raise his head, smile and say with the charm and courage required of victims: 'This happened because I am gay.' ")

Indeed, prior to this undercover operation, the Houston police manifested the insensibility or overt hostility toward gays common among law enforcement officers throughout the country, as Ginny Apuzzo, at the time executive director of the National Lesbian and Gay Task Force (NLGTF), discovered on a trip to the Texas city in the late 1970s. In a Houston hospital she visited Ferrand Gijardo, a twenty-three-year-old Chicano, a victim of a vicious homophobic attack. After picking up a man in a bar, Gijardo had been tracked by two other men to his apartment. Tied to a bedpost, he was beaten, was stabbed twenty-three times, and had his throat slit.

The Houston police refused to investigate the crime.

Roused by Ferrand's outcry, "How could this happen in America?" Ginny resolved henceforth to set homophobic violence as the first priority on her agenda. Returning to New York, she raised funds for an NLGTF antiviolence project employing the tactics, Ginny declared, developed by the Jewish community against anti-Semitic violence: "giving violence a face, putting it in the public eye, with numbers, making the public deal with those numbers. We had an organizing opportunity on the most tangible evidence of our oppression," Ginny insisted, "and an opportunity, too, to get gays and lesbians to say, 'Enough is enough.' " She encouraged Task Force staffer Kevin Barrill to make himself an authority on antigay violence. "The black movement in the South," she told him, "did not win the hearts of white people in this country, but when whites saw dogs jumping on kids and hoses turned on peaceful demonstrators, they said, 'I don't want to be associated with that.' We must let the public see the equivalent in relation to homophobic violence;

we must quantify it and make the injustice so vivid that people will say, 'That's not me; I wouldn't do that.' "

At a meeting of the National Conference of Mayors, Ginny won adoption of a resolution condemning homophobic violence. Building on that success, the Task Force lobbied successfully for similar resolutions at conferences of governors, state attorneys general, and the National Association of Sheriffs. Pressure mobilized by the Task Force impelled a change in attitude within the federal government. Following upon testimony at hearings in October 1986, the House Subcommittee on Criminal Justice began to include anti-gay violence in all considerations of bias-related crime. A study by the Justice Department disclosed that among "victims of hate violence . . . Blacks, Hispanics, Southeast Asians, Jews, and gays and lesbians. . . . homosexuals are probably the most frequent victims." In addition, civil rights organizations like the American Civil Liberties Union and the Anti-Defamation League of the B'nai B'rith joined in documenting bias-motivated attacks against gays and in exposing the growth of homophobic violence among hate groups like the KKK, the neo-Nazis and skinheads.

The development of defense organizations represented a major aspect of the coming out of the gay community nationally. It presupposed, of course, the coming out of tens of thousands of individual gays to form and man these organizations, and in this and in succeeding chapters the reaction of the gay community to homophobic violence is presented through the stories of interviewees who out of their personal coming out experiences felt impelled to participate in gay defense organizations.

THE CHELSEA GAY ASSOCIATION HOTLINE

"It's open season on gay people."

"It is almost impossible for a gay person to get justice."

These two statements in the December 1988 issue of the Chelsea Gay Association's (CGA) newsletter summed up a crisis of homophobic violence in the community just north of Greenwich Village. More than a year and a half earlier, in March 1979, seeking to stimulate a more effective police response to gay bashing (80 percent of the assaults in the area), Lance Bradley, a social worker, organized biweekly consciousness-raising discussions involving police officers and members of the gay community. The program proved short-lived because of resistance among the cops. Through Lance Bradley's initiative, too, CGA established a connection with the Women's Safety and Fitness Exchange. For gay men Lance set up a self-defense training program.

On March 29, 1980, three Chelsea gay men along with a guest from England were attacked on the street by a gang of white youths. One of the gay men succeeded in running off to call for help. Another had two teeth bashed in by the bat-wielding attackers. The English guest was hit on the head. The fourth man required thirty-six stitches on his forehead, his eye was damaged, and he suffered a broken nose and a broken knee. Equally vicious homophobic attacks had occurred in the neighborhood, but on this occasion the victims accompanied by representatives of community organizations and concerned neighbors, including members of the Chelsea Gay Association, marched on the local Tenth Precinct. When the commanding officer rejected their request for additional patrols on the streets, insisting that precinct records indicated no new pattern of homophobic violence, community leaders realized that without a mobilization of the Chelsea gays and lesbians they could not pressure the officials to crack down on perpetrators and to undertake an educational program to change homophobic attitudes among law enforcement personnel and the general population.

CGA issued a call for an emergency Forum on Violent Crime on May 9 at the Church of the Holy Apostles. Cosponsored by fifteen Chelsea-based groups, attended by two city council members and moderated by interviewee Tom Duane, a future gay city councilman, the forum attracted an audience of two hundred. During succeeding weeks, the sponsoring organizations held additional antiviolence meetings in the area and met with the Manhattan district attorney, the city chief of police, and the chairman of the city housing authority.

In face of these spirited community initiatives, the local police chief could no longer ignore the gay-bashing crisis. In consultation with the precinct's community relations officer, CGA members assisted in the establishment of a precinct police council for dealing with gay violence. They also promoted a resumption of consciousness-raising sessions for the cops. According to Tom von Foerster, secretary-treasurer of CGA and an editor of its newsletter, two out of three cops complained, "What the fuck am I doing here?" Once again, with the dwindling of attendance, the sessions were terminated. "We changed the attitudes of very few," Tom admits.

The main source for the developments leading to the establishment of the Gay and Lesbian Anti-Violence Project, Tom von Foerster comes from "a social stratum that rarely has problems with the cops." Born in Berlin in 1941, however, he was aware even as a child of the unrelieved apprehension that oppressed minorities endure. One-quarter Jewish, Tom's father, a physicist, lived under constant threat of denunciation, loss of livelihood, and even deportation to a concentration camp. Split up during the war, Tom's family was reunited only in 1949 after his father found a position at the University of Illinois at Urbana.

In the mid-1960s, while a student at Harvard, Tom first experienced gay insecurity when police raided the apartment of a friend, confiscated his collection of gay pornography, and held him overnight in jail. To avoid a trial and the attendant publicity, the man distributed large sums in bribes. In 1971, after obtaining his doctorate in physics, Tom joined the Gay Academic Union in Cambridge and helped to organize gay conferences at schools and colleges. As a member of the Gay Speakers Bureau in Boston, he lectured on gay issues in college sociology classes and before various gay groups. Upon moving to New York in 1979, he became involved in CGA activities.

Two lesbians, Tom relates, offered to set up a hot line in their answering service. Word of the hot line, unique in the city, spread rapidly by word of mouth and through stories in the gay press. The roster of thirty to forty hot-line volunteers was overwhelmed not only by a flood of calls from every part of the city but also by requests to accompany crime victims to precincts to register complaints and for peer counseling of victims.

As the decade of the 1980s progressed, activists began to focus their energies on the AIDS crisis, and in 1984 CGA disbanded. The hot line, however, renamed the New York Lesbian and Gay Anti-Violence Project (AVP), continued in operation and in 1982 was incorporated as a not-for-profit corporation, "a full service crime victim assistance agency serving the lesbian and gay community in New York City . . . provid[ing] crisis intervention and short-term professional counseling, advocacy and support for survivors of domestic violence, sexual assault, bias-motivated crime and other forms of criminal victimization." Jay Watkins and his lover Russell Nutter, two CGA activists who devoted themselves to the point of obsession to any project they undertook, offered to supervise the hot line's rotation of coordinators and other volunteers. They conducted fund-raising activities and established connections with organizations and agencies with which crime victims often had to deal. With a meticulousness for which they were generally esteemed, they began documenting cases of gay-bashing and maintaining a tally of assaults on a map displaying sites of homophobic violence. With grants of $6,000 in 1983 and $34,000 in 1984 from the New York State Crime Victims Board, the board of directors—Watkins, Nutter, von Foerster, and Lance Bradley—engaged an executive director and opened a headquarters.

Tom, soft-spoken and articulate, accepted the responsibility for resolving conflicts between Jay and Russell, who were determined to do things in their own way, and the new director. Conditions improved in 1985, when David Wertheimer took over. With many years of administrative experience, David did not require supervision by Jay and Russell. Suffering from burnout, they left the city soon after his arrival.

Over the next two years the board raised sufficient funds to add four full-time staff members. At the insistence of Lance Bradley, who had earlier developed the consciousness-raising program with the Chelsea police precinct, all AVP volunteers underwent a special training program. (Dying of AIDS, Bradley did not see his initiative reach fruition.)

Under the loose mode of operation instituted by David Wertheimer, each staff member shared in the decision making and performed a variety of duties, and all received similar compensation. Conflicts over policy threatened the effectiveness of the organization, and upon the recommendations of Roger McFarlane, one of the founders of GMHC and a well-known gay activist, and of a woman business-school graduate hired to review AVP organizational policy and procedures, the board revised the organizational structure and defined the duties, title, and level of each staff member.

Half the staff resigned.

Providing a generous eight-month retirement notice, David Wertheimer hired new staff members and thus assured the continuity of the organization. "Without David Wertheimer," declares Matt Foreman, his successor as executive director, "there would not have been an Anti-Violence Project or anything for us to build on. What he did was to transform an organization without staff or office into a functioning entity with four staff people in a new office. He worked full-time for four years. He took the beeper home every night and was on call twenty-four hours a day and had no private life."

MATT FOREMAN

At thirty-four, Matt Foreman had unique qualifications for succeeding David Wertheimer as AVP executive director. After high school and college in West Virginia, Matt matriculated at the New York University law school. Here he came out as a gay activist in a lesbian and gay organization. In 1979 the group convened a conference on law and gay rights, the first national conference on that subject. The following summer, as an intern in the West Virginia governor's office, Matt was entrusted with responding to general correspondence from prison inmates as well as to appeals for gubernatorial pardons. Impressed by this experience, Matt took a year off from school to work full time in the West Virginia Corrections Department. "It was a field," Matt explains, "for which few educated people applied. I thought I would let people know that I could outthink and outmanage the straight men in the department."

Returning to New York in 1982, Matt became involved with Dignity [the national Catholic gay organization] and served on its board of directors for six years. In 1984 he began five years of activity with Heritage Pride, helping to organize gay pride activities in the city. From 1984 to 1989, he held positions in the New York City Department of Corrections. After he warned that the twenty-year-old prisoner work-release program he supervised would never prove successful under the management of uniformed personnel, who were resistant to programs aimed at reducing the number of inmates, Matt was appointed director of the Marine Annex of Rikers Island, in charge of a 324-bed unit on two ships anchored at the island. Half of the population consisted of regular minimum-security prisoners; the other half either worked outside the prison during the day or were being prepared to participate in the work-release program.

Initially the 180 officers under Matt's supervision expressed skepticism about taking orders from a civilian, but after Matt demonstrated his competence as well as his concern for their personal needs, they concluded that it was easier to work for him than for a uniformed superior. Uniformed administrators on the island, however, on whom Matt's unit depended for transportation and for kitchen facilities, remained uncooperative and even openly hostile.

Until his Rikers Island position, Matt could be numbered among the rare gay men who never suffered unpleasantness because of their sexual orientation. He had no problem with the inmates in his unit. They realized, of course, that he had authority over their lives and could shift them to a harsher jail. ("In fact," Matt insists, "I would never have employed such a punishment.") From uniformed officers Matt never confronted homophobic remarks. Twice, however, his automobile brake lines were cut. In addition, he received threatening telephone calls at home. "I attributed such actions," he says, "both to homophobia and to the resentment of the uniformed force at the appointment of a civilian manager in the prison, particularly a successful manager. They would have preferred me to fail and went out of their way to sabotage my efforts."

While Matt was away on vacation, his opponents filed allegations that he was selling admissions to the work-release program and that money was missing from the inmate account in his unit. Although an investigation exposed the charges as groundless, Matt, discouraged by the slanderous attack, welcomed a transfer back to commission headquarters.

Serving in a legal capacity in his new post, Matt prepared a department response to a drastic court ruling on prison conditions, drafted a manual on investigating inmate abuse cases, issued a new directive on the use of force against inmates, and developed forms for reporting such incidents. He introduced a regulation subjecting correction officers, paid the same salary as police officers and enjoying the same pension plan, to the same proscriptions in regard to beating inmates as governed policemen regarding assaults on citizens on the street.

By 1989 after five years in the Department of Corrections, Matt was ready for a career change. He notes with pride that in appointing him as executive director, AVP became one of the few gay organizations enjoying an orderly transition from one chief officer to another. "Usually," he points out, "the executive director is fired in a nasty scene. In the case of AVP, David Wertheimer resigned after a four-year honorable record in order to seek a new career in Seattle.

"AVP was a well-regarded agency," Matt recalls, "and I didn't come to make improvements." Nevertheless, in keeping with his personal mode of operation, Matt introduced a new aggressiveness in AVP operations; he made the organization "a little more pushy." "I have a difficult time," he explains, "just sitting back and letting things happen."

Matt entered upon his new position during an accelerating crisis in gay bashing. According to the NYPD, whose statistics include only assaults recorded at precinct headquarters, antigay crime increased in 1990 100 percent over that in 1989, the largest increase in five years, and constituted almost 20 percent of all bias crimes, as against 8 percent the previous year. Homophobic assaults were increasing faster than any other category of crime, including homicide, and the violence in the attacks was intensifying, with 49 percent of bias-crime victims suffering physical injury. "For an unprecedented 23 week period, beginning on April 20 [1990]," according to AVP records, "there was at least one such gang assault every week which resulted in serious injury."

"Such has been the intensification of incidents of ever more violent gay bashing," Matt declares, "that people have come to believe that unless you're bleeding on the street it's not antigay violence."

In response to the crisis, the AVP staff was increased from four to seven. They were assisted by a full-time volunteer support person, a community education coordinator, and a coordinator for an HIV-related violence project. During the school year, the staff was supplemented by college students undergoing thirty-six weeks of supervised internship. In the high-crime summer season when interns were not available, AVP employed an additional three or four counselors.

By 1992, after accelerated recruitment, nearly sixty volunteers had undergone training for the twenty-four-hour crisis intervention hotline or for service as peer counselors, court monitors, members of a speaker's bureau, or client advocates. As an immediate defense initiative, AVP began the distribution of eight thousand whistles. With funding from the New York State Health AIDS Institute, AVP developed a resource manual and a training program on HIV-motivated violence.

On June 16, 1990, inaugurating Matt's new activist policy, AVP cosponsored a "take back the streets" march through Greenwich Village. The twelve hundred participants confronted a hail of bottles and cans, and at least three people suffered physical assaults from bystanders, some armed with bats. Ten days later, AVP conducted a community antiviolence forum. On July 22, AVP joined in sponsoring two protest marches in Brooklyn, one through Park Slope against an attack against local lesbians and the other in Borough Park past the homes of two men who had gone to Greenwich Village and bashed gays with golf clubs and baseball bats. A month later AVP promoted the march in Jackson Heights, Queens, in protest of the claw-hammer murder of Julio Rivera.

Matt set himself no regular hours. He conferred constantly, directly or through correspondence, with city and state officials. He visited crime victims in hospitals or at home and appeared as a witness in court cases. Often braving arrest in antiviolence demonstrations, he won the respect not only of gay activists but of the police and city officials as well.

NAOMI LICHTENSTEIN

Among the people hired by David Wertheimer shortly before he resigned as executive director, Naomi Lichtenstein brought to AVP a long and variegated experience as a mental health professional and social worker.

In the summer of 1974, after shifting from one job to another, even working briefly as a beautician, Naomi accepted an invitation to move in as a full-time baby-sitter for two little boys, aged two and seven, sons of a Stony Brook professor of child development. Impressed with Naomi's success with her children, the professor advised her to seek a vocation in which she would be involved with children; and in 1975 Naomi matriculated at the social work school at Adelphi University and did her practicum at the university child-care center. While at Adelphi Naomi became involved in a gay and lesbian caucus. "I was now becoming political," Naomi declares. "Before I had been involved simply in emotional survival."

Naomi's parents provided models for her commitment to radical social activism. Both were involved in the Nassau County Parent Teachers Association, and Naomi's father in affairs of the local temple as well. With a group of friends they mounted a constitutional complaint against prayer in the schools. Naomi herself refused to stand during school prayer, resisting goading by the assistant principal, who insisted, "Come on, don't give us trouble!" At home the family received death threats.

In 1962, two years after the action was initiated, the Supreme Court ruled in favor of Naomi's parents and their associates: School prayer was banned as unconstitutional.

Nevertheless, while her brother, close to her in age, participated in antiwar demonstrations in high school, Naomi was caught up in varsity sports. She admits that not until she was in college did she appreciate the implications of her parents' political activity. "All I knew," she recalls, "was that life was scary during those years." On the other hand, Naomi gained another, contrary lesson within her family. Returning home from work exhausted, her parents often discovered that she and her brother had turned the house upside down with their horseplay. "I would get a slap," Naomi recounted, "and my father used a belt on me a couple of times. I resented being singled out. I think that has something to do with why I'm working in an antiviolence project today." Naomi saw that other first-generation parents in the neighborhood and her aunts and uncles did not hit their children. She became convinced that no one had a right to hit another person.

Naomi performed her social work internship at the Institute for Human Identity, a mental health center for the lesbian, gay, and bisexual community founded by specialists who split off from Identity House after the American Psychiatric Association in 1973 ruled that homosexuality was not a disease. Surrounded by lesbian and gay professionals, Naomi found support to come out formally and had her first experience in discussing political and mental health issues with politically conscious members of the gay community.

Obtaining a position at the Working Women's Institute, a social service and referral agency, Naomi counseled victims of sexual harassment and assisted them in legal matters. Subsequently, at the New York City Victims Services Agency, Naomi worked with battered women and rape survivors and then with children about to testify in abuse cases. At this agency, Naomi comments: "You learned what horrors people can inflict on each other. After work," Naomi recounts, "I put the day behind me. To survive you had to find things outside the job that were very positive."

One day in the summer of 1985, when Naomi offered food from her plate to a cousin's one-year-old daughter, her cousin shouted, "With the friends you deal with, you could give the child AIDS!" The argument that followed convinced Naomi of the importance of struggling against ignorance in the AIDS crisis. As a part-time employee at the New York City Department of Health AIDS Hotline, Naomi gained insight into the issues and problems confronting people at risk from HIV infection. Resigning from her position at the Crime Victims Service Agency, Naomi became involved in counseling people before and after HIV testing. With her new competence, Naomi found a position as a medical social worker on the St. Luke's–Roosevelt Hospital AIDS team. "On this job," Naomi declares, "I learned a tremendous amount from an excellent medical staff—the comprehensive social-psychological aspect of HIV infection."

Late in 1989, David Wertheimer invited Naomi to apply for a position on his staff. He and Naomi had been colleagues four years earlier at the Victims Service Agency, where other staffers often referred cases involving lesbian and gay crime victims to them.

At the time of her appointment at AVP, Naomi, already in her late forties, had achieved competence in working with people of all ages and with varied problems: with children in a day-care center; with teenagers, many on drugs, in a group home; with adults and senior citizens; and, most important, with crime victims and with people with HIV infection. "All my experiences," she declares, "came together here at AVP."

Until she left AVP in 1992, with clients Naomi followed the crisis-intervention victimology model developed in rape crisis and battered women's organizations, a methodology formulated at the Karen Horney school of psychiatry and modified by mental health specialists working with Vietnam veterans. Discovering that victimology models based on men's victimizing women developed at clinics with a feminist ideology are not always applicable to cases of men beating men and women beating women, Naomi had to expand her exploration into an analysis of violence itself. "No one in the field," Naomi points out, "wants to talk about domestic gay and lesbian violence."

When victims called for help, Naomi expressed support of their decision to contact AVP. "We can help you with counseling," she assured them, "and in providing advocacy or in obtaining your entitlements. We will guide you through the criminal justice system if that is what you want."

Crime victims, Naomi discovered, experience symptoms similar to those of many war veterans. "Emotionally," she says, "they are sometimes in denial about the seriousness of what has happened to them and think that they just need to report the crime for statistical purposes or to find out how to get a lawyer." Naomi advises them that weeks or even months later they may need further assistance. AVP will, she assures them, always be available to them.

Crime victim counselors, Naomi advises, often confront difficulties in helping survivors to understand that they are not at fault, that they did not suffer assault because of how they were dressed or because of their being at a particular location at a certain hour. "You could have been running around naked on the street," Naomi insists, "but in no event has anyone the right to touch you."

The majority of victims, Naomi found, would talk about assaults on the telephone. For them a single fifteen- or twenty-minute telephone conversation generally sufficed. Those preferring to come to the AVP office had the option of speaking with either a male or female staffer. In intake interviews, AVP counselors investigated whether clients had previous psychiatric disturbance and whether the crime experience had evoked previous traumas. With the small percentage of clients with previous psychiatric disturbances, AVP made referrals and, where physical injury was involved, assisted in applications to the Crime Victims Board for compensation to pay for long-term treatment and other costs.

Survivors of domestic violence (which affects one out of four or five of all households, homosexual as well as heterosexual) and of sexual abuse, about 7 percent of the AVP caseload, often required many counseling sessions. (AVP offered from one session to a full year of sessions, gratis.) "When you're hit or sexually abused by a lover or ex-lover," Naomi notes, "the betrayal is very intense. It's much more difficult emotionally to overcome. In cases of domestic violence, the pair sometimes still love each other. The issue is of power and control. Sometimes it begins with verbal humiliation, sometimes it occurs only Friday nights, sometimes it arises only after alcohol abuse. Of course, it's not the drug or alcohol that causes the violence."

Naomi agrees with interviewee Shelley Neiderbach, founder of the Crime Victims Counseling Service, that since "sexual assault is the sexual expression of aggression, not the aggressive expression of sexuality," rapists are often indifferent to the gender of their victims.* "Rape in this country," Naomi remarks, "is a feminized crime." Indeed, she notes, most states define rape as forced vaginal penetration, as though the crime involves only women. (AVP defines rape as a forced penetration of any bodily orifice.) Both Shelley and Naomi point out that male rape of both gays and straights, common in prisons, occurs more often on the outside than the general public or the victims will admit. Of the 168,000 or so rapes reported annually in the United States, 13,000 involve male victims; but the male rape figure, Shelley declares, undoubtedly represents a far greater underreporting than that for women. The prevalence of male rape, according to Naomi, is attested by the complaint she repeatedly hears from young gays newly arrived in New York: "Is this what sex is about?" "For men who are raped," says Naomi, "the horror is perceived as too complicated and too scary to deal with. Men are supposed to be in control and not to admit powerlessness." According to Naomi, think-

*Dr. A. Nicholas Groth, author of *Men Who Rape,* cited in "Silent Victims: Bring Male Rape Out of the Closet" in the September 30, 1991, issue of the *Advocate.*

ing of themselves as objects of male affection and love, gay men and heterosexual women suffer similar reactions to rape.

Rape survivors, Naomi has found, may suffer sexual dysfunction because their sex organs were the target of the attack. Most survivors shrink at being touched after an assault. Like victims of battle trauma, they may appear catatonic in the emergency room. "You may have been dating him or her for a long time," Naomi advises gay and lesbian rape survivors, "or you may have picked him or her up at a bar, but when you say no, sex stops and the crime of rape begins."

As the state-authorized crime victims service agency for the West Village and Chelsea sections of Manhattan (though, in fact, it receives clients from all over the Greater New York area), AVP provides service to straights as well as gays, the latter in 1992 composing some 16 percent of its clientele. (The stereotypes of gays, Matt Foreman notes, have become very broad, and it is not uncommon for straight men mistaken for gays to suffer sexual attack.) Because of a heterosexist myth that gay men enjoy being raped, straight male rape survivors wonder what about them made the assaulter take them for gay, and they become troubled about their sexuality. Some hesitated (as, indeed, according to Naomi, did some gay and lesbian rape survivors) to enter the Lesbian and Gay Community Center, where AVP formerly had its offices, out of fear of the "stigma" of being taken for gay or even for fear, in their irrational traumatic condition, of encountering their rapists in the building.

In 1991 five thousand AVP posters on domestic violence, paid for by a grant from the New York State Department of Social Services, were placed in the subways. The posters displayed an outstretched hand alongside the caption, "If your gay or lesbian partner is using one of these to hurt you, we have one to help you." The number of hot-line calls, according to the fall 1991 AVP newsletter, subsequently "skyrocketed."

"In earlier years," Naomi comments, "I was taunted for being Jewish, for being a woman, a tomboy, for being heavy. As a lesbian I am always on guard. I have good locks on the door. I walk strong and tough-looking to give the impression of being secure. If I think I'm being followed, I change direction, cross the street, or go into a store. In the subway I go to the car where the conductor is stationed. I take seriously all the crime-prevention tips we talk about. I watch every person that goes by me. I know what people can do to each other."

HOWIE KATZ

Like Naomi Lichtenstein, AVP fund raiser Howie Katz, forty-eight, exemplifies the talent and rich experience on the AVP staff. Tall and well-built, in appearance and mannerisms, he belies stereotypes of gays. From his earliest school years, Howie excelled in sports. In his family environment Howie, like

Naomi, was exposed early to progressive thinking. His mother, a psychiatric social worker, participated in the 1963 March on Washington, when Martin Luther King, Jr., delivered his "I have a dream" speech. His parents supported Eugene McCarthy in the 1970 election campaign and staunchly opposed the Vietnam War. Howie's sister and brother-in-law participated in the Freedom Rides in the South.

Howie grew up in New Rochelle, an affluent New York suburb, and attended an elementary school where the children were almost all Jewish and the single black student was the daughter of Whitney Young, head of the Urban League. When he was in the fifth or sixth grade, a few black children were bused to the school, and the white children, Howie recalls, were eager to meet children they had not known before. Howie's parents were both active in the Boy Scouts and always involved in the activities of their four children. They read a great deal, attended the opera and ballet, and took their children to museums. Although Howie's brothers taught him to read before he entered kindergarten, he turned out to be an underachiever scholastically. A high school teacher who made a special impact on him was Ann Schwerner, the mother of Mickey Schwerner, one of the three young men murdered by racists in Mississippi in the heyday of the civil rights struggle. She added, Howie recalls, a political moral to every biology lesson.

Howie's father had been forced to drop out of school to help support his family and had not been able to continue on to medical school. His mother obtained her master's degree after her children were grown and worked as a mental health specialist. Thus, when in 1969, his junior year in high school, realizing that he was not getting much out of school, Howie decided to take a year off, his parents were outraged. "They couldn't see a Jewish boy," Howie declares, "dropping out of school." At his mother's suggestion, Howie and his parents consulted a psychiatrist. The psychiatrist thought Howie was making an intelligent decision, and Howie's parents were forced to acquiesce.

At the famous Woodstock concert that summer, Howie confronted the sixties culture for the first time. Someone handed him a piece of paper with a quote from a Bob Dylan song: "You went to the finest schools all right, Miss Lonely, but you don't need to get juiced in it. Nobody ever taught you how to live out on the street, but now you're going to have to get used to it." He wondered at receiving this message just at a time when he was planning to quit school. As he and his friends were walking back to their car, someone handed him a flyer announcing a march on Washington sponsored by the Student Mobilization to End the War in Vietnam. On the way home, he resolved to finish his senior year and to participate in the antiwar struggle.

At George Washington University Howie participated in the hectic activities of the antiwar movement. Once, during an after-Christmas study week, while Howie and his roommate were "tripping" on mescaline, a friend harangued them about poverty in Appalachia, a couple of hours away from Washington. "Why don't I do something worthwhile?" Howie asked himself.

He submitted applications to the Peace Corps and to Vista but was rejected because of a lack of definable skills.

When George McGovern, the presidential candidate universally supported by Howie's circle of friends, won only a single state in the elections, Howie realized that he had no clues to what people were thinking elsewhere in the nation. During the following summer vacation, therefore, he hitchhiked around the country. On the road Howie was surprised to encounter negative reactions to people he admired like Ralph Nader and Cesar Chavez. He was in Wyoming during the Wounded Knee confrontation between Native American activists and federal agents, and in a discussion with a Native American he obtained a different interpretation of life on reservations from what he read in the newspapers. Generally on the trip, Howie says, he learned to listen and to show caution before expressing his opinions.

In 1982 attracted by a notice that Walter Mondale would be speaking at the Waldolf Astoria at a gay Human Rights Campaign* dinner, Howie bought two tickets for the event. The sight of almost a thousand gays and lesbians in tuxedos and gowns impressed him. For the following year's banquet, at which Jessie Jackson appeared as the main speaker, Howie put together a table. "This," Howie declares, "was what I thought gay people should be doing in the political arena. I wanted to be part of it."

Two years later, impelled by a close friend's death from AIDS, Howie joined the Human Rights Campaign's donor's club of some thirty people around the country. He "hit it off" with the Campaign's executive director, like Howie a former antiwar activist, and was invited to a conference in Washington. Here, to his surprise, Howie saw congressmen and senators treating gay people with respect. In 1986 the cochair of the New York chapter of the Human Rights Campaign, Vivian Shapiro, involved him in planning the fund-raising dinner. Early the next year, at Vivian's urging, Howie attended a meeting of a new AIDS activist group organized by Larry Kramer, ACT UP. He saw "everybody I had ever read about in gay newspapers. This is where I belong," Howie assured himself, and he participated in the first ACT UP demonstrations in Wall Street and at the New York City General Post Office.

On June 1, 1987, Howie volunteered to join the sixty-three "heroes of the gay movement," as he calls them, who planned to submit to arrest at the International AIDS Conference in Washington. "On the bus," Howie relates, "the bus captain asked who was getting arrested. I was the only one who raised his hand." At the demonstration, Dan Bradley wanted to be the last one arrested because he had been the highest-ranking federal official (chief of legal services during the Carter Administration) ever to "come out" and a

*The largest gay lobby organization, it employs five lobbyists, sponsors mass letter-writing campaigns and other pressure actions, and contributed one million dollars to political campaigns in 1992.

PWA (person with AIDS) as well. After women demonstrators were packed into buses and a paddy wagon by cops ostentatiously wearing bright yellow gloves as protection against HIV infection, "I saw one of the policeman heading for Dan," Howie recounted. "I stepped out and said, 'I think it's my turn now.' " The others who were arrested wondered who this new man was and were worried because the police handcuffed him so tightly as to stop the circulation in his hand.

Vivian and other New York Human Rights Campaign people were convinced that Howie, one of the best-known gay softball players in the country, might reach out to communities where they had no contacts, and at the Campaign's next meeting he was elected to the national board. In November 1987, at a board meeting just before the second gay march on Washington, the quilt memorializing those who had died of AIDS was unveiled. "I took out a picture of my ball team from 1980 and 1981," Howie declares. "Of the thirty people in the picture, seven were dead and a few others had been diagnosed HIV-positive. That day I decided to work for the community full time."

Howie gave fifteen months' notice at work, plenty of time for his father to train a replacement. "I had always described my occupation as a boring but honest way of earning a living," Howie says. "Now I had no idea how I was going to support myself in the community."

In March 1989 Tom Duane, campaigning for a seat on the city council, offered Howie a job as a fund-raiser. If Tom had been elected, Howie would have been assured of a position on Tom's staff. A year later, concerned that the hate crimes bill remained stuck in the New York state senate, Tim Sweeney, executive director of GMHC, and Jeff Braff, Sweeney's predecessor as executive director, consulted Matt Foreman of AVP on a joint employment of a lobbyist. Tim knew Howie from ACT UP and from the Human Rights Campaign Fund and had heard him speak in public. Tom Duane added his recommendation. With GMHC guaranteeing most of his salary, Howie was appointed to the AVP staff until the end of the legislative session. In the spring of 1991, after the hate crimes bill had once again failed of passage, the AVP board extended Howie's position, at Matt Foreman's suggestion, on condition that he raise money for his own salary above what was required for the lobbying campaign. "I don't like fund-raising," said Howie, "but it is a necessary evil just as a bar is necessary as a place to meet people if you're single." On the other hand, Howie had determined years earlier that the stepping stone to full civil rights for the gay community lay in the hate crimes bill. He foresaw its eventual passage. "Who's going to object to penalties," he asked, "against someone who beats up people because of who they are? Even right-wingers and fundamentalists don't call for beating up gay people. Though they may not want gays as teachers or neighbors, most well-meaning people still say, 'I don't like your lifestyle, but I don't think anyone should beat you up.' "

Like other gay activists, devoting himself wholeheartedly to the defense of gay rights, Howie's association with AVP meant for him the culmination of his coming out. On March 31, 1991, Howie threw a party to celebrate his retirement from his father's business and his forthcoming full-time dedication to the gay movement. The invitation read: "Howie Katz invites you to celebrate the first day of the rest of our lives." Of the almost two hundred people invited, over a hundred showed up; eighty were gay friends, and the rest were relatives and friends of the family. "I prepared a speech to explain, especially to my parents," Howie declares, "why I had chosen this new path in my life and also to make sure that my dad understood that I really cared about him and respected him. I was not running away from him. In fact, I had arrived at my decision because of what he and my mother had taught me. At the same time I also wanted people in the gay community to know who I was and why, on the chance that someone might think I would be a good person to appoint to the staff of a gay organization. It was a wonderful event. I praised my dad in front of all my friends and talked about how I lost one friend after another to AIDS. I made my parents and their friends feel proud. They had never been at a gay event before. This was in a way their coming-out party, too."

At the end of 1991, the AVP board made Howie's position permanent. Howie, at last settled into the kind of job he had long sought, began planning a series of AVP fund-raising activities: dances, house parties, direct mail appeals. . . . Every day, too, he tried to do something on the bias bill.*

ERMANNO STINGO

Volunteers deserve mention because of their major contribution to AVP's activities. Outstanding among them and widely respected, Ermanno Stingo, seventy-five, traced his participation as an antiviolence activist back to a time before the Chelsea program that preceded the founding of AVP.

In the early 1950s Ermanno appeared in court as a character witness for a friend who had been arrested for making an indecent approach in a men's room. Before the case was called, Ermanno saw his friend's lawyer walk out of the courtroom with one of the arresting detectives. Within a few minutes they returned, and the complaint was dropped. A bribe had ended the trial.

Two or three years later, at work Ermanno saw a secretary cringe as she responded to a telephone call. The police, she reported, had picked up Ermanno's lover Boris in a subway-station men's room. An Episcopalian priest accompanied Ermanno to the court and spoke to the judge, noting that Boris had no prior record. The judge agreed that if Boris entered a guilty plea he would let him go. "That'll be the end of it," the judge declared. Boris, unem-

*In 1996, having left AVP, Howie was serving on the staff of State Assemblyman Steven Sanders.

ployed at the time and concerned at the expense of hiring a lawyer, agreed to the judge's demand.

The other man arrested, an executive at the Zeckendorf corporation, a major real estate firm, had been the one who solicited Boris. Upon his entering a guilty plea in response to the judge's offer, his wife, obviously pregnant, entered the court with two lawyers. At her tearful appeal, the judge allowed her husband to change his plea. "I didn't know enough," Ermanno recalls, "to come with a lawyer, and Boris was freed with a crime on his record."

Some years later, after completing a master's degree, Boris obtained a position as a teacher in an inner-city middle school. Because of his creativity in the classroom, he won the respect of his colleagues. He and Ermanno spent a good share of their salaries in providing poor students with school supplies and other necessities. One day, however, Boris was summoned to the Board of Education and charged with failing to disclose his arrest record. Despite the intervention of the Teachers Union, Boris was dismissed. "The anger at that injustice has never left me," Ermanno declares.

Ermanno joined the Mattachine Society, a defense organization composed of gay lawyers, and the West Side Discussion Group. Both he and Boris worked as volunteers at a medical laboratory set up by the Group for venereal-disease testing. They attended Group meetings at which notable guest speakers were sometimes on hand. Gubernatorial candidate Hugh Carey, Ermanno recalls, promised to issue a gay rights proclamation if elected. Subsequently, as governor, he forgot his commitment.

Ermanno and Boris were not barhoppers, but they were aware of raids on bars and on public toilets. The police, Ermanno recalls, were not all vicious. He remembers seeing a cop bang his billy club on a men's room door in the subway as a warning before he entered. "I thought," Ermanno recounts, "if all the cops were like that, wouldn't it be great? I knew that some cops had sex in the men's rooms with gays. So many unfair things were accepted in those days, especially by the older gay people, who said, 'That's part of the price you pay.' I felt it shouldn't be that way. No cop, I argued, would ever arrest a straight couple having sex in a car."

After Stonewall, at meetings of the Gay Activists Alliance and then the Gay and Lesbian Independent Democrats, Ermanno supported activists who demanded bolder public actions. He began attending trials involving homophobic violence and, upon retiring from his job, began to work with the Chelsea Gay Alliance hot line. Chelsea volunteers joined him in monitoring gay-bashing court cases. He recalls two cases that impressed him particularly. One involved a Hispanic man who almost beheaded a gay man, came close to killing a second, and gravely injured a third. Because of the perseverance of a dedicated woman assistant district attorney, the perpetrator received three consecutive sentences. In the Yorkers Five case, after driving about Times Square and harassing prostitutes, five young men decided to go after gays in the Village. During an altercation on Bank Street, a gay man threw a flowerpot at their car. They came out with baseball bats and a golf club and hurt two gays seriously. When the group attacked other people, a straight couple called the cops. The trial lasted three months, with Ermanno present every day. Although ADA John Hogan confronted five strong defense lawyers and the accused were granted youthful-offender status, all five received jail sentences.

Through the ADA in the Yonkers case, Ermanno met Manhattan District Attorney Robert M. Morgenthau. "I invited Jessica Di Grazio, Morgenthau's first assistant, for breakfast," Ermanno recounts. "I told her that no parent ever knows at birth whether their child will be straight or gay." Di Grazio reported back to Morgenthau and persuaded him to add a gay liaison person to his staff. "He is an intelligent man," Ermanno says, "but he didn't even know what a pink triangle was [the insignia the Nazis compelled gay concentration camp inmates to wear]." In the mid-1980s Ermanno invited Morgenthau and members of his staff along with representatives of the gay press to breakfast at his apartment to urge the district attorney to support the city gay rights bill. Morgenthau did speak out in favor of the bill.

Appalled at the direction of the hearings on that bill, Ermanno asked to testify. The witness ahead of him, a representative of the Fire Department, complained of being unable to enter St. Patrick's Cathedral with his children because of the Gay Pride march. Then Ermanno was introduced as an activist member of the Coalition for Lesbian and Gay Rights and other organizations. "I said," Ermanno recalled, "there was an evolving vocabulary in the gay world because so many things were changing. I spoke of my lover of some twenty years, how we were accepted by my friends and relatives. I quoted my father's words when he met my lover: 'Che occhi celesti che ha'—'What beautiful blue eyes he has.' I spoke of how Boris's mother calls me her other son. I talked about the sixty-four children in our lives. How many we were godfathers to, including many Chinese. . . . I was interrupted three times with applause," Ermanno declares with pride, "and got a standing ovation at the end."

Following upon that experience, Ermanno redoubled his volunteer activity, working as though at a full-time job, maintaining the hot line of the Bar Association for Human Rights and continuing his court monitoring. He became a familiar face at court, always identifying himself as a representative of AVP and of Parents of Gays. "It's gratifying," he says, "that when they know that someone from AVP is in the court, they make sure that they're careful.

"Now that I do referrals for the gay Bar Association for Human Rights," says Ermanno, "I hear stories of people who commit suicide because of family or other pressures and their own sense of guilt. There is still much to be done."

In 1990 Ermanno was diagnosed with cancer. On May 25, 1993, Ermanno Stingo died.

Chapter Ten
Gays and the Criminal Justice System

The coming out of the New York gay community has been exemplified in its mobilization not only to protect itself against homophobic violence but also to combat homophobic prejudice within the criminal justice system.

Before serving as a prison administrator, Matt Foreman, executive director of AVP, had "never realized that the law enforcement and judicial systems were so screwed up for victims generally." They were "not designed for inmates or for crime victims [but rather] for the police, the lawyers, the judges, and the court officers." Apart from problems facing all crime victims like losing days at their jobs in repeated interrogations, poring through books of mug shots, attending lineups and meetings with assistant district attorneys, and suffering frustration from changes in trial dates and ADA negotiation of plea bargains without consultation, gay crime victims confront special problems of not being believed and of having their sexual orientation posed as an issue in trials. They face additional handicaps in cases involving police officers as assailants. (In 1990 police assaults represented 7 percent of the total Anti-Violence Project caseload, a 100 percent increase over the number reported in 1989.)

Commenting on a four-year trend of lower reporting of victimization, Naomi Lichtenstein, AVP director of client services, declared that gay crime victims often "are afraid of being revictimized by a callous or insensitive officer. Others are worried about publicity or retaliation by the perpetrator. And still others don't see how going to the police will do any good."

LIZ GARRO, A LIAISON PERSON AT THE OFFICE OF THE KINGS COUNTY DISTRICT ATTORNEY

In background and life experience, Liz Garro was especially qualified for her position. She helped to reduce the problems of gays involved with the criminal justice system.

While holding a job at a community board Liz gained useful experience working with "a lot of decent people, volunteers doing their best with limited funds to help young people and seniors." When her second, part-time job with City Councilman Abe Gerges proved too much of a burden, Gerges offered her a full-time position. When she informed him of her sexual orientation, he declared she could be useful in helping him deal with the gay communities in his district of Brooklyn Heights and Park Slope. Indeed, he brought her to public meetings and invited her to provide answers on gay questions. She developed a constructive working relationship with Mayor Edward I. Koch's director for gay and lesbian affairs and gained a reputation as a source of advice on gay issues for city and state legislators.

Attending a meeting at which Ginny Apuzzo, then Mario Cuomo's liaison to the gay community, was the main speaker, Liz resolved to take Ginny as a role model. To Liz, Ginny was "bright, completely out," and she shared much of Liz's childhood experience in a Catholic family and parochial schools.

After a colleague at Gerges' office died of AIDS, Liz recalls, "I was spending much of my time visiting the sick or going to wakes and crying." She urged a sympathetic Gerges to promote AIDS legislation. He received a flood of hostile mail for his support of the gay rights bill, and a leading Hasidic rabbi, the first rabbi to recognize AIDS as a problem in his own community, turned against Gerges. The day of the city council vote on the bill Gerges invited Liz to be present. She sat with a group called Lesbians in Government. "We were so moved," she recalls, "when Councilwoman Julia Harrison stood up and cried as she dedicated her vote to her brother who had died of AIDS that we were asked to leave the chamber." When the bill passed, Liz exclaimed, "Now we can do anything!"

After more than six years with Gerges, Liz gave notice. She was buying a condominium and needed more money than he could give her. Furthermore, she had a desire to grow in a new experience. Joe Hynes, the Brooklyn district attorney, was developing advisory councils to deal with his various constituencies. Liz was impressed by Hynes' warmth, compassion, and sincerity and was delighted when he offered her a job.

Entering upon her new position on February 1, 1990, Liz telephoned Ginny Apuzzo for advice on organizing the DA's advisory council on lesbian and gay concerns. In May, Hynes appointed Liz to be his gay and lesbian liaison person, with authority to go where she wanted and to contact whomever she thought important to her work. In her new post Liz participated actively in the police council established by Mayor Koch and maintained by

David Dinkins to air problems arising between the police and the gay community. She also attended trials involving gay bashing and made contact with gay crime victims, many of whom would confide in her things they would not tell the ADAs.

At a June 1991 meeting of a community police council, Liz heard a report of an incident of lesbian bashing two months earlier that was rousing widespread indignation in the Park Slope gay community. At 5 A.M. on April 8, five lesbians entered the Purity Diner. Two young men sitting with their dates in the restaurant began to call them names. When the women attempted to leave, one of the men, Michael Cruz, knocked Lisa, one of the lesbians, to the ground, breaking her nose. He spat at Lisa's lover, a black woman. Officers arriving in a police car refused to write up a report or to drive Lisa to a hospital a half mile away. When Lisa demanded that the perpetrators be arrested, the police ordered her to shut up and threatened to arrest her. After speaking briefly to the two couples, the police drove off.

Lisa had never had any association with gay organizations, but she had kept a leaflet from the Anti-Violence Project. She called AVP and then telephoned the local precinct to repeat her demand that her attacker be arrested. Although they insisted that Lisa was exaggerating the incident and rejected her claim of bias in the assault, the police arrested Michael Cruz.

Joe Hynes urged Liz to follow up on the complaint and instructed the civil rights section of his office to institute an investigation. ("Some officials," Liz remarked, "have a problem with admitting that we are getting bashed as gays and lesbians. Joe does not have that problem.") Discovering that the police had failed to provide the DA's office with a record of the incident, Liz called the community relations officer at the precinct. "I don't know what happened to the report," he said, but the next day two police officers hand-delivered the file.

Liz's initial efforts at winning the trust and cooperation of the victims and of the Park Slope lesbian community were rebuffed. At a meeting to plan a protest demonstration, she confronted open hostility. "What are you doing here?" people demanded. "You're part of the system." Liz's assurance that she was on their side was met with hissing, and she was asked to leave during the discussion of specific details of the demonstration.

Although AVP urged Lisa to seek Liz's assistance, she assumed that Liz would be another law enforcement official who would not believe her and would humiliate her. She had had an upsetting experience when three police officers burst through the door of her apartment and announced they were escorting her to a lineup. While she went for a jacket, they studied her books. "I did not know," Lisa said, "whether I could say anything to them."

Cruz arrived in court for arraignment accompanied by several of his buddies. They attempted to intimidate Lisa and her lover by glaring at them. Cruz was charged with second-degree assault. Liz's office added a charge of bias on the basis of the racial slurs Cruz addressed to Lisa's lover. At a subsequent court hearing, Lisa refused Liz's invitation to meet at the DA's office but agreed to talk to Liz in her home. She and her lover described the incident in detail. Liz was infuriated to learn of violations of standard police procedures in the handling of the case.

Upon word that a protest demonstration was being planned, the police called a meeting of gay leaders. Rejecting Lisa's charge that Michael Cruz had attacked her and her friends because they were gay, the precinct commander declared, "I've never had a bias crime in this community. This precinct," he insisted, "has had good relations with the gay and lesbian community." Cruz had become angry, he declared, simply because the five women were given menus ahead of him and his friends.

"That means if I go into a restaurant," Liz snapped, "I can expect this type of treatment over a menu?"

Liz had conferred in advance with Marjorie Hill, director of the mayor's committee on lesbian and gay affairs, and hoped that Hill, an African American, would raise the issue of racial bias, but Hill sat in silence. Nor, Liz asserts, did an NYPD community-affairs liaison with the gay community come to her support. It was left to Liz to ask why the slur "nigger bitch" and the antilesbian remarks of the accused had been omitted from the police record.

The police sought to discredit Lisa's testimony by charging that she had been drinking. The head of the Police Bias Unit remarked that in their dress the women had not given the impression of being gay (thus, presumably, the issue of bias was to be ruled out). When his remark was quoted in the *Village Voice,* he denied making it. Four members of the municipal Police Council on Gay and Lesbian Affairs, however, asserted that they had heard him use just those words.

To spare Lisa additional trauma, the assistant district attorney accepted a request that the cocky eighteen-year-old Cruz be granted youthful offender status. Cruz was sentenced to five years probation and to $2,000 in damages toward Lisa's medical expenses. (Lisa was granted an additional $5,000 by the state Crime Victims Board.) Of the verdict, Liz commented, "Most juries are homophobic. They take the word of the police. We might have lost the case in a trial. Cruz will at least go through life with a criminal record."

At a precinct community board meeting the next day, Liz drew the precinct commander aside. "We got a guilty plea in the Purity Diner case," she announced, handing him a copy of a DA press release on the verdict. "He turned white as a ghost," she recounted, "put the release in his pocket, and disappeared for an hour." During a question period, Liz asked for the floor and announced the verdict to the gathering. The captain pointed his finger at her and said, "You're making it sound as if I did not do my job!" "Yes," replied Liz, "you did not do your job so far as the gay and lesbian community is concerned. You did not believe the victims. You saw the report. It did not say that they were called names."

On January 28 about 150 people, including a councilman and the borough president, assembled at the Park Slope Methodist Church for a follow-up meeting called by the Lambda Independent Democrats. Assured that the audience would be supportive, Lisa agreed to speak. In addition to rehearsing the details of the incident and of her experiences in court, she disclosed that in frequent telephone calls the police had charged that she knew the incident arose merely over menus. They urged her to stop alleging that she had been attacked because she was a lesbian and advised her not to trust Liz.

Asked whether he still believed that bias was not a factor in the handling of the incident, the precinct commander replied, "No, now I think it's bias. I was not informed of all the facts." Liz retorted that the bias relationship should have been clear from the allocution (the formal charge).

"It said nothing about bias," insisted the captain.

Matt Foreman pointed to the epithet "nigger bitch" in the document.

"Well, there it is," admitted the captain. "It is bias; it must be bias."

The next day Liz called the precinct captain's superior to ask why he had not been present at the meeting. The precinct captain, he declared, had asked him to stay away. Liz assured the inspector he would have been embarrassed by the captain's behavior. If the captain had apologized, she noted, and admitted that the police had erred and said right off that he would henceforth call the assault a bias incident, he would have been a hero. Instead, she reported, he yelled angrily and made remarks he would regret when he saw them in print.

"Every step of the way we have to fight the police," Liz asserts. "They discredit the victim and try to disunite us. It is us against them."

Liz established a practice of attending as many gay meetings and participating in as many demonstrations as she could find time for. In recognition of her efforts she was granted an award by the Lambda Democratic Club. "I have learned," she explains, "that we must speak with force because the system is not working; we have to make it work; we must get inside to make a change. My sisters and brothers in Queer Nation and ACT UP are out there, and I belong with them."

BRUCE AT THE CRIME VICTIMS BOARD

With the assistance of the Republican party boss for whom he worked, Bruce obtained a position at the New York State Crime Victims Board. Bruce went for an interview and started work the next day. He took the requisite civil service examination only after being on the job. Initially Bruce was assigned to a newly established unit for senior citizens. Other than dealing with a crotchety grandmother whom he calls "one of the most miserable human beings that ever lived," Bruce had had no experience with seniors. Nevertheless, Bruce had a sense of being useful in winning reimbursement for medical expenses and lost earnings for crime victims. He liked interviewing people and learned to deal with a cross-section of a population in crisis. For the first time in his life, Bruce declares, "I could say, 'I am no longer a failure.'"

The pertinence of some of the crime victims' cases to his own life, Bruce says, struck him particularly when he had his first case involving a gay Asian American stabbed to death by someone he had invited home. "I thought to myself," Bruce recounts, "look what the consequences are. If I were not at the CVB I would have known only what I read in the papers."

Over the years Bruce became convinced that a gay unit was required at the CVB, especially because he like other "closeted" gay staff members felt compelled to remain silent at the frequent homophobic remarks at the agency. "There are people out there," Bruce insisted, "out to hurt us. I'm not just Joe Shmo in a bar reading in the *Native* about a bashing or homicide. I'm in a government agency that is supposed to be doing something." Testifying in 1984 before the Governor's Commission on Gay and Lesbian Concerns, Bruce offered three reasons for the appointment of a gay liaison person at CVB: (1) Gays or lesbians prefer to deal with an openly gay agent and are reluctant to divulge certain information to other people; (2) a liaison person would be more effective in cooperating with gay organizations and in making referrals to them; and (3) homophobia among police and officials makes the appointment of a gay liaison person necessary.

As evidence of the particular service a gay liaison person could provide, Bruce cited a case in which during an interview a crime victim mentioned that his lover had died of AIDS. Bruce wrote in his notes, "Refer to AVP and to GMHC bereavement counseling." "That says it all," Bruce comments. "The community," he declares, "has a vast network to which people need to be referred."

In 1984 Bruce's supervisor declared that Bruce was the only person who could handle an appeal entered against a minimal award to a crime victim approved by one of Bruce's colleagues. Bruce sent for medical and psychological records. After assembling a thick file, he entered a recommendation for a supplementary payment. Because of an objection from the agent who had originally ruled on the case, the commissioner turned down Bruce's recommendation. The agent, Bruce recalls, "told homophobic jokes in my presence and ridiculed the claimant." As a result of Bruce's vigorous lobbying, however, the ruling was reversed.

At Bruce's request, a commissioner agreed to discuss with the other commissioners the establishment of a special gay crimes unit. The chairman of CVB told Bruce privately, however, "Those people can't have their private investigator." Bruce associates the chairman's remark with what he frequently heard from homophobes on the CVB staff: "The gays don't need a civil rights bill, they're all rich." "For them," Bruce explains, "Truman Capote represented the community. They don't think of some homeless kid at the Hetrick Martin Institute [a gay community institution catering to troubled gay youth]."

Once when Russell Nutter and Jay Watkins, founders of AVP, came to the CVB seeking funding from the agency, Burke made himself known to them and urged them to call him if they encountered problems with gay crime victims. Subsequently, in discussing a case AVP was negotiating with a CVB commissioner, Bruce admitted that he had "more than just an academic interest" in the case. Subsequently, after a series of gay-bashing incidents in Greenwich Village, Bruce exclaimed, "Goddammit, I'm going to do something." He "came out." To his satisfaction, colleagues ceased making homophobic remarks in his presence; and sympathetic staff members and, more particularly, one of the supervisors cooperated in assigning gay crime victims cases to him. "I couldn't be doing what I am doing," Bruce admits, "if she hadn't opened the way." When Bruce did an intake on a gay claim, the case was automatically assigned to him. If not, he often had to do fancy footwork, he says, to have it transferred to him. In fact, he began to function informally as the gay liaison person in the office, often confronting resistance from individual commissioner and co-workers, some of whom refused to inform him of gay complaints.

In 1988, after one of his colleagues turned over to Bruce an assault claim involving a PWA, Bruce discovered that the police had not classified the attack as a bias crime. He referred the case to AVP. After AVP contacted the police bias unit, the victim identified his attacker from mug shots. The perpetrator pleaded guilty and was incarcerated. "If my colleague had not been busy and turned over the case to me," Bruce notes, "we would have had a different outcome. I started the ball rolling to get a gay basher off the streets."

Bruce finds satisfaction in lasting friendships he establishes with claimants. "The gay community," he declares, "could find role models among some of the people I've dealt with. I have been honored to work with these people." He has been gratified, too, by some of the tangential rewards he experiences at his job. Once he declared to a gay man whose skull had been fractured by an attacker as he left a disco, "I believe you were attacked because of your orientation even though the police report doesn't say so." The victim nodded in response. "I wasn't sure," Bruce declares, "whether we had communicated with each other." Bruce saw to it that the man received compensation for his medical costs and earning losses and referred the man to AVP for counseling. Just before the gay March on Washington, the man called and said, "I took to heart what you said, and my lover and I are going on the march." "That," exclaims Bruce, "was one of the nicest things ever said to me at the agency. That's the kind of thing that has kept me there."

At Bruce's request, Lee Hudson, Mayor Koch's liaison person with the gay community, appointed him to the Police Council. He and Katie Doran were the only holdovers on the council into the Dinkins administration.

Bruce does consider himself a gay activist despite his reservations regarding militant organizations like ACT UP and Queer Nation. "Over the last ten years," he notes, "I have seen the gamut of violence in our community and of responses from my office. I have paid a lot of people's medical bills. I've buried a lot of our battle casualties. I have handled four to five hundred gay claimants, including numerous PWAs, paying compensation in two-thirds to three-quarters of the cases, whereas generally an equal percentage of claims are rejected by CVB."

Chapter Eleven

GOAL: Coming Out as Cops

Gay police share the general obloquy directed by gay activists against police. In addition, they labor under the handicap of being a beleaguered minority within a paramilitary corps notorious for its homophobia. Thus the coming-out experiences of Gay Officers Action League (GOAL) interviewees differ in numerous respects from those of the other interviewees and deserve separate treatment.

It was a sign of the increasing influence of the gay community in New York City that ten years after the Stonewall "rebellion" officers of the New York Police Department (NYPD) dared to organize their own defense fraternity.

One of the first NYPD officers to come out publicly was Charlie Cochrane.

Ermanno Stingo, the AVP volunteer, recalls how at City Council hearings on the Gay Rights bill in the late 1970s, immediately after the head of the Patrolmen's Benevolent Association testified that there were no gays in the police department, Charlie Cochrane took the stand and announced, "I am a sergeant in the police department, and I am a gay man, and I'm proud of it." Asked by reporters whether his mother knew of his intention to testify at the hearings, Cochrane replied, "Yes, and she said that I should be sure that my suit was neatly pressed."

Such was the fear of exposure among gay officers that when Charlie and a fellow officer set out to build an organization of gay cops they approached only retired officers and their own close friends. Like underground conspirators, they met with potential new members one-on-one in restaurants. Indeed, during the decade of the 1980s only a small proportion of the gay police dared to emerge to demand recognition of their own fraternal organization, the Gay Officers Action League (GOAL). GOAL interviewees related varying experiences in the personal evolution that culminated in their coming out first as gays and then as gay activists within the NYPD.

PETE GUARDINO

In 1982 GOAL marched for the first time as a group in the Gay Pride parade. As the gay officers passed where he was posted, Pete Guardino, a patrolman in his mid-thirties, petrified at his own boldness, walked over to the marchers and shook hands all around. Later that year, Pete recounts, someone put a flyer in his mailbox, a strange message composed of cutout letters. Although fearful that someone was trying to intimidate him, he called the telephone number on the flyer. Charlie Cochrane answered and invited him to a meeting. Pete found about ten men assembled in an office made available by a gay physician. "My first impression? . . . I was scared," Pete says. "I sat and listened." In fact, at meetings during the next four months, Pete said not a word. "Sometimes," he explains, "you have to be sure you know what you're talking about before you speak, and I wanted to get comfortable with the organization."

Although granting that members showed courage simply by attending meetings, Pete was convinced that if they were not prepared to back up the few who like Charlie had come out, their courage had little meaning. "Being invisible," he insisted, "just confirms society's prejudices that we're immoral, we're sick, we're not capable of relationships. For ten years I have struggled," Pete complained, "an individual gay officer without any support, with no one to talk to. Here I joined an organization that wanted to stay in the closet. They weren't publicizing themselves or fighting for our rights. Other groups in the department had their organizations, but this group was not acting like the support organization I was looking for."

Rejecting the rationalizations for continued secrecy, Pete proposed the publication of a newsletter and participation in gay demonstrations. Very quickly in his own precinct he himself became known as Pete of GOAL. "A person has to start by taking pride in himself," Pete declares. "The road ahead is sometimes not as easy as we would like it to be. We have never been recognized as a legitimate section of the society. Stonewall said we have had enough."

Pete, his twin brother, older brother, and older sister were born in Little Italy on the Lower East Side of Manhattan. His paternal grandparents emigrated from Italy; his maternal grandparents, from Hungary. Pete was dark complexioned and looked Hispanic. He did not feel that he was completely American. A loner, he also sensed a difference in himself from the rest of the family. Small for his age and taught at home that fighting did not make a man, Pete was picked on by other boys and called "sissy," "little girl," and "fag."

Pete had his first inklings of being gay as early as age seven. When Pete was about twelve, he "fooled around" with a cousin three years older than he. Two years later someone invited Pete to meet a gay man on the block who sought sex with teenagers. "It was secretive, shameful, a sin," he recalls.

In 1965, after graduating from high school, Pete enlisted in the army. While in basic training, although attracted to men, Pete dated women in his neighborhood. During his service in Vietnam, Pete remained in the closet. He was approached by other men with eye contact and suspected his sergeant and another sergeant were lovers. Once he and another soldier began touching. After they had sex, "the guilt set in," Pete recounts. They never spoke about the experience or repeated it.

Upon returning from Vietnam, Pete took the civil service examination for correction officers and was assigned to a post at the Tombs, a city detention center. It was "rough," he recalls, "to see gay prisoners segregated on a floor of their own. They had no sense of self-worth." Snide remarks from some of the other officers upset him. "But you have to maintain a working relationship with the others," he insists. "I ignored homophobic comments." On the other hand, the inmates recognized that he was different, more compassionate. "Officer Guardino, how are you doing?" they would call out when he came on duty.

While working at the Tombs, Pete married. "I married because I loved the woman," he declares, "because it was the thing to do, and because I thought it could be an answer to the problem of being gay." On the side, Pete continued going to bars and to gay dances. Fearful of transmitting a venereal disease to his wife, he was not promiscuous. In the second year of marriage, Pete started becoming careless with phone numbers and in other ways. When one day his wife confronted him and threatened to expose him to his family, Pete ran to his older brother's apartment around the corner and announced, "We have to talk." "What's the matter?" his brother asked. "You know I've been having troubles with my wife," Pete said. "What's the matter?" "I'm gay." "Yeah, so what?" said his brother. "I didn't expect that response," Pete says. "I expected anger. He's macho, he loves his women." "I'm your older brother," his brother declared, "I'm here for you, if there's ever a problem, come talk to me. If we can't sit down and talk about your problem, we'll find somebody who can."

Pete went on to tell his mother. He found her in the kitchen cooking. He said that they had to talk. "What's the matter?" she asked. "Me and Chris are breaking up," Pete declared. "It's not working out. I'm gay." "What d'ya mean," his mother asked, "you're one of them?" "Yeah!" Pete's mother never mentioned the subject again. Pete did not tell his father, but when his father met Pete's gay friends, he made no remarks. Now when Pete telephones, his father calls his mother and says, "*She's* on the phone." "He's not being vicious," Pete insists. "I think it's amusing."

Pete's sister, divorced with two grown children, knew gay people. Pete had no problems with her. Pete said nothing to his twin brother. "He and I are opposites," Pete explains. "We get along and don't get along. He's been in prison, into drugs.

"If my wife could have understood me," Pete declares, "I could have shared my life with her. She's remarried and has children."

Eager to get out on the street, Pete took the NYPD civil service examination and joined the force in 1973. Although over the years, he says, he has encountered no overt homophobic hostility, at his Midtown South precinct he has not had doors opened to him. After almost twenty years of service he remained a patrolman. Once, indeed, before he came out, someone put pictures of naked men in his locker. Discovering who was responsible, Pete approached the officer and said, "The next time you put pictures in my locker, make them glossy and 5 x 7 so that I can put them over my bed." The officer laughed. "I'm sure," Pete declares, "the rumor had gone around that I was gay because I never went out drinking with the others. I just couldn't be something that I wasn't. People I worked with knew me as a cop, a good cop, before they knew I was gay. I set the tone for my surroundings. I don't let anyone get away with anything." With the three partners he has had over the years, Pete had no problems. He introduced one of them to his friends and lovers and sometimes even talked openly with him about flirting with men.

By the time he joined GOAL, Pete had already completed almost nine years in the NYPD. The years until 1987, Pete says, were a building period. "Out" GOAL members made contact with other gay groups, attending rallies, demonstrations, and meetings of such organizations as Dignity and Parents and Friends of Lesbians and Gays. After establishing a network of support groups, GOAL won the right to make a presentation along with other officers' associations to recruits at the Police Academy and was granted its own room at the Academy. "Now," Pete declares, "we have our own patches on our uniforms. We have our own T-shirt and pins. We hold an annual Christmas party. Numerous articles about us have appeared in newspapers and magazines.

"GOAL is part of my life," Pete declares, "part of my being gay. It provides something I've never had before—dignity, respect, pride, and comradeship. I see how important it is for people to come out in law enforcement nowadays. We don't yet have the freedom that there is in other areas of life. If people say that conditions are so much easier, why don't more people come out? Why are we still demanding representation within the department? No, there is still justification for fear."

FRED ADLER

Fred Adler, a patrolman in the Housing Police, comes from a police family. His father is a retired NYPD detective. His younger brother is a public-housing detective. His sister is married to an NYPD police officer. His uncle is a sergeant in the force. Although Fred's father grew up in an Orthodox family and his mother's family were Conservative Jews, they did not keep a kosher house. In high school Fred and his girlfriend joined the National Federation of Temple Youth and went on weekend excursions throughout New York state, visiting members' homes. When Fred's brother married a gentile, his parents had difficulty in adjusting to the marriage. Fred notes that of his parents' three children he alone has a Jewish life partner. He and his lover attend services on the High Holidays and celebrate Passover in their apartment. "My Jewishness," Fred declares, has proved no complication in my being gay. I was brought up to believe that religion was important but it was not to be allowed to control your life."

In high school Fred was a "regular Joe," a member of the tennis, track, and wrestling teams. He had a "steady" girlfriend. "I did all the things I was supposed to do," he says. At a summer job at the New York City Port Authority bus terminal, "a strange place for a naive sixteen-year-old from upstate," Fred encountered aspects of life of which he had had no conception. One evening on the bus trip home, a young man put his hand on Fred's thigh and invited Fred to get off the bus with him. Fred refused, but he experienced strange excitement at the incident.

After completing a semester at Orange County Community College, Fred quit school and took a job at a New York City bank as a customer service representative. One day after having dinner with a colleague, he returned to the man's apartment with him and had his first homosexual experience. "So this is what sex is," Fred said to himself. "This is it!" Fred then discovered the gay bars and began spending evenings in the city. His fiancée (he had become engaged after graduating from high school) asked whether he was sleeping with other women. Fred said he was not and congratulated himself for not lying; but he was sensing increasing pressure, he recalls, because of his double life. "I had made my decision sexually and was going crazy," he says.

When Fred's prospective father-in-law began making arrangements for a wedding, Fred told his fiancée he could not marry her. "I'm gay," he declared. She was prepared to go through with the wedding. "It's not okay," Fred insisted. "It's not fair to either of us." She told her parents what he said. Her mother accepted the situation, but neither the girl nor her father ever spoke to Fred again.

"We're not ready," Fred explained to his parents. One morning in 1982, however, Fred, then twenty-two, woke up and discovered his father sitting in his bedroom. Easygoing and respectful of his children's privacy, he had never before come into Fred's room uninvited. "Good morning!" Fred exclaimed. "Freddie, are you gay?" his father demanded. "This at eight in the morning!" Fred recalls. "I said I would be right back and went to the bathroom, threw some water on my face, returned and said, 'Yes.' My father walked out of the bedroom. He told my mother, of course. They never said,

'Let's sit down, let's discuss this.' I guess it was easier for them to say nothing. I have no idea what impelled him to bring up the question at that moment."

Fred did not discuss the question with his straight and macho brother, two years his junior, or with his sister, five years younger than he.

"Guilt goes with you through your whole life when you're the firstborn," Fred comments.

Fred floated from job to job. "I wasn't taking life seriously," he relates. "I was just having a good time." At his father's and uncle's urging, he took the police and fire departments' civil service examinations. He passed. Asked whether he wanted to become a cop, he said, "Fine." In fact, although from early childhood he had been aware of police work, he had never had any ambition to join the force. He was assigned to a housing-police unit.

One day, after six months on the job, as he entered the locker room, Fred overheard a police officer from another squad talking about him and complaining that the command was now being forced to accept faggots. "I walked over to him," Fred recounts, "and said, 'If you have something to say to me, say it to my face. Don't talk behind my back.' I didn't come out and admit anything nor did I deny anything. There was total silence. I made up my mind to let them talk and think what they wanted to think."

While still a recruit, Fred had heard about GOAL at the fraternal organizations day at the Academy. Joining in 1984, Fred found in GOAL the support he needed as a gay officer. "I grew up within the organization," he declares. In 1985 Fred agreed to an interview with a reporter from *Newsday* on condition that his name not be mentioned in the article. His photograph, he was assured, would be unrecognizable within the collage. At seven o'clock in the morning about a week after the interview, the telephone rang. "It was Mom," Fred relates. "She was crying." Fred asked what was wrong. "How could you do this?" she exclaimed. "Why didn't you tell me?" "What're you talking about?" Fred asked, still only half awake. *"Newsday."* "Mom," Fred said, "let me call you back." Fred ran out to buy the paper. He saw his picture on the front page, with the caption "Fred X." In the lengthy article the reporter named Fred's housing-police unit. Now not only did his extended family know about him, but the whole world as well. "At first I was mad as hell," Fred recalls, "but afterwards I said, 'It's out now; it's great.' "

The article appeared on a day that Fred was off duty. The next day he went to work, wondering what to expect. "I would not have believed it," he declares. "Cops came up to congratulate me. 'It took a lot of guts,' some officers, including the sergeant, assured me. The reaction was practically unanimous.

"We have to live with it now," Fred said to his mother, "that's the way it is." It did not take his parents long to accept that view. With his brother, however, Fred faced a special problem. He had preceded Fred into the force and was in the same 150-man command. "What I do reflects on him," Fred explains. When the newspaper story broke, Fred said nothing, and for two years his brother ignored the gossip in the squad and said nothing to Fred. "We have never completely resolved the problem," Fred admits. "My brother and I have always been warm, but there has always been a distance between us. Even back in high school we lived differently and had different friends."

One Saturday night Fred invited his brother to go with him to the Saint, a newly opened gay club. "The atmosphere was shocking to him at first," Fred recalls, "but after he met my friends, he had a great time." Early the succeeding Monday morning Fred's brother and his partner came upon a drunk staggering and falling down in the street. The partner gave the man a hard time. The man's wallet fell from his pocket, and a Saint membership card dropped out. Fred's brother told his partner to leave the guy alone, asked the guy where he lived, and put him in the police car and drove him home. "It was nice to hear my brother say," Fred declares, "that he had taken care of one of mine. He thought it could have been me.

"I make sure cops work with me professionally before I come out to them," Fred declares, echoing Pete Guardino. "They can never say, 'He's a bad cop,' but if I'm faced with homophobic cops, I try to make them aware what the job is, who I am. I tell them what we're doing at GOAL. When we're selling GOAL T-shirts, they all buy one, straights as well as gays. I say to them, 'I have to buy a candy bar every time your kid comes in on some charity.' "

Fred estimates that among the thirteen hundred New York City public-housing officers no more than about twenty are gay. Six are members of GOAL. When they bring problems to him as GOAL deputy director for housing police, he calls their captain. "If he isn't cooperative, I'll tell Sam [Ciccone, until 1992 the GOAL executive director]. Sam will call the department head. The department head will send a letter to the captain. "They treat us with kid gloves," Fred remarks, "[not] because they are politically correct . . . [but because] they do not want to lose out on a promotion. It's the departmental right thing," Fred notes, "if not a personal right thing."

Fred belongs to the Jewish fraternal police organization Shotrim as well as GOAL. "People used to think most cops were Irish," he notes. "Now many Jews have joined the force. In my life as a police officer," he comments, "the fact of being gay is a more decisive factor than being Jewish. As far as I am aware there is no problem [in the NYPD] of anti-Semitism, whereas the problem of homophobia is very much alive."

JERRY COX

Jerry Cox, a plainclothes transit police officer in his forties, frequently ran into Pete Guardino in court and had heard about GOAL as early as 1982. Married, with two children, and uncertain about his sexual orientation, he gave no thought to applying for membership. One Saturday in 1987, Jerry recalls, "just after I had admitted to myself who and what I was," he and his police partner appeared at a GOAL meeting to seek assistance for a gay transit officer who had killed his lover in a quarrel. Pete met them at the door, Jerry relates, opened it a crack, listened to what they had to say, and replied that GOAL could do nothing because the cop was not a GOAL member. Convinced that they were straight, Pete refused to let them into the meeting. In fact, as Jerry was subsequently to learn, his partner's lover was inside. Jerry expresses astonishment that during three and a half years he and his partner never had an inkling that the other was gay. "We could read each other's minds about everything else when we worked together," Jerry relates. "He would know in advance if I was going to fart. Such chemistry is necessary because you're covering each other's backs. The uniform helps to stop incidents, but plainclothes officers are utterly dependent upon each other."

Jerry is the first cop in his family. His father's people had settled in Maine in the early seventeenth century. His mother is a third-generation Irish American. Jerry's father died while Jerry was at Sullivan Community College studying to be a chef, and Jerry was forced to drop out to help support the family. In 1977 Jerry took the examination for state corrections officers although, he says, he did not even know what a corrections officer was. He was assigned to the worst state prison at the time, Greenhaven, to which prisoners involved in the bloody Attica prison riot of that year had just been transferred. "It was a powder keg," Jerry declares. "Thank god, we kept everything under control." Finding the work confining and weary of commuting from the city, in 1981 Jerry took another civil service examination, passed "with flying colors," and eight months later, after five years at Greenhaven, joined the transit police.

Because of the way his older brother, who eventually died of AIDS, flaunted his being gay, Jerry suppressed his homosexual urges. In 1976, while still a corrections officer at Greenhaven prison, Jerry married. Some four years later, when he was twenty-seven or twenty-eight, during a free afternoon he wandered into a gay movie house. "I started getting aroused," he recalls. "Next thing I knew some guy came over and started to suck me off. It felt good, but it scared the shit out of me. I thought I was straight. It was not normal for me to do such things. I had a wife, I had a son."

For several years Jerry thought he might be bisexual. In 1987, however, he fell in love with a Japanese man who was living with a friend. "I thought they were just roommates," Jerry relates. After four or five months, forced to choose, the Japanese man left Jerry. "I was depressed over the break up," Jerry recalls. "I had crying spells for apparently no reason. Anything that reminded me of him would set me off. You never really get over your first love," Jerry explains. One day when Jerry was in deep depression, his wife questioned him. Jerry told her not to worry, that he would handle whatever the problem was. She pressed him, and Jerry "spilt the beans. She was in shock," Jerry relates. "We had ceased to have sex for two or three years.

She thought she was responsible. We had a long talk. She seemed to be able to handle the fact that I was gay better than I could." They agreed that Jerry would remain at home because of the children, a boy of twelve and a girl of eight.

Coming out proved a relief for Jerry and for his wife. "I no longer had to sneak around," Jerry declares. They agreed that if Jerry met a lover, he would move out so that she would then be able to get on with her life. They would continue to share responsibility for the children.

When Jerry came out to his mother, she confided that his brother constantly insisted, "You made me this way, it's your fault that I'm gay." "My mother wonders how it was that she had two gay sons," Jerry says. "I tell her she had nothing to do with it. I insist that she was a perfect mother, who did everything a parent can be expected to do."

Transit cops knew that Jerry's openly gay brother had died of AIDS. "So they didn't have to think that I was gay," he says, "to believe that I knew about the disease, and I could talk about it." Nevertheless, Jerry became aware of rumors about him among the 250 men and women in his transit-police district. "Cops," Jerry notes, "love to talk. Some were questioning people who worked with me about me. They all answered, 'Don't ask me, ask him.' It's not easy to come out to people. You don't know how they're going to react." At the 1991 Gay Pride march, Jerry recalls, cops stationed outside St. Patrick's spat at a gay police lieutenant.

One evening after a long conversation with his supervisor in a subway station, Jerry went into the men's room. Two cops told another supervisor that Jerry was hanging out in men's rooms. Fortunately, Jerry's supervisor came to his defense. Now, Jerry says that he hears homophobic jokes or remarks "only once in a blue moon." "Whether I react," he declares, "depends upon the circumstances. It's hard to come out and tell people to stop saying things at a roll call with fifty or sixty people around. There are some men you know you could talk to from now to doomsday and it would do no good to try to correct them. The wall would give you a better response."

According to Jerry, in the force there is more prejudice against gays than against lesbians. "The homophobes will tolerate two women doing things together because that's 'kinky,' " Jerry declares. "If a lesbian comes out, you might hear something but not as much as with a gay cop."

Jerry finds it amusing that the homophobes always think that "because you're gay you're going to attack them, that you want their body. I look at half of these people and think to myself who the hell would want you. You're overweight, you stink." The ones who are always questioning other people's sexuality, he says, are the ones he wonders about being gay themselves.

Jerry has no illusions about the attitude of many police officers toward the gay community. "Any gay person," he says, "is at risk with homophobic cops." At gay demonstrations, he points out, "some cops just love it when you step over the line so that they can beat the shit out of you." He has heard cops warn each other not to stand too close to ACT UP demonstrators. "They don't even know how you get AIDS!" Jerry exclaims. At the Christopher Street subway station, he recounted, a transit cop caught two gays who had jumped the turnstile and took one into the men's room and "beat the shit out of him." One of the gays was politically connected. The cop was tried and found guilty. "It wouldn't surprise me," Jerry remarked, "if he attacked them because they were gay."

On the other hand, Jerry has been mistaken in his judgments of fellow officers. "One guy from an Irish Catholic family in the Bronx, from a background where everything is black or white," Jerry declares, "I find out that he stands up for gays, that his best friend is gay. As long you don't go after kids, he doesn't care what you do in bed. On the other hand, people who seemed liberal have turned out to be very homophobic." To a religious cop who declared "unnatural" sex ought not to be allowed, Jerry retorted, "If two people love each other, what they do in the bedroom is nobody's business. If someone wants to be a Tarzan and swing from a vine and act like a monkey, that's their business. . . . What we're trying to get over to the straight police officers is, 'You might not like us and you don't have to like us. All we say is respect us.' "

(Late in 1991, some months after being interviewed, while on duty in the subway Jerry got into conversation with a Japanese American. Several months later they moved into an apartment together.)

VANESSA

In 1987 at the Lesbian and Gay Community Center, Vanessa, then a patrolwoman at a Bronx precinct, saw an announcement of a meeting of the Gay Officers Action League. "I wasn't sure what the name stood for," Vanessa declares, "whether they were police or military or Coast Guard." At a meeting she found a group of about thirty men and just one other woman. "I was really turned off," Vanessa recalls. "The boys were acting like the cops I knew on patrol. Here was this guy from GMHC talking about safe sex and condoms, and the boys were making wisecracks. With my Catholic upbringing, this was not for me. This was what I was running away from at the precinct. I didn't want to hear it at a GOAL meeting."

Nevertheless, when Pete Guardino and other GOAL members asked her to march in the Gay Pride parade to help add numbers to their contingent, Vanessa agreed. "I was scared," she relates, "but I was also so elated by the celebrations during gay pride month that I did not think of possible repercussions." A sergeant standing among the cops lining the route of the parade recognized Vanessa. Vanessa waved. "I was the last person she expected to see in the parade," Vanessa recounts. "She lowered her glasses, and there was surprise on her face. The truth now was out," Vanessa realized.

Born in New York City in 1962, Vanessa was the youngest of six children, four boys and two girls, of a Spanish merchant-marine father who emigrated with his family to the United States via Cuba in 1958. As a child Vanessa experienced a lot of love in a warm family as well as a lot of passion and conflict. As the youngest child, Vanessa was maneuvered by her brothers and sister to do things for them, but, in turn, she looked to them for love and care. Her second brother, three years her senior, served as a surrogate father to her.

In Vanessa's family, the Spanish macho tradition prevailed. The boys were allowed to stay out later, they got the interesting toys. Vanessa and her sister were given "those sick dolls and silly dresses. I wanted to be like the boys," Vanessa declares. "I competed in games with my brother. For a long time we were pretty parallel." Her acting like a tomboy, Vanessa says, did not trouble her mother. "She is a tough woman," Vanessa explains. "She believes in being independent, and she saw me as the woman she couldn't become. She liked the way I challenged boys." On the other hand, Vanessa's brothers criticized her for not accepting her "proper" place as a girl and as a young woman.

"My earliest memories of sexuality," Vanessa declared, "date to age five or six, when I began to notice the differences between boys and girls and the difference in my attitudes from other girls.' I was intrigued by boys, but I never understood boys, their mentality and psyche, their sense of superiority because they had a penis." By the eighth grade Vanessa had come out to herself. "I was sexually attracted to my best friend," she relates. "I tried to let her know my feelings once, but she got frightened, and I backed off because I didn't want to lose her. My brother used to date her, so there were a lot of problems there." Vanessa has suspected latent homosexuality in this brother. He would make the family laugh by cross-dressing. Though married and with children, he goes to transvestite bars and parties.

When Vanessa broke up with her first lover in high school, her mother, who had become suspicious of the relationship, confronted Vanessa. Vanessa made no admission and was not questioned again for a long time. From the age of sixteen until the age of twenty-two, she dated a Cuban young man, a distant cousin, who did not believe in premarital sex. "I didn't even want to kiss him," Vanessa declares. "I would say, 'It's getting too huffy and puffy, let's get out of here.' " He frequently traveled to Mexico, and they corresponded. When he returned to New York, Vanessa was always eager for him to leave again. "I shouldn't have led him on," she declares in retrospect.

While a physical education major at Queens College, Vanessa did practice teaching in an inner-city high school. "It was scary," she recalls. "I had gone to Catholic schools, where teachers and authority figures were respected. Here students attacked teachers. One day a student set a bulletin board on fire." Close in age to the students, Vanessa did not know how to defend herself. "When my supervising teacher and I handed out basketballs," she relates, "some of the girls started shooting baskets, but others started throwing the balls at the windows and at the clock. The teacher screamed at them.

It seemed that a lot of energy was spent in screaming. I had chosen teaching in order to serve the community. I wanted to teach and not simply to keep order."

Vanessa's eldest brother and a second brother a little older than she, both police officers, provided models for her. "It was a good job opportunity for us," Vanessa declares. "Jobs in the department provide a satisfactory income and financial security. Just as poor youth go into the military, lower-middle-class youth join the police." Vanessa was also attracted to the police because the work offered an opportunity to be of service to the community. "I thought that for what I would be earning, teaching was not for me," she remarked, "and in 1984 I joined the NYPD."

As a rookie at the police academy, Vanessa declares, "it was time for me to grow up, and my mother wasn't allowing me to do so. She wouldn't let me go away on weekends and even screened my telephone calls." Her mother also resented Vanessa's new lover, fifteen years Vanessa's senior. "You're not going to stop this from happening," Vanessa warned. "I love this woman." Her mother shouted, "Don't leave me. I'll take you to Spain. We'll find someone to heal you." When Vanessa announced that her high school friend of six years had also been her lover, her mother was shocked.

Vanessa's brothers urged Vanessa not to "do this" to her mother. "It's against God," they warned. Vanessa's father, however, reacted calmly. "As a sailor in the merchant marine," Vanessa explains, "he was a worldly man with few aspirations. He just wanted me to be happy. I think he wouldn't have been happy if one of the boys had been gay. He never got along with the brother that I suspect may be gay. He called him 'a faggot.' "

After marrying, Vanessa's brothers and sister continued to visit their parents' house every day with their children. "My mother ran everyone's life," Vanessa declares. "I didn't want that." Nevertheless, Vanessa experienced guilt upon leaving home and moving in with her lover. In preparing for her courses at the Police Academy, she recalls, "sitting down to study for an hour was killing me. I couldn't get my head into the books." Her lover helped her through the crisis, showing her a lot of love and bolstering her confidence. "I grew up with her," Vanessa insists. "She gave me a sense of worth and convinced me that I could make it on my own."

During six months of patrol training, Vanessa admits that she was often frightened. One night in the Seventh Precinct near Delancey Street, where her training patrol was assigned, a man, probably a drug dealer, approached her with a bullet wound in his back. "I just got shot," he announced. "It was very scary," Vanessa says, "to deal with people with guns and knives, people who hate you. When I was in Catholic school, my mother walked me to school. Here I was at twenty-two on the street in uniform, naive about a lot of things. I knew nothing about drugs."

After finishing her training and receiving an assignment at the Forty-third Precinct in the Bronx, Vanessa realized that she was expected to share her life with her partner. She hoped to find a woman who thought along the same lines as she or even a man who like her was simply out to do a good job. She worked with various men and women and was always disappointed. Some of her partners, she found, were burned-out. Some were bossy. She didn't like the way they were policing.

Vanessa experienced sexual harassment. "A guy on patrol with me," she related, "would ask what kind of underwear I had on. Did I wear panties, lacey things? I would make a joke. They want to be titillated all the time. They channel the constant tension into sex, eating, and drinking. They make passes. That's macho. Most of the time they don't expect anything. They like a girl they can talk their crap to. If a girl gives in, they'll take advantage of it. The woman always suffers in the gossip. She's looked at as a tramp. The guy doesn't suffer so much. But it is a profession, and they don't want to get into any hassle. It's the discreet cops who advance."

The older cops used to say to Kenny, Vanessa's partner, a veteran with twenty years on the force, "We thought all along you were getting on with her and that was why she wasn't giving it to the rest of us. Kenny snapped back, "What makes you think I'm not?" Occasionally, she and Kenny would walk into the precinct late after lunch. When the sergeant would ask where they had been, Kenny would say, "Sergeant, Vanessa and me, we went to a hotel, and it took a little longer than we expected." The bosses would laugh, Vanessa would laugh, and they would be signed in on time. "You could call that harassment," Vanessa admits, "but I didn't say anything because I was gaining from it, too. By that time I was secure in myself. I was aware, too," she says, "that I was breaking the ice. Other lesbians would follow me and have it easier. The men would say, 'Vanessa was a regular girl, she just wanted to go home with a woman. Other than that she laughed with us, talked dirty with us.' " Other lesbians on the job with her, Vanessa declares, were "very political" and would not stand for any nonsense. "The boys didn't want them around," Vanessa says. "They're afraid of people with causes." Still, Vanessa declares, some of the men were really "dirtbags," but they knew how far they could go, Vanessa insists, "and they never put their hands on me."

On the other hand, Vanessa did not like the subterfuge under which she was living. She was developing warm feelings for the men and women she worked with and resented being dishonest with them. "I knew that the person they cared about," she relates, "wasn't who they thought I was. You guys, I was thinking, really don't care about me because you don't know who I am. Everything I told them was true except the sex of the person I went home to."

When word spread of her marching in the GOAL contingent in the Gay Pride parade, Kenny called and asked, "Is it true?" Vanessa said it was. "What do you want me to do?" he asked. Vanessa replied that she did not want him to do anything. She had already established herself as a good cop.

"The cops liked me," she declares. "I had good relations with the bosses, too." In fact, upon hearing the news about the parade, one officer declared, "I don't think she's gay. She marched probably because one of her friends marched." In fact, Vanessa's lover marched with her. Vanessa wore a GOAL T-shirt. On the back of her lover's T-shirt, Vanessa had pressed letters reading "My lover's on the job."

At the precinct headquarters Vanessa sought out people she cared about, beginning with her commanding officer. "He was like a father to me," she says, "and I wanted him to know that I wasn't any different than I was yesterday." "I'm sorry that you found out the way you did," she declared. "I didn't know how else to do it." "How are you feeling?" he said. "How can I help you?" He asked whether anyone in the command was making things difficult for her. He assured her that if she wanted to talk at any time, she was free to come to him. "He's a caring man," Vanessa notes. "he has a daughter. He was in his fifties and could have been my father. I never really had a father." After he was promoted out of the precinct, he helped Vanessa advance to a new position at police headquarters as liaison to the gay community in the NYPD Community Affairs department.

Next Vanessa spoke to each of the lieutenants at the precinct privately. One of them, who was attracted to her, she knew was hurting especially. He said, "It's okay. I really like you as a person, and this doesn't change my feelings. I may not understand. I may wish that you would go into therapy or let me be the man to try to change you."

Vanessa found it more painful to deal with a young patrolman who was also interested in her. "I should have told him and the lieutenant in advance," she states in retrospect. "I should have said to them: 'People see you're interested in me. You should protect yourselves when the word gets out.' " The young officer responded with silence. "I think he thought I had used him," Vanessa declares. "That was understandable."

Kenny, Vanessa's partner, proved helpful and protective. Sometimes he would launch an attack on Vanessa to get a hostile cop to expose his homophobia. Then he would take the cop to task. If Vanessa complained that Kenny's jokes were abusive, he would stop for a day. At one point, however, she decided she had had enough of him as a partner. The commanding officer offered to intervene, but Vanessa asked him not to say anything. She had needed to vent her annoyance to someone. She would take care of Kenny herself. "In the police department," she explains, "you don't rat on anybody. If you're a rat, you're shut out."

Not all of Vanessa's lesbian colleagues proved sympathetic. "Why did you do that?" one of them exclaimed. "Now they'll start a witch-hunt, questioning who else is gay." Many of the women, both straight and closeted gays, were afraid to talk to Vanessa for fear of being taken for lesbians themselves. Indeed, Vanessa complains of internalized homophobia among lesbians on the force. "At a conference in 1990," Vanessa recounted, "a good 30 percent of the women were lesbians. Yet there were no workshops on lesbian issues or even any mention of lesbians." She arranged with the commanding officer to plant people in the audience to pose gay issues. Someone suggested that the workshop on women of color include lesbians and that the title of the workshop be changed accordingly to "The Minority within the Minority." Some lesbians objected that they did not want special treatment. After the conference, Vanessa maneuvered for the inclusion of lesbian issues at the next conference in the workshop on sexual harassment.

In 1989, five years after she joined the NYPD, Vanessa applied for membership in GOAL. "I wanted to join because it was a place to talk to other gay cops," she declared, "where I would be comfortable." Almost immediately Vanessa found herself appointed GOAL secretary. "They wanted a woman on the board," she says. She also was annoyed to discover that the board was in the closet. "I am working so hard to be proud of myself," she complained, "as a lesbian and to be proud of myself as a police officer, and here you guys are putting me back in the closet." She ceased attending meetings.

In 1990, after a three-year absence from GOAL, Sam Ciccone, by then a retired police sergeant, returned to activity in the organization. "I can't believe that I've come back to GOAL after three years," Vanessa remembers him declaring, "and you people are still voting to remain in the closet." He begged Vanessa to return to active membership. "I told him," Vanessa declares, "I couldn't stand it, those guys were ignorant, the board stank. But I haven't missed a meeting since. We have new blood on the board. The group has grown immensely. You still run into a lot of internalized homophobia, but it's much better than before."

("I was screaming from the beginning," Pete Guardino commented, "that the organization be more visible, but back then Sam was still in the closet. Now, as a retiree, Sam is demanding more openness from all the members." Pete was troubled by Sam's high-handed running of the organization, "acting as though he was still a sergeant at a precinct.")

"GOAL is part of my life," declares Vanessa, "part of my being gay. It has given me something I've never had before—dignity, respect, pride, and comradeship. On the other hand, gays still experience fear within the department, and with justification. Career paths in law enforcement are opening for women and minorities, but though we have homicides in the gay community, we have no gays or lesbians investigating gay homicides and gay bashing."

As liaison to the gay community at the NYPD Community Affairs department, Vanessa regularly speaks to recruits at the Police Academy. "The kids in the class," she says, "have fallen asleep after a series of lectures, but as soon as I say I am a lesbian cop, they wake up. I say to them, 'You're going to be out at demonstrations. Who are those people? Why are they out there? Should you get hot under the collar because they're demonstrating on AIDS? Is it your business that they are lesbians or gays? What is your job as a police officer? People with AIDS are offended if you put gloves on. If you're afraid of mixing blood in an altercation, put gloves on at the last minute. I've come out. Ask yourself what abut the person next to you? Gay or lesbian?' "

Vanessa admits that she is often frustrated in addressing men and women in the force. "You never know who is in your audience," she says. When at a precinct sensitivity session cops expressed their indignation at a gay activist who spat in the Eucharist at St. Patrick's, Vanessa expressed understanding at their being upset. "But," she reminded them, "you are not private individuals, you are police officers in uniform. It's not for you to hit a gay person and call him a faggot because he spat in the Eucharist." An officer raised his hand and declared: "You're not really a cop. You're one of them."

But officers occasionally have volunteered encouragement. One came up to Vanessa and said, "I have not told anyone this before, but my brother is gay. I know that it's tough on him. I think you're really strong to come out." Another cop told her his brother had recently died of AIDS. "I don't understand it," he said, "but I loved my brother very much." He shook Vanessa's hand. Such incidents, Vanessa declares, rare as they are, show that "the work you're doing is paying off. For new gay cops the way'll be easier."

On the other hand, Vanessa notes that when she took the psychological test required of all recruits, "I knew what they wanted to hear, and I answered accordingly. If they had confronted me, I would have denied being a lesbian. I don't know whether they would have accepted me in any case." When applicants for the force ask Vanessa's advice, she does not know what to tell them. "I don't think we're in the place yet to give a clear answer," she says. "There are gay people working in the application process, but if you write down that you are lesbian or gay, you'd better be ready for repercussions. Today they will not document that they are rejecting you because you are homosexual. They'll look for another reason."

GOAL interviewees noted difficulties gay cops undergo in addition to those they confront in coming out. "Most," says Jerry Cox, "think they're being watched and that they have to behave 110, not 100 percent on the job." A gay cop Jerry worked with because no one else was willing to do so let his emotions get the better of him. When someone stuck a gay magazine in his mail box, he made a scene during roll call. "I would have made a joke," Jerry comments, "and said, 'Thank you for the magazine, it's not the one I read.' " On the other hand, Jerry recalls, "Many times when I needed help, this gay cop was one of the first on the scene. If I had to lock up two or three people, I couldn't do it alone. He helped me bring the situation under control."

Vanessa, Pete, Fred, and Jerry all agreed that during their years in the force they had noted a change in the general attitude toward gays, an increased tolerance. According to Fred, among young recruits prejudice has almost disappeared. "The younger gay and lesbian cops coming onto the job," concurs Vanessa, "are activists with experience in the gay movement, with a positive image. They announce, 'Of course I'm out, of course I'm gay.' "

ESPRIT DE CORPS

Striking in the interviews with the four GOAL members was the intense esprit de corps expressed by each of them. They were all gay cops, but above all they were proud cops. "I wanted to show that gay people could do other things besides being hairdressers," said Pete Guardino. During interviews, whenever questions touched solely on police matters, the GOAL members all spoke as members of the department, not as gay officers. "You're a professional policeman who happens to be gay," Pete Guardino explained, "and you are a gay person who happens to be a policeman."

Reviewing his twenty years as a city transit officer, Jerry Cox declared: "Plainclothes is a very tough job, and men in the department know that. If you stop somebody, you have to show your ID, your badge, and hope that in the meantime they don't take a swing at you and, if so, that you're fast enough to stop them." Jerry recalls fighting in a train along with his partner against a man with a gun. "We were between cars, and if the train had made a turn," he says, "my partner and I could have had our hands chopped off. I've had some scary times, but it's part of being a police officer."

Jerry spoke with admiration of a lesbian partner stationed with him at Fulton Street in Brooklyn. "One day we gave chase to some kids through the mall," Jerry recounted. "All I know is that I saw her run past me, take a flying leap like a football player, and take this guy down to the ground and cuff him. I said to myself, 'What the hell is this?' If anyone asked me whether I would work with that woman, I would say that she can take care of people a hell of a lot better than I can."

"Like professional military people," said Fred Adler, "police officers have their lives all worked out for them under strict procedures and discipline. The force becomes a family, and the captain becomes a father. Most cops are eager to adapt. That's what the police department wants." Of the housing police, Fred boasts, "We are the frontline cops. We're the marines of the department. For the number of people we have working we're doing an incredible job. Our creed is 'Second to None.' When I go out on my job, I'm a different person. I am the law, the authority, the Man. That's all people know, that's all they have to know."

When Fred entered the Police Academy in 1983 for the standard six-months' training, he began, he says, "with certain expectations. You think this is going to be a fabulous experience. You're about to become a policeman. You're going to get a badge, a shield, and a gun." He discovered very quickly that in police work, "You become friends or enemies very quickly. Everything is life and death. Now or never. As a cop," Fred explains, "I feel threatened by everybody. I'm blue. Everybody else is not. When I'm in uniform, I don't take anybody for granted. If I let my guard down, some little old lady who is really a psycho is going to stab me in the back with an ice pick. You're still a cop and you're still in public, and so many people hate your guts."

Fred also discovered that a housing police officer hardly had a romantic assignment. "At first I was repelled by conditions at the housing project," he related, "with the bugs, excrement, rats. I was not brought up that way. It's so far removed from my own lifestyle. But you become calloused. The majority of the people living in the projects are good people. That other small percentage, the bad people, what are you going to do? They have to live someplace. Would I do something with them? That's what we have the Bronx for, fence in the Bronx! Of course, that's ridiculous. That's what keeps us on the job.

"Sometimes you want to share your scary experiences with friends and family," Fred declares, "and you can't. That's why the cops are your family, your blue family."

Gay cops, says Fred, are under the same kinds of pressure as straight cops and have the same kinds of problems. "You deal with it by shedding your role as a cop when you take off your uniform. Because your relationship with your friend is the most important aspect of your life, you make a special effort in this regard. He, too, becomes sensitive to the problem. He understands when you say you're not going out tonight, that you have had too hard a day."

While still at the precinct in the Bronx, Vanessa was assigned to work on her own as a print technician with the responsibility of searching for fingerprints in places that had been burglarized. "But if a job came over the walkie-talkie that there was a dangerous situation," she declared, "I was there." Once, responding to a call for assistance, she and an officer confiscated guns on the first floor of a building and then went down to search a dark cellar. "We didn't know who was below," she relates. "It was pitch-black. The officer told me he was going down through the trap door. They could have been waiting for him. I went in right after him. We found a switch and turned the light on. We made a quick canvas to make sure that we were safe. Then he turned to me and gave me a big hug and I hugged him right back. We were safe! That for cops is a highly emotional situation. This person is not your blood, but because you are in uniform you are family."

RELATIONS WITH THE GAY COMMUNITY

Each of the GOAL interviewees expressed a strong commitment to the struggles of the general gay community. All of them would have been sympathetic to the rationale for the decision to come out expressed by NYPD sergeant and GOAL member Edgar Rodriguez at a June 1992 lesbian and gay meeting held at the office of the Manhattan district attorney. While participating in a school drug-prevention program, Rodriguez recounted that he was struck by the fact that gay youngsters in his audience had no role models. He decided that he had an obligation to provide such a role model.

On the other hand, because of the general hostility in the gay community toward the police, Jerry has sometimes found it difficult to deal with gays. When he was first on the job he came upon a gay man smoking in a subway train. The man was sitting on his lover's lap and kissing him. When Jerry started writing out a summons, the man accused Jerry of picking on him because he was gay and because he was kissing his lover. Jerry replied that he wasn't bothered by the man's displays of affection; he could do almost anything with his boyfriend, he said, except have sex on the train, but the fact that he was smoking did bother him. When the man denied that he had been smoking, Jerry ordered him to lift his foot. He uncovered a cigarette still lit. "That's why you're getting a summons," said Jerry. "You're sure you're a cop," exclaimed the smoker. "You're not going to beat my head in because of what I'm doing with my boyfriend?"

"My job as a police officer," Jerry explains, "is to be neutral. I don't look at people and say they're black or Asian or Caucasian or male or female. I just see whether they're committing a violation."

"When I have spoken to gay groups I have been taunted because I'm a cop," Vanessa declares. "I say I am a cop and I am a lesbian but before being a cop and a lesbian I'm Vanessa. I expect you to treat me like Vanessa."

Both Jerry and Vanessa, unattached at the time of their interviews, complained of social ostracism. "I was talking to a guy in a gay bar for maybe two hours," Jerry recounted. "As soon as he found out I was a cop he shut up and didn't want to have anything more to do with me. He just didn't like cops. I said, 'You've got a problem. For two hours you're talking to me, suddenly you clam up.' "

"When I meet lesbians," said Vanessa, "as soon as they find out that I'm a cop, some don't want to have anything more to do with me. Others are attracted because of the uniform. They don't think of me as just another human being."

Constantly confronting hostility and complaints of police brutality among minority groups and gays, the four GOAL interviewees insisted that because of their personal experience as gays they have special compassion for people of color and gays. "I'm a better cop," declared Pete Guardino, "because I'm a gay cop. I have an extra sense that straights don't have. I have to deal with homophobia and discrimination. When I deal with someone who is a victim, I know how to reach out. It's less likely that cases of police brutality are committed by gay and lesbian cops. If more gays in the force were visible, we might have less brutality. Their presence influences the people they work with."

"Gay cops are good cops," concurred Jerry Cox. "Out of their own life experiences they think twice when it comes to questions of prejudice, and they are sensitive generally to the problems of the people with whom they deal. I take it upon myself to point out that there are other people in the world that have needs. That's my job as a gay police officer."

"A gay cop," said Fred Adler, "is a step ahead. He's more aware of different lifestyles." Vanessa agreed: "When you are a victim of oppression, you empathize with people who are down, and those are the people we deal with generally. When you arrest a prostitute, you think, 'I wonder what she went through that put her where she is.' "

Chapter Twelve

The Gay Community and the Police

"When I telephone cops," declares Bruce of the Crime Victims Board (CVB), "who don't know they're dealing with a gay person, you wouldn't believe some of the things I hear." In one case involving a gay man assaulted on the Upper West Side, the officer reported, "We checked this guy out and got reports from neighbors of wild parties. You know what these people are like."

On the other hand, Bruce has had experiences that suggest that not all members of the force are homophobic. He recalls overhearing back in 1981, while he was still in the closet, a conversation between two of his colleagues about a gay man badly slashed on New Year's Eve. "The guy probably invited some guys home," they were saying, "and things got out of hand." Bruce controlled his rage. "If you have a problem with that case," he said, "I'll take it off your hands." The colleague was agreeable. Bruce called the officer on the case. "The perpetrators singled the man out," the cop reported, "and went up the elevator with him intending to rob him. They become more interested in cutting him up because he was gay." ("And this before there was a bias unit in the police department!" Bruce exclaimed.) As a result of Bruce's intervention, the victim underwent massive plastic surgery paid for by CVB. Equally impressive was Bruce's experience with a detective from Midtown North (the precinct responsible for the beating administered to Chris Hennelly), who called to ask Bruce's help in obtaining counseling for a man whose lover had been murdered in a gruesome assault.

Other interviewees did not express such a balanced attitude, generally reporting unpleasant experiences with the NYPD. The tension between gay activists and the police, including members of the Gay Officers Action

League, was exposed in an exchange between Police Lieutenant Don Girac, a spokesman for GOAL, and activist Gerri Wells during a June 1991 PBS "Live Wire" television program moderated by AVP Executive Director Matt Foreman. When Girac admitted that the New York Police Department could take more effective action against homophobic violence, noting that the NYPD employed decoys to catch assaulters of members of other communities but never against gay bashers, Gerri Wells scoffed that such police decoys would "stick out like sore thumbs because they are uncomfortable among gays and lesbians." Teachers on the Police Academy staff, Gerri observed, devote a couple of hours to discussing communication with the gay and lesbian community but spend weeks on nightstick training.

Tensions between the police and the gay community Girac attributed to a lack of understanding on both sides. "The majority of the police officers . . . at demonstrations," he declared, "don't have any idea where the anger is coming from. [They] haven't lost a lot of people [in the AIDS epidemic]."

"If you have a sore temper," the lesbian activist retorted, "be an accountant, be a plumber, don't be a police officer. . . . There's never been an officer injured by ACT UP. It's always ACT UP members who've been injured at demonstrations."

The sharp exchange between Wells and Girac exposed both the potential usefulness of GOAL as a moderating influence within the police department and the ambivalence of GOAL members' loyalties in regard to the department and to the gay community. Gerri's pungent rejoinders exemplified the distrust among gay activists of all police officers.

As the gay liaison person at the officer of the Brooklyn district attorney, Liz Garro has more intensive and continuous involvement with the NYPD than Bruce. Invited as a law-enforcement functionary to join GOAL, she responded with enthusiasm. "The police perceive us as outlaws," she explained. "We need open gays and lesbians on the force."

Liz was especially angered at the hostile silence that greeted her appeal at a GOAL meeting for support in forcing the police to label as bias related the attack on lesbians at the Purity Diner in the Park Slope area of Brooklyn. During the social break in the meeting, Pete Guardino, the only person who would even speak to her, warned Liz that a lot of GOAL members did not want to hear talk against other police officers. "I'm not in my job," Liz replied, "to win friends, but to defend and win justice for gays and lesbians. I need help. There are few enough of us."

Subsequently, at a meeting between gay activists and representatives of the Park Slope precinct, police liaison officer Vanessa pulled Liz aside and chided her. "You're taking the side of the victims against the police," Vanessa complained, "without having been present at the incident." "Nor was anyone else in that room," retorted Liz. "I at least spoke with the victims at length. I believe them. I'm going to be at the protest demonstration [being organized by local gay activists]."

"So you're a sympathizer!" exclaimed Vanessa.

"A sympathizer with whom?" replied Liz. "With victims of bias crime? Spread the word that I am a sympathizer in such cases! I want that reputation."

When the police at last reluctantly designated the Purity Diner case as bias related, both Vanessa and Sam Ciccone, GOAL's executive director, called Liz to congratulate her on the victory. Liz replied, "All of us have to pursue each and every case. Sad to say, you did not believe the victims, you believed the cops. You're not going to do the community any good if you do not believe us."

Liz also resented GOAL's failure to participate in demonstrations on the Rivera and Purity Diner cases or in the protest staged at the Midtown North precinct after the beating by police of the three activists who had painted a slogan outside Cardinal O'Connor's residence.

Liz did not renew her membership. "GOAL," she declared, "did nothing to back me up in disputes with the police brass or to support me in lawsuits involving homophobic violence."

THE POLICE COUNCIL

The rancor of gay activists at the police brass and at GOAL has resulted in conflicts at meetings of the Police Council, established by Mayor Edward I. Koch and composed of top police officials and leaders of gay organizations along with gay liaison people at offices of various city officials.

As director of the Mayor's Office for the Lesbian Community, Marjorie Hill served as the convener and cochair of the Police Council upon its revival by the Dinkins administration. Upon her appointment to the post of director, Marjorie set herself a goal of sitting down with every city commissioner on issues affecting the gay community. She established a committee composed of gay liaison officers in various city agencies. She testified at hearings on plans for AIDS education, organized a forum on problems of gay adolescents, and initiated a library project under which gay organizations donated books with lesbian and gay themes to schools. She arranged for the first reception for gays and lesbians at Gracie Mansion and the first meeting between the mayor and gay and lesbian clergy. She held the first lesbian breakfast in connection with Women's History Month and arranged for a gay and a lesbian to participate n the welcoming committee greeting Nelson Mandela at his arrival in the city. Through her efforts, six gay organizations participated in the city peace corps formed to mediate in minority conflicts. Along with the gay Human Rights Campaign Fund and the Gay Community Center, she called a conference on Invisible Diversity to develop a gay and lesbian agenda in collaboration with business organizations. Her office was able to resist municipal budget cuts affecting the gay community.

Some gay and lesbian organizations expressed dissatisfaction with Marjorie's performance. Once at a Queer Nation meeting she was accused of not caring about homophobic violence. "I am an Afro-American and a lesbian," she replied. "On this job I have received death threats. I go to events all over the city, usually at night, generally alone. I have gay brothers and sisters who have been attacked." By the end of the meeting, she says, "people saw the absurdity of the accusation." (Marjorie resigned her post in May 1993.)

At the initial meeting of the Police Council reconstituted under the Dinkins administration, Liz Garro, a newcomer to the council, listened as Matt Foreman raised the question of denominating the claw-hammer murder of Juan Rivera as a bias-related assualt. Liz was astonished at the angry response from Chief Robert Johnston, the head of the NYPD representation at the gathering. "I worked with your predecessor David Wertheimer," Johnston shouted, shaking his finger at Matt. "David Wertheimer gave us full information on cases, and you're holding it back. Who do you think you are?" "You have the information," Matt retorted. "If you labeled this case as a bias-related case, we could go on to talk about other cases. Whether the community tells the police or not is your business. If there's a lack of trust, you have to work on that problem."

When Liz Garro posed questions about the police handling of the Purity Diner case, Johnston instructed Paul M. Sanderson, chief of the NYPD Bias Unit, an African American, to investigate the status of both the Rivera and the Purity Diner cases.

At the next council meeting, Sanderson reported that a determination regarding the Rivera case was awaiting the arrest of the perpetrators. In the Purity Diner case, he declared, bias did not appear to be an issue. When Liz suggested that the police were concealing facts about the case, "The police representatives freaked out. I realized," said Liz, "that they would only take the word of police officers and would ignore the testimony of the victims or the word of any other agencies or supporting groups." To Liz's warning that the Brooklyn DA was defining the case as bias related, Johnson replied, "If you want to pursue it as a bias case, I don't care. There's no bias here."

Liz had primed GOAL representatives Cam Ciccone and Ernesto Rodriguez in advance on facts omitted from the police records on the Purity Diner case, "Good for you, Liz!" they remarked. "Pursue it if you think that's what happened." During the discussion the two GOAL representatives sat silent.

In subsequent council meetings the NYPD representatives refused to comment on the charge of police brutality in the Chris Hennelly beating at the Midtown North precinct, alleging that an investigation was in progress. Shown video tapes of the incident, they sat, Liz declares, "with arms crossed and said they saw nothing amiss in the police behavior." They rejected the request of the gay council members for the appointment of a special prosecutor on the case. Liz concluded, "The police are not going to investigate themselves."

Frequently at meetings of the council, Gerri Wells, a spokesperson for

ACT UP, pleaded with the police representatives to admit the possibility that one of their officers might be a homophobe and might have used excessive force on one of "our gay and lesbian brothers and sisters." "Not one of my officers!" Chief Johnston invariably replied. "I have argued with the police chiefs until I was blue in the face," Gerri relates.

Gerri Wells's rancor at the GOAL representatives was scarcely less virulent than her anger at the police brass. "The next time you sell me out in one of these meetings," she warned Sam Ciccone, "I'm going to let you have it. If you want to suck up to the chiefs at the expense of the gay and lesbian community, do it on your own time but not as a representative of the community. You're trying to make points with them. When you leave they're saying, 'Look at that sorry sucker.' Do you think they respect you?' Why was the council set up? For bringing us together at a dinner? To resolve an issue, you have to admit first that a problem exists."

Matt Foreman offered a less categorical judgment of the council. "The best thing about the Police Council," he said, "is that it meets regularly with the Chief of Department, and you can raise issues directly with him. Getting an appointment with him otherwise would require going through every layer of the bureaucracy, and that would wear you down." Although asserting that he maintains good relations with GOAL, Matt Foreman echoes the view of many gay activists in declaring, "In uniformed agencies, it's us against them. When people say, 'I'm a gay cop,' they're still cops."

In 1980, Regina began working for the NYPD and advanced to become a supervising police communications technician handling the 911 emergency telephone complex as well as serving as a training officer for both uniformed and civilian personnel. Because of her position Regina was invited to join the Gay Officers Action League, and in 1991 she was appointed a GOAL representative on the Mayor's Police Council. Regina was guarded in her judgment of the council. "Every action requires a slow process," she declared. "We discuss changes, but it takes time to put decisions into effect. It's frustrating."

Marjorie Hill expressed greater optimism regarding the council. She noted that at least through the council good relations had been developed with the administrative offices of the police department.

THE NEW JERSEY STATE POLICE TRAINING PROGRAM

Exhibiting the confidence of a community that has achieved maturity, AVP and other gay organizations have mounted vigorous action to combat police homophobia, conducting sensitivity training at various police precincts following the example set by the Chelsea gay community during the late 1970s, but the first extensive long-range experience in the New York area developed in a program with the New Jersey State Police.

In 1987, after the widow of Vince Lombardi, the famous coach of the

Green Bay Packers, complained that a New Jersey Turnpike rest area named for her husband had gained notoriety as a gay cruising area, the New Jersey State Police instituted an undercover operation at the spot. Over a two-year period, they made almost eight hundred arrests, employing in some cases, or so it was alleged, entrapment tactics. The local township enjoyed a healthy income from a $500 share of the $873 fine imposed on each person arrested.

Following upon a June 1990 meeting between the superintendent of the state police appointed by the newly elected governor Jim Florio and representatives of the New Jersey Gay and Lesbian Coalition, the Lambda Defense League, and AVP, the undercover operation was terminated. The gay representatives did not succeed in having pending charges dropped or in obtaining redress for people previously convicted, but their proposal for the institution of sensitivity training for state troopers did rouse the superintendent's interest. The New Jersey Coalition eagerly embraced the idea. "We simply couldn't let this opportunity pass us by," declared Coalition member David Morris. "This is the first time there has ever been any dialogue between the state police and the gay and lesbian community in New Jersey." GOAL offered to draft an outline for the program but withdrew upon being informed that no compensation would be available for their effort. As a result, the task fell to the New Jersey Coalition and AVP, which, as Matt Foreman remarks, actually had no business becoming involved in a New Jersey project.

The program, the first in the nation, was inaugurated in November 1990 with a perspective of eventually involving all twenty-four hundred state troopers. Groups of approximately fifty officers attended two-day sessions with lectures from representatives of various minority groups. Heidi Jones and David Morris of the New Jersey Coalition assumed responsibility for the first half of each of the three-hour gay community presentations, and Matt Foreman took charge of the second segment. By August 1991, a total of fifty-seven classes had been conducted, and the program was terminated in January 1992.

On the June 27, 1991, PBS "Live Wire" television program, cited at the beginning of this chapter, Sergeant Joseph Kirchhofer, supervisor of the Social Science Unit at the New Jersey State Police Academy, declared that the sensitivity series represented a "commitment to enhancing the professionalism of the troopers. . . . working toward a positive image. . . . It deals also with police ethics, managing culturally diverse societies and communities that we serve as well as developing good community relations." He noted that the troopers had not previously had an opportunity to confront gay community issues firsthand.

Also participating in this television program, David Morris of the New Jersey Lesbian and Gay Coalition estimated that in the sensitivity training sessions 50 percent of the troopers listened part of the time, 25 percent simply refused to listen, and 25 percent gave the lecturers their undivided attention. He hoped there would be a "trickle-down effect" within this elite police force, especially as a program on lesbian and gay issues had recently been inaugurated at the police academy.

At the sessions, the most common complaint he received from police officers regarding gay behavior had to do with the public display of affection. "I think the difficulty comes in people's misunderstanding first of all of what the law is," David responded. "Furthermore, I reply that two people kissing didn't seem to me to represent some kind of crazy overt homosexual activity."

Questioned during a break at a September 1991 session, troopers generally expressed dissatisfaction with the presentations by the gay spokespersons, insisting that the lectures offered them nothing new. A few of the troopers, however, welcomed the encounter with members of the gay community. In the second segment of the session, Matt Foreman disarmed the troopers immediately by admitting he exemplified personally some of the stereotypes about gay men and by recounting a humorous experience he had when stopped by a trooper on the New Jersey Thruway. The room was silent during his discussion of the Kinsey report on male sexuality, according to which, on a scale of zero to six—from exclusive heterosexuality to exclusive homosexuality—a large percentage of men exhibit ambivalent sexual drives.*

At a subsequent session in October 1991, Matt sought in vain to obtain a meaningful critique of an outline developed by AVP for an NYPD sensitivity program. The troopers complained that the situations and issues addressed were pertinent for local police but not for their service. (David Morris admitted that most of the problems gays experienced in New Jersey arose not with the troopers but with the local police. Officers parked in front of gay bars, for example, and harrassed gays coming and going from nearby parking lots.) When as a result of this rebuff, Matt was at a loss as to how to continue the session, a senior citizen whom Matt had invited to observe the session took over. His detailed account of his struggle over decades to overcome his homosexual orientation and to achieve "normality" was received with a hush. When he concluded his account, however, a trooper raised his hand and expressed resentment at being compelled to sit through such a lecture. When the speaker asked whether any others in the audience felt that they, too, had suffered an imposition, not a hand was raised. At the conclusion of the session, several of the troopers congratulated the man for the courage of his presentation; and Jeff Torno, the trooper in charge of the program, informed him that several troopers had declared that all troopers should have the opportunity to hear his story.

At both these sessions the troopers sat quietly, and some were clearly at-

*According to a national survey, nearly 40 percent of males and 28 percent of females in the United States have had homosexual experiences. Estimates of the percentage of homosexuals in the national population range widely from 2 percent to 10 percent. In New York City, which along with San Francisco harbors the largest concentration of gays in the nation, the community certainly numbers in the hundreds of thousands.

tentive; but Matt reported that on other occasions the officers proved undisciplined and even disrespectful to the discussion leaders and openly expressed their homophobia, making remarks Matt considered unbecoming for professionals and impermissible in a country that practices separation of church and state.

At thirty-three, a veteran of ten years on the force and the administrator of the Police Professionalism and Cultural Diversity training program, Jeff Torno exemplified the possibility of achieving increased tolerance and understanding among state troopers. Even as a child, Jeff recalled, he had resented any racist or anti-Semitic remarks in his Italian-American working-class family. During his school years he made friendships with people of all ethnic and racial groups, and in college he had a close gay friend. He had married "a woman of color from the Caribbean."

Open-minded troopers who participated in the cultural diversity program, about a third of the group, Jeff thought, gained something. Some had declared to him, "I had some prejudices and preconceived notions. This program helped open my eyes." Homophobic troopers, he believed, "eased up and saw that it didn't matter what the sexual orientation was, that gays were people like you and me."

Matt Foreman, who carried half the responsibility for the sessions, exhibited more restraint in his evaluation. He considered as positive the fact that the New Jersey State police force had made a commitment and carried it out. The program, he thought, sent a political message that the Florio administration considered such presentations important and that troopers who displayed anti–civil libertarian attitudes or homophobia would face consequences for such attitudes.

NYPD SENSITIVITY PROGRAMS

In January 1991, a subcommittee of the Police Council consisting of Matt Foreman, Regina Shavers, and Marjorie Hill was appointed to plan a pilot long-term, broadly based "sensitivity" program for precincts throughout the city. (To Marjorie this program provided impressive evidence of the usefulness of the council.) According to Matt Foreman, the sensitivity training conducted at the Police Academy by the NYPD had proved ineffective. Matt noted, for example, that the thirty-five discussion leaders, all straight officers, were unable to respond to questions out of direct experience. (There was not a single gay instructor, Matt declares, among almost three hundred at the Academy.)

The Police Council subcommittee set as its goal educating officers about "(1) the diversity of the lesbian/gay communities; (2) issues affecting the lesbian and gay communities; (3) problems which arise between our communities and the police; and (4) the many organizations working in and for our communities."

Only in January 1992, after the appointment of a new NYPD police chief, did the subcommittee obtain permission to initiate a pilot series at the Tenth Precinct in the Chelsea district of Manhattan, selected because of the frequency of antigay assaults in the area, the history of close relations between the precinct and the local gay community, and the accessibility of the precinct to presenters.

On February 10, the subcommittee submitted eight topics to the precinct commanding officer for roll-call presentations at shift changes, that is, one thirty minutes long at 7:15 A.M. and the other twenty minutes long at 3:15 P.M. Posters announcing the sixteen sessions were displayed conspicuously in the precinct headquarters. To avoid the necessity of training presenters, the subcommittee turned to professional specialists. The series was introduced by Marjorie Hill with a presentation on "Myths and Facts regarding Sexual Orientation." Naomi Lichtenstein of AVP followed with "Domestic Violence in Gay and Lesbian Relationships." The pastor of the gay Metropolitan Community Church spoke on religious issues. Matt Foreman discussed antigay and antilesbian crime. A representative of the Gay Men's Health Crisis spoke on AIDS transmission. GOAL took over the sixth session. The Latino Gay Men of New York and Las Buenas Amigas discussed problems of gay men and lesbians in their community, and representatives of ACT UP and Queer Nation concluded the series with a discussion of gay activism.

Naomi Lichtenstein was ambivalent in evaluating her segment of the program. During the morning session a cop who had been standing to the side suddenly strode toward her, shook his finger in her face, and challenged her with undisguised hostility. At the urging of another officer, he backed off. Later he winked at her suggestively. Although the captain subsequently expressed dissatisfaction at the incident, no one rebuked the officer for his behavior. The afternoon session, on the other hand, Naomi believed, went well. "I was more comfortable; I fell into the proper language for the audience. I was able to offer them information on gay and lesbian domestic violence of direct value to them."

In the final session of the series an ugly shouting match between officers and an ACT UP facilitator led to a breakdown of order. Officers recounted incidents they had heard about from fellow officers (but had not experienced themselves) in which ACT UP members had spat at cops. They charged that at every gay demonstration fights erupt and police get hurt. They claimed that a gay activists had dumped a gallon of red paint on Inspector Jonasch's head during the February 11, 1991, demonstration at which Chris Hennelly was brutally beaten. They complained that other activists had shown no reaction to this indignity. (In fact, red paint hurled onto the street had spattered on the inspector's shoes, which so infuriated him that he gave the order to charge the crowd with batons at the ready.) It was clear that as word of the demonstration had spread through the department, the hyperbole had grown. One rumor even held that an ACT UP spokesman had called for burning police cars.

Alden McCane of ACT UP sought to mollify the police, noting that for gay activists the police are the representatives of the enemy but not themselves the enemy. He also insisted that he had never seen violent antipolice actions by gay demonstrators. "We don't believe the cops," he countered, "when they make such charges." The officers were not appeased by his remarks.

"For the last six weeks you have had people come here and ask for special treatment for gay people," one officer exclaimed to Matt Foreman at the end of the program. "No one," commented Matt, "ever asked for special treatment for gay people, but if these programs evoke such a backlash, why should the community expend time and effort in holding them?

"In our twenty-two-year history," remarked Matt subsequently, "we have had exactly one riot, and that was at Stonewall in 1969. The most peaceful parade this city has is the annual Gay Pride parade. Our people don't get drunk, they don't get rowdy. The police never have any problems with the gays that day." In the 70 percent of gay demonstrations that he had attended, Matt had never seen a police officer spat upon or struck or any gay demonstrator resist arrest.

On the other hand, Matt points out, gays believe that the police enforce the law selectively and fail to accept that gays have a right to demonstrate. Matt notes, too, that when an organization calls a demonstration, it does not ask participants to pass an eligibility test. As a result, people with varying levels of discipline take part. Though ACT UP is generally effective in calling to order people who attempt to go off on their own demonstrations, anarchistic acts can and do occur. The police reaction is, "You allowed that to happen." The police expect, Matt says, the same paramilitary discipline from demonstrators as should be expected from the police themselves. Matt rejects the protest of some policemen: "Why should I have to stand there and listen to you shout, 'Shame! Shame!' Why do I have to put up with insults?" Police officers, Matt insists, are professionals paid $45,000 and more a year to behave as professionals and to maintain a professional code of conduct.

Attendance at the Chelsea precinct sessions proved hardly encouraging. Absenteeism of up to 47 percent gave evidence of the inappropriateness of making presentations during roll calls. An evaluation session was long delayed because the department failed to grant overtime to allow officers to participate. A tally of twenty-seven respondents to a questionnaire revealed often contradictory reactions. The presentations on gay/lesbian domestic violence, antigay/antilesbian bias crime, and GOAL were adjudged the most helpful, followed by those on myths and facts about sexual orientation and on AIDS transmission issues. Nine respondents thought the program should be repeated at other precincts; six, only if improved; eight, not at all; and two had no opinion.

Among the questions, comments and suggestions offered by officers were:

"How can you tell who's the dominant one of a pair of fags?"

"Why have they such hatred for the Catholic Church?"

"Why so much attention to gay issues?" ("We spent more on this subject than on any other training ever given!")

"No matter what approach is taken, there is a rulebook that we as police officers must abide by."

"Have a lot of information available after sessions and more on what is expected of us with AIDS infected people."

"You could have stressed that being gay is a way that you're born."

As a result of the evaluations and of their own experience in the sessions, the organizers of the program developed recommendations for future sensitivity training series: that the program be introduced to precincts through a memorandum from the Chief of Police; that precinct commanders inform officers of their support of the program; that a full thirty minutes in the morning and twenty minutes in the afternoon be available for presentations; that precinct and presenters' liaison persons be present at each session; that the sessions be closely spaced, scheduled at least once a week, and held without interruption; that sessions be arranged with specific police squads; that milling about or early departure from sessions be discouraged; that officers of high rank either not be present or be advised not to intervene; that diversity among the presenters be assured; and that printed materials be available for distribution at sessions. The subcommittee urged that the session on religious issues be dropped and that the AIDS transmission topic be presented in two consecutive sessions and be focused on issues of specific concern to the officers (condoms made available at the AIDS session were taken by officers). It was urged that greater attention be paid to "mutual battering" situations and to ways of identifying batterers and that a fact sheet be drafted on the demonstration held at St. Patrick's Cathedral, about which a number of officers had expressed resentment, and on various myths concerning ACT UP. Question-and-answer sessions had proved more effective than a lecture on sexual-orientation myths. The presence of a member of the subcommittee as a back-up person and as a friendly face had proved helpful to the presenters, as had periodic evaluations by the officers during the series.

On May 2, 1992, a second program of six sessions, this one directed to new police recruits, was conducted by five members of a Queens Gays and Lesbians United (QGLU) committee, along with Matt Foreman. (QGLU had been formed in reaction to the savage homophobic murder of Julio Rivera, and the sensitivity project provided an effective first action for the new organization.) Matt felt greater confidence about dealing with recruits, younger, less cynical, and more vigorous in response. In this series sessions lasted at least an hour and fifteen minutes instead of a mere twenty or thirty minutes. "All you could do in the shorter sessions with the regular officers,"

Matt noted, "was to raise an issue and hope to get a few questions. That is not the way to go about a sensitivity program." Only with extensive interaction, the participating committee argued, would the rookies learn "to view us as ordinary members of the community."

The new program did not proceed smoothly. A long delay ensued before the series began. The first session did not take place until after a change in the 15th precinct command. The new captain agreed to a resumption only on condition that the training officer be present as an observer and to provide feedback after every session. Furthermore, he included six hour-long sessions in the standard recruit training program in order to avoid payment of overtime. After selecting topics for the sessions, the presenters, all except Matt Foreman novices in working with police, asked the precinct training officer to assemble fifteen or twenty experienced officers for a discussion of the program. At their request, too, the precinct captain made an announcement of his support.

The committee sought counsel from therapists who had conducted sessions with mentally disturbed police officers. "That meeting," according to Eddie, "made us more realistic in our expectations." The group spent three hours in planning each session and a further meeting in rehearsal. Individual committee members were assigned specific tasks, and educational materials were assembled for distribution.

The new series did not get underway until October 1991, after a six-month hiatus. When at the first session the presenters asked the recruits to write down questions they wanted answered during the six-week program, a sergeant intervened and announced, "They've just met you. They have no questions."

Though taken aback by the officer's hostility, the facilitator proceeded with a standard group dynamics exercise, asking the officers to volunteer words they had heard about gays and lesbians. He then discussed attitudes implied in the epithets. "Who would voluntarily take on such a role in life?" he asked. Some of the presenters then related their coming-out experiences. "We wanted to work with rookies," Eddie Sonderstom of QCLU explained, "since they had not yet been socialized into the system of oppressing and hating us. We found, however, that they had already been told that the most dangerous demos were those conducted by gays."

After the initial session, the group received no replies to repeated telephone requests for the scheduling of the next session. Eventually they learned that the officers had decided not to continue the program. Following up on a letter of inquiry from the group and intervention by Vanessa, a meeting was arranged with the precinct captain. He informed them that he had decided to terminate the program upon receiving a complaint that a facilitator had asked the recruits about their sexual orientation and about what they did in bed. "Clear sign of his homophobia," Eddie remarked. "Would he have accepted without investigation such a charge made against any other group?"

With the benefit of the training officer's suggestions and their own evaluations, the group made revisions as they proceeded. They quickly discovered that the young recruits resented any suggestion that they were homophobic. They insisted that they had gone to school with gays and pointed out that they had already undergone sensitivity training at the Academy. It also became clear that the rookies were yearning for specific suggestions for dealing with problems they were about to confront as police officers. To meet their needs the presenters began organizing sessions about specific working situations rather than about large subject areas. Background material, they found, could be introduced when appropriate. Responding to the objection that the subjective approach in the session on homophobia, for example, seemed of no practical value, the program organizers decided that in the future this topic should be introduced later in the series. They canceled a second session on gay history and substituted one on how to work a gay and lesbian demonstration, during which historical background could be introduced as of more immediate pertinence.

Eight recruits, a sergeant, and the training officer in a final evaluation session accorded the highest marks to role playing, in which recruits participated actively. They were not interested in personal revelations, which they considered not applicable to their job. They found useful the tips on how to address gays and how to find out whether a same-sex pair was a couple. Among the other topics they considered most helpful were community resources, domestic violence, and bias crime.

The session on bias crime proved to be one of the most successful, in part because the presenters showed a video of a "60 Minutes" interview with Houston police officers who had served as gay decoys (an experience described in Chapter 9). The film not only provided evidence of the victimization suffered by gays but also provided a lesson in specialized police work. The segment concluded with an interview with an adolescent working at a gas station who admitted that he and friends were planning to gay bash that very night.

In regard to AIDS, the recruits asked for less lecturing about safe sex and more about what they called "psychological stuff." "Do you get offended," they asked, "if we put on rubber gloves to deal with someone who is bleeding? Do we have to put on rubber gloves first before there's any bleeding?"

A recruit suggested that instead of handing out wallet-sized cards listing gay community resources the committee print a laminated card that would fit inside a police logbook. If officers ran into teenagers hustling on the street, for example, they could check the list and advise a referral to the Hetrick Martin Institute.

By June 1992 gay groups were planning to initiate sensitivity training programs at the Ninth Precinct (the Lower East Side), at the Seventy-eighth Precinct in Park Slope, Brooklyn, and at precincts in Queens and Staten Island.

THE PINK PANTHERS

In face of rapidly mounting, ever more vicious homophobic violence in the late 1980s, New York gay activists decided that they could not rely upon the police for protection. Twenty years after the desperate outburst at Stonewall, the community had come out with sufficient self-confidence and developed a sufficiently high level of organization to mobilize its own security force, the Pink Panthers.

"We were formed," declares Gerri Wells, one of the founders of the group, "in direct response to the rise in gay bashing. We felt that we had to do something because nobody else was doing anything, including the police department."

Gerri Wells had intense personal motivation for combating homophobic violence. Not only had she and her gay younger brother experienced homophobic attacks in elementary and secondary school, but she also had experienced even more savage violence and attendant law-enforcement corruption in the murder of her straight seventeen-year-old older brother. After jeering at him for wearing dark glasses (he was nearly blind), drunks attacked him, killed him, and cut out his heart. At the trial the judge let the perpetrators off. "By putting this Korean War vet in jail," the judge declared, pointing to one of the accused, "we can't bring back the deceased. I'm going to let them go, all three of them." They served only the months they had spent awaiting trial. "We found out," Gerri declares, "that one of the three men was related to TV celebrity Ed Sullivan and had other connections. Two years later the *Village Voice* carried a story charging that the judge made a practice of accepting bribes. It's still hard for me to talk about it," Gerri says. "It taught me how the system works."

With the brutal bludgeoning of Julio Rivera in Queens and then the wanton beating to death of Jimmy Zappalorti, a developmentally disabled gay man, in Staten Island, anxiety at gay bashing in the gay community was transformed into terror and rage. After a further series of assaults, including one in Greenwich Village against Heidi Dorow, Tracy Morgan's lover, and the volleys of beer bottles, heckling, and assaults from bystanders during a "Take Back the Streets" march, "Everybody was talking," Gerri Wells recounts, "but nobody was taking the ball and running with it."

In the face of this crisis, a group of activists, including Larry Kramer (founder of ACT UP), Gerri Wells, and members of Queer Nation gathered at Daisy's Coffee Shop in Greenwich Village to discuss a defensive response. At a subsequent meeting organized by the group and attended by some 150 people, a decision was taken to mobilize Queer Nation and ACT UP members in an antiviolence march through Greenwich Village to publicize the crisis. At a further planning meeting just prior to the march, sixty to seventy people voted to form a new defense organization. Someone suggested calling the group the Pink Panthers in an allusion to the pink triangle worn by gay concentration-camp inmates under the Nazis. "We're drawing from a tradition of communities organizing in self-defense," commented Ming Ma, who designed march T-shirts, black with a pink triangle and paw in front and "Pink Panther Patrol" on the back in English, Chinese, and Spanish.

On August 4, 1990, about two hundred people marched down Christopher Street. "We were announcing," Gerri Wells recounts, "that we were a community under attack, and we were standing up and fighting back." Down by the river, the termination point of the march, Gerri ran around and assigned the sixty or so volunteers into groups of ten and distributed walkie-talkies. Then the groups set out on their first patrol.

The march evoked a positive reaction from straights and gays alike and received good play in the media. Appearing on *Joan Rivers, Good Morning, America,* and other television shows, Gerri denied the charge by some TV channels that the new group were vigilantes. On the other hand, Gerri began receiving death threats and was compelled to cease using her telephone as the Panther contact number.

In a congratulatory statement to the Pink Panthers, Mayor David Dinkins admitted that the city was unable to protect the gay community against the intensifying gay bashing. "The city cannot succeed without your help," he declared. "Community patrols, such as the Pink Panthers, have provided the city and its citizens with a visible and effective means of deterrence."

A gay bar, Two Potato, made available an empty storefront, in front of which the Panthers set up a table and sold buttons and T-shirts. The Spy Shop donated walkie-talkies, one for the command post and one for each group on patrol. The Panthers rejected an offer of training from the local police precinct, but Deputy Inspector Charles Campisi, chief of the Greenwich Village precinct, did respond positively to all requests from the Panthers except for the establishment of a direct line to the precinct, alleging a lack of funds for such a service. "You can't expect everything," remarks Gerri. "The cops are not our friends." The Panthers refused to allow a gay cop to join a patrol but did invite a gay doctor and a gay lawyer to lead workshops on first aid and on legal questions. A representative of AVP gave pointers on how to deal with crime victims.

Some Pink Panthers approached patrolling with trepidation. In its August 29 issue, *Outweek* quoted Panther Carol Anastasion, director of public relations for the Department of Parks and Recreation, as saying: "I felt real proud on patrol, but the entire week before the patrol I was really sad and depressed that there's a need for this type of patrol. I felt that I must be a nut for going out there. . . . But that was balanced by the thought that I would finally have a chance to do something about the violence. . . . This was really empowering." (In December the Parks Department donated ten portable two-way radios to the Pink Panthers.)

On a map of the neighborhood, patrol sections extending over quadrants of ten square blocks centered at Christopher Street and Sheridan Square was marked out. Six groups, each of ten to twelve people, began patrolling Friday and Saturday nights from midnight to three in the morning, the hours when, according to statistics, gay bashing occurs most frequently, "when," according to Pink Panther Steve Machon, "gangs are roaming about looking for trouble." Patrol members identified themselves by their Panther T-shirts or, in cold weather, by their Panther sweatshirts. All wore whistles about their necks. Gerri staffed the command post. Patrol leaders reported on walkie-talkies one by one every fifteen or twenty minutes, either calling in an "all clear" or describing an incident they were about to investigate.

A few weeks after the patrolling began, Gerri received an alarm from a patrol: "Sheridan Square! Sheridan Square! Emergency!" "I got scared," Gerri recounts. "This was it!"

> I called all patrols to respond to the alarm. All of a sudden two groups that had been patrolling down by the river came running past the table. I couldn't believe it. I had never seen a bunch of queers fly so fast in my life. There was Neil, a skinny, frail, effeminate little gay man who had been bashed several times. In the heavy shoes he wears he flew up Christopher Street, nerdy looking with his thick glasses. He just flew, his hair flying in the air. I looked at him, and I saw what it meant to be messed with for years. There was an extraordinary sense in the air. A couple of people ran by who I never thought could move their butts unless there was a fire. Tear-assing up Christopher Street they went. People on the sidewalk drew back astonished at the energy and anger. When they realized it was the Pink Panthers, they started applauding. People ran after them to see what was going on.

A gay man, it turned out, was being harassed by a couple of teenagers. They fled with the approach of the patrol. "That experience demonstrated why we were there," Gerri declared. "Years of gay bashing came to a head. It was frightening but beautiful. The mere presence of the patrols deters gay bashing, a coward's crime. They act in gangs. If there's a tiny possibility of their getting their butts kicked, they stop."

Steve Machon, long an ACT UP stalwart and dedicated gay activist and a member of the West Village Friday Patrol 2, reported that ideally, for moving down sidewalks and through crowds and for maintaining contact and the best interaction, patrols should number no fewer than five people and rarely more than eight or nine. "We look or listen for a situation that seems problematic," Steve noted, "a gang going along the street, people making a lot of noise, someone carrying a baseball bat, a gang in a car. If we see a suspicious group, we watch to see whether they're going to act. If we follow them, we do so circumspectly. We're not there to provoke a situation." Steve says that patrol procedures evolved out of experience and that the Panthers constantly refined their operation. Thus a rule was established that groups stick together; people who slacked off to socialize were to be summoned back into line.

After a few weeks on patrol, encouraged by the goodwill of bystanders and exhilarated by a realization that "we have our gangs, too!" all the Panthers, many of whom had been victims of gay bashing, Gerri noted, "were walking about as though they owned the streets." Steve heard passers-by, both gay and straight, call out, "We love you. We're glad you're here." Shopkeepers offered Panthers coffee and donated money for equipment, including additional walkie-talkies. Gay clubs held benefit nights to raise funds for the Panthers. People in the community respect the Panthers, Steve says, because they discourage all violence. "We don't ask the orientation of people being beaten," Steve points out.

Steve believes that the best remedy for crime-victim trauma is self-defense training, followed by an experience in patrolling. Homophobia, Steve notes, and "queer" identity are interrelated. "So much has to do with an emotional stance," he declares, "and that comes from within. Self-defense class teaches you that you are not defenseless." Steve himself took classes for a year, learning appropriate body language and vocal projection, how to interact on the street and how to prevent incidents. "If you're being approached by several kids," Steve advises, "you don't stand in the middle of the sidewalk as though you're going to take them on. You stand against a wall, you look across the street, you don't focus attention on them as a challenge. You ignore nasty remarks and vocal harassment."

Among the first to respond to the publicity about the new organization was Sharon Levine. Short in stature, gentle, and vivacious, she hardly gives the impression of a fighter, but when she saw a notice in *Outweek* on plans to form security patrols, she urged her friend Doug Brown to join with her. "I roped Denise [Sharon's lover] in," Sharon said. "She didn't want to do it, but she was not going to allow me to patrol the streets without her, and Tom, Doug's lover, wouldn't let Doug do it without him." After developing a problem in her knees, Sharon was unable to continue to patrol. Convinced of the need to approach young people before they engage in gay-bashing sprees, she proposed developing an education program for the schools that would counteract what young people learn at home and elsewhere about gays. "In their patrols," Sharon declares, "the Pink Panthers are stopping the flood, holding back the hatred, but the Cardinal continues to teach people to hate us. Schoolteachers never mention gays and lesbians except negatively. No wonder that kids grow up hating us and wanting to beat us up. Until we reeducate the educators, until we are included in advertising and in media programs, and until a gay or lesbian teenager can see one of his own in a story line that is not negative, we'll have this problem, and it'll get worse."

At the time she was interviewed, Sharon had assembled a five-member Pink Panther education committee and drafted letters and brochures to specially targeted schools. She had also made a presentation before the Board of Education's Committee on Multicultural Education and had asked to be added to the committee's speakers' roster. The Panther's school program, adapted for classes from elementary school through college, was divided into two segments, the first on homophobia generally and the second on gay bashing specifically. Members of the Board of Education were favorably impressed by the committee's materials. (For political reasons, however, the program was never instituted.)

Having gained respect in the areas they patrolled, the Panthers were able to arrange with community planning boards for monthly sensitivity training sessions at police precincts in the West and East Villages. (Gerri, who participated in this program, comments, "It isn't all very pretty.") Six months after the initiation of patrols in the West Village, patrols were established in the East Village; and after random shootings in the cruising area of Central Park known as the Rambles, another patrol was assigned there for Sunday afternoons. Though danger decreases in bad weather, the Panther's continued patrolling through the winter, considering it important to remain visible in the community.

In August 1991, a year after the founding of the Panthers, Deputy Inspector Charles Campisi, commander of the Greenwich Village police precinct, noted that antigay violence in his precinct had declined almost 50 percent, a decline he attributed in part to the presence of the Panthers. "The patrols have served their purpose," Gerri declares. "They have brought attention to gay bashing all over the country and internationally. [Articles on the Panthers have appeared in the press in London, Rome, Berlin, and Tokyo.] They gave a sense of self-empowerment to the people involved. We got to say to the world, 'Enough is enough.' A lot of people heard that message."

Pink Panther patrols were organized in San Francisco, Los Angeles, and Washington, D.C., and in Germany.

Chapter Thirteen

The Hetrick Martin Institute and the Harvey Milk School

The Gay Community Protects Its Youth

> Gay youth are 2 to 3 times more likely to attempt suicide than other young people. They may comprise up to 30 percent of completed youth suicides annually. . . . Suicide is the leading cause of death among gay male, lesbian, bisexual and transsexual youth. . . . The literature on youth suicide has virtually ignored the subject. Research in recent years, however, . . . has revealed a serious problem with cause for alarm.
>
> Report of the Secretary's Task Force on Youth Suicide, Department of Health and Human Services, January 1989

> Nearly one in three young homosexual men attempts suicide, according to a medical study published . . . in *Pediatrics*, journal of the American Academy of Pediatrics.
>
> *Chicago Sun-Times*, May 31, 1989

"A widely accepted American theory holds," declares Matt Foreman, executive director of AVP, "that adolescents need to act out their aggressions. Gays are an open target. Young gays are the most frequent victims." (In 1990 86 percent of AVP clients ranged from eighteen to forty-four years of age.) To protect preteen and teenage gays from homophobic aggression, New York gay activists founded the Hetrick Martin Institute and the Harvey Milk School.

"For the Hetrick Martin Institute and the Harvey Milk School to happen," declared Joyce Hunter, "the right people had to meet at the right time." Such a coincidence occurred in 1979, when A. Damien Martin, an associate professor of communications at New York University, and his psychiatrist lover Emery S. Hetrick heard Joyce speak at a meeting of the gay New York Political Action Committee. Damien and Joyce discovered that the two of them shared a common childhood experience as foster care children. "He and I," says Joyce, "hit it off right away."

Joyce brought an extraordinarily rich perspective to problems of gay youth. The daughter of a Jewish mother and an abusive black father, Joyce spent most of her childhood in an orphanage. Both because of childhood and adolescent trauma that drove her to attempt suicide and because of her concerns as a lesbian mother of two children, Joyce understood from direct experience the sufferings of troubled gay youngsters.*

In addition, after coming out in 1972, when she was in her early thirties, Joyce served on the rape-prevention committee of the National Organization of Women (NOW). Dropping out of NOW because she was convinced that the organization was neglecting lesbian issues, she helped to form Lesbians Rising, "a wonderful organization," she declares, "for someone who had a tremendous amount of rage and a wonderful vehicle to do something constructive with that rage." Older than many of the other members, she served as a spokesperson for the new group. "I found," she says, "that I could be a lesbian feminist without being in NOW during that period. It was an exciting time, before AIDS. We had tremendous hope for the future. We thought of ourselves as facilitators of a better world. Talk about being idealistic! We were going to make it better not just for gay people but for blacks. We were going to be part of a great liberating coalition."

Early in 1972, invited to conduct sensitivity training in a city-college human sexuality class, Joyce had her first experience in gay education. Two years later she helped to found a peer counseling service sponsored by the Gay Men's Alliance and Lesbians Rising. Other students brought in troubled high school students, including teenagers living on the street. Neither gay community organizations nor private agency social workers and therapists to whom Joyce referred these young people were willing to accept them as clients, fearing, Joyce discovered, loss of license on possible charges of child molestation or contributing to the delinquency of minors.

In 1974 Joyce began working with gay and lesbian organizations to mobilize support for the city gay rights bill. In 1976, enrolling in a city college, Joyce quickly won a reputation as "the campus lesbian." She joined with other activists in organizing gay students to combat homophobia. They ran their own candidates for the student government. After the elections, all the candidates who had been in the closet "came out." They invited speakers to the campus and conducted demonstrations. After Anita Bryant began her Moral Majority campaign against gays, Joyce joined the Coalition for Les-

*Joyce Hunter's traumatic experiences prior to her coming out as an adult are related in Chapter 6.

bian and Gay Rights and served as co-coordinator for the 1979 Gay Rights March on Washington.

In 1979, at a conference of the American Public Health Association, Joyce, who was then running a gay and lesbian rap group at college, discovered that her audience not only had no idea that gay youth existed but were not even eager to learn about them. Later that year Joyce met Emery and Damien. Outraged at a report that a fifteen-year-old gay young man, accused of responsibility for the gang rape of which he had been the victim, had been expelled from Covenant House, a homeless youth shelter, they invited Joyce to join them in founding the Institute for the Protection of Lesbian and Gay Youth. With Joyce as vice president and Emery as president, along with Damien and Steve Ashkinazy, they assembled a committee to investigate ways to deal with problems of gay youth.

In 1983, in collaboration with the New York City Youth Bureau and the New York State Youth Commission, they organized the first national conference on "Problems of Lesbian and Gay Youth and Issues in Service Delivery," attracting over two hundred professionals from across the United States, from Canada, and even from England. Participants in the conference, it became clear, did not know how to identify their gay populations and insisted that they did not encounter gay clients in their agencies. They also expressed stereotypes about gay young people and religious and cultural biases.

Following a public report by Emery, Damien, and Joyce on the conference, a wealthy member of the gay community appeared at Emery and Damien's apartment and took $25,000 in cash out of his cowboy boot. Insisting on anonymity, he returned the next evening with another $25,000. With this gift and a grant of $25,000 from the New York City Youth Bureau, the group was able to open an office on Twenty-third Street.

The organizers of the Institute set goals of organizing gay youth defense organizations and of providing services and training to agencies working with gay youth throughout the United States. In traveling about the country, they did not always enjoy a positive reception of their message. At a meeting in Oklahoma City, for example, someone in the audience warned, "You're going to go to hell for your activity." "Thank you for sharing that information with us," responded Damien. Despite resistance, they were able to assist in the formation of gay youth organizations in Washington, D.C., and in Dallas.

In 1984, Joyce, by then a graduate student in social work, stepped down as Institute vice president to accept a position without a salary during the first year as Institute program director. During the next six years she assisted in developing a drop-in center, a counseling program as well as a street-outreach program called Project First Step. In 1987, after Emery's death from AIDS and with Damien ailing with the disease, the Institute's name was changed to the Hetrick-Martin Institute. "Hetrick Martin," Joyce says, "put lesbian and gay youth issues on the map. We made it a big issue within the national youth services." Asked by a *New York Times* reporter to describe the Institute's activities, Damien declared: "We do exactly what the nuns taught us: feed the hungry, clothe the naked, shelter the homeless. The corporal and spiritual works of mercy."

By 1990, grieving at Damien's death and eager to complete a doctorate and to expand the scope of her activities, Joyce resigned from the Institute. As a predoctoral fellow at the HIV Center for Clinical and Behavioral Studies at the New York State Psychiatric Institute, Joyce undertook a three-year study among lesbian and gay adolescents practicing high-risk behavior.

Looking back on her twenty years as a gay activist, Joyce declares: "The most important contribution I have made since I came out has been doing something for lesbian and gay youth. Because I have children, I have been eager to sensitize people to problems of lesbian and gay youth, to get policy changed. I'm a youth advocate in general, but I focus specifically on issues of lesbian and gay youth, the most neglected segment of our society."

STEVE ASHKINAZY

Another founder of the Institute and one of the Institute's original salaried staff members, Steve comes from a radically different background from Joyce's, a prosperous, closely knit, sheltering, extended Jewish family. Nevertheless, in dealing with troubled gay youth, he can apply lessons from his years as a male hustler as an adolescent and from his lengthy struggle to overcome his family's resistance to accepting his homosexuality.

Until his early twenties, Steve had taken no interest in politics generally, and certainly not in gay politics. In 1970, however, he stopped by at the Fire House, then the gay community center in Greenwich Village. "It was unlike any gay place I had ever gone to," Steve recalls. "There was a communal spirit." He sat in on videotapes of gay actions and on panel discussions of gay issues. "It hit me like a ton of bricks," Steve recounts. "Politics affected me! I had been aware of exclusion," he says, "of having to tell lies. Now for the first time I heard people discussing the unfairness of it all, how we were second-class citizens, what the political implications were of being in the closet. These were people being gay politically, not merely 'camping.' " A few days later he participated in his first demonstration.

Steve became active in the Gay Activists Alliance, spending all his free time at the headquarters or at demonstrations. Exploiting his varied personal experiences as a teenager and young adult, he conducted coming-out and orientation groups. Upon coming out politically, Steve, who had never seen anything wrong about having many sex partners, began to seek long-term relationships. His career in the theater, previously all-important to him, now seemed less significant. He began neglecting his work, turning down jobs and suffering a loss of income. Indeed, he determined to transform his life by pursuing a master's degree in social work.

Steve resolved to enter his new career totally "out," and in the personal essay required of all applicants to social work schools he described his hustling as a teenager and his more recent activities in the gay movement. At Columbia, New York University, and Hunter College, interviewers had no problem with his being gay provided that he practiced discretion in classes. They would not permit him to do his field work in a gay agency. The State University of New York at Stony Brook, however, welcomed him and accepted his request to do his practicum at the gay Institute for Human Identity.

At Stony Brook, still burdened with shyness, insecurity, low self-esteem, and depression, Steve, now twenty-four, entered individual group therapy. "I was so raw and exposed, so crippled in exposing myself and in getting to my feelings of unworthiness," Steve relates, "that after sessions I had to arrange a car service to take me home." After two-and-a-half years, he reached a point at which other members of the group began questioning why he continued in therapy.

Steve breezed through his courses. "There was so little literature on gay issues," he declares, "it was easy to read it all. The professors knew nothing about the gay community. Whatever I wrote was a revelation to them. I was able to write most of my papers off the top of my head." In taking his practicum at the Institute for Human Identity, Steve served as a trailblazer. The next semester two other gay students from Stony Brook and a year later five more followed him there. During his second year of study, Steve worked part-time in a residential program for adolescent substance abusers in the Chelsea area of Manhattan. Gay and lesbian clients had not previously been accepted at the agency, and with the support of the director Steve set up a program for them, a program similar to the one he subsequently introduced at the Harvey Milk School.

COUNSELING AND THE DROP-IN CENTER AT THE INSTITUTE

The year Emery, Damien, and Joyce were developing the Institute for the Protection of Lesbian and Gay Youth, Steve was away from New York, studying in Israel. In 1979 he returned to New York, transformed into an Orthodox Jew, dressed in a black suit and black hat and wearing the traditional lovelocks.* Learning that the Institute was searching for a clinical director, he applied for the position. "God does provide!" he exclaims. "I had the thrill of being with the organization at the outset, helping to set its direction, and now this was just the place for me!

"I started," Steve recounts, "to do counseling with gay kids referred to us by people I had met in social service agencies." Institute clients range in age from fifteen to twenty-one, Steve reports. Younger gays and lesbians who come to the Institute are often sent on to other agencies better equipped to handle their problems. Most clients are people of color, and many are substance abusers.

*Steve's religious odyssey is recounted in Chapter 6.

"Class," Steve says, "governs who comes to such an agency; people on the poverty level are accustomed to going to social service agencies." Middle-class blacks, he notes, generally feel more comfortable than middle-class whites in such an environment. (That the Institute has not experienced racial tensions among the young people it serves is due in part, Steve suspects, to the fact that youngsters with racial antipathies exclude themselves.)

According to Steve, the major problems among the young people arise from family tensions, and in his counseling he has sought to prevent dissension from intensifying to the point that youngsters are expelled from their homes. He helps troubled teenagers to understand why parents address them aggressively. Recalling his own lengthy struggle to persuade his parents to accept his homosexuality, Steve tells young people at Hetrick Martin "not to blurt it out, but to set special time aside, to get people prepared for a real conversation." Most parents, he assures the teenagers, learn eventually to accept their children for what they are. "You have to get people to listen to each other," remarks Steve. "When parents reject a gay child who has come out to them, you have to convince them that this is the same child they had loved earlier."

Steve has been astonished at the percentage of young gays and lesbians who have suffered sexual molestation as children. He finds this a difficult problem to deal with, as discussion often evokes a traumatic response. His clients are also victims of general homophobic violence. (Lance Ringel, a member of the board of the Institute, recalled the case of two young men, Institute clients, who in August, 1988, were attacked on the Upper West Side of Manhattan with baseball bats. "We have had kids murdered who were clients," Lance noted.)

"We know that most of our young people are infected with HIV," Steve declared, "though few have been tested." Some have died. For those who have tested positive, special counseling is required. Several members of the staff of the Institute are HIV-positive. Presentations by them about AIDS, Steve says, have a greater impact on the teenagers than those by outside lecturers.

Steve has found the problem of homelessness difficult to handle. Public and private agencies have proved ineffective in assisting Institute clients. Politicians have repeatedly promised to promote the establishment of an Institute shelter, but nothing has materialized.*

A foster parents program inaugurated at the Institute proved abortive. "Many people volunteered," Steve declares, "all white, all with illusions about their own capabilities and about the kind of young people in our care. Some were seeking someone to accompany them to the opera or to the ballet. They did not want blacks or Latinos, the teenagers in greatest need."

*In 1996, having resigned from the Institute, Steve was engaged in organizing a shelter for lesbian and gay homeless young people.

What the young people wanted most from the Institute, Steve discovered, was an opportunity to socialize, for they all suffered from a sense of isolation. When word got about that the Institute was organizing social hours, adults volunteered to serve as group leaders during evening hours. As the major demand, however, was for afternoon socials, the staff made available part of the office space after three o'clock and served cookies and milk.

With the expansion of its activities, the Institute increased its staff and recruited additional volunteers. By 1992 the staff numbered thirty people, including a coordinator with an assistant to supervise the drop-in center and to draw up a weekly schedule of activities—games, theatricals, arts and crafts and creative writing, films, guest speakers (including physicians who conduct health "raps") on such topics as "Relationships," "Coming out to Parents," "Butch and Fem?" and "Safe Sex," and a weekly workshop at which the young people make their own videos.

THE HARVEY MILK SCHOOL

When teenagers began to show up at the drop-in center in the early afternoon, Steve realized that he had to develop a program for truants and dropouts. Young people related harrowing tales of harassment and intimidation at school. The problem affected not only effeminate gays or "butch" lesbians. Some who did not experience hostility directly felt uncomfortable when schoolmates joked about "faggots" and harassed other gays.

In 1984 Steve approached the superintendent for alternative high schools at the city Board of Education on the issue of reintegrating gay dropouts into the public schools. The superintendent recommended three high schools where Steve might expect a sympathetic reception from principals. At two schools Steve arranged for the reenrollment of three of his clients. While two of the boys were willing to report to school counselors on their own, Miguel, the most insecure of the three, insisted that Steve accompany him on his first day. An eager student, he had dropped out of school two years earlier, the butt of jokes regarding his androgynous attire.

Although Steve discussed with him how he should dress on this first day back at school, Miguel arrived in cross-dress. The students at first mistook him for a girl. Whispering, increasingly hostile, spread through the class. Steve sensed that the situation was proving threatening to Miguel, and he led Miguel out of the room.

Neither of the other two students returned to school for a second day.

A fellow member of the Greenwich Village Community Board, a woman active in a committee on the handicapped, informed Steve that the Board of Education provides teachers for approved special education classes outside public school environments. At the Alternative High Schools and Programs Division of the Board of Education, Steve found an official who "didn't require convincing." She visited the Institute and helped draft an application for the appointment of a teacher.

The application was routed to the City Corporation Counsel. Months of delay followed, and only after the threat of a lawsuit did the Board of Education give authorization. Early in 1985 Steve, then thirty-seven, became program director of a school named after the martyred San Francisco supervisor Harvey Milk. He immediately interviewed ten applicants for a teaching post at the school.

In addition to letters of recommendation attesting to his commitment as a teacher and to his accomplishments as faculty adviser in extracurricular activities, Fred Goldhaber, a college friend of Steve's, brought to his interview a scrapbook of his seventeen years as a classroom teacher and as reading coordinator at Wingate High School in Brooklyn. In addition, Fred had personal as well as professional qualifications for the post. Not only had he experienced a troubled childhood and difficulty in coming out to himself, his parents, and his friends, but he also had a black lover and, like many of the prospective students at the Harvey Milk School, he was HIV-positive. In addition, teaching troubled gay and lesbian young people, he declared, was precisely what he most wanted to do. The Institute Informed the Board of Education that Fred was its choice.

In April 1985 a one-room schoolroom for gay students began operation.

For several years Fred served as the only teacher at Harvey Milk, and he takes pride in the fact that he created the school program. His class has ranged from twenty-five to thirty-five students, a large number for a special education program. Fred set as his major objectives helping his students obtain a high school diploma in order to find better jobs. "I also think," he declares, "that a rounded education is an asset, diploma or no diploma, so that they can better appreciate the world. When a student comes to me," he recounted, "with a request to learn something, I always try to respond, especially when I can look forward to learning something new myself. So it was with a student who wanted to learn Ancient Greek and another who wanted to study German. I had to keep a few lessons ahead of them. The kids have a right to learn whatever they want to learn."

Yearning in vain all his life for intimacy and affection, Fred lavished affection on his students as a high school teacher and thereafter at the Harvey Milk School. He recognizes that for some of his students, especially those handicapped by learning disabilities or suffering drug or alcohol addiction, school is an intimidating experience. Occasionally, Fred says, "we get kids who have built walls around themselves. You can't reach them. They don't trust anyone." Fred has to deal with a lot of "acting up" and loud talking. That they sit still for four hours, Fred emphasizes, is "an accomplishment.

"I get frustrated," Fred declares, "when after overcoming problems in math or developing productive work habits, students leave for full-time work or to find a place to live or to build a love relationship. When a youngster who is bright and can do anything I ask disappears for a month or so, it eats me up inside."

Fred has constantly had to find expedients for dealing with special problems among his students. Realizing that one young man became disoriented in math tests if he encountered more than one problem on a page, Fred obtained permission from the Board of Education to place the questions of a statewide examination on separate pieces of paper and for an extension in time for the test. "He insisted upon having Tarot cards spread out on the desk," Fred recounts, "and was allowed to use a multiplication table. When we submitted his exam papers, we thought we had achieved the impossible." In fact, the student achieved a score of forty-seven out of fifty. To Fred's dismay, however, the state examiners lost the examination papers. Upon Fred's vigorous protest, an examination supervisor agreed to allow the student to take the test the next time it was offered, five months later. After much persuasion, Fred convinced the student to try again. This time he achieved a score of forty-nine out of fifty. "When I first met him," Fred recounts with pride, "he couldn't sit still for even a half hour."

Another student, bright enough to confront any academic challenges, had been expelled from a public high school because he was constantly provoking fights. Fred and Steve Ashkinazy imposed limits on his behavior and adapted a program to his particular needs. "We got him through," says Fred. "I went back to his original school and persuaded them to issue him a diploma."

Steve Ashkinazy speaks with pride of an eighteen-year-old man who had run away from Philadelphia after being beaten up at school, expelled as a troublemaker by the principal, and thrown out of the house by his parents. In New York drug dealers turned him into an addict and forced him to work as a hustler. With assistance from the district attorney's office, people at the Institute helped the young man escape from the life of prostitution and end his addiction. At Harvey Milk he obtained a general education diploma. He was assisted in finding a job. His parents came to visit and agreed to let him return home. He continued on to college and was eventually graduated as a nurse.

The Institute helped Randy, a seventeen-year-old runaway and child of an interracial marriage, to go on welfare and to obtain a part-time job. Randy set himself the goal of becoming a rock singer. Living on the streets and sleeping in the subway or in the park, he used his welfare money and wages to rent a recording studio and to hire unemployed musicians to produce a record. He persuaded some stations to air it. A contract followed. Now, says Steve, he drives around in a huge car accompanied by an entourage. He stops by at the Harvey Milk school occasionally to report on his accomplishments.

Steve also recounts Harvey Milk failures.

After completely transforming himself, gaining self-respect, restoring his relationship with his parents, and graduating with honors, an especially effeminate young black, one of the first students at the school, was unable to find work. He started to hustle and to take drugs. "I watched a steady decline," recounts Steve. "His visits grew more and more infrequent. Once he came to visit in drag, looking more like a prostitute than a secretary. Now I don't know where he is."

During his years of work with gay teenagers at the Harvey Milk School, Steve has identified different constructs about gender and sex among the Latino and black students. Unlike the Latinos, most blacks at Harvey Milk have not known a father figure. "For both groups, however, poverty," Steve insists, "makes a difference. If you come from a family of five living in three rooms, the way you deal with problems differs from the way people act who live in five rooms. In my home, if there were tensions, I could go to my room and cool off. Some of these kids don't even have their own bed. They have to wait until everyone is asleep so that they can make up the couch or put two chairs together. In that kind of situation, how do you deal with conflict and tension?"

Fred loses patience with critics who dismiss the Harvey Milk experiment as a failure. The *New York Times* reported, for example, that after more than five years of operation Harvey Milk had graduated a mere sixteen of its hundred or so enrollees. "People do not appreciate," says Fred, "that the failure of these kids to complete their schooling is not a reflection on the school but on the society."*

THE INSTITUTE'S TRAINING PROGRAM

In 1986 Andy Humm ran into Damien at the studio of the Gay Cable Network, where Andy was working as a volunteer. Damien told him that the Institute had just obtained funds to hire an education director. Dissatisfied with his position at the time in a city program for training college students to serve as mentors for high school children, Andy expressed interest. Within weeks Andy was training teachers and social workers to work with gay young people.

Concerned at the spread of AIDS among adolescents, youth agencies approached Andy for advice on dealing with gay young people. Funds from the Department of Health enabled Andy to hire two assistants. The Institute staff gained a national reputation as a leader in the field of AIDS education.

PROJECT FIRST STEP

When in the Institute's counseling or socializing programs problems arose between street teenagers, often flaming prostitutes employing crude language, and young people from more sheltered backgrounds, it became obvious to Joyce Hunter and Steve Ashkinazy that an outreach program would have to be housed in a separate headquarters with a separate staff and operating at different hours from the other programs of the Institute.

In March 1991 Juan Mendez was appointed assistant director of the outreach program, Project First Step. At the time the staff consisted of a direc-

*In 1996, suffering severely with AIDS, Fred resigned his positon.

tor, an assistant director, and two counselors—two white lesbians, an African-American gay man, and Juan.

Juan had undergone a transformation since his arrival in New York from Puerto Rico in 1988. Working at the Strand Bookstore, Juan found himself in a bohemian atmosphere. He met writers and began going to poetry readings. He moved to the Lower East Side. "It was perfect for me," he declares. "There were gays, Puerto Ricans, and other Latinos." One day, shortly after his arrival in New York, he saw silhouettes of bodies on the sidewalk with a caption stating that Mayor Koch had blood on his hands and showing the number who had already died of AIDS. "It was," he recounts, "the most liberating and empowering thing I had ever seen." Given a notice of an ACT UP meeting by a co-worker at the bookstore, Juan went to the Lesbian and Gay Community Center and found the room packed with three hundred people. Although he felt lost in the large gathering, he persisted, and for more than three years he attended ACT UP meetings every evening, rarely averaging more than five hours of sleep a night. At the December 1989 demonstration at the St. Patrick's Cathedral, Juan filmed the scene of the cops running their motorcycles into the crowd of demonstrators. Those who lay down on the street, including Juan and his lover, were arrested.

Upon obtaining a position as assistant to the vice president for administration at Orion Pictures, Juan used computers and other machines in the office for ACT UP work. After a year, finding conversations in the elevator and in the offices banal in comparison to what he heard at ACT UP meetings and depressed by the empty and sad faces he saw every morning on the subway, he left his job and found a position at the Lower East Side Family Union, an agency with a Latino, Jewish, and Chinese staff offering family services. Juan visited the homes of clients with AIDS and made assessments of their needs. He also lectured about AIDS in schools, before community organizations, and at workplaces and parks. Initially Latino audiences reacted with uneasiness. "Our popular culture," Juan declares, "is very sexual, but it is necessary to adjust one's language in talking about sex, avoiding clinical or scientific terms."

Juan admits that in his social service activities he has frequently been overwhelmed with despair. One day as he walked along the East River after visiting a woman dying from AIDS, he passed some ten buildings in each of which he knew at least one person was dying of the epidemic. Ten years in the future, he thought to himself, the Latino community will be wiped out, and those buildings will be gentrified. "I went back to my office," he said, "and started to cry."

Upon his appointment as assistant director of the Institute's outreach program, Juan underwent special training, read widely on dealing with disturbed young people, and accompanied experienced staff members on their rounds. Three times a week for three-hour stretches Juan and other staff members went out to areas where gay and lesbian street people congregate—Times Square, the Port of Authority terminal, East 53rd Street, and sections of Jackson Heights—moving in pairs for security reasons, though Juan insists he has never encountered a menacing situation. The staff was planning to extend operations to the Bronx and to other parts of Queens.

In public toilets the staff drop off cards with the outreach address and telephone number. The program has become known, says Juan, among the young street people, in great majority people of color (only 10 percent of the clients are white), usually supporting themselves by prostitution. The staff provides counseling, food, changes of clothing, shower facilities, and referrals to other agencies to a constantly changing clientele of about one hundred people. (Almost half of New York's homeless, according to Juan, are gays and lesbians. Many are infected with the AIDS virus.)

Juan has felt particularly frustrated in working with transsexuals, who number about one-third of the Outreach clients. "There is nothing I can do for transsexual clients," Juan declared, "except offer them showers, show them respect and understanding, and counsel them."

Many of the homeless young people choose to live on the streets. "I have to respect their choice," Juan says. "A lot of them will be dead in two years, but at least they will have lived a free life for a brief time." For the 90 to 95 percent of clients addicted to crack, there is no agency providing help. With the limited resources of the Institute, the staff can do nothing for these people. "We recognize the problem," he says, "but we can't tailor our services to deal effectively with them."

After six months of the outreach program, Juan admitted that the staff had much yet to learn. "We cannot assume every gay or lesbian we meet has had our kind of experience. We have not succeeded in getting people off the street, cured of drug addiction, and employed in constructive jobs. Sometimes you wonder whether you're part of the solution or part of the problem. As a social worker you are glossing over the problems so that people who should be assuming responsibility don't have to deal with them."

On a more positive note, Juan declared, "I think that being a gay Puerto Rican, politically progressive, when there are not many, means that I serve as an example. A lot of people of color are on the street because there was no one to show them an option."

CARLA AND OUTREACH TO TEENS

Codirector of the Outreach to Teens program of the Community Health Project (CHP), which provides health services to homeless gay and lesbian young people, Carla, who had endured a difficult life from her earliest years through young adulthood, had always felt a profound connection to the Hispanic community and was eager to participate in programs to educate the community about homophobia, AIDS, and parenting. Informed that the CHP, which provides social services and health care to the gay community, was looking for a driver who could also handle vehicle maintenance, Carla applied for the position and was hired.

Pending the acquisition of a van for an outreach program and a specialized driver license for herself, Carla was assigned to a program called "Health Outreach to Teens" (HOT) providing information about HIV prevention and teaching safe-sex practices. She participated in counseling, in making referrals and health-care appointments, and in assembling statistical data for the Department of Health.

When adolescent clients come into HOT headquarters at the Community Center, Carla recounted, staff members explain the program and assure them of confidentiality, since most are concerned at the possibility of information reaching their parents. Some of the teenagers, she says, come in merely for a bag lunch. They want an ear, someone who will listen to talk about their parents and their loneliness.

Like Juan Mendez, Carla finds dealing with cross-dressers, the majority of the clients in the HOT program, especially frustrating because she can do so little for them. Most support themselves as male prostitutes. Carla and her colleagues direct them to places where they can obtain meals and take showers. "They live in an underground world," she declares. "Rarely having fixed addresses, they have problems obtaining Medicaid. They resist referrals to other agencies. You have to establish trust," Carla notes. "Otherwise nothing you say will have an effect. They test us constantly. If they don't get immediate attention, they walk out. You can't question their lifestyle, and it's not our place to be judgmental. They are hesitant to open up about their personal lives. When they do, you discover fear and unhappiness.

"The gay community," Carla remarks, "is slowly acknowledging that we have a problem with cross-dressing adolescents. At CHP we are creating a safe space for them."

To better understand and help cross-dressers, Carla began attending a Gender Identity group established for men who have undergone a sex change. Carla says she can identify with such men. "There have been moments," she declares, "when I wished I was a guy. I'd love to experience the intimacy of penetrating my lover. I had to decide that it was all right for me to be a woman loving another woman." She has heard members of the group relate how they had felt trapped as women in men's bodies and how they suffered as children. "I think, my God," she declares, "some people do share what I went through. Looking at their lives, I realize that if you don't go through struggle, it's not worth it. Without struggle you don't grow."

Constantly facing the threat of burnout, the CHP staff sets aside one day a week as a "down" day, when they sit together and talk about their own lives. They also participate in support groups to strengthen themselves against the stress they experience in dealing with clients who lead, in great part, lives of desperation.

Carla completed the two-year course at Hostos Community College and was planning to go on for a master's degree in social work. "I'd like to do this kind of work," she says, "for the rest of my life."

Chapter Fourteen

The Gay Community and the AIDS Crisis

> On the deepest personal level most of us [activists] can say that AIDS is the tragedy of our era. We experience deeply personal pain and shame in watching our government fail us, in many instances intentionally, watching with indifference while against all odds people struggle for their lives, demonstrating on the streets or working on the inside. . . .

So spoke Ginny Apuzzo, some of whose closest associates in the gay movement were among the first to die in the AIDS epidemic.

Among the sixty or so interviewees, six had tested positive for the HIV virus; one parent was dealing with the sorrow of watching her son suffer with AIDS; two interviewees had endured the loss of brothers to the disease; and several had undergone the travail of nursing lovers dying of AIDS. Indeed, the AIDS crisis loomed as a backdrop to the experience of almost all the interviewees, and a number expressed poignantly the pall the epidemic cast upon their lives. "I have lost more contemporaries than my parents have," exclaimed Andy Humm, an activist in his late thirties. "My parents," declared Lance Ringel, "lived through war and depression, and I'm living through the AIDS crisis. I can't keep track of my acquaintances who have died." Though he has tested negative, Lance says that years ago he ceased thinking of growing old. "The future has shrunk."

"If I run into someone from my past," said Steve Ashkinazy, "I never ask about other people. If someone is mentioned, I grip myself, ready for word of death. You take care of all these people until they die, and wonder why you are left behind. It is a concentration-camp syndrome. I can tell my ninety-six-year-old grandmother how my friends have died. She's at the end of her life, and I'm in the same place emotionally. I think it must be like what it was in the Warsaw Ghetto, when after a transport train, people would go out to the street to see who was still alive."

Sharon Levine, a computer technician and longtime volunteer at the Gay Men's Health Crisis, summed up the intensity of grief among many lesbians at the tens of thousands of deaths in New York City. "From now on, when a man talks to you," she told her employer, "I do not want to meet him, to go to dinner with him. I don't want to get to know him because he's going to die." Liz Garro expressed an even stronger reaction to the deaths multiplying about her, declaring, "As a lesbian, I even feel guilty that none of us have AIDS."

At the initial outbreak of the epidemic, when PWAs still numbered only in the hundreds, a few farsighted New York gay activists took measures to defend their community. As head of the National Gay Task Force, Ginny Apuzzo along with other activists presented demands for action to Mayor Edward I. Koch. In the first discussion gay activists ever conducted with the top officials of the Social Security agency in Washington, they negotiated rapid disability coverage for persons with AIDS (PWAs at the time were dying within two years after diagnosis). "We were successful, too," Ginny recalls, "in preventing the use of the HIV test to exclude people from insurance." In a meeting with Assistant Secretary of Health and Human Services Ed Brandt, a conservative Republican from Oklahoma, Ginny warned, "We are not going to get to the bottom of this disease until we deal with homophobic discrimination." Without a guarantee of confidentiality, she also noted, people at risk would hesitate to undergo testing. When Ginny charged that the Reagan administration was "out to get us," Brandt looked at her, Ginny recalls, "as though I was out of my mind." Subsequently, Ginny declares, "he found that the things we were telling him were right, that people did hate lesbians and gays, and our lives were not valued. He became our staunchest ally in the Reagan administration," Ginny recalled. He sent a confidential message to Secretary Margaret Heckler supporting the request of gay leaders for an immediate appropriation of a hundred million dollars to fight the disease. After a meeting of Ginny and her colleagues with Heckler, "the first time lesbians and gays met with a cabinet officer," however, the secretary turned down the appropriations request.

"In our very first testimony before a congressional committee," Ginny recounted, "we predicted everything that was going to happen. We warned that the administration's closing its eyes to the plague would result in havoc in health care in this country and drive insurance rates off the wall."

Gay activists demanded that AIDS agencies be run by gays, the individuals immediately affected by the epidemic, not by heterosexuals. "We said that we can best serve the special needs of the infected," recalled Ginny Apuzzo. In 1981, alarmed at the whirlwind spread of the HIV infection and at the reluctance of government at all levels to recognize the threat of a national epidemic of vast proportions, prescient New York activists founded the Gay Men's Health Crisis (GMHC). Within a few years GMHC expanded into a large-scale AIDS service organization that won international renown for the variety of its services to an ever-increasing number of clients.

By the end of the decade, the face of the epidemic began to change, with mounting infection among IV drug users, women, and children, predominantly people of color. Gay activists addressed the new circumstances both by expanding services within established service organizations and by establishing new organizations. In New York City activists developed more than a hundred organizations and agencies serving those, gay and straight, infected with the virus. "Tragically," as Ginny Apuzzo noted, the gay community "are the most experienced people in dealing with the problems of all the groups suffering from the infection. We have become the best organizers, the best administrators in the world in this bloody epidemic. How well we share our experience with others ravaged by this disease is a measure of the challenge that we face."

To expand its clientship beyond middle-class gay white males, GMHC appointed to its staff minority people to establish contact with other endangered communities.

GUILLERMO VASQUEZ

One of these new minority specialists was Guillermo Vasquez, appointed coordinator of the AIDS Prevention Program for People of Color. Guillermo had varied experience as an activist in the New York Latino community. Emigrating to the United States from Colombia as a young man, Guillermo appreciated not only the problems confronting Latinos but also the problems of all newcomers to the country. Furthermore, he had undergone an intense personal odyssey in coming to terms with his sexual orientation and in transforming himself from a pampered youth raised in affluence to an adult with an understanding of class and ethnic discrimination.

Guillermo had early displayed leadership and organizational abilities. In secondary school he helped to organize a gay mutual-support system. Upon settling in New York he developed an informal mutual-assistance group among Latino friends in Queens, some members of which had immigration problems; others, problems relating to work. Guillermo himself suffered homophobic assaults. He was called names on the street and once was attacked by teenagers in "Vaseline Alley" in Jackson Heights (where Julio Rivera was later bludgeoned to death). In a mugging he was cracked on the head with a blackjack.

After deaths of close friends from AIDS, Guillermo began to attend GMHC workshops and entered a clinical study of sex practices among gay men. In addition, he volunteered at the GMHC education and policy departments, working twice a week as supervisor of the New York City AIDS lobby. He also became active in Latino AIDS activist groups, joining the AIDS education committee of Boricua Gay and Lesbian Forum, a group seeking to empower the Latino gay and lesbian community through participation in the political process.

In 1988, on the strength of his volunteer work at GMHC and his experience with Latino gay groups and as assistant director of education at the AIDS Center for Queens County, Guillermo was hired as a GMHC education coordinator, charged with community development in the Latino community. Encountering resistance among Latinos to attending GMHC workshops, Guillermo developed AIDS presentations at Latino gay bars. He obtained the cooperation of a popular drag entertainer, Mario de Columbia, as well as of the owner of the bar where Mario was performing and of the physician in charge of the AIDS Center at St. Vincent's Hospital in Greenwich Village. The program they evolved won an award from the State Department of Health.

Guillermo also persuaded a Latino playwright to write an educational play posing questions about testing, denial, and safe sex and exposing misinformation about the infection. Summers, Guillermo organized a "Love in the Time of AIDS" health fair in an outdoor park with a theater performance and the distribution of educational materials. A physician was on hand as a consultant.

It was at such events, Guillermo declares, that his efforts achieved greatest success. Gay Latinos, who used to insist that they had no need of condoms, began picking them up at bars; but much, he says, still remained to be done. Among Latinos, he points out, the aggressive partner, "the man" in homosexual anal sex, is not considered to be gay or to be at risk of infection, while the receptive partner, the one "playing the woman's role," is scorned and considered to be potential spreader of the disease. Thus in approaching gay and bisexual Latinos, Guillermo declares that he misses half his audience.

Guillermo also encounters difficulty in his education efforts because frank talk about homosexuality, he explains, "does not fit with our Latino culture. We can speak about sexual acts, but we can't ask people to volunteer their experiences." An additional complication arises from the male-chauvinist machismo that proclaims, "I want my pleasure, and I don't give a damn about you. I just want to get my rocks off. I don't care if you get infected." "One man I know," Guillermo relates, "wouldn't tell his wife he was infected or use condoms with her even when she became pregnant. He didn't want her to know that he had been having sex with a guy." Indeed, families prefer to say that their infected men shot drugs. Because of machismo, too, Latino men at risk refuse to go to a doctor. "I'm as strong as a bull," they boast. As a result, when they finally seek medical treatment, they are often in an advanced stage of the infection. Doctors tell Guillermo that if some of their patients had consulted them a year earlier, they would still be alive.

"Day by day," Guillermo recounted, "I meet with people from other organizations to evolve ways to educate the Latino community and to exchange information, but we need many more programs, involving up to five thousand staffers and volunteers in a massive education program. Latinos, about 10 percent of the nation's population, account for 16 percent of all AIDS cases. . . . We Latinos carry a lot of burdens—poverty, lack of information, discrimination. AIDS is way down in the list of problems."

Regarding his contribution in this complex struggle, Guillermo insists "I am doing good work and not hurting anybody, really doing what Christ asked, to love and help one another."*

KEITH CYLAR AND HOUSING WORKS

At the time of his interview Keith was director of Housing and Services at Housing Works, "a minority controlled not-for-profit organization that provides housing services and advocacy for homeless individuals with HIV infection."

Keith first developed political awareness while still in high school. He was moved by the Kent State incident, and during riots in 1965, he slipped out of the house and joined in the "long hot summer" riot. A tear gas canister thrown by a national guardsman, he recalled, fell near his feet and rolled down the street. During his undergraduate years, while working at a Boston psychiatric hospital, Keith joined a group called Black Gay and Lesbian Youth (BLAGLEY) and facilitated at it meetings. "There is a process that leads to your being able to stand up at work and say, 'I am a gay man,' " Keith declares. "At twenty-four or twenty-five I reached the point at which I understood who I was, a gay man, not a bisexual. My friends were gay, my world was gay."

In 1986, at twenty-eight, after working three years as a therapist in Boston, Keith enrolled at Columbia University for graduate study. "If you were going to be gay," he explains, "New York was the place to be. I was ready for New York." While at Columbia, Keith helped organize an AIDS awareness day on campus. While pursuing his graduate studies, Keith resolved to ease up on his intense gay life until he became oriented to his new environment. He was, after all, he reasoned, starting a new life. "I knew," he says, "that if I did a lot of drugs in New York, I would get into trouble." Keith's resolution foundered upon his meeting a new lover at the Spike, a gay leather bar. "We went home and had the best sex I had ever had," he recalls. "The next morning we went out for breakfast, had sex again, and walked down Riverside Park arm-in-arm. It was a wonderful spring day. I was so happy." His new friend had been a fireman and an undercover cop and a founding member of GOAL. He was at the time a drug dealer. Although Keith de-

*In 1996, overwhelmed by disease, Guillermo was no longer reporting to his position at the GMHC.

clares he was in love and could not keep his hands off his new lover, he sent him away, convinced that in his new life he had to remain free of complications. The man called the next day, however, and they remained together for two and a half years, when Keith's lover fell ill with what appeared to be a severe case of influenza. At the hospital his illness was diagnosed as pneumocystic pneumonia. His lungs filled up, and within four days he was dead. "My world collapsed," Keith exclaims. Within a two-month period, Keith lost two other friends. "I wanted to die. I started taking drugs heavily and drinking."

Keith took over his lover's drug trade to support himself.

Upon obtaining his master's degree, Keith found a position as a social worker in the AIDS ward at Montefiore Hospital in the Bronx, working under Dr. Gerald Friedlander, a physician renowned for his dedication to his numerous AIDS patients. At Montefiore, the patients were all black or Hispanic and all close to death. Keith's job was to help patients obtain their entitlements. "I couldn't get through the red tape at the hospital and at the public agencies," he recalled. He became convinced that the only way to accomplish anything was to go outside the system.

As a result of his frustration at Montefiore and his sorrow at his lover's death, Keith began to attend ACT UP meetings. At first he sat and listened, trying to decide how he fit in. It bothered him that the attendance was almost entirely white and even more that people of color were not taking the epidemic seriously, insisting that AIDS was a disease of white gay men and that people of color had too many other problems to be concerned about the epidemic. (Paradoxically, although he had been clipping articles about AIDS since 1982, Keith had not himself practiced safe sex. He discovered after his lover's death that he himself tested HIV-positive.)

Invited to join the Majority Action Committee, the ACT UP caucus of people of color, Keith was disappointed with what he encountered. "I opposed their analysis of the political situation," he says, "and their proposals for becoming more effective within ACT UP." Though heavily on drugs at the time, he opposed a needle-exchange program. (Subsequently, he admitted his error.)

One day at a committee meeting, Keith spoke his mind about what troubled him. Encouraged by appeals that he take leadership in dealing with problems of PWAs of color, Keith accepted responsibility in helping to organize ACT UP demonstrations and served as spokesperson at a demonstration at the National Institutes of Health (NIH). He participated in a panel with Anthony Fauci, the head of the NIH AIDS program, and in an AIDS discussion at ABC television.

A turning point in Keith's activism occurred at a People of Color conference in Washington in 1989. The Majority Action Committee of ACT UP and the people-of-color caucus chose him to deliver a major address on AIDS in the black community as well as the summation speech before the five thousand people in attendance. Out of that conference, Keith notes, the Latino and Asian caucuses of ACT UP developed. The black caucus, however, left ACT UP and formed Black AIDS Mobilization. Keith helped organize the Minority Task Force on AIDS. He expresses pride that the Task Force staff quickly expanded from five to about thirty. Thereafter he undertook to transform the ACT UP caucus dealing with homeless PWAs into a new and separate organization—Housing Works.

But Keith still confronted a critical subjective problem. "I was a recreational drug user who crossed the line," he recounts. "It was part of the culture of the 1970s and 1980s. You worked certain hours and after work you did drugs, alcohol, sex, kinky sex—you partied hard. We believed that you defined yourself as a gay man by having sex, and you were to have sex as often as you could. In the bars there was a kind of community, a family of sorts. That was a good life if you could also do your job."

But in undertaking a major organizing effort, Keith had to face head-on the fundamental contradiction between his vision of himself as an ethical human being dedicated to fighting for justice and the reality of his disorganized personal life. "There was the Keith," he relates, "who was selling drugs and taking drugs and drinking at night to the point that his memory was failing. There was also by day the social worker and therapist, the advocate. Two distinct people." His drug addiction was out of control. After a hard day at the office, he would stop at a bar for a drink and remain until closing time, 4 A.M. "I was an alcoholic and a drug addict," he admits, "and I couldn't function at work." As a dedicated activist, he had given up the right, he says, to do drugs and alcohol. He entered a therapy program.

Keith describes Housing Works as a minority-controlled corporation, the majority of whose staff, directors, and clients are people of color. (Gerri Wells, one of the founders of the Pink Panthers, was one of the few white staff members.) As the chief clinical person, Keith helped design and develop the philosophy of the agency, and he supervised its various programs. Funded by subsidies from foundations, by direct mail fund-raising and other fund raising activities, and by contracts with the City Division of AIDS Services and the State AIDS Institute, Housing Works provides services to homeless PWAs referred to it by public and private agencies. Keith derives satisfaction in his post because he is providing services that he believes are "intellectually and therapeutically appropriate for this very difficult population." Some of the Housing Works clients, he says, have been helped to remain in their apartments or to find housing. Some are overcoming their drug addiction.

Housing Works had developed plans for an apartment residence that would be licensed as a treatment and diagnostic center. It would differ from Bailey House, the city residence for homeless PWAs, in that it would not exclude PWAs on drugs and would place greater emphasis on individual independence by providing private kitchenettes and bathrooms.

Keith sat on various committees set up to streamline procedures in the city and state AIDS bureaucracies and participated in a group called Fair Share, which sought a fair distribution of AIDS funds to affected populations. He was a member of AIDS Action, a coalition of eighty AIDS organizations pressing to place AIDS issues on the agenda in political campaigns.

GAYS COME OUT FIGHTING

To demonstrate how the dynamism in the gay community intensified during the decade after Stonewall, Ginny Apuzzo contrasted the struggle to include a gay rights plank in the Democratic Party platform during the 1976 presidential campaign process with the invitation to the White House she and other activists received in 1980 to hear an appeal from Carter aide Anne Wexler for gay support in the election that year. With the outbreak of the AIDS epidemic at the beginning of the 1980s, however, the confidence and militancy evoked by Stonewall dissipated almost from one day to the next. Beleaguered by the rapid spread of the infection and the decimation of gays in major centers like New York, the epicenter of the disease, and San Francisco, the gay community also confronted an intensification of homophobia promoted, in part, by leaders of the Moral Majority, who gloated that gays were suffering just punishment for their "sinning against God's law."

In its 1988 Final Report, the Presidential Commission on the Human Immunodeficiency Epidemic called attention to "increasing violence against those perceived to carry HIV." In 1991 the New York Lesbian and Gay Anti-Violence Project (AVP) reported 133 incidents in the city motivated by fear of AIDS, "a sharp increase over 45 such cases in 1990." Bea Hanson, Coordinator of AVP's HIV-Related Violence Program, noted "a common scenario . . . is neighbors attacking and harassing persons who they think have AIDS."

By 1986, frustrated by the indifference to the epidemic of Reagan officials to the suffering of those infected by the virus, the gay community had replaced despair with rage; and many lesbians and gays yearned for leadership in militant action. In March 1987 at a meeting at the Gay Community Center, dramatist Larry Kramer issued a call to "fight back," and the AIDS Coalition to Unleash Power (ACT UP) was born. Thereafter the AIDS community throughout the nation underwent a resurgence even more aggressive than that following upon the Stonewall uprising.

By 1990 ACT UP chapters had been formed in cities across the United States as well as in several foreign countries. After mounting demonstrations involving up to hundreds of thousands of gays and lesbians outside federal, state, and municipal agencies and at the annual International Conferences on AIDS here and abroad, ACT UP came to exemplify the fighting spirit evolving in the community as well as the community's renewed and increasing political clout in the nation. Its bold and dramatic actions inspired courage among the timid and provided organizational training to hundreds of gays and lesbians who had never before participated in public protests. Activists displayed courage and dedication rarely matched in the immediate post-Stonewall years. "I get up every morning to go to war," says Juan Mendez. Describing the feelings of many AIDS militants, long-time activist Ginny Apuzzo declares, "Sometimes you just feel like a kamikazi fighter."

In a development potentially decisive in the struggle for the achievement of full citizenship for the community, lesbians in ever-greater numbers joined gay men in the struggle. Indeed, the AIDS crisis impelled the development of an unprecedented unity between gays and lesbians. "I was just enjoying life," recounted Gerri Wells, "but everything changed when my brother was diagnosed early in 1987. I was hurt and angry at his getting AIDS. There was no place to yell about it." Upon her brother's death, at the urging of Larry Kramer, Gerri attended an ACT UP meeting. A friend encouraged her to express her intense feelings. "I had never been able to speak before a group," she said, "but I felt so passionate about what I felt that I forced myself to speak. O my god! They loved what I had to say. People said that I inspired them because I spoke from my heart."

Apart from the state and municipal officials interviewed, all but a very few of the interviewees for this book gained their experience in gay activism in ACT UP. Several underwent a six-hour ACT UP civil disobedience (CD) course conducted, in great part, by Quaker ACT UP members, learning the rationale of civil disobedience and studying tactics of nonviolence. Trainees underwent role-playing exercises in preparation for arrest situations. "Our aim," says Steve Quester of ACT UP, "is to be able to go into the streets on the AIDS issue without getting killed." Often individual CD classes remained together as action groups. "When the police arrest you," explained Steve, "you need to know that someone has seen you get arrested."

STEVE QUESTER

As early as sixth grade, Steve asserts, he had leftist sympathies. "I remember," he recounts, "reading articles about the percentage of the world's population and wealth in the United States. I thought that was wrong." His thinking was influenced by experiences during three summers at a camp for Jewish children, where a rabbi lectured them on political issues, took them to Washington to meet with the Egyptian ambassador, and exposed them to people concerned about disarmament and abortion rights. In high school, with his mother's encouragement, he served as coordinator for the John Anderson for President campaign and represented the progressive viewpoint in a continuous school newspaper debate on current issues. At a school model congress, representing himself as a "straight" civil rights advocate, he introduced a bill for equal rights for gays and lesbians.

As an undergraduate Steve joined Gay People Columbia, a social organization that ran monthly dances. By the end of his freshman year he was completely "out" on campus and politically active in numerous causes. Asked by a sociology professor to explain his participation in an antiapartheit blockade at the university, Steve replied that he had adopted his mother's set of beliefs and carried them to their logical conclusion. Although Steve's mother was concerned at his neglecting his schoolwork, she was proud of his activity and told him so. "My brother," says Steve, "was at the State University at Oneonta drinking beer."

Steve became impatient with the political apathy of Gay People Columbia. In the spring of 1983, when the gay rights bill was once again defeated in the city council, he called upon the members to join a demonstration at City Hall. Few of the members followed him to participate in a sit-down at Seventh Avenue and Sheridan Square. "We were being so bad," Steve recalls. "It was very exciting."

After graduation, Steve spent two years as an Intern for Peace in an Israeli Arab town. The interns were warned to be careful of their behavior in the traditional Arab communities, and Steve came out of the closet to Americans and to some of the Israelis but to none of the Arab interns. "I don't ever want to be in that position again," he remarks. In this experience he says that he learned to work with people, to listen, and to accept people at their point of development without being judgmental.

Upon returning home, Steve obtained a position teaching in a New York private school. He wanted a rest from intensive politics and needed time to obtain a perspective on his Israel experience. One day he saw an ACT UP leaflet. "I shook my head," he recalls, "and thought, 'Isn't this pathetic; these people are angry at a virus. What's needed is science, not politics.' " When at a Passover dinner Andrew, a college friend who served as chairperson of the ACT UP action committee, explained the purpose of an ACT UP demonstration about to be held at Wall Street, Steve asked what Wall Street had to do with AIDS. What kind of action did they want the corporations to undertake?

In May 1988 Andrew invited Steve to participate in a demonstration in Washington at the Federal Civil Rights Commission. Demonstrators were going to wear clown masks to express their sentiments about the commission's effectiveness. At the urging of a school colleague Steve took off a day and participated. Returning to New York, the demonstrators appeared in their masks at an ACT UP meeting and were greeted with applause. "That was my first ACT UP meeting," Steve declares, "and I have been going back ever since." ACT UP, he says, provides a continual learning experience. "You pick up the leaflets on the table at the back of the room," he explains. "You listen to what people say. Everything becomes clear."

Steve joined Andrew on the Action Committee and experienced his first of many arrests at a takeover of the New York City health commissioner's office in August 1988.

With the passage of the years, noted Steve Machon, another ACT UP activist, "our focus changed as the crisis changed." ACT UP expanded its activities to encompass issues sometimes only indirectly related to the AIDS struggle. Individual ACT UP members began forming either ad hoc committees or loosely organized "affinity groups" that came together usually with the purpose of civil disobedience on particular issues. Some twenty ACT UP members, one of whom was Steve Quester, who demonstrated at the 1988 party conventions formed such an affinity group, the Delta Group, a name recalling their attendance at the Republican convention in New Orleans, where they had been surrounded and threatened by enraged Republicans. Delta Group members assumed a role as a defensive vanguard in demonstrations—"people ready to put their bodies on the line," declares Steve Quester. In one demonstration in Washington the Delta Group marched headlong into a police line in order to divert attention from ACT UP members advancing at another point.

Steve also participated in the formation of an ad hoc Police Violence Working Group in response to the police brutality against Chris Hennelly in February 1991. "The incident at the Midtown North precinct was not the first time," Steve declared, "that we had encountered police violence, but gays never saw them move in and beat us up like that. It had happened in Chicago but never in New York." Suspicious of all police, the ad hoc committee refused to confer with GOAL. "We don't want to talk to cops," remarked Steve.

The Police Violence group assembled a hundred people for a demonstration at Gracie Mansion, the mayor's residence. They found five hundred mounted police in riot gear awaiting them. The group met with Bill Lynch, the deputy mayor of intergovernmental affairs, and mobilized leading political figures in support of their demand for an independent investigation of the Hennelly incident. When the demand was rejected, they chained themselves to the doors of City Hall. Five of the group were arrested.

Subsequently, the ad hoc group infiltrated a $2,500-a-plate fund-raising dinner for the Police Athletic League hosted by District Attorney Robert M. Morgenthau. At Columbia University, they disrupted a speech by the police commissioner, but when they attempted to picket at the residence of the chief of police, they were cordoned off a block away. They chanted: "The boys in blue are bashers too!"

When the group sought to build a coalition about the issue of police brutality with organizations like the National Congress for Puerto Rican Rights, the Medger Evans Center, and the Committee against Anti-Asian Violence, Steve became aware of how the police terrorized communities of color. "I will never accept," he declares, "what happened to Chris Hennelly, but what has happened to us since Stonewall pales next to what is done to Latino and African-American young men every day."

STEVE MACHON

In the late 1980s Steve assumed responsibility in ACT UP for responding to prisoners who appealed to ACT UP for help for themselves or for infected friends in combatting the regulation excluding them from clinical trials, their only hope for obtaining satisfactory medical care. During the 1990 March on Washington, Steve was outraged by a report of the horrendous treatment accorded HIV-infected women in the District prison. After consulting Judy Greenspan of the ACLU national prison project, Steve approached various New York prison officials. At the State AIDS Discrimination Unit someone recommended that he speak with the commissioner of prisons, Thomas Coughlin. Coughlin told Steve to mind his own business. AIDS, whether caused by sexual contact or drugs, Steve explains, was supposed not to exist in the prisons, and the New York State Department of Correctional Services did not recognize the existence of an AIDS crisis.

Hired by the Correctional Association of New York, an independently funded organization that works with parolees, to assemble data on the recruitment of prisoners in AIDS clinical trials, Steve obtained permission to speak with prison inmates. "People working on AIDS issues develop an intense rapport with HIV-infected prisoners," he declares. Infected prisoners, he discovered, led a completely confined existence, segregated and subject to abuse and lacking adequate medical care. One prisoner, he learned, was placed in solitary confinement and deprived of all medication after an outburst of anger upon being informed that the infirmary had run out of his medication. PWA prisoners, Steve discovered, were shackled at the ankles and wrists during transport to hospitals and within hospitals. A prisoner in a New York prison suffering from diarrhea, vomiting, and nausea in the final stage of AIDS underwent six hours of pain while being transported to a hospital. The guards stopped on the way for snacks. When he asked to be allowed to use a toilet, a guard beat him. By the time he arrived at the hospital he had messed all over himself.

AIDS status is supposed to be kept confidential, but prisoners, Steve learned, cannot insist upon their rights. A doctor passing an inmate waiting on line for his test results announced for all to hear, "Gil, you have AIDS." The man had received no counseling to prepare him for the news. He went berserk. Guards rushed up, beat him, and threw him into solitary confinement.

Steve helped organize the ACT UP Prison Issues Committee, an interracial committee with a membership varying from six to eight individuals, including a doctor, a lawyer, and a nurse who works with adolescents with HIV. As a result of protest demonstrations promoted by the committee, PWAs were granted conjugal visits like other prisoners. "After a public outcry," Steve remarks, "the prison authorities yielded on the easiest issue." In April 1992, the committee's demand for compassionate release for critically ill PWAs was approved.

The committee was still demanding AIDS education for prison staffs as well as inmates, the establishment of peer support groups, distribution of condoms and clean needles, provision of adequate medical treatment and a definition of a standard of care. Now, Steve says, HIV-infected prisoners know that there are places where they can get assistance and information.

His years of ACT UP activism, Steve declares, have given him "a place to hook into all the problems." It has also made him comfortable with being gay. "I've learned that you can be intimate with another gay man without necessarily having to go to bed with him. It has opened up new possibilities for being with and working with other gay people, including lesbians. All of us can be close to one other without society's homophobia intruding into our interaction."

By the 1990s, with its tremendous increase in membership, ACT UP began to undergo strains, and the original ACT UP members began to drift away. Many AIDS activists were suffering burnout and frustration at the realization that, as Steve Machon noted, a resolution of the AIDS crisis would take more time than people had anticipated. "AIDS is so caught up in politics," he declared. "The crisis is putting a strain on health care, ethics, racial issues. That's why ACT UP has so many committees working on so many issues."

A sizable number of ACT UP people, while sometimes retaining their association with ACT UP, moved on to form new organizations dealing with critical problems to which ACT UP, as an AIDS-activist organization, was not devoting attention.

QUEER NATION

"The catalyst for the formation of Queer Nation, a new organization for direct action on gay and lesbian issues," recounts Alan Klein, "was Andy Rooney's snide homophobic remarks on television. When Rooney was reinstated after being briefly barred from *60 Minutes*, Michelangelo [Signorile, an editor of the gay publication *Outweek*] called me in panic and anger. He insisted that we do something. We realized that there was no activist mechanism for handling such a problem or for dealing generally with gay bashing, antigay discrimination, and domestic partnership and all the other pressing issues affecting the community."

Alan, Michelangelo, Alan's lover Karl Soenlein, and Tom Blewitt urged Jay Blotcher, like them an active member of ACT UP, to join them in forming a new activist gay organization. "They were incensed," Jay recalls, "at a rising tide of pubic homophobia—not only the offensive remarks from Andy Rooney but also the antigay jokes from Andrew Dice Clay and homophobic lyrics from rap artists, along with mounting statistics of gay bashing throughout the country."

By word of mouth and a telephone campaign the group assembled some sixty people at the Community Center. Insisting upon informality and loose organization, people at the meeting even opposed adoption of a name. After a lengthy debate at a second meeting with a larger attendance, however, the decision was taken to call the new group "Queer Nation," in defiance of the homophobic epithet. The name had, in fact, been employed in the gay press and in gay conversation to denominate gay activists. It offered the advantage of covering both gays and lesbians. The members set an objective of serving as a grassroots expression that avoided the kind of bureaucracy with which ACT UP was becoming burdened.

Jay Blotcher and Alan Klein are representative of the gay activists who founded Queer Nation.

JAY BLOTCHER

As a child, Jay Blotcher watched his parents going to meetings at the local temple. "Now I wonder," he declares, "why I was not interested in such activities." Their activism, he admits, did have a delayed effect on him. "As an adult active in gay and lesbian activities," he declares, "I am essentially doing what they used to do."

In 1982, after graduation, Jay moved to New York and began writing for gay publications and for a cable television gay and lesbian magazine show called "Our Time." He met Vito Russo, a well-known, longtime activist. "Russo," Jay declares, "wasn't saddled by any narrow preconceptions, he saw the whole picture. From him I learned about the community, its history."

When "Our Time" was discontinued in the spring of 1983, Jay, impatient with factional bickering in the community, felt no inclination to become involved in any of the gay organizations. "I thought," he says, "I would make a personal statement. I would just talk about gay life and serve as its best example." Becoming more politically aware and comfortable with himself, in March 1987 Jay participated in the first ACT UP demonstration, on Wall Street. Thirteen people were arrested. During the summer he joined a second demonstration at Memorial Sloan-Kettering Medical Center. Inspired by the march on Washington later that year, he joined ACT UP. "Something about it," he recalls, "fired my imagination, its visibility and refusal to apologize for its actions."

During this time of his increasing militancy, Jay met a man with whom he was to remain for two years. "When we grew apart," Jay recounts, "ACT UP became my family, my friends, my lover." In 1989 Jay took over as ACT UP media coordinator, and his face and name and statements began appearing in the media. "I was in a key position in the biggest and most well-known AIDS activist group in the country," he declares. "My job was to transform the yelling in the streets into explanations for the press and to the public with the aim of changing public policy on AIDS."

In April, 1989, Jay participated in the break-in at the Burroughs-Wellcome headquarters in North Carolina, an action that helped to persuade the corporation to reduce the price of AZT by 20 percent. That summer Jay distributed press kits at the International AIDS Conference in Montreal and was one of the ACT UP members who stormed the conference. At a subsequent ACT UP meeting he gave a report of how ACT UP had broken into the press all over the world. When he finished, an older woman, a 1960s activist, stood up and declared: "I want the group to know that Jay was always there, always at work." The meeting gave Jay an ovation. When someone reported that Jay had worked through his birthday and had not even mentioned it, everybody sang "Happy Birthday." "I felt loved," Jay declares, "and as though I had done something."

After the Stop the Church demonstration at St. Patrick's Cathedral on December 9, 1989, as media coordinator Jay had "to turn a situation that got out of hand into a palatable news story with an explanation of why we did what we did." He talked at length with a *New York Times* reporter, and on January 2 an article appeared on the first page of the "Metro" section of the *Times* praising ACT UP for its accomplishments. "You couldn't buy that publicity," declares Jay. "It turned things around. People reconsidered who we were and what we did." Jay adjudges his role in that incident as the zenith of his ACT UP experience.

While Jay was media coordinator for ACT UP, his phone was ringing all day long. "I felt," he says, "as though I was in the center of the universe, in the middle of it all. I would call somebody at a newspaper, and the next day I saw my release in print." After participating in the attempt to block the appointment of Woodrow Myres as New York City Health Commissioner in January 1990, Jay, at the point of burnout and harassed by hate mail, took a break from activity.

"I certainly did not anticipate that I would become associated with another activist organization," Jay insists. "I thought I was settling in for a nice long rest." It was not merely that he was exhausted from his intense ACT UP activity. ACT UP, he began to think, had grown too big, too complex. He was no longer able to move without consulting someone, and the organization had so widened its focus that its aims were becoming blurred—AIDS and women, AIDS and prisoners, AIDS and the homeless. "It's necessary to be concerned about varied issues," Jay grants, "but ACT UP was taking on too much."

The concept of Queer Nation excited Jay. He was attracted by the energy, enthusiasm, and freshness in the new group. Many of these people, like Jay himself, were burned-out ACT UP members committed to fighting homophobia and determined to streamline the bureaucracy hampering the struggle on gay issues. The attendance at Queer Nation meetings represented more of a cross section of the community, including both young and older activists. The members said, "Of course you'll do the media work for Queer Nation." Jay agreed.

ALAN KLEIN

At Ithaca College Alan Klein was exposed to left-wing thinking in some of his courses, but his education as a gay activist began after graduation, when he attended a student health conference at Columbia University. It was the first time, he says, that he met a PWA and the first time he heard Larry Kramer. Karl, with whom Alan was living at the time, attended a series of AIDS lectures sponsored by the *Village Voice* and was persuaded that he and Alan should become involved actively. In June 1987 they went to a planning meeting for the march on Washington scheduled for the fall. Repelled by the contentious atmosphere, they walked out. Finding that an ACT UP meeting was proceeding simultaneously at the Center, they stopped by. "It proved to be the most incredible gathering I had ever attended," Alan recalls, "passionate, with an energy I had never experienced. I had never been so inspired." Shortly thereafter, when Karl served as a marshal at an ACT UP demonstration at Federal Plaza, Alan came alone, wearing a baseball cap and dark glasses. When he saw people being arrested on the steps of the federal court house, he thought to himself, "What am I doing with dark glasses? This is a question of life or death, and here you are thinking about yourself." He pulled off his dark glasses, turned his cap around, and continued to demonstrate.

While Karl served as an ACT UP facilitator, Alan helped organize demonstrations. In 1989 he worked on the largest AIDS demonstration the city had as yet seen, at City Hall. Thereafter, to avoid burnout, he took a break from intensive activity. In fact, like Jay Blotcher, he was sensing a change in ACT UP. With the flood of new people, ACT UP seemed less like a family.

In March 1990 Alan and Karl, who retired from activity following upon his mother's death, participated in the formation of Queer Nation. The new organization made its presence known quickly. In late April, the morning after a pipe bomb injured three people in Uncle Charlie's South, a gay bar in the Village, Jay Blotcher, who had been present at the explosion, and Alan were on the phone calling activists to a demonstration. That evening more than a thousand people assembled at Uncle Charlie's and set out on a march behind a banner reading "Gays and Lesbians Bash Back!" "This success,"Jay declares, "told us that something about QN touched people, they wanted to be part of it."

In a second action, under the slogan "Take Back the Night," a larger procession with Mayor Ed Koch at its head was heckled by homophobes who shouted epithets and pelted marchers with bottles.

With this event Jay was able to break into the media. "The press," he says, "was especially intrigued by our choice of name. We were on the cover of the *Voice* and appeared in articles in the *Daily News*. We captured their imagination and drew attention to the problem of gay bashing." Subsequently, Jay managed to get an article in the weekly *New York* on the brutal murder of

Julio Rivera, "a very good article, exactly what we needed, good ammunition in support of the hate crimes bill coming up in Albany."*

During the succeeding winter, Queer Nation expanded, spreading throughout the nation so rapidly that unanticipated problems developed. (It was Queer Nation that pressured the Houston police to deploy decoy cops after a brutal homophobic murder.)** New members were seeking to involve QN in varied issues only loosely associated with gay problems—apartheit, Central America, Haiti, and so on. After a reexamination of the organization's charter and mission, Queer Nation was transformed into a smaller and tighter organization relying less on "theatrics and sex appeal."

In September of 1990, convinced that with their specialized experience in publicity and films there were more effective actions which they could undertake, Jay and Alan ceased participation in QN and developed a national Anti-Violence Campaign entitled "Public Impact," under which they produced television video spots exposing homophobic violence. "We could no longer just sit back," Jay declared, "while friends were getting bloodied in the streets."

In June 1991, on the anniversary of QN's "Take Back the Night" march, Alan returned to help mobilize five thousand people in one of the largest gay antiviolence demonstrations the country had ever experienced. This time, he declares, the "queers" were well organized. Marshals were equipped with walkie-talkies. The police were on hand and quicker in their response to taunts and threats of violence from homophobic bystanders. "People had a good time," Alan recounts. "It was a serious event conducted in a good spirit."

On Saturday, September 26, 1992, the *Los Angeles Times* announced that two local television stations were running thirty-second spots on gay bashing. The article described one spot as displaying a montage of average-looking people making disparaging remarks about gays and lesbians. "A young man walks out of an office," the article recounted, "and begins to make his way down a sunlit street. The sound of breaking glass—a beer bottle being smashed against a wall—is the first sign that something is wrong. A gang of thugs—shouting antigay epithets and wielding a baseball bat and the jagged bottle—chase him, surround him, and finally trap him against a chain-link fence." "Public Impact" had been launched!

*See page 160.
**See page 173.

Chapter Fifteen
Gays in the Military

Upon the exoneration of Admiral Frank B. Kelso II, "the officer who saw no evil," of responsibility for the flagrant display of macho arrogance at a September 1991 convention of naval aviators, *New York Times* columnist Frank Rich commented ironically (February 20, 1994): "Now that the Tailhook scandal has been swept under the Navy's rug—140 marauding Navy and Marine pilots, 83 assaulted women, 0 courtsmartial—connoisseurs of poolside sex can turn to happier pursuits." If after "a civil rights movement, the Vietnam War and a sexual revolution," he noted, women officers could obtain no redress for male-chauvinist humiliation at a public gathering, then what protection against homophobic assault could gays, unprotected by a military antidiscrimination policy, expect?

In the inquiry following the Tailhook incident, male officers scrupled to blame the female victims for the outrages. In the debate over gays in the military, during which the nation confronted as never before the issue whether lesbians and gays were to be accorded full citizenship, homophobes did not labor under such compunctions. "If you were not gay," they in effect insisted, "straight servicemen would not ridicule, bash, or murder you." Incidents like the savage fatal beating in Japan late in 1993 of a gay sailor by a homophobic shipmate demonstrated that the problem lay no more with gay service personnel than did the problem of male chauvinism lie with women in the military.

When earlier that year President Bill Clinton attempted to lift the ban on gays in the military, he encountered vehement opposition from the military brass, members of Congress, and homophobic elements in the civil society.

In the controversy the African-American Colin Powell (Chairman of the Joint Chiefs of Staff until September 1993), among other opponents, dismissed any comparison between their arguments and those of opponents of racial integration of the services forty-five years earlier. Powell drew no lesson from the fact that almost fifty years after Truman's order desegregating the armed forces a marine colonel could declare publicly and without fear of a reprimand that blacks lacked capacities for leadership. In a disingenuous, melodramatic maneuver, Sam Nunn, surrounded by a battery of television cameras, questioned servicemen and servicewomen on an aircraft carrier as to their reaction to the president's proposal. Lo and behold! the senator discovered that except for a few individuals brave enough to defy the hysteria whipped up by people like the chairman of the Senate's Armed Services Committee, the men and women expressed adamant opposition to serving alongside gays and lesbians.

In December 1993, the Pentagon published the procedures for implementing a compromise "don't ask, don't tell" policy. According to this document, military personnel who came out in their units would be discharged from the service. Mere presence at a gay bar invited no penalty, but, presumably, servicemen and servicewomen would run a risk if they put their arms around the shoulders of someone of the same sex; same-sex kissing, it appeared, posed a clear and present danger to the national security.

"To those struggling to counter hatred toward gay people," remarked the *New York Times* editorially on December 26, "homophobia is a phenomenon at once unique and terribly familiar. It shares with other prejudices like racism and anti-Semitism and many others the same roots: an intolerance toward otherness; a fear of lives, perspectives and practices that one doesn't understand and a visceral desire for a social hierarchy that puts some people on the rungs below you."

From the Revolution through Desert Storm, noted interviewee Rene Puliatti, an Annapolis graduate and former naval aviation officer, gays have served in the military. He considers discrimination against any segment of the population a violation of the principle that all men are created equal. Exclusion from sharing in the defense of the nation, Rene asserts, means second-class citizenship for the excluded group. "I doubt," declared Rene, "that any officers, including Colin Powell, have not had experience with gays in the military whether they choose to admit it or not, and the sooner the military comes to grips with reality, the better for our military preparedness and for our society as a whole." Studies conducted by the military, Rene points out, have shown that gays and lesbians discharged from the services because of their sexual orientation are generally above-average performers. ("We suffer a handicap," Rene explains, "and work harder to compensate.") "It is ironic," Rene declares, "that after spending so much money on training these superior people, the services should spend additional large sums to kick them out." Under the "don't ask, don't tell" policy, he says a double subterfuge is fostered: "The military pretend that gays do not exist, and gays pretend they are not who they are." Furthermore, under the new policy, according to Rene, "the military not only insist that we hide our identity, they also demand that we be celibate—a stipulation that is outrageous and humiliating." While on duty in the Philippines, on the other hand, Rene saw that the command accepted "guys' sleeping with three women in one night or married men's having affairs with different girls every night. That was macho! For me to have a long-term relationship with a man was outlawed."

In a January 1990 memorandum to his commanding officer, Rene described how the discriminatory policy of the military impelled him to resign from the Navy:

> I thought I could bury myself in my work and remain isolated from personal relationships in order to keep my secret safe and the frustration manageable. . . . Only recently have I taken the time to thoroughly examine my life and weigh the consequences of my actions or lack of actions, and I have come to the conclusion that the only real solution for me is to be honest to the Navy and to my fellow officers. My decision to come forward about my homosexuality and submit my resignation . . . is a very hard decision and will affect me the rest of my life. I have risked my career, my security, my reputation, and some of my closest friendships in order to reaffirm my personal values and beliefs.

Under the new "don't ask, don't tell" policy, according to Barbara de Lamere, a veteran of service prior to the Vietnam War, gays are under a greater burden than Rene or she herself confronted. "Before if you *said* you were gay," she noted, "they didn't do anything to you. You had to be caught in the act. With his campaign promise Clinton encouraged people to come out who otherwise would not have done so, and now they face persecution."

From what he has seen of military integration of women and people of color, Rene is not hopeful regarding the rapid development of an effective training program to overcome homophobia in the ranks, no matter what new antidiscrimination policies may be adopted. (Sensitivity training against racism and more recently against male chauvinism, Rene notes, is limited to a week of lectures during basic training, and nothing more is said thereafter.) Despite professions of dedication to equality for women, he points out, the services tolerate blatant male chauvinism. At the Naval Academy, Rene recalls, women were constantly on the defensive. They had to be "butch" to be accepted as "regular guys," but if they did not respond to the advances of the men, they were ridiculed as lesbians. To achieve recognition, they were forced to put in twice the effort of their male classmates.

"It is just hard for a woman to be in service no matter whether straight or gay," concurs Shirley Gerow, a bisexual who was married and the mother of three children at the time she joined the Army. "I found playing both roles equally difficult."

Regulations exist governing the sexual behavior of all military personnel. Rejecting the rationales for maintaining special restrictions on the gay minority, courts in a series of decisions from 1993 through 1996 have ruled that the military must judge personnel on performance and not on what they do in the privacy of their bedrooms. Indeed, the experiences of three interviewees—Ken, Shirley Gerow, and Rene Puliatti—provide evidence that clear direction and bold personal example by commanding officers can provide an environment in which gay service people enjoy acceptance.

All the gay military interviewees, with the exception of Ken, who lives in Washington, D.C., and does not belong to a gay veterans organization, are active members of the New York Gay, Lesbian, and Bisexual Veterans Association. The association dates back to an informal get-together at a Washington gay bar on the occasion of the "Welcoming Parade for Vietnam Veterans" in June of 1984. Upon failing to obtain authorization to participate in the Veteran's Day Parade both that year and the next, the vets brought suit against the American Legion, the organizer of the event. The Legion contended that the gays were agitators and not bona fide veterans, and the suit failed. Mayor Edward I. Koch threatened the Legion with a denial of a parade permit the next year, and the publicity resulting from the controversy evoked letters from throughout the country expressing interest in the organization of a national gay veterans organization. By 1994 the New York Gay, Lesbian, and Bisexual Veterans Association had achieved full recognition in the city as a member of the New York City Veterans Council, and other chapters had been established in many cities throughout the nation.

The following accounts provide insight into the status of lesbians and gays in the military and evidence of the feasibility of their full integration within the armed forces. Often living in fear and forced to conceal their sexual identity, all the interviewees performed their military duties effectively and even with distinction. Before entering the services, two had heterosexual experiences. Shirley Gerow had married before joining the armed forces. Ken became aware of his sexual orientation only during his military service and, like Eddie and Shirley, maintained a clandestine homosexual relationship in service. Like police officer Peter Guardino (Chapter 11), Ken married after leaving the service and, like Pete, remained married until his homosexual drive reasserted itself irresistibly.

EDDIE (INTERVIEWED AS BARBARA, TWELVE YEARS AFTER A SEX CHANGE)

In 1959, Eddie, nineteen years old and confronting an imminent draft, volunteered for the air force. A friend of his sister's, rejected because of a glass eye, was ostracized by his friends; and Eddie realized, "It would have been a disgrace for my parents if I, their only son, didn't serve in the military." On the other hand, having no confidence in his ability to resist his urge to cross-dress while in the service, he confessed to a priest that he had often put on his mother's and sister's clothes and that he masturbated. ("I had never confessed my cross-dressing before because I did not think it was a sin," Barbara remarks. "It wasn't anything like stealing or lying or the other evils which teachers in the parochial school warned us against.") The priest advised Eddie to see a psychiatrist and expressed doubt about Eddie's decision to delay until he could consult an air force therapist. (In fact, Eddie did not seek help while in the service.)

Over the years Eddie had developed an ability to "size up" people. If in conversations he received a negative response to a remark about an effeminate man, he knew he could expect no sympathy for his own idiosyncratic behavior. On one occasion, Barbara recalled, during basic training, "Four of us were sitting at a table. One guy, Larry, got up to get something to drink. The jerk across the table from me said, "That boy's a fag!' I immediately took a liking to Larry and decided I would have nothing to do with the other guy." In fact, Eddie and Larry, both assigned to training as medics, arranged to room together along with a congenial black recruit named Danny.

During basic training, in the stalls of the toilets Eddie masturbated, calling up his customary fantasy of finding himself in a beauty salon with a group of undifferentiated women. But it was about his cross-dressing, an obsession that overwhelmed him unexpectedly like an epileptic fit, that most concerned him. If caught, he faced dishonorable discharge, which could ruin him for life. On occasions when he was summoned to the sergeant's office, Eddie trembled with fear that someone might have caught him applying makeup. Nevertheless, he did take risks. One day, for example, seeing an attractive dress in a Dayton, Ohio, shop window, he entered the store and asked about it. To his delight, the sales clerk, who had her back to him, addressed him as "Miss." Eddie bought the dress. In the men's room of the Dayton library he tried it on. Back at the barracks, he put the dress in Larry's locker. "I had learned," Barbara explains, "that you can get away with almost anything if you make a joke of it. This was my was of testing Larry."

That afternoon, Eddie found Larry laughing hilariously and cursing him in good humor. Some days later, finding Larry lying naked, Eddie draped the dress over him. Larry became aroused. He in turn draped it over Eddie. They were both aroused. Eddie had necked with girls, but Larry's was the first naked body he had ever touched. Larry taught him how to kiss, and Eddie liked kissing Larry. Though more sophisticated about sex than Eddie, Larry did not think of himself as gay. He called their activity "a distraction." "You're distracting me from reading," he would say. Eddie loved what they did together, and he loved Larry. "I didn't give a name to what we were doing," Barbara recalls, "nor did I think we were doing anything wrong." Nor, apparently, did their roommate Danny. He made oblique, good-natured remarks that revealed that he was aware of Eddie's cross-dressing and of his having sex with Larry, but he kept their secret.

After completing training, Eddie was assigned to an air force base in Libya, and Larry to one at Izmir in Turkey. On one occasion, during a five-hour lay over in Libya on Larry's way to Wiesbaden to undergo surgery, he and Eddie filled the time in kissing and hugging. "It was the love of my life," Barbara remarks.

Once in Libya Eddie's new roommate caught him drunk and with lipstick on his face and elsewhere on his body. "You've got the stick on again," he said. Clearly, he had caught Eddie before. Like Danny at the Dayton camp, he did not report what he had seen.

Recalling the "wonderful years" of their relationship, Barbara remarks, "We were simply enjoying each other. What harm were we doing? How the hell was that innocent love play incompatible with the military? Today I can say the military's attitude is bullshit. Thirty years ago I couldn't say that."

(Discharged at the same time, Eddie and Larry moved together into an apartment on the Lower East Side of Manhattan. They remained together from 1963 until 1967, when Larry married.)*

After undergoing a sex change in 1982, Barbara sought to find a community with gays and lesbians and became active in gay organizations. In 1990, after the Gay Veterans Association was excluded from the Veterans Day Parade, Barbara joined the association. "We did our bit in the services," she insisted. "They can't stop us from marching." Since the association attracted few women members, the officers keep saying to her, "As a woman you must . . . !" But Barbara protests, "I can't represent lesbian veterans. I wasn't a lesbian in the military." Nevertheless, she became a member of the board and editor of the association's newsletter.

In 1993 Barbara marched in the unofficial St. Patrick's Day parade organized by ILGO, the Irish and Lesbian Gay Organization, and was one of those arrested on that occasion. She intended to march with them again in 1994.

KEN, A VIETNAM VET

In 1965, anticipating a draft notice, Ken, a twenty-three-year-old college graduate who grew up in a prosperous WASP Washington suburb, volunteered for a three-year stint in the Army. "I thought the war in Vietnam was a noble cause," he recalls, "the good guys versus the bad guys, and enlistment seemed to me to be the thing to do." During basic training at Fort Gordon in Georgia, he experienced cultural shock, finding himself for the first time in his life with a group of school dropouts. Out of a company of 120 men, only four had completed high school and only one, Ken himself, had graduated from college. At Fort Bliss in Texas, he and Tommy, a nineteen-year-old from Tennessee with "beautiful blue eyes" whom Ken had met earlier at Fort

*The remainder of this segment of Barbara's life is recounted in Chapter 2.

Gordon, frequently drove over to Juarez "to get laid." Once when Tommy, drunk, dozed off in the car, Ken fondled him. Thereafter he repeated the experience at every opportunity until one time Tommy woke up and exclaimed, "Enough of that, I'm not that way." Ken accepted the rebuff.

Recruits were frequently shown a film warning them of possible "communist" blackmail. After each showing, a sergeant announced that any soldier who suspected he might somehow be a security risk should report his problem to the commanding officer. Conscientious and naive, Ken confessed to his captain his fear that he might be homosexual. Since at the time no "don't tell" policy was in force, the captain took the news calmly. He advised Ken to consult the camp psychiatrist. Ken recalls, however, that his sergeant, present during the conversation, did not conceal his disgust at Ken's "confession." "I was not surprised at his reaction," Ken relates. "I thought I deserved his scorn. I did not like myself as a 'queer.' "

A "normal" teenager, "one of the guys," Ken participated in high school drinking sprees. Weekends until 2 A.M. he cruised with friends around their suburban town. Although during his last years in high school and again in college he often had sex with young women, he never felt satisfied with the experience. Indeed, he had long had inklings of being different. When, abruptly, after vacation before eighth grade, his friends began boasting about their exploits with girls, Ken was shocked. "I didn't understand," he recalls, "what had happened to them over the summer. I had friends who were girls, but I had no sexual interest in them." In elementary school and even more in high school Ken had crushes on boys, particularly on boys like Garry, who was "cool," had a suave way with girls, owned a convertible, and always carried a condom in his wallet. Having no reference point or gay models, Ken was troubled by his feelings. "I thought it was wrong; I felt guilty." The general conception of "queers" among his friends was of effeminate cross-dressers. Ken joined in making fun of a group of "sissies" who regularly ate together in the high school lunchroom. One Friday night, invited by a buddy to have some fun with "queers," Ken drove to Lafayette Park, a gay cruising area across from the White House. His friend had Ken sit on a park bench. "They'll come up to you," his friend insisted, "and invite you into a toilet. I'll be right behind you, and we'll steal a guy's wallet." The adventure proceeded "successfully." "I was disgusted with myself," Ken declares. "I knew it was wrong to make fun of people and to hurt people."

In his freshman year in college, Ken developed a serious crush on a classmate. Neither of them had a girlfriend, and Friday nights they went out drinking together. When they changed in the car before playing intramural softball, Ken watched with fascination as his friend undressed. He became aroused, too, when they took showers in the gym. Next year his friend found a girlfriend. "It broke my heart," Ken recalls.

Ken detailed his sexual anxieties at weekly sessions with the Army psychiatrist. On one occasion he announced that he was going to inform his parents of his "problem." What reaction, the psychiatrist colonel inquired, did Ken expect from them? "They will be shocked," Ken admitted. Then what was to be gained in telling them? the colonel asked. Ken reminded the colonel that two men caught "fooling around" in the showers had just been summarily discharged. Had Ken done anything that made him fear a similar punishment? the colonel asked. No, Ken admitted. "Then what are you afraid of?" said the colonel. Ken wrote nothing to his parents.

At the colonel's urging, Ken participated in group therapy. At one session, Ken decided to speak out about his sexual problem. After a soldier related how when he encountered a "queer" he was roused to such fury that he wanted to beat him up, Ken kept silent. But Ken felt pressured to confess to someone among his buddies, and he "came out" to Rick, a "surfer" from California, more broadminded and worldly than most of the other men. "That's no big deal," Rick responded. "Why don't you just go with the flow? As long as you don't come on to me, it doesn't make any difference." Rick reported, however, that Tommy was gossiping about Ken in the unit. Ken noticed no change in attitude toward him, nor did he suffer from snide remarks. "When I think back on my experience," Ken comments, "I can't understand all this hullabaloo today about people coming out in the service."

Ending his relationship with Tommy, Ken began to drive over to Juarez with others in his unit. No longer compelled to prove that he was a "regular guy," he stopped visiting the brothels. With his new companions, he never talked about his sexuality.

When the colonel concluded that Ken had homosexual tendencies but was not a homosexual, Ken felt totally reassured. His propensity, he decided, represented no more than a dirty obsession like smoking. With will power, he was convinced, he would overcome his "problem." "I'll just have to go cold turkey," he assured himself, "and in six months this will all be behind me."

During a tour of duty in Vietnam and in Guam, still taking seriously the "threat" of enemy blackmail and determined to do nothing that might jeopardize his military career, Ken remained celibate. Reassigned to a missile-and-radar unit in Fuerth, a German town a few miles from Nuremberg, he advanced rapidly to staff sergeant and even turned down an offer to enter officers' training school. He was instructed to orient a new arrival to the unit's duties. Nicknamed the "Deek," a happy-go-lucky soldier with a huge grin, the newcomer and Ken immediately took to each other. Like Ken, Deek had been a history major in college and like Ken was interested in making a career in special education. The two men shared a room in the barracks and became inseparable. "I don't know how it started," Ken relates. "The attraction was mutual. You look at each other and you know."

Though by this time Ken realized that the danger of enemy blackmail was exaggerated, he and Deek maintained discretion on the base. Only when they took trips did they behave as lovers. "I had never had a complete experience before," Ken recounts. "Deek had had only a transient experience in high school. We came out together. It was so wonderful that all guilt disappeared."

Since Deek's discharge was slated for three months after Ken's, they decided that Ken should remain in Europe so that they might travel together before returning to the States. They would go to Washington and then to Rhode Island, Deek's home, to tell their parents that they were going to join the national teacher corps and teach in a ghetto and that they were going to live together. They were prepared to face their parents' shock.

That was not to be.

Invited to participate in an Army quiz contest, Ken asked Deek to take over his evening duty assignment. At the conclusion of the contest, one of the men in the unit came up to Ken and asked gravely, "Have you heard?" "I knew instantly something had happened to Deek," Ken recalls. "I grabbed him and shouted, 'What?' " "Deek's been injured," he answered, "and they've flown him to the hospital in Nuremberg."

"I rushed to the gate of our compound," Ken relates. "Inexplicably the taxi station was empty. Panic-stricken I ran all the way, I don't know how many miles, to the Nuremberg military hospital. I raced into the emergency room. Everyone was there—my captain, my sergeant. . . . I didn't have to ask. Deek was dead.

"The whole world ended for me at that moment. The captain put his arm around me and said he was sorry. I walked back to the barracks, bawling, cursing Deek, mad as hell. 'Damn him!' I cried to myself. It was pounded into us that in the event of a radar breakdown we were to turn on the safety switch. Deek found a unit out of order. Without turning on the safety switch, Deek, ever carefree and oblivious of procedures, opened the back to make an adjustment. The man on duty at the central control room a half mile away saw the signal that the repair had been made and turned on the unit. The radar crushed Deek with the power of a Mack truck. 'How dare you ruin our life,' I kept shouting, 'and over something as stupid as this.'

"The next morning, Deek wasn't there, and he wasn't there all day, nor the next day."

Ken obtained leave to accompany Deek's remains home. In Rhode Island he met Deek's family. He said nothing about his relationship with their son. "They were a wonderful family," he recalls. "They thanked me for being Deek's friend."

Returning to the base, Ken discovered that the general grief for Deek was over. "I felt like a hollow man," he recounts, "shell-shocked, but I couldn't show it or people would have figured out that something had been going on between us, and I didn't want that."

In January 1968, his tour of duty completed, Ken returned home and found a teaching position. A year and a half later, at twenty-seven, he married Jane, on June 28, 1969. (Twenty years later he realized that that was the day of the Stonewall riot that started the mass gay liberation movement!) Neighbors, Ken and Jane had known each other since childhood. Ken's two brothers were already married. Ken's homosexual experiences had not been reassuring. With Tommy he had suffered ridicule, and he and Deek had had to engage in subterfuge. "Who wants to spend his life in hiding?" Ken asked himself. With his marriage he believed he was putting the tragic experience with Deek behind him. "That's it, no more," he said to himself. "Now I am back in civilian life, and I want to be a regular person. Once again," Ken remarks, "I went along with the crowd, being one of the guys."

Ken and Jane had a daughter and remained married for seventeen years. During thirteen of those years he lived a life of satisfaction and never glanced at a man. At his teaching position, however, Ken became frustrated with the bureaucracy. In general, he had a sense of falling into a routinized existence. Jane, on the other hand, was content to have her life revolve about her garden and her ailing mother. More and more it became clear that they were staying together only for the sake of their daughter.

Ken left his teaching position, went back to school for a master's degree, and found a new job as an educational consultant. His work required traveling about the country, and he spent many lonely nights in hotels. One evening in San Diego, Ken discovered he had forgotten to bring anything to read. Going out to buy some magazines, he came upon an adult bookstore, where, naively, he thought he would be able to buy the *Atlantic Monthly* and the *New Republic.* Astonished at what he found in the store, in panic, he left without buying anything. Returning the next night, however, he bought two or three gay magazines. The third night he discovered projectors for porno films in the rear.

Thereafter in his travels, Ken regularly sought out adult bookstores. On the way to the airport, he threw away whatever magazines he had bought. On one occasion, carelessly, he returned home with some in his briefcase. His daughter Susan, then twelve years old, had been assigned a school project on careers. Not understanding precisely what Ken did at work, she looked in his briefcase and found the magazines.

Returning home late and exhausted, Ken found Jane waiting up for him. "You're gay," she announced. "What the hell are you talking about?" Ken demanded. She told him what Susan had discovered. Ken agreed to go with Jane to a marriage counselor. The counselor asked whether they were happy with their lives. "I had to say no," Ken relates. "Jane admitted she was not happy, either." The marriage counselor asked whether they could live together as friends as many couples do. "He's out at night," declared Jane, "and I don't know where he goes." Ken often worked late, going to bed after Susan and Jane. After finding a copy of the gay *Washington Blade* newspaper on the subway, however, and learning about gay organizations, bookstores, and bars, Ken began to slip out nights to go to gay bars. Sipping a diet soda, he hid in a corner, convinced that at forty-four he was old and unattractive. Gay life, he thought, was for people in their twenties like Deek and himself many years earlier.

Jane imagined that he was engaging in promiscuous sex and was worried about AIDS and about violence on the streets. In November 1985, she delivered an ultimatum. "You have to live the kind of life you want," she announced. "The question is when we should separate." Ken could not argue with her. They decided to wait until after Christmas. Then they postponed the date until summer. In June, Ken says, "We ran out of excuses."

The first weekend of August 1986, Ken moved into his own apartment. "I sat in my room," he recounts, "wondering what I had done with my life. I would have returned immediately if she invited me back. On several occasions, one of us would say that I should return. On each occasion the other said no. It couldn't be.

"In many ways," Ken declares, "my life began in 1986. It was only after I left home that I began to think seriously about who I was. At first I made gay life the center of my existence. I had one unpleasant experience after another, and then eventually as I became more sophisticated about gay life I had some encounters that were satisfying.

"I'm totally 'out,' Ken declares, "except in some business situations. My career is now my big push. I won't let anything interfere with it. My current straight friends are good friends. Generally, they don't want to talk about my sexual life. Their attitude is: 'In spite of being gay, you're a wonderful guy.' "

Ken is unhappy that his relations with Jane and Susan are strained. Susan did not invite him to her high school graduation. He is disappointed that she refused to go on to college and that she goes out with young men whom Ken does not respect. He remains silent when his brothers and their wives boast about their children.

"Nevertheless, I'm more pleased with myself now that my orientation in life is clear," Ken declares. "I lived with a Japanese fellow for a year, but he's back in Japan. I have not found another Deek."

SHIRLEY GEROW, A POST-VIETNAM VETERAN

Shirley Gerow had become enured to discrimination against women long before she confronted sexism in the military. Until she was ten, when her mother ran off from Shirley's father with her three children, Shirley and her two older sisters suffered from unpredictable harassment whenever their alcoholic father drank too much and watched in terror as he physically abused their mother. Marrying at twenty in 1965, Shirley discovered that the man she had admired as a kind and gentle fiance proved to be selfish and psychologically abusive as a husband, exhibiting the male-supremacist contempt for women he had learned in an immigrant Italian family with traditional values. "I quickly discovered," Shirley declares, "that Joe wanted me at home, barefoot and pregnant, leaving all decisions to him." As he refused to turn over his paycheck—"I earned this money, it's mine," he insisted—Shirley was compelled to find part-time work in order to feed and clothe their three children and to meet the mortgage payments.

When after seven years of marriage, Shirley asked her mother's advice about obtaining a separation, her mother expressed astonishment. In her eyes, Shirley enjoyed a perfect marriage. Joe went to work every day, came home every evening, did not run around with other women, and did not abuse Shirley physically. He did not even smoke. She refused to believe that Joe did not contribute to the children's support. In any event she urged Shirley to make no decision until her youngest child was old enough to start school.

In 1976 Shirley gave Joe an ultimatum: one or the other of them was to move out. Although astonished at her contention that their marriage had failed, he packed his things and moved in with Shirley's mother. "My mother and sisters," Shirley explains, "think he walks on water." Shirley's neighbors, however, exclaimed, "My God, Shirley, it's time you woke up. That man's been abusing you for years." Shirley agrees. "I should have put my foot down," she admits, "but I had my own victim syndrome, and my twenties were years of growing up."

With Joe continuing to refuse to contribute to the support of the children, Shirley was compelled to find secure part-time employment. Uncles she admired had served in the military, and while still in high school Shirley had made inquiries at a recruiting station. Now once again she thought of a career in the Army. "Even before I signed up," she recalls, "I encountered military sex discrimination." As a married woman and a mother, she was required to obtain her husband's permission for her enlistment. "If he were enlisting, would he have to obtain my permission?" she asked the recruiting sergeant.

Joe agreed to sign the document upon the advice of his lawyer, who noted that in a fight for custody of the children Joe would be able to cite her enlistment as evidence that she was an unfit mother. A year after her separation from her husband, Shirley joined the Army reserves. Her children were then five, seven and ten years old.

During basic training at Fort McCullough in Georgia, Shirley turned to her mother and neighbors to care for her children. As an experienced school bus driver Shirley was eligible under a Civilian Acquired Skills program for immediate assignment to a military transport unit. During her first year, Shirley was called to duty for only two weeks. As the years went by and she was advanced in grade, she spent ever-longer periods away from home. The first year Joe failed even to visit his children. "He loved them," Shirley declares, "but he was confused. Like me, he had to grow up." The next year Shirley reminded him that in signing the document granting her permission to enlist he had made a commitment to assume parental responsibilities when she was on duty. Accordingly, Joe moved back to the house during her absences.

Separation from her children was painful. "I never talked about them," Shirley relates. "That made me too homesick. I felt guilty at leaving them." At home, however, things went well. The eldest child assumed responsibilities beyond her age. Joe and the children developed a new and close relationship.

"It turned out to be a learning and growing-up experience for him," Shirley asserts, "and I found that the kids survived, and survived well."

Shirley was assigned to the Seventy-eighth Division at Edison, New Jersey, a transport unit. Reporting for duty at a busy motor pool, she was confronted with an abrupt silence. One of the men pointed to the first sergeant's office. Shirley entered and waited to be noticed. "Ah, you, the first female!" exclaimed the sergeant. He and the other 150 men in the company did not hide their displeasure at the new policy of integrating women in all army units. The sergeant assigned Shirley to secretarial busy work.

After four days of sorting and filing papers, Shirley rebelled. "I'm not here to do your paperwork," she announced. "I'm here to drive trucks." The sergeant assigned her to a maintenance crew. The men made snide remarks. "What are you doing here, bitch?" they demanded. "Why aren't you home with your husband and your kids?" "I was called all the names," Shirley recounts, "cunt, whore, bitch and sweetheart, honey, and baby, and it was a pinch here and a squeeze there." When Shirley turned down their requests for dates, they muttered, "Probably a lesbian." The harassment abated after Shirley struck back. When a man grabbed at her while the company was out marching, Shirley dropped out of formation and shouted, "If you ever touch me again, any one of you guys, I'll kick your balls up into your throat, and you'll wear them as earrings." Shirley caught up to her place in line. "They were testing," she declares. "They were raised with a macho image that they had to live up to. They were all right if you got them over their crap."

A few weeks before the unit was to depart for summer camp, Shirley approached the motor sergeant and asked him to set a date for her driver's test. He procrastinated. When Shirley persisted, he asked for a volunteer to go out with her. None of the men volunteered, and the sergeant was compelled to accompany her himself. "When we got back," Shirley recounts, "he got out of the truck and announced to all the guys that I drove better than three-quarters of them. That was the first verbal support I heard."

During her third year Shirley was joined in the unit by a woman much younger than she. Not unsophisticated about the gay world, Shirley recognized immediately that Kathie was a lesbian. In fact, Shirley had entered a lesbian relationship as a freshman in high school, and for three years she and Carol, a fellow trumpet player in the school band, were inseparable. Though they frequently spent nights together in each other's homes, they also dated boys, Carol as a cover for her lesbianism, and Shirley because she found pleasure in also having sex with boys. "I enjoyed both relationships," Shirley recounts. "I can't say that one offered me more pleasure than the other."

Shirley's mother condemned her relationship with Carol as "unnatural," but an older family friend in whom Shirley confided offered reassurance. Because she was straight, this woman declared, she was unable to have sex with other women, but she loved "queers," she found them "so interesting."

On the other hand, she could not understand bisexuals, who didn't know who they were and just could not make up their minds. At this remark Shirley abruptly realized who and what she was: She was a bisexual.

During her senior year in high school, with Carol away at college, Shirley accompanied a lesbian classmate to the Duchess, a lesbian bar in Greenwich Village. Although ill at ease that first night, she returned several times on her own. When, shortly thereafter, Joe asked her to marry him, Shirley told him that she was bisexual and returned his engagement ring. A few weeks later Joe called and said he wanted to share his life with her. They married, and for the next ten years Shirley broke off all contact with lesbians. "I made a commitment to Joe," she explains. "I was in love with him. I decided that I would always maintain monogamous relationships, regardless of gender." After she and Joe separated and she joined the army reserves, Shirley knew, she declares, that her next involvement would be with a woman.

By the time Shirley entered a lesbian relationship with Kathie, she had advanced to the grade of sergeant and felt secure in her unit. "For a long time I pulled shitty duties," she relates. "I proved myself." She and Kathie behaved with professional discretion. One day, however, she and Kathie, who was hotheaded, had an argument. Noticing that their relations were strained and that Shirley failed to call Kathie to account for falling down on the job, several sergeants invited Shirley to a meeting and asked her why she was displaying indulgence toward Kathie's poor performance. "Two of the sergeants in particular felt threatened by me and had long been out to get me," Shirley recounts. "At the meeting they made remarks about my personal life. 'Either you're a lesbian,' they sneered, 'or you're fuckin' the captain.' " Shirley responded that what she did on her own time was her business. She warned them that they were breaking regulations in calling a meeting without the knowledge of their superior officer.

The next day the captain approached Shirley. He had heard, he said, about an unofficial meeting in which she was involved. "Since I was in charge of a company," Shirley relates, "I was constantly in contact with the captain. We had a good personal relationship with never a suggestion of male chauvinism on his part. One of the best commanders you could have," Shirley asserts. Undecided what action she was prepared to take against the other sergeants, Shirley merely confirmed that she had been called to a meeting. That evening as she was leaving the base to go for dinner, the captain came by in his car and invited her to join him at a restaurant. He questioned her about the meeting. "They don't like what I'm doing in my personal life," Shirley declared. "I can just imagine what I'll hear tomorrow about having dinner with you." The captain asked her to decide whether she wanted to press charges for sexual harassment against the two most hostile sergeants, and the next day Shirley informed him that she had decided to let the incident pass. The men, she reported, had been quiet that morning.

Closing the door, the captain asked Shirley whether she was having an affair with Kathie. "We're friends," he assured her. "Whatever you say won't go any further than this office."

"Yes," replied Shirley, "I'm a lesbian, she's a lesbian, and we're having an affair."

"You're a good soldier," responded the captain. "You perform your duties well, and Kathie is good at her work. That's all that concerns me."

When Shirley admitted that the two hostile sergeants had accused her of being a lesbian and of having sex with the captain as well, the captain declared, "This is my company. I won't stand for sexual harassment. The issue of lesbianism won't come up if you bring charges. I'll back you all the way."

Shirley did eventually bring charges against the two sergeants. One kept up his derogatory remarks and grew ever more belligerent. When he pushed a nineteen-year-old woman who had just joined the unit into a dark corner, she fled into Shirley's office and burst into tears. Shirley urged the young woman to pursue the matter and promised to support her. She assured her of the captain's backing.

During the days preceding the sergeant's appearance before a military court, officers and NCOs appealed to Shirley to withdraw the charges. "You'd protect this man?" she retorted. "He's totally out of line, and it's time he grew up." The sergeant received a dishonorable discharge six months before he was due for a discharge after thirty years of service.

Though forewarned, the other sergeant continued his obnoxious behavior. Speaking in a loud voice so that she would be certain to hear, he reviled Shirley as a "whore, lesbian, and cunt." Since he served as one of her platoon sergeants, Shirley summoned him into her office. "I'm a soldier," she announced, "here to do a job. I'm not going to put up with this shit. Get down to business."

When this warning proved of no avail, Shirley informed the captain that she wanted to press charges. Would you be satisfied, he asked, if they merely sent him away to some dead-end job. "I had compassion this time," Shirley recounts. "What I want is to get him out of my company," she replied.

For her remaining six years in the service, Shirley experienced no sexual harassment. "I established myself," she says. "Above all, I had the captain on my side."

During Shirley's eleven years as a reservist, her husband did not contribute at all to the children's support. She did not initiate divorce proceedings, fearing that he would demand custody of the children. In addition, she discovered that she could claim an additional $35 a month from the Army with him as her spouse. At last in 1991, fourteen years after their separation and three years after she left the Army, Shirley obtained a divorce. But her relationship with Joe did not end. When their son, an Army ranger, was sent off on the Panama police action, Joe realized he might become a casualty. Suddenly, Shirley declares, he became aware of what it meant to be a father. He even, belatedly and grudgingly, began to accept his financial responsibilities. "He grew up," says Shirley, "and we remain friends." Joe lives upstairs in their old home; she lives downstairs. A Catholic, he does not believe in sex except for reproduction. He has no difficulty in accepting Shirley's lesbian lover. "The Joe of then and now are two different people," remarks Shirley. "Now he behaves like a brother. I never had a brother."

Shirley looks back on her Army experience as an important, growing-up segment of her life, and for several years she served on the board of the New York Gay, Lesbian, and Bisexual Veterans Association.

RENE PULIATTI

After five years as a naval officer, Rene Puliatti came out to his superiors and submitted his resignation, unable to endure any longer the life of frustration and subterfuge he was compelled to lead as a gay man.

Rene was born in Syracuse, New York, in 1963, the youngest of four sons of an Italian immigrant father, a barber who subsequently opened an Italian restaurant, and an American-born mother, daughter of the editor of the local newspaper and head of the advertising department of a local department store. When Rene was five years old, his mother died suddenly of cancer. One day three years later, without any forewarning, Rene's father introduced a stranger to his children, declaring, "This is your new mother." She brought with her four children of her own whose ages matched those of her new husband. Tension developed between the two sets of children and between Rene and his brothers and their stepmother. "I learned not to make waves," recounts Rene, "in order not to make things more difficult for my father and to avoid rejection and ridicule."

When Rene was nine, he and his brothers were sent off to the school in Hershey, Pennsylvania, established by the Hershey chocolate family for boys missing one or more parents. Rene was glad to leave home and easily adapted to living in a house with thirteen other boys and a pair of houseparents. During the years from fifth grade through high school, Rene met Ari, the brother closest to him in age, every day at school, but did not see his older brothers more than once a month. "I learned to be independent," Rene declares.

Leading his class academically and active in student government and in extracurricular activities, Rene enjoyed school. He sang in the glee club and ran on the track team ("I wasn't very good," he admits). As an upperclassman, he served as a trainer for the school gymnastics team. He was troubled, however, by the requirement to attend a weekly religious assembly with a definite Christian tone. "I very early learned to question everything that I didn't understand or thought was wrong and unfair." In the compulsory religious education class, he protested the discrimination against non-Christians. When the teacher responded, "We have both Old Testament and New Testament readings," Rene asked whether the Jewish students should not be excused after the Old Testament readings were concluded. "What if you don't believe at all?" he added. He displayed a similar sensitivity to racial prejudice. When he was a high school senior, a black student (blacks represented about one-third of the school enrollment), said that he respected Rene because he could see that Rene cared about people. "I do care," Rene insists, "and my caring engenders trust in people."

On the other hand, from the age of six, Rene had intimations of being different. Unlike his brothers but like many other gay boys, Rene did not enjoy competitive sports, preferring solitary pursuits. During these early years, Rene recounts, he always felt incomplete, somehow less than a man. While his brother Ari began to chase after girls at an early age, Rene, self-conscious and shy, did not enjoy the church dances attended by Hershey boys. "I tried to compensate," he declares, "by excelling where I could. If anyone found out that I was gay, they would say, 'He's gay, but he's above average.' "

Rene was aware of homosexual activity among his schoolmates through gossip and jokes. Boys who were weak, small, and effeminate were derided as sissies or fags. Boys made jokes about "queers." Brought up as a Catholic, Rene felt that his attraction to boys and to some of his teachers was sinful. After Rene returned from vacation while in seventh grade, his father called to announce that a woman's brassiere had been found in his closet at home. (Rene suspects that one of his stepbrothers had taken the brassiere from a stepsister and hidden it there.) "If I thought you were gay," his father exclaimed, "I'd pull you out of that school right now." The next year, wrestling with his roommate, "an arrogant son of a bitch," led to a sexual experience. The roommate boasted falsely that he had "fucked" Rene. Fortunately for Rene, the boy was generally disliked, and the other boys in the house did not take seriously anything he said. "It was a scary incident," Rene recalls.

Once, as a sophomore in high school, drinking with an older boy (a serious offense in the school) while watching a raging storm, Rene touched the boy's leg. When he did not resist, Rene moved his hand up his thigh. They kissed and went to bed. They repeated this experience several times until the other boy called an end to it. Rene feared that the boy might gossip about what they had been doing. "My reputation would have been ruined," Rene remarks.

As a senior and president of the glee club, Rene came out to Greg, a close friend and the glee club vice president. "You have to risk to gain anything," Rene reasoned. "If I do not say anything, and he is attracted to me, we both will miss out." He handed Greg a note in which he declared his attraction. Greg read the note, shook his head, and said nothing. When soon thereafter Greg quit the glee club, Rene thought he did so because the club was preparing a show in which there were routines in which Greg would have had to touch him. The remainder of the school year they rarely talked. Years later at a class reunion, however, Greg declared that he had appeared troubled and aloof because he was having problems with his girlfriend. Greg could have saved him much anguish, Rene replied, if he had given that explanation five years earlier.

Rene was offered a scholarship to Cornell University, but because the brother of Ari's girlfriend attended the Naval Academy at Annapolis, Rene investigated the military academies, where he would obtain a first-class education at no expense and be able to join good glee clubs. Besides, he wanted to serve his country, and for him that meant joining the armed forces. When he reported his plans to his brothers and father, "Their jaws dropped." Rene chose the naval academy because unlike the two other academies, it was located within a town and was not far from Baltimore and Washington. Rene certainly had no thought of engaging in urban gay social life. He knew nothing of gay bars, gay literature, or gay life generally. ("To this day," Rene declares, "I have a lot of catching up to do.") At his graduation from high school, Rene was beginning to accept that he was gay, though maintaining a hope that his attraction to boys represented merely a phase that he would overcome.

During Rene's first year at Annapolis, an effeminate man in Rene's company (about thirty people) was ostracized and jeered at as a "fag." "I was no help to him," Rene admits. "I was intent on guarding myself." The man dropped out.

Rene was not aware of any homosexual activity at the academy. He did hear a rumor that an upperclassman who attempted suicide was probably gay. It was clear to him that exposure in the hypermacho atmosphere could result in danger. "It can get you kicked out, beaten up, even killed." In fact, in sports or in leadership training, instructors shouted, "You fag, you sissy, you girl!"

Rene's participation in the glee club made him suspect to some in his company. But others retorted to the doubters, "He goes off campus on trips every weekend and can meet babes everywhere, while you're stuck here drilling." Rene protected himself by talking about his girlfriend, a student at a nearby college. She made no sexual demands on him, and "gentleman" that he was, he made no advances. When Rene reported that he had gone horseback riding with her, men in his company would exclaim, "Oh, so that's what it's called."

Failing to receive encouragement from men for whom he felt an attraction, Rene did not come out to them. "It would have meant," he says, "putting my career and life on the line." On the other hand, during a vacation with some members of his company at Daytona Beach, Florida, he had an embarrassing experience. Sitting around a jacuzzi, Rene's friends noticed that a woman was clearly attracted to him. "Hey, Rene," his friends said, "Here's your chance. She has the hots for you." "Fine," Rene replied, "but I don't have the hots for her." Inviting the woman and her friends back to the apartment, Rene's friends pushed him into a bedroom with her. "Have fun!" they exclaimed as they shut the door. "I made an effort," Rene recalls. "She realized that it wasn't working and got up and left. I felt angry at being used. I determined then that I would never make up stories, pretend to relationships that did not exist, never play games."

During his four years at the academy, Rene remained celibate. He did come out to Joel, the brother to whom he felt closest, and Joel with his "big mouth" told his other brothers; but at Annapolis Rene had no one to talk to or confide in. "If I had not had outlets in music and the glee club," Rene asserts, "I would have gone crazy."

After a six-month assignment as a liaison officer in Munich, Germany, following upon his graduation in 1985, Rene was sent from one training center to another. He risked several tentative attempts at coming out to people. At Pensacola while his roommate was away on vacation, he hung a male poster on his closet door. When his roommate returned, he made no comment. Once Rene found himself alone in the communal showers with an officer named Sandy. Sandy exclaimed, "Hey, you have a really nice tan!" Rene took note of the remark. He wrote Sandy a note saying he would like to meet for dinner. "I didn't use the word sex," Rene declares, "but I think he understood what I wanted." When Sandy left the base some weeks later, Rene wrote to him again. This note, he realized, was "a giveaway." Sandy gossiped. Friends warned Rene, "Watch your back." Nevertheless, at a Virginia training center, Rene came out to an officer who invited him to stay in his apartment. He reported that Sandy had warned him about Rene. Fortunately, nothing came of Rene's indiscretion.

In January, 1988, Rene was posted to a top-secret intelligence unit headquartered on Guam. Aware that the military considered gays to be security risks, he remained "squeaky clean." In despair at his inability to act on his emotions, he withdrew into the bachelor officers quarters, living alone, a recluse. "Here I am in my twenties," he murmured to himself, "my life is going by and I'm wasting my opportunities." Abruptly, he opted to room with a newly arrived officer with whom he hit it off well. For a whole year he wrestled with an impulse to come out to Steven. When news of the Joe Steffan case reached the squadron (upon announcing that he was gay, Steffan was dismissed from the Naval Academy only weeks before graduation), Steven joined others in jeering, "We don't need fags in the navy. Why the hell did he even join?"

In December of 1989, a year and a half after his arrival on Guam, Rene jotted down in his journal an evaluation of his situation—in relation to his career, his reputation, his friendships and his security level. "Can I live in the closet the two and a half years I am to remain in the Navy," he asked himself, "and hope then to go quietly into civilian life to pick up my life?"

Rereading his journal a month later, Rene came to a decision: He could not continue the way he was living. He needed to be honest with the men and women with whom he spent fifteen or more hours of every day. Above all, he needed to be honest with himself. On January 21, 1990, he drafted the following letter addressed to his commanding officer and his executive officer, with copies to the special security officer and the officer in charge of his detachment:

Subj: Letter of Resignation

1. I hereby submit my letter of resignation from the Navy. . . . I am a homosexual and I have kept this fact concealed from the Navy since my induction into the Navy until the present. If the Navy should determine me fit to serve, despite my homosexuality, I will continue to serve.

2. This situation has been developing over quite a long time, yet I made the decision only yesterday to come forward with the truth. My reason: I am not able to effectively perform my duties because of frustration resulting from 1) repression of my feelings and 2) being dishonest with those people I consider my friends. Attempts to avoid and/or weaken friendships in order to avoid these conflicts have not proved a satisfactory solution.

3. I do not consider myself a security risk because of my homosexuality, and I am certain that an investigation will attest to this statement. I am aware that homosexuals have been considered poor security risks. . . . I have been especially careful to maintain proper security procedures . . . throughout my naval career.

4. Although it is not my intention to cause the Navy public embarrassment, I request permission to explain my decision to the members of the VQ-1 wardroom. I do not intend to seek out publicity, but nor will I deny the truth of the situation if I am asked.

5. I do not make this decision lightly, but I do so freely and in good faith. No particular event has prompted this decision, but only the slow realization of my own personal values and beliefs.

Very respectfully submitted,

Before submitting the letter, Rene informed Steven of his intention. "I couldn't base my life on how things affected other people," Rene relates, "but I had an obligation to warn Steve and give him an opportunity to end our rooming together." Steven refused to believe that Rene was gay and urged him to seek counseling. "Do you want me to prove it to you?" Rene challenged. Steven didn't want to be shown any proof, but he dismissed Rene's warning that Rene's coming out might make things difficult for him.

At the Japanese base where Rene was temporarily stationed, the executive officer, the head of Rene's detachment, and the special security officer reacted civilly to Rene's letter. They warned him to attest in any security investigation that he had had no gay experiences while in the service. They took away Rene's top-secret security rating and had him flown back to headquarters in Guam. There Rene's commanding officer pointed out that an admission of homosexuality could result in a discharge. Rene replied that he loved the

Navy and considered his years of service "an incredible experience, but it's not worth living like this."

At the regular Friday squadron meeting, the CO announced that a member of the squadron wanted to make a statement. Rene stood up, his legs shaking. "I'm sure everyone has noticed," he declared, "that I'm wearing a yellow [low-level clearance] instead of a blue [top] security badge. You're probably wondering what's happening, and I want to be up front with you. I'm gay. I know this is a personal issue, but I consider you my family and my friends."

To Rene's astonishment, the officers applauded; some stood up to express their sympathy. Two junior officers approached and said that they did not agree with him but appreciated his forthrightness. "It took a lot of guts to do what you did," they declared.

Rene next made a statement to the Automated Data Processing division, which was under his command. The men and women responded in silence. As he left the meeting, Rene urged the chief of division to conduct a discussion until the group felt comfortable with what he had said. Later he learned that they talked for two hours before concluding that his declaration changed nothing for them.

Rene had heard of horrendous incidents in other commands in which people accused of being gay on mere hearsay had suffered a loss of reputation and had even been incarcerated. "I was lucky because of the kind of CO I had," he declares. "A CO sets the tone in a command. Of course, I was not responding to an accusation but coming out voluntarily. Besides, I gave assurance that I did not want to make a public issue of my action. Then, too, the personnel in intelligence units tend to have more education and greater sophistication than in other units."

Rene's CO provided him with a letter of recommendation which Rene subsequently used in applying for admission to law schools. After describing Rene's duties in his command, Commander Bruce N. Coburn wrote, "Mr. Puliatti's performance was far above average with extremely strong emphasis in initiative and problem-solving. . . . A tremendous asset to the command, Mr. Puliatti is totally reliable. Once he assumed or was assigned a task, I never had to follow up to ensure its completion. He is a man of exceptional integrity and unwavering principle. His dedication to his country and the Navy, and his care and concern for those in his charge, garnered him the utmost respect from every member of the command."

Rene remained on the Guam base for an additional five months, no longer permitted to fly intelligence missions but continuing to serve as head of his computer unit. He made a point of appearing at all social events. "I wanted them all to see me for who I was, that I was the same person I had been before." He encountered only minor unpleasantness. His roommate Steven, in particular, became openly hostile, making snide remarks when Rene was within earshot and snapping at him when they were alone. At the weekly volleyball game, some men seemed intent on besting him, determined not to be beaten by "a fag" (though Rene never heard the term directed at him). Some delayed entering the locker room while he was there. "That's your problem," Rene assured them.

Rene frequently confronted what he describes as silly questions. He answered them all:

> "Why would you choose to be gay?" "I didn't choose. Who would choose to be kicked out of a career and be ostracized?"
>
> "What about the Bible?" "First of all you have to believe in the Bible, and then you have to believe in it literally and not metaphorically." "Then what parts do you believe?" "Do you accept Leviticus as a whole?"

Some of his questioners, Rene discovered, were more offended at his declaring that he was not a Christian than at his declaring he was gay.

A security investigator found no evidence of misconduct and recommended that Rene be granted an honorable discharge. Naval Military Personnel Command accepted the recommendation. "I think I could have remained in the Navy," Rene declares, "but I wanted out. I didn't see the Navy as my life's career."

Like other departing officers, Rene was given a farewell party. The CO praised Rene's contributions to the squadron and did not mention the issue involved in his leaving. Departing officers were customarily presented with a plaque along with a photograph of a plane signed by most of the officers. Two who signed Rene's photograph snidely added "O's" and "X's"—"love and kisses." In responding to the CO's remarks, Rene announced to general laughter, "I may take them up on it." Other officers urged him to ignore the childishness of the two men. "In effect," Rene declares, "there was no difference between my farewell party as far as warmth and friendship were concerned; perhaps there was even more warmth because of my particular situation. Most people thought that I was a victim of an unfair military policy." Officers told him of others they knew in the Navy who were forced to live in the closet. Several said that they would miss him and urged him to keep in touch.

On July 3, 1990, after an incredulous processing clerk at the Treasure Island base in California called Washington to confirm that a confessed homosexual was to receive an honorable discharge, Rene was separated from the Navy.

Upon enrolling in computer science courses at Syracuse University, Rene went back into the closet. In the summer of 1991, however, after *Time* magazine quoted two sentences of a letter he had written in response to an article on gays in the military, Rene came out to the supervisor of the university science library, where he was working. She thanked him for displaying trust in her and asked permission to post the page on which he was quoted. "This," Rene declares, "was my first coming out to the world."

For the first time in his life, Rene, now twenty-seven, ventured into a gay bar. He was repelled by the atmosphere. "Like a hypocrite, I resented the meat market unless I was the one who took the initiative." He did meet transient sexual partners, but he did not experience an explosion of sexual promiscuity after his many years of enforced celibacy. "I had disciplined myself for so long," he explains, "and I continued to do so."

Deciding that computer science was not the career he wanted to follow, Rene applied for admission to several law schools and in the fall enrolled at the Rutgers University law school in Newark, New Jersey. Once again he returned into the closet. When a fellow student learned in casual conservation that Rene had served in the Navy, he made an angry remark about the treatment of gays in the military. Rene then declared that he himself was gay. The gossip following this admission "forced me to come out publicly," Rene declares, "and confirmed to me once and for all the necessity of ending denial and subterfuge." He joined the school's Gay and Lesbian Caucus and wrote articles on gay issues for the undergraduate newspaper and for the publication of the student chapter of the National Lawyers Guild.

During Bill Clinton's 1992 presidential campaign, Rene read in some gay publication that Michael Garry, a West Point graduate, was organizing a gay alumni association. He learned, too, of the New York Gay Veterans Association and attended a meeting of the group at the Lesbian and Gay Community Center. After beginning to contribute to the association's newsletter and giving talks for the association, he was elected the association's vice president. He participated in protest demonstrations at the Times Square recruiting station and marched under the Gay Vets banner in the Veterans Day parade. (The American Legion and the Catholic War Veterans, he notes, outvoted in rejecting the gay vets' participation by the other members of the United War Veterans of Greater New York, were compelled to hold a separate parade.)

At the time of his interview, Rene had not established a long-term relationship. "I have difficulty opening up to people," he declares. "I grew up learning to be quiet, to be the good boy. Having lived in subterfuge for so long, it still takes a long time to gain trust in people. I hope one day to settle down with someone and to adopt children."

Despite the many years of frustration, self-denial, and self-hatred, Rene is certain that he made no error in going into the Navy. "I grew in discipline," he declares, "and learned to analyze situations and to solve problems, to work with people as a leader. I became aware of other people's suffering, the darkness in people's lives. My experience made me more compassionate."

Rene remains in contact with three officers from his squadron and six members of his company at the Naval Academy. He considers them to be among his closest friends. All know that he is gay.

The interviews recounted in this chapter all provide illumination about the unfairness and the ineffectiveness of the "don't ask, don't tell" policy. The following statement issued by the Washington-based Servicemembers Legal Defense Network in August 1994, six months after the inauguration of the new policy, sums up the initial experience with the new regulation:

GAYS IN THE MILITARY: FACTS ABOUT THE NEW POLICY

1. Commanders *will ask* personnel if they have ever stated they were gay and use this information to investigate and discharge gay military members. Investigators *will ask* questions about sexual orientation during security clearance investigation and may, with a waiver from the Pentagon, discharge personnel based on such information.
2. Investigators continue to interrogate suspected gay personnel about the details of their private lives and sexual activities and to pressure service members to name others who might be gay. Information gathered in witch hunts has already been used to discharge and criminally prosecute servicemembers.
3. Commanders may seize and read *personal diaries,* letters and computer files to search for evidence of homosexuality. Even servicemembers' off-base homes may be searched.
4. Clergy, doctors and psychiatrists may reveal confidential conversations regarding servicemembers' sexual orientation or activities to commanders, information which can lead to discharge or imprisonment.
5. Gay servicemembers face up to fifteen years *in jail* for engaging in the same adult, consensual acts as heterosexuals: holding hands, hugging, kissing and sex, even if such acts occur off-base and in the privacy of one's home.
6. Going to a gay bar, marching on gay pride day, reading gay magazines, displaying a pink triangle or even an innocent glance may constitute credible evidence to start an investigation when reported by a third person.

In reality, the new policy should be called "Do Ask, Force to Tell, Do Pursue."

Chapter Sixteen

Parents and Friends of Lesbians and Gays (PFLAG)

As was apparent in the experiences described in Part I, attitudes of parents are often crucial in the coming-out process of lesbians and gays. Indeed, 37 percent of the troubled young people who seek assistance from the Hetrick Martin Institute have suffered violent abuse from homophobic parents; 20 percent have run away from home; 30 percent have attempted to commit suicide; and only 10 percent have enjoyed family acceptance of their sexual orientation.

Like their children, parents of gays also undergo a coming-out process, often lengthy and painful. Alice Wong relates that after a strained relationship during her lesbian daughter's childhood, she and Ellen grew ever closer as they both underwent the coming-out experience. "If she were straight, she wouldn't have needed me as much," Alice declares. "When your child is gay and is able to come out to you and you are able to show support, the gratitude the child shows for your support is overwhelming."

Ellen concurs. "At fifteen," she declares, "I could tell my mom things about my life that I could not tell my classmates or my friends. I knew that if the world outside rejected me, if my school friends beat up on me, there was one person who would never turn her back on me."

Grateful to supportive parents, the gay community welcomes no other allies with as much warmth, love, and gratitude as it accords to PFLAG (Parents and Friends of Lesbians and Gays). "The easiest way to get a high on undeserved kudos," declares Alice Wong with self-deprecating modesty, "is to march in the Gay Pride Parade among the parents. Everyone applauds wildly when the PFLAG contingent marches by; people cry. If you need a little stroking, it is the easiest way to get it."

PFLAG dates to the 1972 gay march commemorating the Stonewall "uprising." Marching with a handlettered sign reading "Parents of Gays, Unite in Support for our Children" was Jeanne Manford, the first straight parent ever to participate in a gay parade. She was overwhelmed by the response of onlookers. "The young people were hugging me," Jeanne subsequently recounted, "screaming, asking if I would talk to their parents. I realized we just had to form a group, Parents of Gays." Ermanno Stingo (the septuagenarian with long service as a volunteer observer at trials involving victims of homophobic violence) offered to assist her in forming an organization of parents of gays. When Jeanne was awarded an honor by the organization, she recalled that during the 1972 march Ermanno had rushed over to her and kissed her. She said, "I think of Ermanno as another son." "And I," exclaimed Ermanno, "was older than she was!" (In the late 1980s, Jeanne's gay activist son died of AIDS. She continued her activism.)

At the 1993 PFLAG convention, President Mitzi Henderson proclaimed in her keynote address, "Despite our sometimes gray hairs and our generally middle-class backgrounds, we are a new breed of revolutionaries. . . . redefining 'normal' to include homosexual and bisexual. . . . If a major shift in public attitude is to come, it will be not only gay groups that will make it happen. It will be the PFLAG mom in Iowa and those of us in this room and our thousands of members not here in New Orleans, who make it happen."

At the same convention, the organization changed its name from Parents of Lesbians and Gays to PFLAG (Parents and Friends of Lesbians and Gays). By then it had expanded to include 265 chapters and contact groups throughout the United States, Canada, France, Israel, and five other countries (including a chapter in Moscow). At its Washington national headquarters, an executive director and a full-time staff carry out policies developed by a board of directors. Among its honorary directors, it has listed seven clergyman and four bishops. The organization issues a national quarterly newspaper in addition to the numerous bulletins and educational pamphlets published by individual chapters.

Though PFLAG membership is overwhelmingly straight, the Washington gay newspaper the *Blade* included PFLAG in its 1993 survey of "national gay political groups" and praised PFLAG for taking "a more and more visible role in lobbying for Gay-related bills, against antiGay initiatives . . . providing a unique voice for equal treatment of Gays." The newspaper further noted that PFLAG surpassed all gay political organizations in contributions to the campaign funds of openly gay and lesbian candidates for public office.

Although PFLAG conducts family support and educational activities "designed to lead gay people, their families and friends, and our society to understand and accept homosexuality," its prime emphasis is on parents of gays.

"Just as coming out is difficult for gay people," asserts a national PFLAG document, "the coming-out process is equally difficult for parents who often crawl right into the closet their children have left." According to a pamphlet issued by the New York City chapter, the most common initial reactions of parents to the coming out of their offspring are:

> Why did he or she have to tell us? Why did he or she do this to us? What did we do wrong? Will he or she be ostracized, have trouble finding or keeping a job or even be physically attacked? Will he or she be lonely in his old age if he does not have a family of his own? Will he or she get into trouble with the law? Should we send our child to a psychiatrist to be "cured"? Should we tell the family? What will the neighbors say?

The pamphlet concludes:

> Accepting your child's homosexuality and educating yourself on the subject takes time. Sons and daughters often expect their parents to understand immediately, but many cannot do this. Do not be impatient with yourself, however long it takes. If you really want to learn and understand, you will.

This chapter explores the coming-out experiences of some PFLAG members. The process of their acceptance of their children's sexual orientation can provide models to all parents of gays:

GISELLE

"I'm not the PFLAG member you ought to interview," Giselle protested. "When my daughter and son came out to me, I accepted them as they were. When you love someone, your prime concern is for their happiness. My children had no problems with me, and I had no problems with them."

Giselle married in 1951. David, her first child, was born five years later; Alan and Elaine, both gay, followed at two-year intervals. (Giselle and her husband had met at meetings of the Ethical Culture Society, an organization dedicated to humanistic ideals. They sent their children to the Society's Sunday school. Until their marriage began to deteriorate about 1975, Giselle relates, "We had the marriage of the century. People were jealous of our apparent happiness." In 1981, with their children all grown, they were divorced.)

Early on, Giselle and her husband recognized that Alan was different from other boys. He played with dolls and was not interested in sports. Nevertheless, he had many friends and experienced no difficulties socially. Noting that in high school he never went out on dates, Giselle and her husband wondered whether he was gay, though they expressed no concern at the possibility.

The athlete in the family, Elaine played tennis with her father from the age of seven and joined boys in sports. Self-assured and popular, at seventeen she asked to be fitted with a diaphragm. When at eighteen, without offering any explanation she asked to be allowed to visit a therapist, Giselle hesitated, aware of Elaine's frequent short-lived enthusiasms. Elaine, however, prevailed. (Only years later did Giselle learn that Elaine was at that age discussing with her brother Alan, with whom she is very close, her concerns about her sexual orientation.)

In November 1980, Giselle and her husband received *the* letter from Elaine:

> . . . there is no right way to tell you I am a lesbian. I suspect that however I do it will be somewhat of a shock. I choose to write because I realize this is a hard issue for all of us, and I think we need time to organize our thoughts and reactions before any of us lash out in fear. . . .
>
> I have been struggling for a long time, and it has been scary. Every belief I've grown up with has had to be turned upside down and shaken loose. I've had to relearn who I am. I am changing and growing all the time. . . . Even with all the fears: fear of rejection . . . of a new life style . . . I am feeling warm and capable . . . powerful . . . in control. I am learning to be gentle with myself, to love myself. . . . In some ways I perceive the world differently now: it is harsher, but I am stronger. And if I live alone the rest of my life it will be by choice.
>
> I do not hate men. My lesbianism is an outgrowth of positive experiences and connections with women. I allow myself to share more, to go deeper into myself and make myself more vulnerable. It's almost harder to have relationships with women because I invest so much more of myself, risk more. . . .
>
> Be happy for me. I am being honest with myself, and I want to be honest with you. Trust me.

At Thanksgiving, two weeks later, Elaine and her parents had a discussion. Elaine insists that Giselle cried, but Giselle has no recollection of tears. "I accepted it; it didn't trouble me," says Giselle. "I saw that Elaine was content, and that was all that was important to me." Unlike many parents, Giselle did not exclaim, "Why me?" though she did wonder to her therapist whether she had done something to cause Elaine's lesbianism. When he reassured her, she accepted his word immediately, "and," she declares, "I didn't trouble myself with the thought thereafter." Giselle does recall, however, being concerned for Elaine's safety, aware that lesbians and gays suffer insult and even injury from homophobes.

"Do you want us to tell anybody?" Giselle asked. "You can tell anybody that you're comfortable telling," Elaine replied, "because after all if people know that someone like me is gay, it can't be bad." "I was so proud of her," Giselle recalls.

When Giselle mentioned Elaine's news, invariably friends responded, "We suspected Alan might be gay, not Elaine." Apparently, Elaine's coming out to

Alan in 1978 did not impel him to self-investigation, and not until years later did he come out to himself.

In 1982, two years after she had received Elaine's coming-out letter, Giselle received a coming-out letter from Alan:

> . . . As you may have suspected, I am gay. . . . It is only two months since I have embraced this identity. I've had my suspicions for much longer, but I've been able to avoid the issue. I think that living with you in New York may have inhibited this process . . . being in a situation with friends, colleagues and family that was comfortable. Why rock the boat?
>
> Moving out here freed me of any past expectations, my own as well as those of others. San Francisco is especially hospitable to gays, but this really did not play a role in my decision to move. I did not expect to confront myself for a much longer time and had assumed that therapy would be the instrument I would have to use. As it turned out, I went to a concert that was attended primarily by gay men and felt such warmth of security that I was uplifted and realized that there was no alternative. . . .
>
> In the face of total insecurity—no job, no permanent home and a questionable future—I am feeling better more often than I ever have. . . .
>
> And, as I hope is clear to you, being gay is not simply a question of sex—it is a way of life. I must learn that way and become secure in my identity in an accepting environment so that I can face the world.

"Alan's announcement was anticlimatic," Giselle recalls. "We always suspected it with him."

Giselle attributes her easy, unproblematic acceptance of the homosexuality of two of her children to her childhood experiences in wartime France. "I suffered enough for being different," she declares, "and have no patience with people who are intolerant of difference."

Born in Nice in 1929, Giselle was eleven in 1940 at the fall of France. Even before the war she had been made aware of her difference as a Jew. The daughter of her father's superior at the bank where he was employed called her a "dirty Jewish snake," and a classmate muttered, "You're a true member of your race!" when Giselle refused to whisper an answer to her during a test. When she was eight, her anti-Semitic teacher never said anything overt, but she was quick to penalize Giselle. "She looked at me with contempt," Giselle recalls. In 1940, upon receiving orders from the Rome headquarters, Giselle's father was dismissed as the head of the foreign exchange department in an Italian bank branch. He continued to make a living by conducting black-market money exchange out of their home, sometimes using Giselle as a courier. In 1941 her father and mother packed their things, prepared to take a train on a Monday for Bilbao in Spain, where they were to board a ship for New York. During the weekend, however, the Americans invaded North Africa, and the Germans marched into unoccupied France and closed the frontier.

Immediately the Germans began to round up the Jewish refugees in Nice, first deporting non-French Jews who had arrived since 1939 and rapidly widening the razzia to include other Jews. By the summer of 1943 Gestapo agents were conducting nightly surprise descents on Jewish apartments, and Giselle's parents moved daily from place to place. The family of Giselle's best friend, French Catholics living in the same apartment building, agreed to place Giselle, then fourteen, and her four-year-old brother with relatives in Valence in central France for safety. Giselle's parents obtained false papers for her and her brother and sent them off on their own one night. "Many French are anti-Semitic," Giselle remarks, "but during the war individuals were good, and there will never be a way to repay what my friend's parents did for us." They even sheltered Giselle's grandmother, who spoke little French and thus could not pass as a Catholic. They nursed her when she suffered a stroke and buried her when she died.

With false papers Giselle's parents made their way from town to town. On one occasion, a family active in the Resistance that sheltered them received an anonymous warning that it was known that they were harboring Jews. Departing at night, Giselle's parents escaped the Gestapo, who arrested the family the next day. They made their way to Valence. When in 1944 the Germans began withdrawing, Giselle and her brother left their hiding place to rejoin their parents. After returning briefly to Nice, they emigrated to the United States.

"Because I was a victim of anti-Semitism and prejudice," Giselle notes, "I've always felt that nobody had the right to reject anyone else for being different. As long as you're not hurting anybody, you should be allowed to pursue whatever is right for you."

Giselle sees Alan and his lover of seven years at least once a year, either in San Francisco or in New York. "For me," says Giselle, "Alan's lover is another son." The lover had been married for some twelve years and has a grown son. His wife came out to him as a lesbian before he came out to himself. She now lives in her own apartment in the two-family building owned by him and Alan. "They live together as an extended family," declares Giselle with satisfaction.

Elaine began a relationship at the same time as Alan, and her lover became "a second daughter to me," says Giselle. The couple separated, however, after five years.

Giselle's experience with the Holocaust not only proved a decisive factor in her formation but also helped to shape the attitudes of her children. Speaking as the daughter of a survivor at a Holocaust commemoration ceremony in a temple in Cambridge, Massachusetts, Elaine recounted her mother's wartime experience living in hiding "under painful conditions of little food and forced labor." She herself sought, Elaine said, "to understand what it must have been like to not know if her parents were dead or alive, to lose her home, to be solely responsible for her brother, to live in constant fear of being caught, to watch friends deported and killed, to experience the pinnacle of anti-Semitism as a young Jewish girl." She declared herself the heir of "her mother's pain" as well as of her mother's "deep belief in justice, truth, and equality." What she herself faced now each day as both the daughter of a Jewish Holocaust survivor and a lesbian, she continued, "is the choice of when and how I inform the world, [wondering] if I will be persecuted for who I am. . . . Every one of us here," she declared to the audience, "has our own struggles and pain. But each of us also has the obligation to carry forth the lessons of the Holocaust: that life is rich and precious, that a just society ceases to be just when bigotry and oppression exist. That is the challenge before us."

Both Elaine and Alan work for AIDS organizations. For several years Alan served as a buddy to people with AIDS.

For her part, Giselle was determined to do something in the gay movement, "for my children." Elaine suggested that in PFLAG she could help other people, "not because I needed support in dealing with my children's sexual orientation," Giselle remarks. "Most of us in the group go to the meetings because we are comfortable with other people who, like us, have come out. . . .

"At meetings I sometimes get upset when I hear the anger in some people. Loving someone is wanting that person's happiness, with no conditions. I do not understand how parents can stop loving their child after the three seconds it takes to say, 'Ma, I'm gay.' I get angry with these people because to me they are saying to their children, 'I don't love you.' How can you inflict such pain on your child?"

ALICE WONG

Like Giselle, Alice Wong protested that she would not be a good interviewee. "I have had no problems with my daughter's lesbianism," she insisted. Alice is the daughter of a Canadian mother, a lapsed Catholic, and a WASP father with a trade-union background. In Astoria, Queens, Alice's parents chose to attend a Dutch Reformed church because it accepted black parishioners. Alice went through the New York City public school system and then attended St. Lawrence University in Upstate New York. Upon graduating, she joined the Peace Corps and in 1968 in Borneo met and married a Malaysian-born Chinese who was teaching English there. They went to Hawaii, where he completed his education, and Ellen was born. When he obtained a position at the United Nations in New York, they moved in with Alice's parents in Brooklyn. Alice found a position, which she still holds, at the United States Customs Service.

From Ellen's earliest years, Alice was aware that her daughter was a loner, quiet like her father and shy in groups, and she had an inkling of a more profound difference when as an eight year old Ellen refused to wear dresses. "I simply accepted Ellen's insistence upon wearing pants," Alice recounts. "After all, I wore pantsuits myself." Alice recalls that at some time in her childhood Ellen did not want to go to Chinatown, as though troubled at being Eurasian.

When Alice and her husband caught Ellen stealing money from them, they sent her to a psychiatrist for therapy. In retrospect, Alice thinks that Ellen's stealing might have been related to unconscious anxiety at being different. "We're not introspective people," she remarks.

The psychiatrist informed Alice that Ellen was undergoing a sexual identity crisis. "My reaction was," declares Alice, " 'What do you expect me to do about it?' Ellen was only eight, and I had other things on my mind than Ellen's sexual identity." Alice does not recall even mentioning the therapist's announcement to her husband. After all, she explains, they had put Ellen in therapy because of her stealing, and they were content that that problem had apparently been resolved.

In 1981, when Ellen was twelve, after six months of illness, her father died of cancer. Ellen remembers him as always being quiet and patient. "I bent over backwards to please him," she recalls. He never raised his voice and only rarely punished her.

Compelled now to assume full responsibility for her daughter, Alice realized she would have to make a considerable effort to prove a successful single parent. "The previous years had been a difficult time for Ellen and me," Alice declares. "We didn't get along. I was unhappy as a mother. A perfectionist like my father, I made constant demands on her. She was untidy, she didn't do her homework. I found myself screaming at her all the time. My husband was wonderful. He took over the parent's role entirely and acted as a buffer between Ellen and me. He was perfect." With his death, Alice resolved to learn patience and tolerance as a parent. She set aside Wednesday evenings after work to be with Ellen and frequently took Ellen out to dinner. The more she practiced mothering, the more she came to like the role.

Alice had no suspicion of the "miserable experience" Ellen was undergoing at Packer Collegiate, a private school she attended from the age of eight through high school. "I was the goat of the class," Ellen recalls, "the social outcast. I was aware of being different and unwilling to conform." By the ninth or tenth grade, however, she ceased caring when the others made fun of things she said or did, called her names, or even pushed her down the stairs. She found some relief with her few friends, "other outcasts."

Ellen declares that she had always known she was different from other girls. "I didn't have the same interests," she says. "As a child, I didn't play with dolls. I played sports with boys; my best friends were boys." She also had crushes on female teachers and on girl classmates from an early age. When she was in fourth grade, she cornered a girl in the cloakroom. The girl called her a "lezzie." Ellen did not know what the term meant, though she had heard it before. But she did not feel uncomfortable at being different. "My actions," she insists, "seemed natural, a part of me. I didn't particularly want to be like other girls." By the time she entered adolescence, "a difficult time," Ellen says she had a label for what she was. She had no role model and no one to talk to about her sexuality, except her mother.

Alice had never heard homophobic remarks from her parents. She knew gays at college and worked with gays at her job. She socialized with a gay couple at the Unitarian church she and her husband attended. When once she heard Ellen remark that there was "a faggot" in the school, she recounts, "I had a fit at her using that term. I said kids call names just to hurt people, and just because they call him faggot doesn't mean he's necessarily a homosexual, and if he is a homosexual, there is no reason to make his life miserable. I was upset because I assumed that Ellen had been part of the crowd calling him a faggot."

Alice had noticed that Ellen showed no interest in boys and was not upset at not having dates. At their Wednesday evenings together, Ellen began bringing up the subject of lesbianism. One evening Alice asked point blank, "Are you gay?" Ellen answered with equal directness, "Yes." "Are you sure?" Alice asked. "Yes," said Ellen. "It was all very matter of fact," recalls Alice. "I made no fuss, and Ellen felt comfortable at my reaction. After all, I hadn't lost a loved one. My kid hadn't died or changed from the day before."

With trepidation, Ellen came out to close friends, former classmates no longer attending Packard. She feared that henceforth they might be concerned if she showed affection to them, but she had never been demonstrative and, indeed, she experienced no problem with them.

Alice, on the other hand, did not mention Ellen's coming out to her acquaintances with the exception of a single friend at work, who traveled with her and Ellen during vacations. If the news bothered this woman, Alice reasoned, she would have the choice of not traveling with them again. Her friend, however, took the news calmly. "I didn't come out to anybody else for a long time," Alice declares. "I didn't recognize Ellen's coming out as a problem. I accepted my child. I was happy with how I handled her coming out. Nevertheless, I did realize that her life would be tougher as a lesbian."

When Ellen was a senior in high school, Jocelyn, one of the friends to whom she had come out, a mature young woman and a member of the Unitarian church Ellen and Alice attended, read a notice in the *Village Voice* of a gay softball league. She encouraged Ellen to join and even accompanied her to her first meeting with the group. "It was a life-changing experience," Ellen recalls. "For the first time in my life I had a community." The league members, however, were older, and most were gay men. "When we socialized after playing, I just listened," Ellen relates. "We had little in common."

Before Ellen left for Tufts University in 1987, Jocelyn told her about the March on Washington to take place that November and urged her to participate. The March proved to be another pivotal experience for her. "To see hundreds of thousands of gays, from every walk of life," she recounts, "of every age group, from everywhere, to know that wherever you would go there would be gays, that was a revelation to me. I spent the entire weekend with a smile on my face." Thereafter at college Ellen became active in the gay student group. She helped to organize a speakers' bureau and participated as a lesbian spokesperson in the freshman orientation program.

Unable to make travel or room arrangements until a day or two before the event, Ellen had not informed her mother of her decision to participate in the March on Washington, but Alice read an article in the *Times* by a parent who declared how proud he was of his child's participation. "If I see gay in the title of an article," she explains, "I read it. I was certain Ellen had been there. I wondered why I hadn't gone myself." She called Ellen and said, "You go on a march, and here's your mother sitting here dumb, fat, and happy and not doing anything." "Reading that newspaper article, I realized I should be doing something. I had been taught to fight for what you believe in. My father was a member of the NAACP. I had been a feminist and active in the women's movement. This was the next step."

Alice contacted the Washington office of PFLAG and obtained the number of the New York chapter. She was disappointed, however, in the first meeting she attended. PFLAG, she discovered, was primarily a support group. She was convinced she needed no support; she had no problem with Ellen's lesbianism. "When I listened to parents bemoaning their fate at having gay children," she recalls, "I found it difficult to believe that in this day and age people could react this way." After attending a board meeting, Alice became involved in various PFLAG activities. In 1992 she became the chapter's vice president. She began to speak in public. (Subsequently, she became president of the Brooklyn chapter.)

"Although I had always claimed that I had no problem with Ellen's lesbianism," Alice admits, "at PFLAG I came to realize that I had been very private about her coming out. I wasn't as comfortable as I had assured myself I was. I suffered from a residue of homophobia. I decided that I had to be completely out." When she and Ellen were invited to appear on the "Geraldo" television talk show as representatives of PFLAG, she announced the program in advance at church. "We really came out then," Alice declares, "and nobody expressed any hostility or criticism."

Of her sexual life, Ellen declares that she had her first "trick" when she was nineteen, someone she met on the train on the way home from college. She knows that her mother objects to one-night stands. "The very concept of a trick," Alice admits, "is objectionable to me, the idea of spending one night with someone with whom you have no emotional involvement. It's a difference in generation, I guess."

"I don't see anything wrong with one-night stands," Ellen counters. "I'm always honest about my relationship or lack of relationship. As a senior at Tufts, I had a relationship with a woman a few years older than I who worked in the locality. With mutual agreement, it was an open relationship. With my emotions I'm monogamous, but I also want experiences without involvement."

In 1992 at the PFLAG annual dinner dance, Ellen met her lover. Alice, the organizer of the affair, had hired Barbara as the disk jockey. She gave Ellen Barbara's telephone number, and they have been together ever since. Ellen alternates in staying at home and at Barbara's apartment. Barbara is twelve years older than Ellen, and they are going through a trial period before making a lasting commitment. Barbara, Ellen notes, is established in her career and set in her ways. She wants to buy a house in the suburbs. Ellen considers herself a city person. "We don't talk about a long-term commitment," Ellen declares. "I have never thought about having children. Neither of us can stand children. We are career oriented. If we are together for another three years, I would like a formal commitment ceremony."

"The fact that we are both activists," remarks Alice, "makes it easier for us to talk. For the twenty-fifth anniversary of Stonewall [June 28, 1994], the assumption is that this house will be wall-to-wall with Ellen's friends. Because I am an activist I know how important the Stonewall celebration will be. Gay Pride Day, too, is a big day for both of us. I march with PFLAG; Ellen, with a lesbian motorcycle group."

WILLY AND FRANK JUMP

"I knew Frank was gay since he was two," insists Willy Jump. "I just knew." She was troubled by her intuition. In Holland she had had gay friends. When she was sixteen, one of them exclaimed to her, "O God, why was I made gay? I could have married you otherwise." Shortly thereafter, he turned on the gas in his apartment and died. Another friend, Peeter, Willy's hairdresser, told her that he had suffered so from shock treatments prescribed to "cure" him of his homosexuality that he had frequently thought of jumping to his death from a bridge in Amsterdam. "I never asked my friends why or how they came to be gay," Willy declares. "Such questions never occurred to me. That was the way they were, but listening to what they went through scared me for Frank."

Frank did not appear especially effeminate, although on home movies he declares, "You can see that I was a nellie little kid, running around flinging my arms about. It was a put-on. Even today I sometimes camp it up." But he did delight in using his mother's makeup. One day when he put on her slip and a wig, a friend of Willy's did not recognize him. "Who's that kid?" she asked. "I thought she was kidding me," Willy recalls. "That's Frank," she replied. Her friend snatched the wig from Frank's head and threw it on the ground. "I didn't mind his actions," Willy recounts, "but I did object to his wasting my expensive cosmetics. One day I threw my hair hot rollers on his bed and told him that I had bought another set that he was not to touch." "During my whole life," Frank remarks, "my mother's attitude has been, 'If that's what you want, it's all right.' "

In 1965, when Frank was five, Willy brought him to a psychiatrist. He advised her to wait until Frank reached puberty before taking any action about his behavior. Frank's second-grade teacher took Willy aside and told her that Frank had effeminate tendencies. The other boys wanted to be Superman or Batman, while Frank wanted to be Mary Poppins. "Of course," Frank quips, "Mary Poppins opened up her umbrella and flew through the air."

Frank recalls a mixed childhood. His parents were not well matched and were constantly arguing. (They met while his father was a soldier stationed in Germany. Willy arrived in the United States in 1958. They divorced in 1986, when Frank was twenty-six.) His father was undemonstrative by nature but showed affection by buying toys that Frank enjoyed and even took him fishing.) At the nearly all-black Laurelton, Long Island, suburban elementary school, Frank was uncomfortable as one of only three white students. "Why do all the kids hate me?" Willy recalls him complaining. "Why do they call me a white cracker?" Often when five or six boys ganged up on him, Frank would pull himself up on a wire fence and fight back with his feet. "I was fighting all the time. I was bigger than the others and so scared that I would fight for my life. I was shell-shocked from my experiences." At the principal's orders, Frank was not allowed to go to the boys' room alone. One of his classmates volunteered to accompany him. "We'd start to kiss as soon as we closed the door," Frank recounts. "I would go five or six times a day."

Always feeling threatened by male aggression, Frank played with the black girls during recess. He learned to jump rope to their rhyming patter and to like the popular music they liked. When the family moved to the all-white Howard Beach area, Frank, then nine, had already been socialized, he says, "as a little black girl." His new classmates called him "fairy," and he had to fight once again. He recalls having a crush on "a beautiful boy" in his class. "I don't remember being tortured about my feelings," he declares. "I didn't hide my feelings. If I wanted to kiss a boy, I did so. Some showed annoyance, others kissed me back."

On the other hand, Frank spent four happy months every year in Holland. His father worked for Pan Am and took advantage of his traveling privileges to allow Willy and Frank to visit Willy's family and friends in Amsterdam. In Holland, Frank encountered no hostility or name-calling from his playmates. He was popular as "the American" and taught his friends English and American popular songs.

When Frank was about nine, Willy recalls, he began to test her about his sexuality. Once at Macy's department store, Frank started to mimic and ridicule a man applying makeup in a cosmetics demonstration. "Frank, never do that," Willy admonished him, "that's not right." When he called someone a faggot, she slapped him. Reassured as to her attitude, increasingly, Frank dropped hints about his sexual preference. On visits to Amsterdam, Willy voiced her concerns to her gay friend Peeter. "Why don't you just leave him alone?" Peeter urged.

At thirteen, Frank announced to Willy that he was bisexual. "I thought my mom would accept that more easily than if I admitted I was gay." Alarmed, Willy consulted Frank's pediatrician. He suggested that Frank might be confused about his sexual identity and recommended that she bring Frank to a psychiatrist he knew. "It was a bad experience," Frank relates. "He asked me whether I wanted to change. I said yes. I saw how much pain I was causing my mom. She was crying and was a nervous wreck."

"Yes," Willy admits, "previously I had sensed that he was gay. Now I knew." It was a bad time otherwise for her. She was suffering from a herniated disk and was frequently hospitalized. She was constantly worried about him. "Frank and I were always together," she explains. "He was my buddy, my whole life. My husband was always traveling. I had no family here. None of my gay friends in Holland were happy. I didn't know what caused homosexuality and was afraid that I loved Frank so much that I made him gay."

The psychiatrist suggested that if Frank really wanted to change his sexual orientation he should try to think about girls instead of about boys when he masturbated. Frank followed this advice without success; but to make the psychiatrist and his mother happy, he declared that the suggestion worked. Willy assumed that Frank's "problem" was resolved. "I wanted to believe it," she declares.

In fact, Frank, physically precocious, had sex with girls from age eleven through age seventeen as well as with boys. In high school he had a lesbian lover as well as a gay lover. Elaine, a "butch" young black woman, welcomed him as a boyfriend to stop her mother's badgering. She lifted weights, while Frank wore seven-inch platform shoes and let his hair grow long. "I looked like Cher from behind," he declares. He and Elaine double-dated and played, "Let's seduce the straight couple." "I never was uncomfortable in having sex with girls," Frank says. "I have always felt at ease with whomever I was with, but it was a little boring."

At the age of thirteen Frank seduced the drama counselor at a summer camp, a man twice his age. When Willy again asked the counselor whether he was gay, the man denied that he was, frightened at being involved sexually with a minor. Once Frank's father caught them together in bed and ordered the man out of the house. Nevertheless, they continued to meet. Frank's father subsequently caught him in bed with Elaine. He walked away, chuckling. "I think he knew that we were two queers experimenting," Frank declares. "When after graduating from high school, I told him I was gay, he patted me on the back and said, 'You know about my sister. She is a lesbian.' My father's not a stranger to homosexuality."

Though completely "out" in high school, Frank had little trouble because he was identified as a "freak." Besides, he says, a whole group of students were "out." "We'd pass each other in the halls," he recounts, "and say, 'Hi, girlfriend!' It was the 1970s, when anything went. I think the 1970s was a perfect time to grow up gay."

Although Willy was not aware of Frank's hectic sexual life during his high school years, she sensed that he was drifting away from her. "We were no longer having a good time together," she says. "I sensed an imminent war." ("I didn't like you at the time," Frank admits.) "He thought I was rejecting him," Willy declares. "Finally, I asked him, 'Do you have something to tell me?' 'I'm not bi, I'm gay,' he replied. I screamed. The problem had not been resolved with the psychiatrist three years earlier!" In panic Willy called Frank's pediatrician. "Don't take this problem to bed with you," he counseled. "Frank is the same human being today that he was yesterday. Love him!" He said that he had gay friends who were doctors, lawyers, and judges. "Just ask him one question," he advised Willy, "Is he happy? If he says yes, get on your knees and kiss the floor." Willy put the question to Frank. He said he was happy. "Once I knew that he was happy and was not going to suffer like my gay friends in Holland, I went on with it. The doctor's word was decisive."

Frank does not recall that his mother's anxiety disappeared immediately. "It took a few months," he says, "before I felt that my mother was looking at me and not thinking about my being gay."

Nineteen seventy-six, the year he came out to his mother, Frank recalls as "an incredible year for us." Willy read an article about Jeanne Manford and Parents of Gays. "O my God," she exclaimed, "now I have people to talk to! If I had spoken to my friend Barbara, she would have told me to throw Frank out of the house. I didn't go to my first meeting to cry, but to learn. I heard gays say they knew they were gay at a very early age. So it wasn't strange what I had sensed when Frank was only two or three! Going to Jeanne Manford's group was a further step in my coming out."

In 1976, too, Frank entered Queens College and became president of the gay club there. Willy began to go to gay bars with him and to dance with him and his friends. "It was a time of ferment for both of us," Frank declares, "and we both grew in the experience." When Anita Bryant made gay rights a national issue, Frank and his mother began to discuss the question of gay rights. "For the first time I saw what an issue homosexuality was in this country," Willy recounts. "I remember how during the war my Jewish neighbors were ordered out of their houses. We put our lives on the line for Jews. When I arrived here, I heard people cursing the Jews. I heard remarks about blacks. I had gone to black clubs in Amsterdam. I had black friends. I certainly did not think that I would have to worry about my child's safety in this country."

Frank participated in the planning of the first gay March on Washington in 1979. Willy marched with the Parents. "We met friends for life in Washington," she recalls, "people from all over. This was my coming out to the world. I haven't been the same since." The next year Willy marched with the Parents in her first Gay Pride march. Thereafter she appeared on numerous television talk shows. "I have been warned to be careful at demonstrations,"

Willy remarks with regret, "since I'm not a citizen and am subject to deportation."

Frank attended only a few Parents' meetings with Willy. "Some parents," he recounts, "were looking for excuses to lash out, and I didn't want to sit there as a target for their anger." On the other hand, he criticized his mother for showing impatience with parents who expressed hostility to their gay children. "If you can't say something helpful to parents who are complaining about their children," Frank said, "maybe you shouldn't say anything." On one occasion, he recalled, she pulled a father out of the room and pushed him against the wall in her anger. "I heard terrible things," Willy protests. "I remember a parent saying she would prefer her kid had cancer or was a murderer."

Willy no longer speaks out at meetings. "I'm better," she says, "speaking one-to-one. After the meeting we go off with the newcomers and have a discussion. I ask parents, 'Is he healthy? Is he HIV-positive?' "

Willy had yet to undergo a further stage in her coming out.

In the late 1970s, Frank participated in a lengthy Hepatitis B clinical study. In 1984 blood not used in the study was frozen, and in 1987 the New York Blood Program asked whether Frank would let them use his blood from the former study in an HIV study. "I knew people who had died," Frank declares, "and thought I was probably positive since I was sexually active."

Willy went on a Parents' group trip to the Centers for Disease Control for information about HIV infection. Upon her return to New York, she called Frank to report what she had learned. "You know, just because people test positive," she assured him, "doesn't mean they will get AIDS." She asked him for the result of his HIV test. "It came out fine," Frank replied. A few minutes later he called back. "Ma," he said, "I can't lie to you." He admitted that he had tested positive.

"I've been one of the lucky ones," Frank declares. "I have not come down with any of the opportunistic diseases associated with AIDS, but I have watched my blood count diminish." He considers himself lucky in another respect. "I know so many people who came out to their parents only after learning that they were infected. They had so little time thereafter for their parents to learn who they were. Some have died without ever coming out to their parents, and their parents buried strangers. My mother did not jump for joy upon learning I was positive, but at least I had no hesitation about telling her that I was gay. We had some years together when being gay was not a death sentence. We have marched together. We continue to go on marches.

"When I received the test result, I was told," Frank recounted, "that there were only a few years left. I went wild, buying all kinds of things I wanted. The threat provided a push to do things. It also holds me back. I don't make commitments. The fear of falling sick makes you look at the future differently. My mother told her friends that I was positive before any of their children became sick. They assured her they would stand with her, and a lot of their children who later died were supports for me."

"Yes," remarks Willy, "I think of some of the parents with whom I went to Atlanta to learn about AIDS. Their children refused to be tested and then fell sick. I have lived the whole experience with them."

After breaking with his first lover, the camp dramatics counselor, Frank had series of relationships, the first, which lasted for five years, with a man who, like Frank, was a founder of ACT UP. In 1989 he met Vincenzo. "I told him on our first date that I was HIV-positive. His previous lover had died of AIDS; he himself tests negative. We're registered as domestic partners. My mother loves him. They do fight a lot, but he's the first one she considers as a real son-in-law. Vincenzo knows who he is. He'll kiss me on the street and hold my hand in the subway. That could be dangerous, but I feel we have to come out this way in order to change attitudes."

"My life is not worry free any more," declares Willy. "I'm no longer happy-go-lucky. No matter how blue the sky, for me there is always a haze. Frank has become my baby again; I want to pick him up and protect him. I have a constant fear that I'm going to lose him. We live day by day. I'm afraid sometimes to ask him how he feels. I watch myself against becoming overprotective. That's not good for him. At least Frank became politically active. That has helped him, and I'm proud of him. We're living through a war. When she was pregnant with my father, my grandmother lost her husband and her fifteen-month-old daughter in a typhoid epidemic. Now I am going through a plague. I'm angry, so angry at the whole society. I feel so helpless."

RACHEL AND DANIEL

While attending the New York City High School of Performing Arts, Rachel had no negative reaction to the gay and lesbian students, many of whom were dancers. They were "all part of the gang."

The only homosexual Daniel could recall from his childhood was a boy in elementary school notorious for giving oral sex to whichever boy or man was available. Because of his upbringing, Daniel did not join his friends, athletes like him, in gay baiting, but he did not oppose it. Daniel never heard his mother use a derogatory term for any group of people. She encouraged him to read *The Well of Loneliness,* a classic novel about lesbians written in the 1920s. "She was a tremendous influence on who and what I am today," Daniel declares.

After their marriage, Rachel and Daniel bought a country house in an upstate liberal community with as large a percentage of gays, they say, as Greenwich Village. Indeed, they had as next-door neighbors two gay men with whom they socialized comfortably. Nevertheless, she declares, "Our perceptions came from the media." The stereotype of someone prancing about was not appealing to her, and the gay lifestyle was not what she wanted for her child.

Rachel and Daniel had forewarning regarding Joshua's sexual orientation. When he was only three, his nursery school teacher expressed concern at his playing exclusively with the girls in the doll corner. "We were among the progressive parents," Rachel relates, "who bought boys dolls to play with and girls trucks. The teacher suggested that I send him to school in a shirt and tie instead of turtleneck shirts and sweatpants. He was three years old! I thought she was an idiot."

Rachel did wonder that all the friends Joshua invited home were little girls with whom he played house and marriage ceremonies. When he was about seven years old, she learned that he had been the only boy invited to a little girl's birthday party. She called the mother and expressed her chagrin. "Didn't it occur to you to invite other boys?" she asked. "I never thought about it," the woman replied. "I invited my little girl's close friends, and he was one of them."

In high school Joshua found companionship within the theater department. (Only years later did Rachel and Daniel learn that a sizable percentage of the boys were gay.) When he began to date young women whom Daniel describes as "a bevy of beauties," Rachel remarked to Daniel, "Whew, we got away with that one. A close call, but we got away."

Rachel and Daniel did not feel particular concern at Joshua's frequently locking himself in his room. "He was impossible to live with," Rachel recalls, "fun one minute and cranky the next. I was so tired of living with a person whose moods were all over the place. We walked on eggshells with his moods. I thought it was a part of his actor's self-centeredness."

When Rachel took her mother-in-law to visit Joshua at his out-of-town college, they discovered that he had dyed his hair red and set it with a permanent wave. He was also wearing a strange kind of pantaloons and high-top sneakers, along with an earring. "He's adorable," remarked his grandmother. Rachel felt relieved by her reaction.

When, two months later, Joshua came home for Christmas vacation, his hair was back to normal, and he had given up his earring. A temporary fad, Rachel and Daniel decided.

On a subsequent visit, Joshua introduced his parents to a beautiful girl with whom he had apparently developed a serious relationship. They took the two young people out to dinner. "She was physical," Rachel recounts, "all over him in the restaurant, crazy about him. He held her hand, but I could see he had no interest. That struck me, but I never thought 'gay.' "

One summer, with a girlfriend with whom he had seemed madly in love for about two years, often sleeping over in her room, Joshua went off to act in summer stock. A week or two into the summer, she quit and returned home. Fearing that Joshua would follow her, abandoning his first professional acting job, Rachel drove up to the theater in Massachusetts. "I hope you're not planning to leave the theater," she declared. "This is a wonderful opportunity. You can always write and call her after the summer." "I'm not going to quit," Joshua responded. "But I'm concerned that I don't feel anything. I don't understand it." "She's just not the right one," remarked Rachel in reassurance.

During a subsequent summer, on a visit to a stock company in Maine where Joshua was acting, Rachel and Daniel found him strangely abstracted. Ordinarily talkative and gregarious, he remained silent most of the day, tense and nervous. He seemed to be counting the minutes until they left. "But it didn't occur to me," Rachel declares, "that anything serious was wrong."

Some weeks after Joshua returned home, Rachel found a letter in his room. "It lay out there right near the door so that I couldn't miss it," she relates. "It made me think that he wanted me to see it." The letter was from an actor from the summer stock company, an extremely handsome young man whom Rachel and Daniel had met. From the contents it was clear that he and Joshua had had a summer "fling." The man had somebody in the city, and now he was seeking to break off his relationship with Joshua. From what she could infer from the letter, Rachel gathered that Joshua resisted the rupture.

That evening Daniel discovered Rachel in the bedroom, crying. "Our son is gay," she declared, showing him the letter. Daniel put his arms about her. "We don't know for sure," he said in an attempt to comfort her. "Maybe he's just been experimenting or is passing through a phase."

During the following months, Daniel recalls, "We weren't beating our breasts or throwing ourselves out the window. On the other hand, we weren't talking about it." Joshua was leading a busy life as an actor and was rarely home. Besides, he was not involved with anyone. "It's easy to deny," Daniel asserts, "when they don't present you with someone." In addition, Rachel was caught up in her work as a choral director, and "Lots of good things were happening with me," she notes. "I was able to tuck the problem away. That's so unlike me. I'm always direct about facing things."

While Daniel and Rachel kept silence with each other about their anxieties, Rachel issued warnings to Joshua. Whenever the subject of homosexuality came up in the media or somehow in conversation, she made remarks like, "Oh my God, what a life! What a way to live!" "I was giving him the message," Rachel admits, " 'You better not tell us you're gay. It's not going to be something I'm going to like.' "

A year after the discovery of the revealing letter, on the way home from an evening movie, Daniel remarked, "Wouldn't it be nice if you and Sheila [a young woman with whom Joshua had had a long friendship] and Rachel and I could double-date some night and go to the movies together?" Joshua did not reply.

Upon their arriving home, Joshua announced, "I have something to tell you." He appeared, Daniel recalls, "dry-eyed and determined, very dramatic." "We have to talk," he began. "I think you know what I'm about to say," he went on, speaking rapidly as though under pressure. "I'm gay. The reason that I am telling you is that I feel we can have a very close relationship if I'm truthful." "You always say to me," he continued, directing himself to Rachel, 'Isn't it wonderful that we're so close?' I have answered that we were, but in some things we weren't. Well, now you know what was the wall between us. I want to be close. Like Adam [his older, straight brother], if I have a partner in life, I want to be able to bring him to the family Seders, to Chanukah parties, to all family celebrations. I want a nice apartment, I want you to visit, I want everything that everybody else has."

Rachel was moved by his words. She had always felt a special bond to Joshua. ("He looks like me; he is in the creative arts like me," Rachel explained.) "Besides, there is nothing more you want to hear from your child," she declared, "than that he wants to be close to you, to come to all family affairs. Nevertheless, he was saying it all so dry-eyed and so quickly, and it was obviously rehearsed. When he finished, for me it was as though he had announced that he had terminal cancer. The hair on the back of my neck stood up, and I felt excruciating pain. Of course, we said all the right things. The three of us embraced in a circle and said how much we loved each other."

Euphoric, Joshua raced up to bed as though he had just tossed a brick off his shoulder.

Rachel had kept herself under control. "The emotional reaction lags behind," she insists, "and takes more work." She resented the matter-of-fact tone with which he had passed his burden on to her. The problem was old business to him. Now he was free. She was not.

Joshua informed his parents that he had earlier come out to close friends of the family, an open-minded, nonjudgmental interracial couple. "I understood intellectually why he came out to them first," Daniel declares. "He needed a dress rehearsal. But I felt hurt. I could see his going to his peers but not to people of our generation ahead of us."

Joshua explained that he involved the couple so that they would be able to provide support to his parents. Rachel did call them. "I was sobbing on the phone," she recalls, "and I said, 'I can't stand the idea that I am just going to be known as Rachel, the mother of a gay kid.' I had just won an Academy Award and an Emmy, and I had a reputation of being so competent. I was not going to be that person any more."

For Rachel and Daniel, there followed seven years of struggle before they fully adjusted to Joshua's announcement.

"It didn't take me seven years to accept him," Rachel insists. "It took me that long to start to tell other people. With him I don't remember how long it took—a couple of seasons. During those months I couldn't talk to him beyond asking whether he would be coming home for dinner. My throat locked."

Daniel did not suffer as intense a reaction as Rachel, but he did experience shame. "Despite my background," he declares, "I fell victim to the job society has done on us. You hear the limp-wristed jokes on television, you hear them in the grocery store, you see the sneering on the streets. It percolates inside you." But whereas Rachel became resentful and found it difficult to talk freely with Joshua, Daniel made an effort to become closer to him. From the time of Joshua's birth, Daniel had spent little time with his son. While Joshua was a child, Daniel was involved in graduate school and was constantly out of the house. "I remember one evening," Daniel relates, "after supper when I was leaving the apartment, Joshua asked where I was going. I said that I was going to school. 'Again!' he exclaimed. I turned around and stayed home that evening. All the years thereafter I hadn't a chance to really spend time with him. When he came out, Rachel went into a seven-year period of numbness. I used the seven years to get closer to Joshua."

"I behaved terribly," Rachel admits, "but Daniel came forward immediately and enveloped Joshua in emotional support and love."

During the weeks following his coming out, Joshua clarified past events for his parents, relating, for example, how in junior high school the rougher boys tormented him, calling him "sissy." Passing him in the hall, they would give him a push on the head. When he went to his room at home and closed the door, he often cried himself to sleep.

In high school, he had girlfriends, but he was forcing himself into the relationships. Only after graduating did he realize what was different about him.

Rachel never felt guilty for Joshua's being gay. "Most parents find that hard to believe," she says. "But I never felt it was the result of something that we did wrong. I was convinced that he was born that way. I do have guilt for his suffering a long time without any support from us and for it taking me such a long time before I could discuss with him freely. I froze him out."

"It makes me crazy to think that he suffered so," exclaims Daniel, "and we didn't suspect what was happening. All those nights that he was up there crying behind a closed door I was not there for him. I may even have fed into his suffering. Your kid comes home from a dance, from camp, from school, and you say, 'Did you meet a nice girl?' An innocent remark. But now, knowing what he was going through, I realize I was adding to his struggle. On the other hand, once one regains the role of parent, you feel very good. That provided the sense of satisfaction I had upon coming out as a parent."

Both Rachel and Daniel express gratitude for the strength Joshua displayed during the difficult years. "He hung in there with us," declares Daniel. "He could have walked out of our lives, but he didn't."

"Joshua has a good feeling about himself," Rachel explains. "He didn't bring as much negative baggage to his coming-out struggle as I've seen among some gays." During the months when she was in the process of adjusting to Joshua's being gay—"I was never proud of how I acted," Rachel declares—she frequently appealed to him to give her time. "I'm working on it," she assured him. "I know I'll get there." "He realized," Rachel asserts, "that that was the best he could have from me, but he was always confident that we would come around. He knew that we would not walk away from our kids."

Rachel and Daniel underwent an intensive education. "When your own child comes out to you," declares Daniel, "you begin to see through the stereotypes. I thought, too, that if it happens to me, it must happen all over the place in families just like mine."

Some experiences during their years in the closet shocked Daniel and Rachel into a clearer realization of their responsibilities. Encountering one day the mother of one of Joshua's elementary school classmates, Rachel and the woman showed each other pictures of their now adult sons. "What a hunk!" the woman exclaimed to a friend who was with her. "You should have seen Joshua years ago, he was such a sissy!" "That remark," Rachel relates, "went through me like ten knives. For the first time I realized that kids had called him a sissy. The mother knew it, and I didn't."

"Once at a New Year's Day party with people whom we knew as confirmed liberals," recounted Daniel, "a woman I was talking to pointed to a woman who had just arrived and said, 'Her daughter's a lesbian.' I spoke with that woman and found her a fascinating person. I said to Rachel later, 'In one sentence she was reduced to nothing. Her dimension was flattened: Her daughter was a lesbian!' "

Two years later, toward the end of the "seven-year silence," Daniel had another, similar experience at a dinner party. Someone mentioned Noel Coward. The host remarked, "Oh, he's a fruit, you know." "He reduced the brilliance of Noel Coward to 'He's a fruit,' " Daniel remarked to Rachel, "and they're going to do that to my son! People will say, 'You see that kid there, he's gay,' my wonderful son who's loving, kind, decent, and talented. Once I arrived at that point, I said to myself, 'I have to come out to protect my son.'

"Thereafter we started to come out swinging," recounts Daniel. "We had spent a good deal of our lives in liberal causes. We'd marched the correct marches, fought the good fight against the wrong wars and for the right causes. We fought for people who were having a hard time—it was a natural extension to fight for our gay son."

Achieving this stage of awareness, they had not, however, completed the process of coming out. Rachel still confronted the hurdle of accepting the reality of never having grandchildren from Joshua. "You have this overwhelming love for another human being when you're a parent," Rachel declared. "You're prepared to give your life for your children, but that doesn't stop you from wanting things for yourself. It's not so terrible to think that you might expect a few dividends for your devotion and sacrifice. I was always unhappy as an only child. I dreamed that one day the dining room would be filled with our family. You hear from your friends, 'Wait until you have grandchildren!' I want them so badly, I can't tell you how much. It's what keeps me from going out of my mind when I have bad days.

"Joshua doesn't have the same needs as I," Rachel admits. "Even if he were straight, he would not want children. He's so involved in his career. When I told my mother-in-law of his coming out, she expressed regret that he was not going to have a family. 'That's not what he's looking for,' I replied. 'All right,' she responded, 'as long as he's happy.' Her words helped me a lot. I don't think about the problem so much any more. I have come to the point of accepting that he'll be the single uncle. Maybe he'll meet a permanent partner. Maybe he won't."

Another continuing anxiety, particularly for Rachel, was the threat of AIDS. "The gay issue is so clouded over with the AIDS thing," she exclaims. "I have been paralyzed with fear for him."

As a former chairperson of the HIV/AIDS committee of the New York State Mental Health Counselors, Daniel was knowledgeable about the problem. At the high school where he served as a guidance counselor, he was "the condom-availability man." Joshua assured him that he had undergone GMHC counseling and was aware of the necessity for safe sex.

"There are different levels of accepting," Daniel notes. "The first level for us was in accepting that the boy Joshua was and the man we thought he was becoming was no longer the case. The next level was to tell people who he was and that we still loved him for who he was. Those were the easy levels. Then we had to grapple with the question of homosexual private life. As long as my son was unattached, the question remained abstract. When he said he was going with some guy, the graphics came in to play."

Daniel recalls the discomfort he experienced upon overhearing Rachel in a telephone conversation with Joshua. Joshua had met someone. Rachel asked his name, whether he was attractive, whether Joshua liked him. It had taken her a long time, Rachel says, before she could discuss Joshua's dates freely. During an earlier relationship of Joshua's, when he frequently stayed overnight at the man's apartment, Rachel knew she should ask Joshua about his friend, "but," she recalls, "I couldn't get the words out."

On the other hand, when Joshua brought a new companion to the family country house, Rachel declares that she had no problem at all. "We opened the door," Daniel relates, "and in walks this preppy, good-looking guy." (Subsequently Joshua admitted that he had dressed his friend in everything that he knew would appeal to Rachel.) "He was blond and blue-eyed like a California surfer," Rachel declares. "Very sweet and very polite. They shared a bedroom," Rachel recalls. "This time I was completely relaxed."

"Whether they did anything that night, I don't know," declares Daniel. "The picture of two guys holding hands or hugging never bothered me. I kiss my sons and my male friends without any hangups. Even the thought of oral sex between two men does not trouble me especially. The picture of anal sex, however, upsets me. Upon reading the letter disclosing Joshua's affair with the summer stock actor, I burst into tears at the thought of Joshua's participating in anal sex with another man."

A turning point for Rachel and Daniel came with their attending PFLAG meetings. "My coming out really didn't take me seven years," Rachel declares. "We had decided that we weren't going to let anyone know about Joshua because we were determined to keep the news from my mother-in-law. That had me in the closet much longer than I needed to be." (Ironically, when Rachel did tell her mother-in-law that Joshua was gay, she said, "Yes? He's my grandson. I love him. All I want is his happiness." "Here we had been hesitating all these years," Rachel exclaims, "and she was far ahead of us all that time!")

"Since we have come out to our family and friends," Rachel declares, "our social functions have been transformed. Before, when we sat down with our friends, we never knew when the subject would come up in a joke. When you discuss gays in the military, you can't anticipate what may be said. Now at the Seder or other celebration, our attitude is, 'You'd better accept us as we are or you're not going to be welcome here again and we're not going to visit you.' That's what we mean when we say that coming out is a liberation, a brick off your shoulder."

"I had had a very easy life," Rachel continues. "We had no crises. We enjoyed comfort, jobs we liked. I had been protected like a little child. I feel proud at what I have been able to do in this situation. My kid is happy and at ease. We've drawn closer than ever. If anything interesting happens at a PFLAG meeting or in relation to our gay friends, I call Joshua. We share our lives with each other as we had never done before."

"Since coming out," says Daniel, "we have been on a trip that is almost heady, with a tremendous pride in ourselves. Rachel frequently has lunch with parents who are a little further behind her in dealing with the problems of coming out. She and I have undertaken responsibilities at PFLAG. We have helped to organize an annual lesbian and gay 'liberation Seder.' "

"A new, fascinating world has opened up to us," Rachel declares, "a whole world that my friends know nothing about, and it's hard for me to discuss certain things with them. I have moved far ahead and left them behind. My perception is no longer, 'Poor me, I'm in the closet and I have this shame.' "

"I will not kid you," Daniel cautions. "If I could have my son as he is but otherwise straight, there is no doubt that I would trade sides. Who wouldn't? But after all, I'd also rather do the work I've been doing than some other kind of work. I have to say, too, that after my son came out, he blossomed into a different kind of person. He was a pain in the ass for many years. Now we have such a wonderful relationship. If what I see now is part of his being gay, if his personality is formed by his being gay . . .?"

Daniel admits that he has an additional level of struggle to go through. Their older son is in a relationship. "If there were to be a wedding, and

Joshua had found a partner," Daniel recounted, "I would have no trouble with his arriving with his friend, but when the orchestra strikes up a slow dance and the corny MC announces, 'Now take the one who you love most,' and my son were to get up to dance with his partner . . .? After all, it would be our first meeting with some of the in-laws. That would represent a hurdle for me.

"We're entering the Passover season," Daniel declared as a final comment. "In the gay and lesbian Seder we have helped to organize, we have emphasized the liberation theme, a theme evoking the best strains of Judaism—the humanism, the dedication to social justice. A heritage that comes to us through our mother's milk, one that is so appropriate for the gay struggle."

Chapter Seventeen
Problems and Perspectives

"We have read the same newspapers," advises Gerri Wells, "watched the same television programs, seen the same movies, experienced the same education, and also submitted to the same history books excluding gays and lesbians." Indeed, gays and lesbians, individually and in organizations, exhibit the attitudes and prejudices of the general society, attitudes and prejudices that undermine solidarity within the community and render the struggle for equal rights more difficult.

In assessing the discussion of organizational problems and perspectives in this final chapter, readers should keep in mind that the gay community is as varied as the general community, comprehending differences in age, gender, religious beliefs, political ideologies, class, race, and ethnicity as well as levels of education and cultural interests. Furthermore, interviewees differed according to the extent of their activism. Billy E. Jones, an African-American city official, never participated in gay organizations and movements. Even at the height of lesbian and gay activism as exemplified in the attendance of hundreds of thousands from all over the nation at the 1987 March on Washington, a majority of lesbians and gays throughout the nation either remained in the closet or stood on the sidelines during demonstrations. Billy E. Jones, for example, had progressed from one success to another professionally and in private life, rarely encountering incidents of homophobia and always dealing effectively with racism. He never joined any gay organization. Indeed, the most impelling experience of his life had little association with his sexual orientation but much with his military service. "In Vietnam," he recounted, "your exclusive concern was maintaining yourself. When you got back home, you began to put things into focus. I realized that America is hardly the land of opportunity. There is no genuine concern about people. It's about capitalism, about making money. Not what we can do for everybody, not about opening up things to everybody. A lot of blacks grow up with the realization this country is not there for us. There are no jobs. How do you maintain esteem if there is nothing for you to do?"

ORGANIZATIONAL PROBLEMS

Chafing under intense social pressures to conform, many gay activists, like other Americans of the Reagan-Bush "me" generation, reject organizational discipline. At ACT UP, Steve Quester points out, action guidelines presented at general meetings have been voted down as imposing too much structure. As a result, Steve declares, "Actions have been undertaken by individuals that are not discussed in advance by the organization." Thus, after being fined $9,000 for drilling a metal plate onto the entrance door at the North Carolina headquarters of Burroughs-Wellcome, the manufacturer of the AIDS drug AZT, a group of ACT UP members successfully requested reimbursement from ACT UP though they had provided the organization with no advance notice of their action. More blatantly adventurist was Scott Sensenig's painting of a slogan outside the residence of Cardinal O'Connor. Scott subsequently berated himself for his imprudence, muttering to himself, "I should have sought advice from people involved in previous actions at St. Patrick's [Cathedral]. I wanted to do something on my own," he explained. "I have always had trouble doing things with people. If I hadn't gotten caught, I wouldn't regret it so much. If I hadn't gotten beaten, I wouldn't think it was so stupid, a college prank." His action led to the fracas between ACT UP members and the police and the unconscionable beating of Chris Hennelly at the Midtown North precinct.

A concomitant to this rejection of group discipline is the frequent expression of resentment against leaders. "Society has made gays feel fucked up about themselves, insecure about their own power," declares Gerri Wells. "When I started organizing the Pink Panthers, some people stopped talking to me. 'How come you're on all the TV shows,' they demanded. 'How come you're so often in leadership positions?' 'Credit where credit is due,' is my answer. 'I was the one out there hustling.' We have to trust one another and be more supportive of our spokespeople."

Matt Foreman and Tracy Morgan expressed resentment against entrenched leaders who prefer to compromise with government officials with whom they have formed close relations rather than to employ direct action to force action on issues. Matt complained, for example, that those in charge of finances at the Community Center bargained with the city over the rate paid on the Center's mortgage instead of demanding cancellation of both the mortgage and municipal taxes in compensation for the massive services provided by the Center that would otherwise have to be underwritten by the city.

"When men long established in leadership positions meet with officials," Tracy declares, "I always wonder what is being traded off. I believe in educating people through public actions. I have begun to feel that everyone who wants to take action is being undermined by such meetings with officials." Juan Mendez, a Puerto Rican gay activist, shares Tracy's belief that "struggles are to be won in the streets and not in boardrooms of organizations. Locked out of power centers," he declares, "are women, advocates of IV-drug-users as well as people of color."

Jay Blotcher, one of the founders of Queer Nation, on the other hand, was "leery that people have become 'demo' crazy. Every time something happens they take to the streets and squander their energy and undergo pointless arrests. I think arrests should be reserved for important issues. On some occasions, people should say, 'No need to get arrested today. No need to drown out that person or to stay so long in blocking a street or to get into a fruitless impasse with the cops.' "

Some militant activists do not classify as "queers" gays who work "inside" and even criticize them for "selling out" to the establishment. In a television discussion with Dennis de Leon and Marjorie Hill, Bill Dobbs, an ACT UP activist, charged that when people in official positions say the right things and advocate the right policies it becomes more difficult for activists to oppose government. In response, Dennis rejected the implication that he had been coopted by government, pointing out that one-third of the caseload of the city commission on human rights, which he heads, was directed against the city.

Sensitive to the charge that as a state employee he undermines the activist movement, Bruce attributes the difference on strategy to a generational conflict. "A lot of people in ACT UP and Queer Nation," he noted, "are younger. They say to people of my age, 'What have you done during your lifetime? The problems are still here.' " These organizations, Bruce insists, "are important but they are not the whole community, and theirs is not the only way to do things. I think you also have to have people talking and networking with the people in power." In discussions with his critics, Bruce asks, "Have you any idea what I've been through at my job and the shit I've had to take to get justice for some of my claimants?" "Maybe as they grow older," he suggests, "they'll understand me a little better. They think that working from the inside means compromising. I have to compromise."

Luke expressed concern about a different kind of generational conflict within the Pink Panthers. "It seems that the only new people we can recruit into the Pink Panthers," Luke complains, "are in their late teens or early twenties and know nothing about Stonewall." According to Luke, these young people reject the nonviolent reactive policy originally adopted by the Panthers and press for aggressive preemptive action against potential gay bashers. Carrying self-empowerment to its limit, they insist, Luke says, that it is pointless to fight within the system. They believe, he asserts, that all gays should carry guns and "blow away anybody they suspect is a gay basher." (Although Gerri Wells considered Bruce's concern exaggerated, she warned, "If we were to practice violence without direct provocation, what would distinguish us from the gay bashers?")

SEXISM

Out of their particular experience, Tom Duane declares, many gay men have come to appreciate the importance of feminism. "The lesbian feminist movement," he says, "has brought us light years ahead." Nevertheless, he no longer believed that gay men were not threatening to women. "Gay men," he says, "can be sexist pigs. I am often appalled at our behavior." Among the women interviewees, Tracy Morgan expressed herself at greatest length and with the most passion on what she sees as a failure of middle-class white male activists to accept women as equals or to appreciate the significance of problems specific to lesbians and to other women in the general AIDS struggle. Before attending ACT UP meetings she had heard stories about how men in the organization did not trust women or respect women's opinions. At meetings of the Treatment and Data Committee, she recounts, she encountered "a room full of men from privileged backgrounds. When a woman made a comment," Tracy relates, "no one really listened. Everyone talked while a woman was speaking. Then a man would say the same thing, and everyone would say, 'Oh, he's right.' I get out of such environments. Why be turned into an Anita Hill?"

Disgusted at what she considered male ignorance of women's problems, Tracy concentrated her efforts primarily within the ACT UP women's caucus. She participated in demonstrations to pressure the Centers for Disease Control to broaden the definition of AIDS among women and to force the National Institutes of Health to include women in AIDS clinical tests. In these actions, she declared, she found herself in conflict with the original founders of ACT UP. "No one in Treatment and Data would speak to me," she declares.

LESBIAN SEPARATISM

Less critical than the conflict over women's issues but still a threat to gay community unity is the antimale sentiment among some lesbians. "I have never known gay men who hated women as a class," Marsha S., for many years an active member of PFLAG, declared, "but it is not uncommon among lesbians to hate all men, whereas many straight women say they like the company of gay men." According to psychologist Shelley Neiderbach, women who see men as universally untrustworthy exhibit an adolescent view of the world. "A part of the lesbian separatist movement insists," she pointed out, "that no males over the age of seven be permitted at their meetings. What is a lesbian to do if her son is eight years old? Men have the power and men oppress," she admits, "but we're in the world with men, gay and straight. We can't pretend they don't exist."

"There are women who really need women's communities," notes Joyce Hunter, a divorcée and a lesbian mother, a survivor of incest as an adolescent. "They need space and time to heal and for personal growth." On the other hand, she notes that since the AIDS epidemic a lot of the lesbians who she knew as separatists were no longer separatists.

Attitudes of lesbians toward gay men, say Gerri Wells and Rita, depend in part upon the extent of their contact with gay men. While the only woman employee in a male movie theater, Gerri came to understand that gay men had more sexual freedom than lesbians, and she learned from them to enjoy life more. "I knew," she declares, "that if we could create a family of gay men and lesbians it would be better for all."

"It would be understandable," declares Rita, "if I shared the hostility to men of lesbian separatists in view of my antagonistic relationship with my father. I understand gay men," she declares, "and enjoy their company. With them I feel no threat of sexual attraction—except that I have to listen to their penis stories and exclamations at handsome men."

RACIAL AND ETHNIC SEPARATISM

"When the gay rights bill was being discussed," recounted Bruce, "I heard opponents argue that if the bill passed the next thing would be quotas for gays on the job. I wondered, 'Is that what they're afraid of? Look at the city council reapportionment program aimed at seeing to it that each ethnic group has a certain number of seats. How many New Yorks are we going to have?"

Bruce was posing an issue that some Americans see as threatening the integrity of the nation: balkanization through racial and ethnic and other separatist movements. In its continuing struggles for full civil rights and for more vigorous measures against the AIDS epidemic, the effectiveness of the gay community would be gravely threatened if racial, religious, and ethnic conflicts disrupted the solidarity that has been developing since Stonewall. "I thought that my being a Jew and being black would make no difference in the gay community," recounted Joyce Hunter. "I had a rude awakening. I found that at the Fire House they were not supportive of lesbian mothers. I also found some of them to be racist."

Although, as Joyce's remarks attest, the racial and ethnic tensions straining the national social fabric are not absent from the gay community, none of the white activists interviewed for this book displayed a hint of prejudice toward African Americans. Without exception they expressed resolute solidarity with the African-American struggle for full citizenship, a struggle that they all considered critical for the future of the nation. Ginny Apuzzo recalled how as executive director of the National Gay Task Force in the early 1980s, after a discussion with the head of the National Coalition of Black Gay Men, she recognized the necessity of dealing with the struggles of people of color at every speaking engagement.

Luke's bigoted father refused to allow him to play with Catholic neighbors and expressed contempt for blacks and Jews. Luke's older brother, an unabashed neo-Nazi, kept a picture of Hitler and a Nazi flag hidden under his bed. He said Hitler should have finished the job with the Jews. After service in Vietnam, however, he completely changed his attitudes and never again spoke against Jews, blacks, or homosexuals. Uncomfortable as a gay in this intolerant environment, Luke sympathized with all the groups his brother and father despised.

Liz Garro, who experienced an unhappy childhood, recalls her years at a multiracial public high school as among the happiest in her life. When she invited Gloria, a black classmate, home, however, her mother practically "shooed" the young woman out and then gave Liz a beating, shouting, "How dare you bring her into this house!" On the other hand, visiting Gloria's home, Liz was amazed to find that no one there was ever beaten. Gloria's mother offered Liz a glass of milk and cookies and even smiled. "This let me know," Liz recalls, "that there was another kind of world."

Fred Goldhaber initially shared his parents' suspicions of blacks. When he began teaching at an inner-city high school, he recalls, "I had fears from what I saw on TV, and the first year and a half I treated the black kids badly. I couldn't put my hand on a shoulder. The kids were patient with me, as warm and honest as I could ever hope for. After reading their compositions and talking to them, I lost my prejudice and felt stupid." He warned his father never to use the word "nigger" in front of him again. He himself was among the first members of the gay Black and White Together organization. He participated in its consciousness-raising programs.

Some white activists expressed appreciation of the harsher repression suffered by people of color. Thus at a demonstration protesting the musical *Miss Saigon,* for example, Steve Quester noted that the police singled out people of color and "beat the shit out of them."

A number of the white, Latino and Asian interviewees, however, were troubled by an intensifying go-it-alone separatism among some blacks. Some white activists attributed this phenomenon to an intensifying frustration among African Americans with the persistence of racism in the nation three decades after the civil rights movement. Tracy Morgan remarked that government agencies found little difficulty in reaching accommodations with white middle-class gay PWAs, but expressed in action or inaction the attitude, "Who needs blacks in this society?" "Our contention [as white lesbian activists]," she declared, "is that women of color are always at the bottom of the barrel in crises." She discovered, however, that some black women activists reject as culturally uncongenial or impracticable tactics that white lesbian activists employ in AIDS struggles. At a 1991 demonstration in Washington, black women, Tracy related, screamed, "Racists, racists!" The problem of racial division within the gay community, she asserts, is exacerbated by white gays who have never collaborated with blacks.

At initial meetings of Queer Nation, according to Jay Blotcher, blacks accused the group of racism. "As persons of color," some declared, "we don't feel comfortable. There aren't enough people of color here." "We said," Jay related, " 'Why don't you bring your friends and every other person of color you know? If you come in, other people will follow. We white middle-class gay men need your input.' " "No," blacks retorted, "judging by who you have here, there's obviously a racist bias." "Under such circumstances," Jay notes, "whites become apologetic, and open discussion becomes difficult."

To such remarks black gay activist Keith Cylar offered a persuasive rejoinder. "Few of us still go to ACT UP meetings," he declared, "frustrated by the overwhelming racism. There were constant fights to get things translated into Spanish and to put people-of-color issues on the agenda as priorities." Blacks, he notes, were not involved in planning demonstrations in opposition to the appointment of Woodrow Myres as city health commissioner (because of Myres's stance on some AIDS issues). Myres, a black man, the black activists pointed out, had been nominated by a search committee and appointed by a black mayor. According to Keith, people of color should have been allowed an opportunity to explain gay concerns to the people who nominated Myres before any protest action was undertaken. The whites, according to Keith, simply dismissed this argument. "That's too damn bad," they said. "We're right." "Maybe," Keith declares, "we could have changed things, maybe not. Instead, we had a group of white gay men publicly attacking a black person nominated by other blacks. That attack was perceived as an insult and as arrogance on the part of white gay men. Whites are not respectful of our needs. They say that they're in control of this show, and they're going to do what they need to do to protect their interests."

"One reason," Keith says, "there is no longer an ACT UP black caucus is that people got tired of such struggles. I don't think there will ever be a space in ACT UP for people of color to get things done that they need done. We had to create another forum in which people of color feel they can participate comfortably and effectively." Keith directed similar criticism at the leadership of GMHC. "They come in and offer a time line," he says, "and they want things to happen their way. They have lots of documents, everything printed, and insist theirs is the way things should go. People of color say we want to discuss the strategy, we want to feel that we're part of planning, that we are empowered. Ours is a different approach. The outcome may be the same. There's a distinct clash when you bring the two cultures together."

Juan Mendez, a Puerto Rican activist, concurred with Keith's observations. "All gay organizations," Juan declared, "must recognize that gays and lesbians are not only white and middle class, and this recognition must be reflected in their programs and their language. There has to be a level of trust, and trust has to be demonstrated in a real share of voice and power. When people create carbon copies of white organizations to deal with the AIDS problem among peoples of color, the result is a bureaucratic approach. People are doing work in the South Bronx among people of color without large amounts of money, conducting education, distributing food, and running support groups."

On the other hand, Keith notes, "there are situations where we are being forced to come together. We had an interracial meeting at [Councilman] Tom Duane's office on Enoch Williams [a black city councilman accused of homophobia]. 'For the first time,' people of color said, 'we are meeting together. We don't want you to do anything until we have had a meeting of our own to discuss the problem and to reach an agreement on action. We understand your urgency, but we are going to shape our own response.' We asked for another meeting to present what we decided and to discuss a strategy. The result was that a joint press conference was arranged to call for Williams's resignation."

Tensions between blacks and whites do not represent the only threats to community solidarity. Dennis de Leon was concerned at the influence of black-white separatism upon other communities. A segment of the Puerto Rican population, he noted, was complaining that Hispanic groups arriving in later immigrations were impinging upon some of their prerogatives. "Such separatist tendencies," he asserted, "are dangerous. They pit friend against friend."

"Whenever there are debates about race," noted Juan Mendez, "it's always black or white, rarely Hispanic." Guillermo Vasquez noted that in the struggle for more equitable apportionment of voting districts, opposition to the redistricting came from the African-American community, who thought the Latinos were taking away power from them. Latinos, Juan Mendez pointed out, have problems within their own community, arising in some cases from their having different countries of origin. Among Latinos, Indians suffer special oppression from whites. There is prejudice against people whose skin color is "too dark." "No one," he warns, "should expect to come out the winner from this kind of antipathy."

ANTI-SEMITISM, ANOTHER THREAT TO GAY AND LESBIAN UNITY

Black anti-Semitism was denounced in a July 20, 1992, *New York Times* Op-Ed essay entitled "Black Demagogues and Pseudo-Scholars" by Henry Louis Gates, Jr., chairman of the Afro-American Studies Department at Harvard. After citing a recent survey showing "not only that blacks are twice as likely as whites to hold anti-Semitic views but . . . that it is among the younger and more educated blacks that anti-Semitism is most pronounced," Gates quoted Princeton Professor Cornel West's observation that "attention to black anti-Semitism is crucial . . . in no small part because the moral credibility of our struggle against racism hangs in the balance."

Commenting on Gates's statement, Lance Ringel remarked, "Here is a group [the Jewish community] that historically has been most helpful and sympathetic [to the black community]. To utilize them to advance your own separatist agenda and to attack a people also at risk, who for historical reasons respond almost hysterically, is self-defeating. If you can succeed in demonizing the Jewish people, you don't have to confront the actual dangerous elements. Pat Robertson is not unhappy about such a tendency among blacks."

"I'm scared of black anti-Semitism and homophobia," remarked Chris Hennelly. He was dismayed at a decision taken by Queer Nation to leave it to the black community to protest anti-Semitic remarks by City University Professor Leonard Jeffries.

Commenting on the anxiety of white staffers like Fred Goldhaber at the hostility to whites and openly expressed anti-Semitism of a people-of-color caucus at the Hetrick Martin Institute, Juan Mendez remarked, "I can understand the distrust and resistance to having anyone not of color speak for them, but I have to look far ahead . . . [The question was never posed whether black staffers could work with white clients.] But we must demand not just lip service but commitment from our so-called leaders to fight for and with everyone."

Marjorie Hill, director of the Mayor's Committee on Lesbian and Gay Affairs, called for action "upon issues of diversity-inclusion in an integrated and effective way. We're taught to be with people who are like us. If we [gays] address public safety and bias attacks as they effect women, people of color, Jews—then we will have much more potential for success than if we just call attention to attacks on our own community."

One interviewee, Martha, an African American with whom I initially established a warm personal relationship, abruptly expressed blatant anti-Semitism during an interview.

Martha posed strict conditions for her interview, insisting upon the right to bring it to an end at any point. As the hours passed, however, Martha began to volunteer intimate details of her life, including incidents of sexual molestation as a child. Walking me to the subway station, she shook my hand and exclaimed, "I have found a new friend."

During the following weeks, apparently assuming we were good friends, Martha confided her sorrow at her father's approaching death from cancer.

At the end of a second interview conducted over the telephone after her father's funeral, Martha reported that in his will her father had listed as his sole heir the wife he had married only a year earlier, thereby depriving Martha, her sister, and her niece of any inheritance. "She's Jewish," Martha declared, "and we're going to see whether what people say of Jews is true." When I demurred at her wholesale stereotypical judgment, she continued, "You Jews think only of your own suffering. What has happened in South Africa has been as bad as your Holocaust." In the face of this outburst, it would have served no purpose to point out that wanton murder of any people is horrendous. Nevertheless, comparison of the barbarous shooting of the seventy-nine black youths in Sharpsville—which Martha adduced as an example of a horror equal to that of the Holocaust—to the annihilation of a million and a half Jewish children through exhaustion from forced labor, starvation, gassing, barbarous "medical" experiments, and even burning alive in ovens is not only pointless but obscene. In a comment appended to the transcript I mailed her following this telephoned interview, I noted that if Martha was indeed being victimized by her stepmother in her father's revised will, such an injustice could have been committed by women of any ethnic, racial or religious background.

Weeks later I received a letter in which Martha declared, "Hopefully you have learned from these many hours of labor that trust is not automatic in the lesbian and gay community and even harder to come by in the black community. You appear with little or no credentials and expect a person's whole life in return for a project that you will eventually reap the benefits from . . . I must bow to the fact that you are a white Jewish Man and everything you heard in your interviews will be utilized, interpreted and prioritized in a form that corresponds to your needs."

In reply, I made no mention of her earlier anti-Semitic remark, declaring: "Except in the case of a tiny percentage of the nearly fifty people I have interviewed so far, I found that within an hour or so I convinced interviewees of my determination to represent them honestly and honorably to the limits of my ability. . . . I consider myself primarily as a recorder and think of my book as a compilation of biographical accounts that should be told not only to provide a historical record of struggles but also to provide role models for young people in the community."

To demonstrate my credentials, I recounted some pertinent events of my life—my childhood in a Ku Klux Klan town, my leadership at the age of twenty-two of an antisegregation struggle in a large World War II War Department agency and my subsequent participation in struggles at the side of W.E.B. Du Bois and Paul Robeson.

I asked Martha to note corrections, additions, and comments on the transcripts of her two interviews so that I could be confident of expressing her views precisely and fully. "I may not be the ideal person to write this book," I remarked, "but no one else to my knowledge is writing a book like it."

Six weeks later, having received no reply from Martha, I sent a second letter. "It seems clear," I wrote, "that after our initial meeting your attitude toward me and the book underwent a transformation. You expressed suspicion of me as a man, as a white and, in particular, as a Jew and even implied that you resented the possibility of my profiting from my effort. If you feel that you are being exploited, your life experience should not and will not be included in the book.

"What you now have to determine," I went on to say, "is whether inclusion of your experiences will produce a book closer to what you would write if you were the author. . . . If some time in the next weeks, you reach such a conclusion and send me the corrected transcripts as evidence of your trust, we may return to what seemed to be the understanding we had at the end of the first interview."

Martha never replied to this letter.

"Everyone is used to seeing only their own pain," Dennis de Leon declared in a general comment about divisive prejudice. "It's a big part of my mission [as Commissioner of Human Rights] to get people to see the links between their exclusion and someone else's." In his attempts at developing unified action on issues of civil rights, Dennis says he has encountered greatest resistance among African-American and women's groups. On the other hand, in the case of a black student who charged that she had been raped and sodomized by white athletes at St. John's University, Dennis succeeded in building a coalition of African-American and women's groups but could not involve other groups. He did succeed, however, in uniting representatives of the Jewish, women's, and black communities with the gay community in demanding the passage of a state civil rights bill that included the gay community as well as the other communities. "But that was difficult to accomplish," he remarks.

THE ISSUE OF EUROCENTRISM, A FURTHER THREAT TO GAY AND LESBIAN UNITY

The campaign mounted in certain circles in recent years against what is called Eurocentrism, a campaign that received a particular impetus during the 1992 Columbus quincentennial, has provided an intellectual rationale for a potential balkanization of the United States. Anti-Eurocentrists, especially the black nationalists among them, denigrate the contributions to world civilization of the ancient Greeks and concomitantly exalt the contributions of the ancient Egyptians. In such movements, dogmatism often precludes scholarly investigation and renders open-minded discussion difficult.

Admitting that "you always take note, of course, of the extremes," Lance Ringel, state assistant commissioner for human rights, pointed to the attack of a black leader on what he called "the Eurocentric tendency among young people in the black community to disrespect their elders." "Eurocentrism," Lance commented, "has become a term to characterize anything bad," even as within the gay community "the response to anything that someone doesn't like is 'They're acting straight.' "

An inadvertent introduction of a topic related to Eurocentrism and to African-American nationalism led to the elimination from this book of an interview with

Arnold (the pseudonym for an African American in his mid-thirties, a staffer at a leading gay organization). Upon my using the term "Black Africa" during the interview, Arnold jumped up, pointed to the door and shouted, "There is only one Africa! Get out of my apartment!" Loath to abandon an interview already in its third hour and eager to continue an exploration of Arnold's views, I succeeded in appeasing him, not, however, without having to submit to the admonition, "You should have investigated what African Americans are thinking before coming here."

Although an ancient historian by profession, I did not attempt to respond to Arnold's contention that "there is only one Africa, and the term Black Africa is merely an invention of European imperialists." Nor did I volunteer facts about ancient Egyptian history that run counter to Arnold's preconceptions. (Several months later, upon my recounting the exchange with Arnold, a Ghanaian physician, son of a distinguished political figure in his native country, laughed and declared, "We don't even consider the North African countries to be part of Africa.") Arnold recounted that older-generation relatives of his in New Orleans took pride in their light complexions and looked down upon darker-skinned blacks. An hour later, in an exemplification of the alienation with which many African Americans contend, after proclaiming, "I'm proud of all the strains in my background, African, Native American . . . " Arnold hesitated, uncertain how to deal with another strain obvious from his light complexion.

At the conclusion of the interview, Arnold listened patiently to my account of my friendship with Paul Robeson and the renowned black historian W.E.B. Du Bois and then to my response as a former Classics professor to the allegation of an overemphasis of the Greek contributions to world civilization. Articulate and precise in speech, Arnold could only respond lamely to my observation that our discussion over several hours had been conducted in a language that embodies the multimillennial history, traditions and culture of Europe, a language Germanic in structure with a vocabulary of 69 percent Latin and 9 percent Greek origin, a language universally adopted (especially in Africa) as a lingua franca. More specifically, the terms and concepts of political debate, I pointed out, not only between the two of us but, indeed, throughout the contemporary world, originated in Greece and Rome and not in Egypt or in Africa generally.

Within weeks I received a letter from Arnold requesting that I not include his interview in this book. He did not have time, he declared, to make essential additions to round out his story.

Any account of Arnold's attitudes would be incomplete and unfair without any note of his categorical rejection of anti-Semitism. He insisted that he never heard an anti-Semitic remark among his African American friends. He condemned unequivocally the 1991 lynching in the Crown Heights section of Brooklyn of an Australian Jew by a gang of young blacks who shouted "Kill the Jews!" and "Heil Hitler!" He distanced himself emphatically from openly anti-Semitic African Americans like City College professor Leonard Jeffries, who had recently accepted an invitation to attend a conference of white racist "scholars" who pretend that the Holocaust was a mere invention. In fact, along with his letter requesting the elimination of his interview from this book, Arnold sent a poem he had written associating the horrors of the slave trade with those of the Holocaust.

Among the Chinese interviewees, Li (an interviewee eliminated from this book because he failed to return a signed release form) displayed the anti-European Centrism to be found among some Asians. In our interview, he exhibited more interest in exposing the interviewer's possible violation of "politically correct" separatist conceptions than in revealing details about his own life.

> *In response to Li's prodding for my political insufficiencies, I related how upon a visit to a dim sum restaurant in Chinatown I refused a waitress's offer of coffee, declaring, "I don't come to Chinatown to drink coffee." The waitress asked what I meant. "When I come to Chinatown," I replied, "I want to drink the traditional Chinese drink." The waitress translated the response to the other workers in the restaurant. Although assured that the staff smiled in approval at my response, Li denounced my remark as racist. "Didn't you understand," he demanded, "that you were* paying *for a bit of Chinese culture? Didn't you recognize that times have changed and people now drink coffee or even coca-cola with Chinese food?" Nor was Li appeased when I assured him that following this incident I developed a warm relationship with the restaurant staff. Indeed, if I missed a Saturday at the restaurant, they inquired where I had been and always offered me a seat immediately when there was a waiting line. "I suppose you find them especially polite, too," Li challenged. He was dubious of my response: "Not always." He did, however, find acceptable my attendance at performances of Chinese operas.*
>
> *Of his studies at Cooper Union, Li remarked sarcastically, "Of course, they filled us with the standard diet of Western art." In response, I noted that not all Asians shared his derogation of Western cultural achievements. Thousands of Asians, I pointed out, were flocking to American and European conservatories and subsequently joining orchestras or touring the world as concert artists. "You're talking about classical music?" Li scoffed.*

None of the other Asian interviewees—Charles Ching, Scott Hirose, June Chan, or David Eng—shared Li's hostility to European culture or his suspicion of gays and lesbians of other racial or ethnic origins. While maintaining pride in her Chinese heritage, June Chan did not share Li's disdain for Western cultural achievements. At college, in addition to courses in her science major she enrolled for pleasure and personal enrichment in courses in Western literature. The Eurocentric issue appeared to be of little concern to David Eng. He recounted the satisfaction he experienced upon being accepted as a student at the Parsons Institute, a school of design devoted primarily to the transmission of an aspect of European civilization. On the other hand, he felt alienated from his Chinese heritage.

PROGNOSTICATIONS

ACT UP activist and Pink Panther Steve Machon was hopeful of a decline in the rate of homophobic violence because more and more gays were emerging from the closet. "The stereotype that faggots are limp-wristed and can't fight to protect themselves and what they're about," he contended, "is being broken down." He noted that gays had won cases in court and that laws were being enacted against discrimination. "Homophobes know," he pointed out, "that we will prosecute and sue the hell out of them, and hostile public officials have learned that we will demonstrate at their homes. I'm talking power."

Assistant State Commissioner for Human Rights Lance Ringel, however, worried that gays were falling into a victim mentality, seeing enemies and prejudice where they did not exist. "We must distinguish," he declared, "between bureaucratic inertia and outright homophobia. To assume homophobia behind every action of nongays is a self-fulfilling prophecy." The majority of Middle America, Lance was convinced, were indifferent to issues affecting the gay community. "In the last twenty years," Lance noted, "we have had a community under siege, confronting an uncaring attitude about AIDS in the general population. But more people have become aware of gay people. In the midst of a backlash against gay activism, four states have passed gay civil rights bills. California is about to pass a bill. In upstate New York Syracuse passed a bill at first reading. It's hard to see progress," he declares, "when you're in the middle of the struggle."

"The situation with homophobic violence," concurred Gerri Wells, "has to get better. It can't get worse. If I didn't believe it's going to get better, then why all this work, time and energy?"

Tom Duane offered the perspective of an elected gay officeholder. The election of an increasing number of gays to office throughout the country, he believed would result in an improvement of the status of the community. "My being on the city council," Tom declares, "means we are no longer excluded. When a lesbian or gay wants access to the council, I'm there." His very presence, he asserts, guarantees that gay issues will be posed and that straight council members will display greater sensitivity to gay issues or at least mute their expressions of homophobia. Tom would urge gays and lesbians throughout the country to seek public office. "You can make a difference," he declares. The election of Harvey Milk as a city supervisor in San Francisco, he noted, reverberated in New York. To those who express fear of confronting homophobia in political life, Tom declares, "You meet homophobia in every area of your life. You won't find more in politics. To be elected, you must have a unified gay community behind you and you must take a broad stance on issues. You cannot be effective by being involved merely in lesbian and gay issues."

Dennis de Leon had a generally hopeful long-range vision for the gay community. Many mainstream companies, Dennis noted, had developed an equal-employment infrastructure and were ready to implement antibias regulations and to facilitate access for gays and lesbians. In employment statistics, Dennis points out, blacks, Latinos, women, Asians, all are counted, and attempts can be made to increase their proportionate numbers. Dennis was convinced that problems of gays would not be understood until they, too, were counted in censuses. Only when their numbers are known, he believed, would there be an appreciation of the importance of integrating gays and lesbians at the highest levels of companies and government.

Other interviewees expressed less optimistic views of the future.

"Until government makes antigay violence odious," declared Bruce of the Crime Victims Board, "homophobes are going to have a green light. As long as there is no moral imprimatur against it by government and by the churches, it's going to continue."

AVP executive director Matt Foreman drew no hope from the general atmosphere within American society. "I have no doubt," he declared, "that gay kids continue to be beaten up just as frequently in high school, and gay people are being beaten up all over the city. I see a higher level of verbal harassment on the street every day." Nevertheless, Matt saw indications of a possible long-range change. He expected a positive impact from the increased police presence on New York City streets and from Pink Panther patrols as well as from the increasing sensitivity to homophobic violence as a result of the increasing dissemination of information about the gay community. "Some of the myths," he noted, "are gradually fading away."

Naomi Lichtenstein, who dealt more directly with AVP clients than Matt Foreman, was less sanguine about the future. "We are an extremely violent culture," she declared, "and no one is doing anything about that. Since people in authority are not standing up against homophobic violence, there is a tremendous increase throughout the country." Although encouraged by the formation of AVPs throughout the country and by the building of coalitions with other antiviolence movements, Naomi insisted that since passing her fortieth birthday she had become more pessimistic. "I won't see the end of gay bashing in my lifetime," she insists. For a decrease in violence, a fundamental social change, she asserted, was required. "This country is getting worse."

Noting that, infected with HIV, he lives day to day, Keith Cylar nevertheless maintained cautious optimism about the future. "I think," he declared, "we're headed for some real fights. The social and economic system is going to have to address some issues unaddressed over the last twelve years. There has to be a change in the distribution of wealth and resources or there will be a blowup. It will be a very painful process. People are not going to give up power or their accustomed way of life. The environment is going to be critical issue. There will be decisions as to who lives and who dies. A lot of people of color throughout the world are going to die."

A TRANSFORMATION IN THE COMMUNITY

By the early 1990s, many dedicated activists were beginning to express weariness and despair. "For more than three years I went to a meeting every day," Juan Mendez exclaimed, "working during the day. I was averaging five hours of sleep a night. There came a point when I had to stop for my own sake to remain effective." "First and foremost," declared Steve Quester, "I am an AIDS activist, and most of my friends are infected. I don't see what victories ACT UP can win that are going to keep the great majority of my friends from dying before the year 2000. Any progress the gay and lesbian movement makes is not really very comforting to me."

"There's a lot of despair in the community, and I worry that we have forgotten how to fight and to take care of ourselves," said Scott Hirose. "There's been a disintegration in the movement. People have decided that they can learn to live with the epidemic."

Rita had no hope of a solution to the critical problems of the community within her lifetime. "There have been some positive developments in regard to AIDS," she admitted, "but AIDS is just an additional problem for communities of color above the problems of homelessness, poverty, unemployment, drug addition . . . all the evils." To resolve these problems, she was convinced, a radical change was required, a revolution. "The prognosis," she concluded, "is not a good one."

Lance Ringel expressed an equivocal view of the impact of AIDS activism on the gay community. "The AIDS crisis," Lance declares, "has brought both greater unity and increasing splintering within the gay community." Lesbians, he points out, "as a group came through for gay men. That kinship might not otherwise have developed. I think, on the other hand, that the crisis has exacerbated a gap between my generation and the succeeding one. A lot of the anger and frustration that we all feel gets directed into a strong impulse to separate from the uncaring majority community and to go it alone. We're going to have to get through this as part of a larger society."

Ginny Apuzzo shudders when she hears people say that the AIDS crisis has had its positive aspects. "Yes," Ginny admits, "we are maturing, we are increasing our experience, demonstrating an extraordinary resilience that will be tested every step of the way, but," she exclaims, "at what cost all this has come about!"

Thus at the time the first interviews for this book were conducted, with the rapid spread of the HIV epidemic outside the gay community and with the recognition that no cure could be anticipated for many years, the passionate activism of the decade began to flag, the unity of the many disparate groups within the broad anti-AIDS coalition weakened, and all the differences within the community—of race, ethnicity, age, gender, class, and ideology—became ever more exposed.

As evidence of the fragility of the variegated coalition within the community, Scott Hirose adduced the "*Miss Saigon* incident" in December 1990. At a meeting of GAPIMINY (Gay Asian and Pacific Islander Men of New York), a member noted that the Lambda Legal Defense and Education Fund, an agency defending gay civil rights, was preparing to do a fund-raiser with a theater party at *Miss Saigon,* a play with racist and sexist overtones. GAPIMINY protested both to Lambda and to the Lesbian and Gay Community Center, which had also planned a similar fund-raising event. The Center cancelled its fund-raiser, but the governing board of Lambda, complaining that it would lose a sizable sum of money, refused to drop its theater party. GAPIMINY mobilized a multiracial coalition to set up a picket line the night of the Lambda function. Aware of NYPD hostility to ACT UP, Lambda advised the police to be prepared for an ACT UP demonstration, and the picketers found a powerful police presence at the theater. Violence erupted, and several demonstrators were injured by the police.

In a blatant rejection of community unity, a major lesbian and gay civil rights organization appealed to the police for action against a multiracial gay protest.

Alarmed at a flagging of energy and threats to unity among lesbian and gay activists, Ginny Apuzzo warned, "If we give up the struggle, all of the blacks, the Asians, the older people, the younger people . . . what will happen to them?" Jay Blotcher agreed. "I have always believed that we are everyone," he declared, "we are everywhere, as the song goes. If we are everyone and everywhere, then this struggle will not end until everyone, everywhere is free to be who they are. At the March on Washington I said, 'For as long as ignorance can bully and as long as justice is frail, we have not made our full contribution.' "

Tom Duane concurred that lesbians and gays have a particular contribution to make. They can assist, he suggested, in winning recognition of nontraditional family relations and in providing an example in the way gays interact with each other. "Gays and lesbians in their very existence," Tom was convinced, "pose a threat to straight white male domination of the world. If we could turn things around," Tom insists, "we could help straight white men to make a better world for everybody."

"I think that part of what being gay is about is being able to embrace multiple identities," declared a staffer at APICHA (Asian and Pacific Islander Coalition on HIV/AIDS), probing for a new and comprehensive definition of the gay community. "For me," he asserted, "being gay means accepting all of me, all the identities, all the political views—my total life experience. When the community is engaged solely in fighting discrimination, homophobia, and heterosexism and in conducting the struggle against AIDS, we pathologize our identity. It becomes something negative, a source of pain. We must think instead of our positive contribution to the world. Gayness does not refer merely to our having same-sex relationships. There's something qualitatively different about how we see the world." But this APICHA staffer had difficulty defining that "difference." "We don't give ourselves a chance to center ourselves as a people," he admitted, "to figure out what it is that we do bring to the human experience, and I don't have the answer as to what it is." Indeed, he expanded the boundaries of "his community" to preclude a definition. "Who I choose for my community," he declared, "has less to do with whether they are lesbian or gay. I am much more interested in people who have a vision of the world, whatever their sexual orientation, a vision that includes lesbian and gay people along with political prisoners, people with AIDS, people of all races, older people, and so on."

This hope for a grand coalition comprehending both gays and straights seems all the more illusory when one considers that at least half of the people interviewed for this book in the early years of the 1990s had by 1996 dropped out of all gay and lesbian activity. One had died. Two were dying of AIDS. The others had left either because of burnout or disillusionment.

A Native American gay man whose interview is not included in this book was resolute in his rejection of any such coalition as advocated by the API-CHA staffer. "I don't see myself as part of the perspective of the gay community," he declared. "It hasn't embraced what motivates me to do what I do and that is the abolition of the political relationship that currently exists between the federal government and the sovereign Indian tribes of this hemisphere. The gay leadership does not understand what I am about. The general community is just concerned with comfort, it just wants to be part of America."

Tracy Morgan was equally adamant about distancing herself from lesbian-gay activism. "Looking backwards," Tracy declared, "I find the generation I came up and out with is in so many ways unrecognizable. What brought us together subsequently tore us apart. People whom I cried with at so many wakes, with whom I stood for hours at Xerox machines or collating teach-in packets, now scarcely say hello. As for me, I count myself among the 'lesbian disappeared.' With the decline of our movement, our identity lost shape, and my lesbianism no longer felt like an act of resistance. By 1993, like a number of other prominent lesbian activists, I was in a love relationship with a man."

Don Lemke, a Lutheran pastor and a continuing member of various activist organizations, and Scott Hirose, a Japanese-American activist, did not consider their sexuality to be central to their lives, nor were they convinced that one could define a gay culture or a gay community. "Being gay," declared Don Lemke, "does not represent my totality. I am a man of faith, a Lutheran, a Norwegian and a German, a Midwesterner, a New Yorker, a six on the Kinsey scale." "You can be in a business suit working on Wall Street one day and the next day on Fire Island having a gay party," agreed Scott Hirose. "Our identities are fluid and multiple," he explains. "People may see me as an Asian man, but my identity is much more complex. Depending upon the setting, I reveal, more or less comfortably, different aspects of myself. Our sexuality or homophobia are not enough to make us a community,"

Scott insists. "Everyone who is gay deals with multiple existences. We all deal with our identities, and these are all different. Each of us creates a space where we think we're safe. If there is a gay community," he declares, "it's an artificial construct."

Some issues represented as community issues, Scott notes, like those of gays in the military and of domestic partnership, he points out, actually concern only a segment of the community. "Someone like me," he contends, "really has no choice as to what the next issue will be. Issues are thrust upon us by individuals, and we all are expected to take a stand." On the other hand, Scott finds a common denominator in common problems "on a very introspective level. We've all had to undergo," he notes, "difficult journeys in coming out." (In fact, as is clear from the accounts of interviewees like Matt Foreman, Tom von Foerster, Marjorie Hill, and Billy Jones, a significant percentage of lesbians and gays undergo nearly problem-free coming-out experiences.)

With new questions about aims and identity being posed in the evolving struggle, some former activists were beginning to adopt as their primary goal acceptance within the general society. "Many gays," admitted Dennis de Leon, "say that they want the question of their identity to become irrelevant. I, too, look forward to a time when the question of sexual orientation will not even be posed, but today," he countered, "you can't escape the fact that you're gay. Being gay means, for example, that you have different family arrangements—the domestic partnership issue."

Reflecting a questioning, not despair, Scott does not foresee a disappearance of gay activism, but he declares, "We need something to replace ACT UP, something that rouses energy and passion." Indeed, since before Stonewall the gay community has showed a capacity to adapt to changing circumstances and displayed courage, vigor, and imagination in varied struggles toward full citizenship. These qualities, as the accounts in this book demonstrate, have not been lost.

In an Op-Ed statement appearing in the New York Times *on May 16, 1993, two years after being interviewed for this book, Dennis de Leon disclosed that since 1986 he had known that he was HIV-positive. The next day he expressed to a* New York Times *reporter his conviction that his announcement of his HIV status would "allow him [as New York City Human Rights Commissioner] to more forcefully speak out and write on the subject of AIDS-related bias. The more of us that do it," he added, "the easier it gets for somebody who is living in terror of being exposed. This is a statement that you don't need to chalk off your life, that you can keep working, that there are more of us around . . . that we're going to fight efforts to exclude us. People should know: If you don't treat us with respect, we intend to fight back."*

Suggestions for Further Reading

Compiled by G. Nick Street

Berubé, Allan. *Coming Out under Fire: The History of Gay Men and Women in World War II.* New York: Free Press, 1990.

Blasius, Mark, and Shane Phelan. *We Are Everywhere: A Historical Sourcebook in Gay and Lesbian Politics.* New York: Routledge, 1995.

Boswell, John. *Christianity, Social Tolerance, and Homosexuality.* Chicago: University of Chicago Press, 1980.

Browning, Frank. *The Culture of Desire: Paradox and Perversity in Gay Lives Today.* New York: Crown, 1993.

D'Emilio, John. *Sexual Politics, Sexual Communities: The Making of a Homosexual Minority in the United States.* Chicago: University of Chicago Press, 1984.

______. *Making Trouble: Essays on Gay History, Politics, and the University.* New York: Routledge, 1992.

Doty, Alexander. *Making Things Perfectly Queer.* Minneapolis: University of Minnesota Press, 1993.

Foucault, Michel. *The History of Sexuality.* Vol. I, *An Introduction.* New York: Vintage Books, 1978.

Greenberg, David. *The Construction of Homosexuality.* Chicago: University of Chicago Press, 1988.

Gross, Larry. *Contested Closets: The Politics and Ethics of Outing.* Minneapolis: University of Minnesota Press, 1993.

Harry, Joseph. *Gay Children Grow Up: Gender Culture and Gender Deviance.* New York: Praeger, 1982.

Herdt, Gilbert. *Gay Culture in America: Essays from the Field.* Boston: Beacon Press, 1992.

Hertzog, Mark. *The Lavender Vote: Gay Men and Bisexuals in American Electoral Politics.* New York: New York University Press, 1996.

Kaufman, Gershen, and Lev Raphael. *Coming Out of Shame: Transforming Gay and Lesbian Lives.* New York: Doubleday, 1996.

Kayal, Philip. *Bearing Witness: Gay Men's Health Crisis and the Politics of AIDS.* Boulder, Colo.: Westview Press, 1993.

Leyland, Winston. *Gay Roots.* Vol. 1, *Twenty Years of Sunshine: An Anthology of Gay History, Sex, Politics, and Culture.* San Francisco: Gay Sunshine Press, 1991.

———. *Gay Roots.* Vol. 2, *An Anthology of Gay History, Sex, Politics, and Culture.* San Francisco: Gay Sunshine Press, 1993.

Likosky, Stephan. *Coming Out: An Anthology of International Gay and Lesbian Writings.* New York: Pantheon Books, 1992.

McNaught, Brian. *On Being Gay.* New York: St. Martin's Press, 1988.

Mohr, Richard. *Gay Ideas: Outing and Other Controversies.* Boston: Beacon Press, 1992.

Sedgwick, Eve. *Epistemology of the Closet.* Berkeley: University of California Press, 1990.

Shilts, Randy. *Conducting Unbecoming: Gays and Lesbians in the U.S. Military.* New York: St. Martin's Press, 1993.

Signorile, Michelangelo. *Queer in America: Sex, the Media, and the Closets of Power.* New York: Random House, 1993.

Sullivan, Andrew. *Virtually Normal: An Argument about Homosexuality.* New York: Knopf, 1995.

Sutton, Roger. *Hearing Us Out: Voices from the Gay and Lesbian Community.* Boston: Little, Brown and Company, 1994.

Warner, Michael. *Fear of a Queer Planet: Queer Politics and Social Theory.* Minneapolis: University of Minnesota Press, 1993.

Woods, James, and Jay Lucas. *The Corporate Closet: The Professional Lives of Gay Men in America.* New York: Free Press, 1993.

Index

About the Author

ARTHUR D. KAHN is Professor Emeritus of Classics at Colgate University. His previous publications include *AIDS, the Winter War: A Testing of America.*